CIVIL LIBERTIES AND THE STATE

CIVIL LIBERTIES AND THE STATE

A Documentary and Reference Guide

Christopher Peter Latimer

Documentary and Reference Guides

GREENWOOD

AN IMPRINT OF ABC-CLIO, LLC
Santa Barbara, California • Denver, Colorado • Oxford, England

Library of Congress Cataloging-in-Publication Data

Latimer, Christopher P.
Civil liberties and the state : a documentary and reference guide / Christopher Peter Latimer.
p. cm. — (Documentary and reference guides)
Includes bibliographical references and index.
ISBN 978-0-313-37934-5 (alk. paper) — ISBN 978-0-313-37935-2 (ebook)
1. Civil rights—United States—History—Sources. I. Title.
KF4744 2011
342.7308'5—dc22 2010041535

ISBN: 978-0-313-37934-5
EISBN: 978-0-313-37935-2

15 14 13 12 11 1 2 3 4 5

This book is also available on the World Wide Web as an eBook.
Visit www.abc-clio.com for details.

Greenwood
An Imprint of ABC-CLIO, LLC

ABC-CLIO, LLC
130 Cremona Drive, P.O. Box 1911
Santa Barbara, California 93116-1911

This book is printed on acid-free paper ∞

Manufactured in the United States of America

CONTENTS

READER'S GUIDE TO RELATED DOCUMENTS AND SIDEBARS

Note: Some documents appear in more than one category.

Legislation, Congress

Due Process

Free Speech

Lower Federal Court Rulings

Politics of Civil Liberties

Privacy

Right to Privacy

War on Terror

Supreme Court Decisions

Due Process

Equal Protection

Free Speech

Privacy

War on Terror

PREFACE

The discussion concerning civil liberties and arbitrary state action is an enduring issue in American politics and constitutional analysis. National debate over our civil liberties extends back to before the founding period and has intensified at various times throughout our nation's history. In particular, the protections of due process, equal protection, privacy, freedom of speech and press have been essential instruments for the safeguarding of individual freedom and liberty against arbitrary state action. In response to 9/11, Congress, the president, and the Supreme Court are continually deliberating about possible restrictions on these civil liberties.

The historic and complex decision of *Boumediene v. Bush* in June 2008 has also opened the door to reexamine these fundamental rights in relation to arbitrary state action and the war on terror. The purpose of this book is to compile a wide range of documents, organized by chronology and subject matter, to provide the reader with a more complete understanding of the history, evolution, scope, and consequences surrounding the relationship between our civil liberties and arbitrary state action. The selected documents will expose readers to the historical underpinnings of four critical constitutional guarantees that provide important protections against government intrusion. This proves to be of particular value to the reader because so much of the writing and commentary on arbitrary state action in relation to due process, equal protection, privacy, freedom of speech and press focuses on what the nation's founders achieved and thought, on laws, executive orders, court cases, and other commentaries that provide alternative points of view on the issues discussed.

Chapter 1 opens with documents from the founding era with a particular emphasis on the development of the aforementioned constitutional guarantees including the Fifth Amendment's due process clause, the Fourteenth Amendment's due process and equal protection clauses as well as the historical foundations of the First Amendment freedoms of speech and press and the right to privacy. This includes a number of treatises and early legislative enactments. Chapter 2 contains a number of early often overlooked Supreme Court rulings on due process, equal protection, the First Amendment, and privacy. Chapter 3 focuses on early statements, executive orders, and federal laws concerning equal protection, the First Amendment, and privacy. Chapter 4 contains a treasure trove of Supreme Court cases during the

20th century dealing with the four guaranteed rights during several periods when the United States was in a constitutionally declared state of war such as World War I and II and during times when Congress authorized engagement without a constitutional declaration such as Vietnam. Chapter 5 examines 21st-century federal resolutions, bills, and laws that were responses to the September 11, 2001, attacks and the continuing war on terror. Chapter 6 provides the texts of Supreme Court decisions and lower federal court decisions from the 21st century concerning the war on terror, due process, equal protection, the First Amendment, and the right to privacy. Chapter 7 concludes with an examination of the major two-party platforms concerning individual rights.

The style of presentation is uniform throughout this book. Every document is introduced with a brief outline giving the name of the document, the document's date, its location, and a brief summary of its significance to the topics discussed. The document is then reprinted, most likely in an edited form (a necessary step given the sheer length of the documented), and then followed by an analysis sections that summarizes its significance, context, and consequences. These edited versions will make it easier for the reader to understand the issues presented. Further readings are then offered for the individual seeking additional information. Each chapter also includes a number of sidebars that highlight important side issues related to the topic areas. The book also includes a listing of additional resources including pertinent government Web sites. A quick note about the language used in some of the older documents. In order to maintain accuracy to the original source material, the language and punctuation used were not updated to meet our current standards of modern writing conventions. As such, a number of legal opinions and legal writings predating the 20th century will contain phrases and arcane language that may be unfamiliar to the reader. The documents and sources offered in this book provide an opportunity for the reader to gain a better understanding of the debate surrounding civil liberties and arbitrary state action.

ACKNOWLEDGMENTS

I would like to thank Greenwood/ABC-CLIO for the opportunity to contribute to their Documentary and Reference Guide series, and especially editor Sandy Towers. She was very helpful during this process, and I value her patience with me as well as her expertise, knowledge, and professionalism. At Cortland, I would like to extend thanks to my colleague Robert Spitzer and our department secretary, Debby Dintino. I would like to reserve special gratitude to my research assistant and SUNY Cortland senior Matthew G. Pennello. Matt's efforts were critical to the completion of this book. He pulled together numerous documents from sources with which he was formally unacquainted and helped me with related technical matters. He did an outstanding job and is one of our institution's many success stories. I also received support from Cortland student Steven Dray, who graduated in 2007. Finally, I would like to acknowledge Bill, Kim, Brian, and Wendi for their continued support and especially my mom, dad, and Joel McCarthy, to whom this book is dedicated.

INTRODUCTION

The terrorist attacks on September 11, 2001, served as a catalyst for federal government action, opening the door to federal and state legislation and presidential executive orders. Terrorists are murdering Americans and our allies, recruiting new members and spreading propaganda, utilizing wireless communication devices to detonate bombs, and using credit card scams and identity theft to raise millions of dollars for illegal activities. The government is compelled to respond, but to what extent? There is a deep-rooted association between our individual liberty interests and the use of government power during times of crisis. This dichotomy underlines an inherent tension in the United States:

> [t]he choice is not between order and liberty, [but] between liberty with order and anarchy without either. There is danger that, if the Court does not temper its doctrinaire logic with a little practical wisdom, it will convert the constitutional Bill of Rights into a suicide pact.[1]

Presiding over the Nuremberg trials, Justice Jackson's fears were based on witness testimony concerning genocide and terrorism. This experience shaped his views that civil liberties could only exist under governments with the power to protect those liberties from assault. It is not order per se that conflicts with individual rights but the government's approach to preserving security that may challenge civil rights in this country.

This type of response is often couched in terms of trade-offs—the extent to which civil liberties should be sacrificed for security. An examination of polling data right after 9/11 demonstrated that a majority of citizens would be willing to give up some civil liberties in order to combat terrorism.[2] Support for this position has steadily fallen as we move further away from 9/11 and as more stories of possible governmental abuse are reported by the media.[3] The policy and legal debate concerning the appropriate balance between liberty and national security presents a paradox: government power is viewed both as a threat to and as a defender of our liberty. These documents will enhance our understanding of this debate as well as the relationship between our civil liberties and arbitrary state action.

COLONIAL AND FOUNDING DOCUMENTS (Chapter 1)

The first chapter begins with colonial-era documents that reference some antecedent to what influenced the structure and writing of the U.S. Constitution. Most agree that the wording from the Magna Carta, the British Habeas Corpus Act, the British Bill of Rights, and the Massachusetts Constitution found its way into the First and Fifth Amendments of the American Bill of Rights of 1791, the suspension clause of Article I, Section 9, Clause 2 as well as the equal protection and due process clauses of the Fourteenth Amendment. The Constitution was ratified in June 1788, but because ratification in many states was contingent on the promised addition of a Federal Bill of Rights, Congress proposed 12 amendments in September 1789. Ten of the amendments were ratified by the states, and their adoption was certified on December 15, 1791. The framers were also especially concerned with limiting the power of the government and securing the liberty of citizens. The Constitution's separation of the legislative, executive, and judicial branches of government, the checks and balances of each branch against the other, and the explicit guarantees of individual liberty were all designed to strike a balance between power and liberty. An understanding of the influences of the words, phrases, and structure of the U.S. Constitution will provide much needed context for why certain individual liberties and privileges were included.

EARLY COURT RULINGS ON DUE PROCESS, EQUAL PROTECTION, THE FIRST AMENDMENT, AND PRIVACY (Chapter 2)

The second chapter begins with a series of British court cases from the 17th and 18th centuries that provide several examples of individuals who were imprisoned for challenging and disobeying the British monarchy and parliament. These first documents demonstrate the importance of having a system which allowed individuals who were incarcerated an opportunity to be heard by a court. This did not always make a difference as often times the King's Court was just an extension of the monarchy and their views. However, there were several instances in which the mere process of a public trial led to the release of the prisoner. These early cases also led to the serious examination of slavery in both England and the United States. Finally, the last set of 19th-century court rulings include an assessment of the suspension clause, the writ of habeas corpus, the use of military tribunals, and the freedom of speech in relation to one's government during a time of war and the implications of executive and congressional powers with this regard.

20TH-CENTURY STATEMENTS AND ENACTMENTS (Chapter 3)

Chapter 3 includes a series of legislative acts and executive orders responding to World War I, World War II, the red scare of the early and later part of the 20th century, and the war on terrorism. During this time arbitrary state action was almost entirely justified as necessary for protecting our national security. The consequence of this was a curtailment of our civil liberties at the hands of the federal government. During and after World War I, the Espionage Act and the Sedition Act were used in a number of prosecutions and convictions against individuals who other than being affiliated with the Communist and Socialist Party had no criminal record or affiliations with any saboteurs or subversives. While many of the laws were repealed in 1921, major portions of the Espionage Act remain part of U.S. law. This time also led to Japanese immigrants and Americans of Japanese descent living on the West Coast to be assembled, registered, and moved to internment camps during World War II. The second red scare continued through the later part of the 20th century, providing an opportunity to enact a loyalty order. Finally, starting with the Watergate scandal of the Nixon administration, the federal government began to enact laws that would protect our privacy. All of these examples will continue to contribute to our understanding of the relationship between arbitrary state action and liberty.

20TH-CENTURY COURT RULINGS (Chapter 4)

The fourth chapter provides court cases that respond to the legislative acts and executive orders that were enacted during World War I, World War II, the red scare of the early and later part of 20th century, and the war on terrorism. The results of these cases vary tremendously in terms of their analysis of the due process clause, equal protection clause, the freedom of speech, and the right to privacy. One unusual example is the case of *Korematsu*, concerning the constitutionality of Executive Order 9066, which ordered Japanese Americans into internment camps during World War II. This case is unusual because the ruling is significant both for being the first instance of the Supreme Court applying the strict scrutiny standard to a regulation based on a racial classification and for being one of only a small handful of cases in which the Court held that the government met that standard. These cases also dealt with whether noncitizens whose countries were engaged in hostilities against the United States could use our judicial system and apply for a writ of habeas corpus. The implications of these cases have far reaching effects on the current war on terror. This is also a time in which the Supreme Court begins to selectively incorporate the Federal Bill of Rights to the states through the Fourteenth Amendment. The cases start to include individuals challenging state laws based on the First Amendment and the right to privacy.

21ST-CENTURY ENACTMENTS CONCERNING THE WAR ON TERROR (Chapter 5)

The fifth chapter includes documents that were enacted as a direct response to the September 11, 2001, attacks on the United States. The terrorism which occurred on September 11 not only had political and international results, the events of that day also significantly impacted American society and culture. In the foreign policy arena, one of the first outcomes was Congress providing a grant of power to the Bush administration. The limits of this power would eventually be tested in the courts. These federal laws provided a basis for many of the actions committed by the Bush administration. In particular, the Authorization for Use of Military Force (AUMF) was touted by the Bush administration for justifying the war in Iraq, for designating prisoners as enemy combatants, detaining these prisoners indefinitely without an attorney or a hearing as well as for justifying domestic surveillance of possible terrorists without obtaining authorization of the special court created by the Foreign Intelligence Surveillance Act (FISA) of 1978, as amended. In the policy arena was the enormous and controversial omnibus USA PATRIOT Act that was passed without much debate. Despite the almost unanimous congressional passage, the PATRIOT Act became controversial very quickly with many Americans greatly concerned about its far-reaching mandates. The enactments also help to discern the continuing power struggle between the executive and legislative branches of government and the importance of checks and balances for protecting our civil liberties from arbitrary state action.

21ST-CENTURY COURT RULINGS (Chapter 6)

Chapter 6 provides a series of significant cases regarding the war on terror and the actions by the Bush administration. This set of Supreme Court cases deals with controversial issues concerning the power of the executive and also Congress to set up military commissions, the ability of the executive and legislative branches of government to strip the jurisdiction of the federal courts to hear cases, the designation of prisoners as enemy combatants, the permanent detainment of enemy combatants without access to an attorney or a court to be formally charged, and the rights under the constitution for American citizens who are terrorists versus resident aliens versus noncitizens. These cases are sometimes confusing especially since the same issues seem to be adjudicated multiple times. Once it appears as if the Court has ruled on a particular legal issue, another case comes before the Court with a similar issue. These cases are extremely important because the Court not only revisits a number of previous and controversial decisions but the Court also begins to provide a framework for understanding our civil liberties in relation to the federal government. This chapter also includes a number of lower-court cases concerning the First Amendment and the curtailing of our speech and press access to certain hearings and events. Finally, there is an examination of our right to privacy in a world where technological advancements allow for greater surveillance by the government.

ARBITRARY STATE ACTION AND POLITICS (Chapter 7)

Chapter 7 concludes with an examination of the political part of the issues. The two main political parties have very different ideas about what types of rights should be protected and how the government should respond to national security threats. The political parties have an additional element to worry about as they solidify their positions about issues concerning our individual liberties; namely, the additional motive of getting reelected to public office. The party must balance this truism about

American politics with the positions they support especially regarding controversial subjects such as same-sex marriage and affirmative action. With this in mind, the broad scope of the national party platform is designed to attract a broad range of voters to that party, in the hopes of generating party loyalty and potentially creating voters who will automatically select candidates associated with that party. Interest groups also play an important part of the process. This is because these organizations look to influence political and policy decisions as well as promote their issues. They usually have both well-defined political agendas and the financial resources necessary to exert broad influence on the political and regulatory process. Understanding the politics will provide another important perspective about the relationship between our government and our individual liberties.

NOTES

1. *Terminiello v. Chicago*, 337 U.S. 1, 37 (1949) (Jackson, J., dissenting).
2. Humphrey Taylor, *The Harris Poll #49: Overwhelming public support for Increasing surveillance Powers and, in spite of many concerns about abuses, confidence that these powers would be used properly*. Retrieved August 2, 2009, from http://www.harrisinteractive.com/harris_poll/index.asp?PID=260; Pew Research Center for the People & the Press. American psyche reeling from terror attacks. Retrieved August 2, 2007, from http://people-press.org/reports/display.php3?PageID=30.
3. Jill Darling Richardson. Poll analysis: Concern growing over loss of civil liberties. Retrieved on August 2, 2009, from http://www.latimes.com/news/nationworld/timespoll/la-463pa3an,1,457920.story?coll=la-news-times_poll-nation.

1

COLONIAL AND FOUNDING DOCUMENTS

The Magna Carta

- ***Document:*** An excerpt from The Magna Carta or "Great Charter"
- ***Date:*** June 15, 1215
- ***Where:*** Runnymede (Surrey), England
- ***Significance:*** This was a signed agreement between King John I of England and his nobles, limiting the crown's authority to arbitrarily hold or imprison freemen, impose excessive bail, or to take away liberties normally granted, without a hearing. The Magna Carta is one of the first embodiments of due process and influenced the common law and the U.S. Constitution.

DOCUMENT

Magna Carta

Date: 15 June, 1215

1. In the first place we have granted to God, and by this our present charter confirmed for us and our heirs forever that the English Church shall be free, and shall have her rights entire, and her liberties inviolate; and we will that it be thus observed; which is apparent from this that the freedom of elections, which is reckoned most important and very essential to the English Church, we, of our pure and unconstrained will, did grant, and did by our charter confirm and did obtain the ratification of the same from our lord, Pope Innocent III, before the quarrel arose between us and our barons: and this we will observe, and our will is that it be observed in good faith by our heirs forever. We have also granted to all freemen of our kingdom, for us and our heirs forever, all the underwritten liberties, to be had and held by them and their heirs, of us and our heirs forever....

13. And the city of London shall have all it ancient liberties and free customs, as well by land as by water; furthermore, we decree and grant that all other cities, boroughs, towns, and ports shall have all their liberties and free customs....

17. Common pleas shall not follow our court, but shall be held in some fixed place....

20. A freeman shall not be amerced for a slight offense, except in accordance with the degree of the offense; and for a grave offense he shall be amerced in accordance with the gravity of the offense, yet saving always his "contentment"; and a merchant in the same way, saving his "merchandise"; and a villain shall be amerced in the same way, saving his "wainage" if they have fallen into our mercy: and none of the aforesaid amercements shall be imposed except by the oath of honest men of the neighborhood....

38. No bailiff for the future shall, upon his own unsupported complaint, put anyone to his "law", without credible witnesses brought for this purposes.

39. No freemen shall be taken or imprisoned or disseised or exiled or in any way destroyed, nor will we go upon him nor send upon him, except by the lawful judgment of his peers or by the law of the land.

40. To no one will we sell, to no one will we refuse or delay, right or justice....

45. We will appoint as justices, constables, sheriffs, or bailiffs only such as know the law of the realm and mean to observe it well....

52. If anyone has been dispossessed or removed by us, without the legal judgment of his peers, from his lands, castles, franchises, or from his right, we will immediately restore them to him; and if a dispute arise over this, then let it be decided by the five and twenty barons of whom mention is made below in the clause for securing the peace. Moreover, for all those possessions, from which anyone has, without the lawful judgment of his peers, been disseised or removed, by our father, King Henry, or by our brother, King Richard, and which we retain in our hand (or which as possessed by others, to whom we are bound to warrant them) we shall have respite until the usual term of crusaders; excepting those things about which a plea has been raised, or an inquest made by our order, before our taking of the cross; but as soon as we return from the expedition, we will immediately grant full justice therein.

53. We shall have, moreover, the same respite and in the same manner in rendering justice concerning the disafforestation or retention of those forests which Henry our father and Richard our brother afforested, and concerning the wardship of lands which are of the fief of another (namely, such wardships as we have hitherto had by reason of a fief which anyone held of us by knight's service), and concerning abbeys founded on other fiefs than our own, in which the lord of the fee claims to have right; and when we have returned, or if we desist from our expedition, we will immediately grant full justice to all who complain of such things.

54. No one shall be arrested or imprisoned upon the appeal of a woman, for the death of any other than her husband.

55. All fines made with us unjustly and against the law of the land, and all amercements, imposed unjustly and against the law of the land, shall be entirely remitted, or else it shall be done concerning them according to the decision of the five and twenty barons whom mention is made below in the clause for securing the pease, or according to the judgment of the majority of the same, along with the aforesaid Stephen, archbishop of Canterbury, if he can be present, and such others as he may wish to bring with him for this purpose, and if he cannot be present the business shall nevertheless proceed without him, provided always that if any one or more of the aforesaid five and twenty barons are in a similar suit, they shall be removed as far as concerns this particular judgment, others being substituted in their places after having been selected by the rest of the same five and twenty for this purpose only, and after having been sworn.

56. If we have disseised or removed Welshmen from lands or liberties, or other things, without the legal judgment of their peers in England or in Wales, they shall be immediately restored to them; and if a dispute arise over this, then let it be decided in the marches by the judgment of their peers; for the tenements in England according to the law of England, for tenements in Wales according to the law of Wales, and for tenements in the marches according to the law of the marches. Welshmen shall do the same to us and ours.

57. Further, for all those possessions from which any Welshman has, without the lawful judgment of his peers, been disseised or removed by King Henry our father, or King Richard our brother, and which we retain in our hand (or which are possessed by others, and which we ought to warrant), we will have respite until the usual term of crusaders; excepting those things about which a plea has been raised or an inquest made by our order before we took the cross; but as soon as we return (or if perchance we desist from our expedition), we will immediately grant full justice in accordance with the laws of the Welsh and in relation to the foresaid regions.

58. We will immediately give up the son of Llywelyn and all the hostages of Wales, and the charters delivered to us as security for the peace.

59. We will do towards Alexander, king of Scots, concerning the return of his sisters and his hostages, and concerning his franchises, and his right, in the same manner as we shall do towards our owher barons of England, unless it ought to be otherwise according to the charters which we hold from William his father, formerly king of Scots; and this shall be according to the judgment of his peers in our court.

60. Moreover, all these aforesaid customs and liberties, the observances of which we have granted in our kingdom as far as pertains to us towards our men, shall be observed by all of our kingdom, as well clergy as laymen, as far as pertains to them towards their men.

61. Since, moveover, for God and the amendment of our kingdom and for the better allaying of the quarrel that has arisen between us and our barons, we have granted all these concessions, desirous that they should enjoy them in complete and firm endurance forever, we give and grant to them the underwritten security, namely, that the barons choose five and twenty barons of the kingdom, whomsoever they will, who shall be bound with all their might, to observe and hold, and cause to be observed, the peace and liberties we have granted and confirmed to them by this our present Charter, so that if we, or our justiciar, or our bailiffs or any one of our officers, shall in anything be at fault towards anyone, or shall have broken any one of the articles of this peace or of this security, and the offense be notified to four barons of the foresaid five and twenty, the said four barons shall repair to us (or our justiciar, if we are out of the realm) and, laying the transgression before us, petition to have that transgression redressed without delay. And if we shall not have corrected the transgression (or, in the event of our being out of the realm, if our justiciar shall not have corrected it) within forty days, reckoning from the time it has been intimated to us (or to our justiciar, if we should be out of the realm), the four barons aforesaid shall refer that matter to the rest of the five and twenty barons, and those five and twenty barons shall, together with the community of the whole realm, distrain and distress us in all possible ways, namely, by seizing our castles, lands, possessions, and in any other way they can, until redress has been obtained as they deem fit, saving harmless our own person, and the persons of our queen and children; and when redress has been obtained, they shall resume their old relations towards us. And let whoever in

the country desires it, swear to obey the orders of the said five and twenty barons for the execution of all the aforesaid matters, and along with them, to molest us to the utmost of his power; and we publicly and freely grant leave to everyone who wishes to swear, and we shall never forbid anyone to swear. All those, moveover, in the land who of themselves and of their own accord are unwilling to swear to the twenty five to help them in constraining and molesting us, we shall by our command compel the same to swear to the effect foresaid. And if any one of the five and twenty barons shall have died or departed from the land, or be incapacitated in any other manner which would prevent the foresaid provisions being carried out, those of the said twenty five barons who are left shall choose another in his place according to their own judgment, and he shall be sworn in the same way as the others. Further, in all matters, the execution of which is entrusted, to these twenty five barons, if perchance these twenty five are present and disagree about anything, or if some of them, after being summoned, are unwilling or unable to be present, that which the majority of those present ordain or command shall be held as fixed and established, exactly as if the whole twenty five had concurred in this; and the said twenty five shall swear that they will faithfully observe all that is aforesaid, and cause it to be observed with all their might. And we shall procure nothing from anyone, directly or indirectly, whereby any part of these concessions and liberties might be revoked or diminished; and if any such things has been procured, let it be void and null, and we shall never use it personally or by another. . . .

63. Wherefore we will and firmly order that the English Church be free, and that the men in our kingdom have and hold all the aforesaid liberties, rights, and concessions, well and peaceably, freely and quietly, fully and wholly, for themselves and their heirs, of us and our heirs, in all respects and in all places forever, as is aforesaid. An oath, moreover, has been taken, as well on our part as on the part of the barons, that all these conditions aforesaid shall be kept in good faith and without evil intent. Given under our hand—the above named and many others being witnesses—in the meadow which is called Runnymede, between Windsor and Staines, on the fifteenth day of June, in the seventeenth year of our reign.

SOURCE: http://avalon.law.yale.edu/medieval/magframe.asp

With the introduction of the printing press to England some five centuries earlier, the Crown had become fearful of the widespread dissemination of information to the general public. In 1534, in order to control the flow of information, the Crown decreed it illegal for anyone to publish without a license. To aid in enforcing this censorship control, the Crown in 1557 granted a charter and, effectively, a publishing monopoly to the Stationers' Company, a private group of London printers and booksellers who therefore had a large financial stake in censoring works deemed objectionable to the government or the Church. This basic method of censorship for monetary reward remained unchanged for the next one and one half centuries. In force between 1662 and 1679, and then again between 1685 and 1695, the Licensing Act was the culmination of the Crown's efforts to censor the press. In 1695, when the House of Commons refused to renew the Licensing Act, censorship of the English press ended except during wartime. In an intriguing twist, the Licensing Act helped to lay the foundation of the copyright laws that today protect authors. In this 19th-century drawing, King John of England swears vengeance against the barons who forced him to sign the Magna Carta. In 1215, dissatisfaction with John was so widespread in England that a revolt broke out and London was taken by the rebels. The rebel barons forced John to accept the Magna Carta, which limited his powers. (Ridpath, John Clark, *Ridpath's History of the World,* 1901.)

ANALYSIS

For centuries it was the practice of European royals to claim absolute authority over their subjects, including the landed nobility. England had a tribal history of making the ruler of all tribes answerable to a council of other trial chiefs. This relationship had evolved over time, and by the 13th century, it was made clear by the actions of King John I that the monarch could not be trusted with absolute authority. The feudal system that England operated under at that time required the nobility to provide the crown with soldiers, trained and armed, to fight in wars, but also to pay taxes to the crown. Decades of expensive wars with France and in the Crusades had left the nobility drained financially. In particular, King John I lost an important battle to King Philip II at Bouvines and attempted to rebuild his coffers by demanding "scutage," which is a fee paid in lieu of military service from the barons who had not joined his war against Philip. The Barons in question objected, condemning John's policies and insisting on a reconfirmation of Henry I's Coronation Oath (1100), which would limit the king's ability to obtain funds. But John refused to withdraw his demands. The rebelling barons faltered against John's superior resources, but after the surprising capture of London, they were able to bargain. As a result, John agreed to grant a charter. Although a document seeking redress for many grievances, the Magna Carta is at its heart a tool used by the people—a contract between the ruler and the governed that limited the power of the king and forced the crown to recognize that there are common rights which could not be infringed upon.

FURTHER READING

Holt, James Clarke. *Magna Carta*. Cambridge: Cambridge University Press, 1965.
Pallister, Anne. *Magna Carta: The Heritage of Liberty*. Oxford: Clarendon Press, 1971.
Thompson, Faith. *Magna Carta; Its Role in the Making of the English Constitution, 1300–1629*. Minneapolis: University of Minnesota Press, 1948.

The Habeas Corpus Act of 1679

- ***Document:* The Habeas Corpus Act:** An Act for the better Securing the Liberty of the Subject, and for Prevention of Imprisonment beyond the Seas
- ***Date:*** May 27, 1679
- ***Where:*** London, England
- ***Significance:*** The English parliament passed the Habeas Corpus Act in 1679, formally establishing the legal right to a writ of habeas corpus, which limited the power of the king to arrest and detain without cause.

DOCUMENT

The Habeas Corpus Act, 1679

31 Car. 2, c. 2, 27 May 1679

Whereas great delays have been used by sheriffs, gaolers and other officers, to whose custody any of the King's subjects have been committed for criminal or supposed criminal matters, in making returns of writs of habeas corpus to them directed, by standing out an alias and pluries habeas corpus, and sometimes more, and by other shifts to avoid their yielding obedience to such writs, contrary to their duty and the known laws of the land, whereby many of the King's subjects have been and hereafter may be long detained in prison, in such cases where by law they are bailable, to their great charges and vexation:

II. For the prevention whereof, and the more speedy relief of all persons imprisoned for any such criminal or supposed criminal matters; (2) be it enacted by the King's most excellent majesty, by and with the advice and consent of the lords spiritual and temporal, and commons, in this present parliament assembled, and by the authority thereof, That whensoever any person or persons shall bring any habeas corpus directed unto any sheriff or sheriffs, gaoler, minister or other person whatsoever, for any person in his or her custody, and the said writ shall be served upon the said officer, or left at the gaol or prison with any of the under-officers, under-keepers or deputy of the said officers or keepers, that the said officer or officers, his or their under-officers, under-keepers or deputies, shall within three days after the service thereof as aforesaid (unless the commitment aforesaid were for treason or felony, plainly and specially expressed in the warrant of commitment) upon payment or tender of the charges of bringing the said prisoner, to be ascertained by the judge or court that awarded the same, and endorsed upon the said writ, not exceeding twelve pence per mile, and upon security given by his own bond to pay the charges of carrying back the prisoner, if he shall be remanded by the court or judge to which he shall be brought according to the true intent of this present act, and that he will not make any escape by the way, make return of such writ; (3) and bring or cause to be brought the body of the party so committed or restrained, unto or before the lord chancellor, or lord keeper of the great seal of England for the time being, or the judges or barons of the said court from whence the said writ shall issue, or unto and before such other person or persons before whom the said writ is made returnable, according to the command thereof; (4) and shall then likewise certify the true causes of his detainer or imprisonment, unless the commitment of the said party be in any place beyond the distance of twenty miles from the place or places where such court or person is or shall be residing; and if beyond the distance of twenty miles, and not above one hundred miles, then within the space of ten days, and if beyond the distance of one hundred miles, then within the space of twenty days, after such delivery aforesaid, and not longer.

III. And to the intent that no sheriff, gaoler or other officer may pretend ignorance of the import of any such writ; (2) be it enacted by the authority aforesaid, That all such writs shall be marked in this manner, Per statutum tricesimo primo Caroli secundi Regis, and shall be signed by the person that awards the same; (3) and if any person or persons shall be or stand committed or detained as aforesaid, for any crime, unless for felony or treason plainly expressed in the warrant of commitment, in the vacation-time, and out of term, it shall and may be lawful to and for the person or persons so committed or detained (other than persons convict or in execution by legal process) or any one on his or their behalf, to appeal or complain to the lord chancellor or lord keeper, or any one of his Majesty's justices, either of the one bench or of the other, or the barons of the exchequer of the degree of the coif; (4) and the said lord chancellor, lord keeper, justices or barons or any of them, upon view of the copy or copies of the warrant or warrants of commitment and detainer, or otherwise upon oath made that such copy or copies were denied to be given by such person or persons in whose custody the prisoner or prisoners is or are detained, are hereby authorized and required, upon request made in writing by such person or persons, or any on his, her or their behalf, attested and subscribed by two witnesses who were present at the delivery of the same, to award and grant an habeas corpus under the seal of such court whereof he shall then be one of the judges, (5) to be directed to the officer or officers in whose custody the party so committed or detained shall be, returnable immediate before the said lord chancellor or lord keeper, or such justice, baron or any other justice or baron of the degree of the coif of any of the said courts; (6) and upon service thereof as aforesaid, the officer or officers, his or their under-officer or under-officers, under-keeper or under-keepers, or their deputy, in whose custody the party is so committed or detained, shall within the times respectively before limited, bring such prisoner or prisoners before the said lord chancellor or lord keeper, or such justices, barons or one of them, before whom the said writ is made returnable, and in case of his absence before any other of them, with the return of such writ, and the true causes of the commitment and detainer; (7) and thereupon within two days after the party shall be brought before them, the said lord chancellor or lord keeper, or such justice or baron before whom the prisoner shall be brought as aforesaid, shall discharge the said prisoner from his imprisonment, taking his or their recognizance, with one or more surety or sureties, in any sum according to their discretions, having regard to the quality of the prisoner and nature of the offence, for his or their appearance in the court of King's bench the term following, or at the next assizes, sessions or general gaol-delivery of and for such county, city or place where the commitment was, or where the offence was committed, or in such other court where the said offence is properly cognizable, as the case shall require, and then shall certify the said writ with the return thereof, and the said recognizance or recognizances into the said court where such appearance is to be made; (8) unless it shall appear unto the said lord chancellor or lord keeper, or justice or justices, or baron or barons, that the party so committed is detained upon a legal process, order or warrant, out of some court that hath jurisdiction of criminal matters, or by some warrant signed and sealed with the hand and seal of any of the said justices or barons, or some justice or justices of the peace, for such matters or offences for the which by the law the prisoner is not bailable.

IV. Provided always, and be it enacted, That if any person shall have wilfully neglected by the space of two whole terms after his imprisonment, to pray a habeas corpus for his enlargement, such person so wilfully neglecting shall not have any habeas corpus to be granted in vacation-time, in pursuance of this act.

V. And be it further enacted by the authority aforesaid, That if any officer or officers, his or their under-officer or under-officers, under-keeper or under-keepers, or deputy, shall neglect or refuse to make the returns aforesaid, or to bring the body or bodies of the prisoner or prisoners according to the command of the said writ, within the respective times aforesaid, or upon demand made by the prisoner or person in his behalf, shall refuse to deliver, or within the space of six hours after demand shall not deliver, to the person so demanding, a true copy of the warrant or warrants of commitment and detainer of such prisoner, which he and they are hereby required to deliver accordingly, all and every the head gaolers and keepers of such prisons, and such other person in whose custody the prisoner shall be detained, shall for the first offence forfeit to the prisoner or party grieved the sum of one hundred pounds; (2) and for the second offence the sum of two hundred pounds, and shall and is hereby made incapable to hold or execute his said office; (3) the said penalties to be recovered by the prisoner or party grieved, his executors or administrators, against such offender, his executors or administrators, by any action of debt, suit, bill, plaint or information, in any of the King's courts at Westminster, wherein no essoin, protection, privilege, injunction, wager of law, or stay of prosecution by Non vult ulterius prosequi, or otherwise, shall be admitted or allowed, or any more than one imparlance; (4) and any recovery or judgment at the suit of any party grieved, shall be a sufficient conviction for the first offence; and any after recovery or judgment at the suit of a party grieved for any offence after the first judgment, shall be a sufficient conviction to bring the officers or person within the said penalty for the second offence.

VI. And for the prevention of unjust vexation by reiterated commitments for the same offence; (2) be it enacted by the authority aforesaid, That no person or persons which shall be delivered or set at large upon any habeas corpus, shall at any time hereafter be again imprisoned or committed for the same offence by any person or persons whatsoever, other than by the legal order and process of such court wherein he or they shall be bound by recognizance to appear, or other court having jurisdiction of the cause; (3) and if any other person or persons shall knowingly contrary to this act recommit or imprison, or knowingly procure or cause to be recommitted or imprisoned, for the same offence or pretended offence, any person or persons delivered or set at large as aforesaid, or be knowingly aiding or assisting therein, then he or they shall forfeit to the prisoner or party grieved the sum of five hundred pounds; any colourable pretence or variation in the warrant or warrants of commitment notwithstanding, to be recovered as aforesaid.

VII. Provided always, and be it further enacted, That if any person or persons shall be committed for high treason or felony, plainly and specially expressed in the warrant of commitment, upon his prayer or petition in open court the first week of the term, or first day of the sessions of oyer and terminer or general gaol-delivery, to be brought to his trial, shall not be indicted some time in the next term, sessions of oyer and terminer or general gaol-delivery, after such commitment; it shall and may be lawful to and for the judges of the court of King's bench and justices of oyer and terminer or general gaol-delivery, and they are hereby required, upon motion to them made in open court the last day of the term, sessions or gaol-delivery, either by the prisoner or any one in his behalf, to set at liberty the prisoner upon bail, unless it appear to the judges and justices upon oath made, that the witnesses for the King could not be produced the same term, sessions or general gaol-delivery; (2) and if any person or persons committed as aforesaid, upon his prayer or petition in open court the first week of the term or first day of the sessions of oyer and terminer and general gaol-delivery, to be brought to his trial, shall not be indicted and tried the second term, sessions of oyer and terminer or general gaol-delivery, after his commitment, or upon his trial shall be acquitted, he shall be discharged from his imprisonment.

VIII. Provided always, That nothing in this act shall extend to discharge out of prison any person charged in debt, or other action, or with process in any civil cause, but that after he shall be discharged of his imprisonment for such his criminal offence, he shall be kept in custody according to the law, for such other suit.

IX. Provided always, and be it enacted by the authority aforesaid, That if any person or persons, subjects of this realm, shall be committed to any prison or in custody of any officer or officers whatsoever, for any criminal or supposed criminal matter, that the said person shall not be removed from the said prison and custody into the custody of any other officer or officers; (2) unless it be by habeas corpus or some other legal writ; or where the prisoner is delivered to the constable or other inferior officer to carry such prisoner to some common gaol; (3) or where any person is sent by order of any judge or assize or justice of the peace, to any common workhouse or house of correction; (4) or where the prisoner is removed from one prison or place to another within the same county, in order to his or her trial or discharge in due course of law; (5) or in case of sudden fire or infection, or other necessity; (6) and if any person or persons shall after such commitment [Volume 3, Page 312] aforesaid make out and sign, or countersign any warrant or warrants for such removal aforesaid, contrary to this act; as well he that makes or signs, or countersigns such warrant or warrants, as the officer or officers that obey or execute the same, shall suffer and incur the pains and forfeitures in this act before mentioned, both for the first and second offence respectively, to be recovered in manner aforesaid by the party grieved.

X. Provided also, and be it further enacted by the authority aforesaid, That it shall and may be lawful to and for any prisoner and prisoners as aforesaid, to move and obtain his or their habeas corpus as well out of the high court of chancery or court of exchequer, as out of the courts of King's bench or common pleas, or either of them; (2) and if the said lord chancellor or lord keeper, or any judge or judges, baron or barons for the time being, of the degree of the coif, of any of the courts aforesaid, in the vacation time, upon view of the copy or copies of the warrant or warrants of commitment or detainer, or upon oath made that such copy or copies were denied as aforesaid, shall deny any writ of habeas corpus by this act required to be granted, being moved for as aforesaid, they shall severally forfeit to the prisoner or party grieved the sum of five hundred pounds, to be recovered in manner aforesaid.

XI. And be it declared and enacted by the authority aforesaid, That an habeas corpus according to the true intent and meaning of this act, may be directed and run into any county palatine, the cinque-ports, or other privileged places within the kingdom of England, dominion of Wales, or town of Berwick upon Tweed, and the islands of Jersey or Guernsey; any law or usage to the contrary notwithstanding.

XII. And for preventing illegal imprisonments in prisons beyond the seas; (2) be it further enacted by the authority aforesaid, That no subject of this realm that now is, or hereafter shall be an inhabitant or resiant of this kingdom of England, dominion of Wales, or town of Berwick upon Tweed, shall or may be sent prisoner into Scotland, Ireland, Jersey, Guernsey, Tangier, or into parts, garrisons, islands or places beyond the seas, which are or at any time hereafter shall be within or without the dominions of his Majesty, his heirs or successors; (3) and that every such imprisonment is hereby enacted and adjudged to be illegal; (4) and that if any of the said subjects now is or hereafter shall be so imprisoned, every such person and persons so imprisoned, shall and may for every such imprisonment maintain by virtue of this act an action or actions of false imprisonment, in any of his Majesty's courts of record, against the person or persons by whom he or she shall be so committed, detained, imprisoned, sent prisoner or transported, contrary to the true meaning of this act, and against all or any person or persons that shall frame, contrive, write, seal or countersign any warrant or writing for such commitment, detainer, imprisonment or transportation, or shall be advising, aiding or assisting, in the same, or any of them; (5) and the plaintiff in every such action shall have judgment to recover his treble costs, besides damages, which damages so to be given, shall not be less than five hundred pounds; (6) in which action no delay stay or stop of proceeding by rule, order or command, nor no injunction, protection or privilege whatsoever, nor any more than one imparlance shall be allowed, excepting such rule of the court wherein the action shall depend, made in open court, as shall be thought in justice necessary, for special cause to be expressed in the said rule; (7) and the person or persons who shall knowingly frame, contrive, write, seal or countersign any warant for such commitment, detainer or transportation, or shall so commit, detain, imprison or transport any person or persons contrary to this act, or be any ways advising, aiding or assisting therein, being lawfully convicted thereof, shall be disabled from thenceforth to bear any office of trust or profit within the said realm of England, dominion of Wales, or town of Berwick upon Tweed, or any of the islands, territories or dominions thereunto belonging; (8) and shall incur and sustain the pains, penalties and forfeitures limited, ordained and provided in and by the statute of provision and praemunire made in the sixteenth year of King Richard the Second; (9) and be incapable of any pardon from the King, his heirs or successors, of the said forfeitures, losses or disabilities, or any of them.

XIII. Provided always, That nothing in this act shall extend to give benefit to any person who shall by contract in writing agree with any merchant or owner of any plantation, or other person whatsoever, to be transported to any parts beyond the seas, and receive earnest upon such agreement, although that afterwards such person shall renounce such contract.

XIV. Provided always, and be it enacted, That if any person or persons lawfully convicted of any felony, shall in open court pray to be transported beyond the seas, and the court shall think fit to leave him or them in prison for that purpose, such person or persons may be transported into any parts beyond the seas, this act or any thing therein contained to the contrary notwithstanding.

XV. Provided also, and be it enacted, That nothing herein contained shall be deemed, construed or taken, to extend to the imprisonment of any person before the first day of June one thousand six hundred seventy and nine, or to any thing advised, procured, or otherwise done, relating to such imprisonment; any thing herein contained to the contrary notwithstanding.

XVI. Provided also, That if any person or persons at any time resiant in this realm, shall have committed any capital offence in Scotland or Ireland, or any of the islands, or foreign plantations of the King, his heirs or successors, where he or she ought to be tried for such offence, such person or persons may be sent to such place, there to receive such trial, in such manner as the same might have been used before the making of this act; anything herein contained to the contrary notwithstanding.

XVII. Provided also, and be it enacted, That no person or persons shall be sued, impleaded, molested, or troubled for any offence against this act, unless the party offending be sued or impleaded for the same within two years at the most after such time wherein the offence shall be committed, in case the party grieved shall not be then in prison; and if he shall be in prison, then within the space of two years after the decease of the person imprisoned, or his or her delivery out of prison, which shall first happen.

XVIII. And to the intent no person may avoid his trial at the assizes or general gaol-delivery, by procuring his removal before the assizes, at such time as he cannot be brought back to receive his trial there; (2) be it enacted, That after the assizes proclaimed for that county where the prisoner is detained, no person shall be removed from the common gaol upon any habeas corpus granted in pursuance of this act, but upon any such habeas corpus shall be brought before the judge of assize in open court, who is thereupon to do what to justice shall appertain.

XIX. Provided nevertheless, That after the assizes are ended, any person or persons detained, may have his or her habeas corpus according to the direction and intention of this act.

XX. And be it also enacted by the authority aforesaid, That if any information, suit or action shall be brought or exhibited against any person or persons for any offence committed or to be committed against the form of this law, it shall be lawful for such defendants to plead the general issue, that they are not guilty, or that they owe nothing, and to give such special matter in evidence to the jury that shall try the same, which matter being pleaded had been good and sufficient matter in law to have discharged the said defendant or defendants against the said information, suit or action, and the said matter shall be then as available to him or them, to all intents and purposes, as if he or they had sufficiently pleaded, set forth or alledged the same matter in bar or discharge of such information suit or action.

XXI. And because many times persons charged with petty treason or felony, or as accessaries thereunto, are committed upon suspicion only, whereupon they are bailable, or not, according as the circumstances making out that suspicion are more or less weighty, which are best known to the justices of peace that committed the persons, and have the examinations before them, or to other justices of the peace in the county; (2) be it therefore enacted, That where any person shall appear to be committed by any judge or justice of the peace and charged as accessary before the fact, to any petty treason or felony, or upon suspicion thereof, or with suspicion of petty treason or felony, which petty treason or felony shall be plainly and specially expressed in the warrant of commitment, that such person shall not be removed or bailed by virtue of this act, or in any other manner than they might have been before the making of this act.

SOURCE: http://press-pubs.uchicago.edu/founders/documents/a1_9_2s2.html

ANALYSIS

The English Civil War ended with the execution of King Charles I and the exile of the royal family. After years of the militaristic Commonwealth, led by Oliver Cromwell, it was decided to invite the Stuart family back from exile and return the monarchy to its former position, although a deep distrust of the Stuart family still existed. Long respected in common law, the writ of habeas corpus had never formally been recognized by Parliament. In 1679, the Habeas Corpus Act—also called Shaftesbury's Act, after the principal sponsor, Lord Shaftesbury—was passed by Parliament, which made it clear that the territorial scope of the protections afforded by habeas corpus—the guarantee against arbitrary detention—was intended to be broad. The preamble described the act as "An Act for the better securing of the liberty of the subject, and for the prevention of imprisonment beyond the seas." This was an important element because no longer could the King or council ship prisoners beyond the jurisdiction of the courts to avoid the reach of habeas corpus.

The additional consequence of the Act of 1679 was that it clarified the English law of habeas corpus, codified it, and compelled sheriffs and others who kept persons in custody to justify that custody by reference to law rather than personal will. The act codified the principle as a matter of law and provided for the accused to have their complaint heard before a judge to determine if the state had a strong enough case to hold the prisoner. It was passed during the reign of Charles II and meant that even a political prisoner, an opponent of the king, as well as a common criminal, could have a fair trial and not just be thrown into prison to be forgotten about. The English Habeas Corpus Act of 1679 is the most significant part of the English law of habeas corpus for its impact on American law and the suspension clause from the U.S. Constitution. Though amended over time, the Habeas Corpus Act remains on the statute book to this day.

FURTHER READING

Hallam, Henry. *The Constitutional History of England from the Accession of Henry VII to the Death of George II*. Buffalo, N.Y.: W.S. Hein Co., 1989.

Kenyon, J. P. *The Stuart Constitution, 1603–1688; Documents and Commentary*. Cambridge: Cambridge University Press, 1966.

The British Bill of Rights

- ***Document:*** An excerpt from The British Bill of Rights; subtitled, "An Act Declaring the Rights and Liberties of the Subject and Settling the Succession of the Crown"
- ***Date:*** December 16, 1689
- ***Where:*** London, England
- ***Significance:*** The British Bill of Rights established that the monarchy's power came from Parliament, and that the crown and whoever held it, were bound to respect long respected civil liberties.

DOCUMENT

Whereas the late King James the Second, by the assistance of divers evil counsellors, judges and ministers employed by him, did endeavour to subvert and extirpate the Protestant religion and the laws and liberties of this kingdom;

By assuming and exercising a power of dispensing with and suspending of laws and the execution of laws without consent of Parliament;

And whereas of late years partial corrupt and unqualified persons have been returned and served on juries in trials, and particularly divers jurors in trials for high treason which were not freeholders;

And excessive bail hath been required of persons committed in criminal cases to elude the benefit of the laws made for the liberty of the subjects;

And excessive fines have been imposed;

And illegal and cruel punishments inflicted;

And thereupon the said Lords Spiritual and Temporal and Commons, pursuant to their respective letters and elections, being now assembled in a full and free representative of this nation, taking into their most serious consideration the best means for attaining the ends aforesaid, do in the first place (as their ancestors in like case

The British Parliament offers the crown to William and Mary. (Library of Congress.)

have usually done) for the vindicating and asserting their ancient rights and liberties declare.

SOURCE: http://avalon.law.yale.edu/17th_century/england.asp

ANALYSIS

For centuries, the religious struggle between Protestants and Catholics had led to the unfair treatment of each side by the other, and culminating under James II in his attempt to reestablish the Catholic Church by force. Under this threat, Parliament passed the Bill of Rights, effectively ending the absolute power of the monarchy and making the parliament the source of power in England. With James II overthrown, Parliament invited William of Orange and his wife, Mary, eldest daughter of James II, to take the throne and rule jointly. In adopting the 1689 Bill of Rights, the English parliament sought to condemn punishments that were illegal because they were contrary to the common law. The Bill of Rights was ratified by a formal parliament in December 1689, and the Scottish parliament approved it as the Claim of Right.

Notwithstanding its importance as a precursor of the American Bill of Rights, the English bill was quite narrow in the range of its protections, even against the crown.

In fact it established no new principles, except, perhaps, for the provision against standing armies in time of peace without parliamentary approval. The Bill of Rights nevertheless confirmed several old principles of major significance, including the freedom of petition; and prohibitions on excessive bail, excessive fines, and cruel or unusual punishment. The foremost significance of the English Bill of Rights most likely comes through the symbolism of the name, conveying far more than the document itself actually protects. As a symbol of fundamental law and the rule of law it was a strong precursor of the larger number of rights developed by the U.S. states and in the U.S. Constitution. A century later, the American founders took this language of their English heritage and applied it as a constitutional limitation upon the validity of federal action.

FURTHER READING

Hoppit, Julian. *A Land of Liberty?: England 1689–1727*. The New Oxford History of England. Oxford [England]: Clarendon Press, 2000.

Kenyon, J. P. *The Stuart Constitution, 1603–1688; Documents and Commentary*. Cambridge: Cambridge University Press, 1966.

The Massachusetts Constitution

- ***Document:*** Preamble and Declaration of Rights, Massachusetts State Constitution, 1780
- ***Date:*** March 2, 1780
- ***Where:*** Cambridge, Massachusetts
- ***Significance:*** Ratified before the federal Constitution, the Massachusetts Constitution served as an important guide for setting guidelines to due process with regard to the rights of citizens accused of a crime.

DOCUMENT

Massachusetts Constitution, 1780

A CONSTITUTION OR FRAME OF GOVERNMENT, Agreed upon by the Delegates of the People of the STATE OF MASSACHUSETTS-BAY,—In Convention,—Begun and held at Cambridge, on the First of September, 1779, and continued by Adjournments to the Second of March, 1780.

Preamble

The end of the institution, maintenance and administration of government, is to secure the existence of the body-politic; to protect it; and to furnish the individuals who compose it, with the power of enjoying, in safety and tranquillity, their natural rights, and the blessings of life: And whenever these great objects are not obtained, the people have a right to alter the government, and to take measures necessary for their safety, prosperity and happiness.

The body-politic is formed by a voluntary association of individuals: It is a social compact, by which the whole people covenants with each citizen, and each citizen with the whole people, that all shall be governed by certain laws for the common good. It is the duty of the people, therefore, in framing a Constitution of Government, to provide for an equitable mode of making laws, as well as for an impartial interpretation, and a faithful execution of them; that every man may, at all times, find his security in them.

We, therefore, the people of Massachusetts, acknowledging, with grateful hearts, the goodness of the Great Legislator of the Universe, in affording us, in the course of His providence, an opportunity, deliberately and peaceably, without fraud, violence or surprise, of entering into an original, explicit, and solemn compact with each other; and of forming a new Constitution of Civil Government, for ourselves and posterity; and devoutly imploring His direction in so interesting a design, DO agree upon, ordain and establish, the following Declaration of Rights, and Frame of Government, as the CONSTITUTION of the COMMONWEALTH of MASSACHUSETTS.

Part the First. A Declaration of the Rights of the Inhabitants of the Commonwealth of Massachusetts.

Art. I.—All men are born free and equal, and have certain natural, essential, and unalienable rights; among which may be reckoned the right of enjoying and defending their lives and liberties; that of acquiring, possessing, and protecting property; in fine, that of seeking and obtaining their safety and happiness.

II.—It is the right as well as the duty of all men in society, publicly, and at stated seasons, to worship the SUPREME BEING, the great creator and preserver of the universe. And no subject shall be hurt, molested, or restrained, in his person, liberty, or estate, for worshipping GOD in the manner and season most agreeable to the dictates of his own conscience; or for his religious profession or sentiments; provided he doth not disturb the public peace, or obstruct others in their religious worship.

III.—As the happiness of a people, and the good order and preservation of civil government, essentially depend upon piety, religion and morality; and as these cannot be generally diffused through a community, but by the institution of the public worship of GOD, and of public instructions in piety, religion and morality: Therefore, to promote their happiness and to secure the good order and preservation of their government, the people of this Commonwealth have a right to invest their legislature with power to authorize and require, and the legislature shall, from time to time, authorize and require, the several towns, parishes, precincts, and other bodies-politic, or religious societies, to make suitable provision, at their own expense, for the institution of the public worship of GOD, and for the support and maintenance of public protestant teachers of piety, religion and morality, in all cases where such provision shall not be made voluntarily. And the people of this Commonwealth have also a right to, and do, invest their legislature with authority to enjoin upon all the subjects an attendance upon the instructions of the public teachers aforesaid, at stated times and seasons, if there be any on whose instructions they can conscientiously and conveniently attend.

DID YOU KNOW?

Protection of Rights in State Constitutions

Under our system of federalism, in which power is separated between the national government and the states, each state creates its own system of governance through its own distinctive constitution. Although there are similarities between the federal constitution and the state constitutions, there also are a number of differences, based in part on the traditions, history, and desires of a particular state. The variety of rights incorporated into the state constitutions is one such area of difference. Each state constitution has a bill of rights (sometimes entitled a declaration of rights), and some state bills of rights provide greater protections from government intrusion than does the federal Bill of Rights.

Several state constitutions recognize individual rights that are not explicitly expressed in the federal Constitution or in other state constitutions, such as the right of privacy. Ten states include an explicit right to privacy: Alaska, Arizona, California, Florida, Hawaii, Illinois, Louisiana, Montana, South Carolina, and Washington. State bills of rights will continue to be an important bulwark against arbitrary state action as well to play an important role in the shifting views of individual liberties and federalism in the 21st century.

Provided notwithstanding, that the several towns, parishes, precincts, and other bodies-politic, or religious societies, shall, at all times, have the exclusive right of electing their public teachers, and of contracting with them for their support and maintenance.

And all monies paid by the subject to the support of public worship, and of the public teachers aforesaid, shall, if he require it, be uniformly applied to the support of the public teacher or teachers of his own religious sect or denomination, provided there be any on whose instructions he attends: otherwise it may be paid towards the support of the teacher or teachers of the parish or precinct in which the said monies are raised.

And every denomination of christians, demeaning themselves peaceably, and as good subjects of the Commonwealth, shall be equally under the protection of the law: And no subordination of any one sect or denomination to another shall ever be established by law.

IV.—The people of this Commonwealth have the sole and exclusive right of governing themselves as a free, sovereign, and independent state; and do, and forever hereafter shall, exercise and enjoy every power, jurisdiction, and right, which is not, or may not hereafter, be by them expressly delegated to the United States of America, in Congress assembled.

V.—All power residing originally in the people, and being derived from them, the several magistrates and officers of government, vested with authority, whether legislative, executive, or judicial, are their substitutes and agents, and are at all times accountable to them.

VI.—No man, nor corporation, or association of men, have any other title to obtain advantages, or particular and exclusive privileges, distinct from those of the community, than what arises from the consideration of services rendered to the public; and this title being in nature neither hereditary, nor transmissible to children, or descendants, or relations by blood, the idea of a man born a magistrate, lawgiver, or judge, is absurd and unnatural.

VII.—Government is instituted for the common good; for the protection, safety, prosperity and happiness of the people; and not for the profit, honor, or private interest of any one man, family, or class of men; Therefore the people alone have an incontestible, unalienable, and indefeasible right to institute government; and to reform, alter, or totally change the same, when their protection, safety, prosperity and happiness require it.

VIII.—In order to prevent those, who are vested with authority, from becoming oppressors, the people have a right, at such periods and in such manner as they shall establish by their frame of government, to cause their public officers to return to private life; and to fill up vacant places by certain and regular elections and appointments.

IX.—All elections ought to be free; and all the inhabitants of this Commonwealth, having such qualifications as they shall establish by their frame of government, have an equal right to elect officers, and to be elected, for public employments.

X.—Each individual of the society has a right to be protected by it in the enjoyment of his life, liberty and property, according to standing laws. He is obliged, consequently, to contribute his share to the expense of this protection; to give his personal service, or an equivalent, when necessary: But no part of the property of any individual, can, with justice, be taken from him, or applied to public uses without his own consent, or that of the representative body of the people: In fine, the people of this Commonwealth are not controlable by any other laws, than those to which their constitutional representative body have given their consent. And whenever the public exigencies require, that the property of any individual should be appropriated to public uses, he shall receive a reasonable compensation therefor.

XI.—Every subject of the Commonwealth ought to find a certain remedy, by having recourse to the laws, for all injuries or wrongs which he may receive in his person, property, or character. He ought to obtain right and justice freely, and without being obliged to purchase it; completely, and without any denial; promptly, and without delay; conformably to the laws.

XII.—No subject shall be held to answer for any crime or offence, until the same is fully and plainly, substantially and formally, described to him; or be compelled to accuse, or furnish evidence against himself. And every subject shall have a right to produce all proofs, that may be favorable to him; to meet the witnesses against him face to face, [Volume 1, Page 13] and to be fully heard in his defence by himself, or his council, at his election. And no subject shall be arrested, imprisoned, despoiled, or deprived of his property, immunities, or privileges, put out of the protection of the law, exiled, or deprived of his life, liberty, or estate; but by the judgment of his peers, or the law of the land.

And the legislature shall not make any law, that shall subject any person to a capital or infamous punishment, excepting for the government of the army and navy, without trial by jury.

XIII.—In criminal prosecutions, the verification of facts in the vicinity where they happen, is one of the greatest securities of the life, liberty, and property of the citizen.

XIV.—Every subject has a right to be secure from all unreasonable searches, and seizures of his person, his houses, his papers, and all his possessions. All warrants, therefore, are contrary to this right, if the cause or foundation of them be not previously supported by oath or affirmation; and if the order in the warrant to a civil officer, to make search in suspected places, or to arrest one or more suspected persons, or to seize their property, be not accompanied with a special designation of the persons or objects of search, arrest, or seizure: and no warrant ought to be issued but in cases, and with the formalities, prescribed by the laws.

XV.—In all controversies concerning property, and in all suits between two or more persons, except in cases in which it has heretofore been otherways used and practised, the parties have a right to a trial by jury; and this method of procedure shall be held sacred, unless, in causes arising on the high-seas, and such as relate to mariners wages, the legislature shall hereafter find it necessary to alter it.

XVI.—The liberty of the press is essential to the security of freedom in a state: it ought not, therefore, to be restrained in this Commonwealth.

XVII.—The people have a right to keep and to bear arms for the common defence. And as in time of peace armies are dangerous to liberty, they ought not to be maintained without the consent of the legislature; and the military power shall always be held in an exact subordination to the civil authority, and be governed by it.

XVIII.—A frequent recurrence to the fundamental principles of the constitution, and a constant adherence to those of piety, justice, moderation, temperance, industry, and frugality, are absolutely necessary to preserve the advantages of liberty, and to maintain a free government: The people ought, consequently, to have a particular attention to all those principles, in the choice of their officers and representatives: And they have a right to require of their law-givers and magistrates, an exact and constant observance of them, in the formation and execution of the laws necessary for the good administration of the Commonwealth.

XIX.—The people have a right, in an orderly and peaceable manner, to assemble to consult upon the common good; give instructions to their representatives; and to request of the legislative body, by the way of addresses, petitions, or remonstrances, redress of the wrongs done them, and of the grievances they suffer.

XX.—The power of suspending the laws, or the execution of the laws, ought never to be exercised but by the legislature, or by authority derived from it, to be exercised in such particular cases only as the legislature shall expressly provide for.

XXI.—The freedom of deliberation, speech and debate, in either house of the legislature, is so essential to the rights of the people, that it cannot be the foundation of any accusation or prosecution, action or complaint, in any other court or place whatsoever.

XXII.—The legislature ought frequently to assemble for the redress of grievances, for correcting, strengthening, and confirming the laws, and for making new laws, as the common good may require.

XXIII.—No subsidy, charge, tax, impost, or duties, ought to be established, fixed, laid, or levied, under any pretext whatsoever, without the consent of the people, or their representatives in the legislature.

XXIV.—Laws made to punish for actions done before the existence of such laws, and which have not been declared crimes by preceding laws, are unjust, oppressive, and inconsistent with the fundamental principles of a free government.

XXV.—No subject ought, in any case, or in any time, to be declared guilty of treason or felony by the legislature.

XXVI.—No magistrate or court of law shall demand excessive bail or sureties, impose excessive fines, or inflict cruel or unusual punishments.

XXVII.—In time of peace no soldier ought to be quartered in any house without the consent of the owner; and in time of war such quarters ought not to be made but by the civil magistrate, in a manner ordained by the legislature.

XXVIII.—No person can in any case be subjected to law-martial, or to any penalties or pains, by virtue of that law, except those employed in the army or navy, and except the militia in actual service, but by authority of the legislature.

XXIX.—It is essential to the preservation of the rights of every individual, his life, liberty, property and character, that there be an impartial interpretation of the laws, and administration of justice. It is the right of every citizen to be tried by judges as free, impartial and independent as the lot of humanity will admit. It is therefore not only the best policy, but for the security of the rights of the people, and of every citizen, that the judges of the supreme judicial court should hold their offices as long as they behave themselves well; and that they should have honorable salaries ascertained and established by standing laws.

XXX.—In the government of this Commonwealth, the legislative department shall never exercise the executive and judicial powers, or either of them: The executive shall never exercise the legislative and judicial powers, or either of them: The judicial shall never exercise the legislative and executive powers, or either of them: to the end it may be a government of laws and not of men.

SOURCE: http://press-pubs.uchicago.edu/founders/documents/v1ch1s6.html

ANALYSIS

The Massachusetts Constitution is the oldest state constitution. Having been authored primarily by John Adams, the document was more sophisticated than many of the other state constitutions due to its construction. For example, instead of just listing provisions, it had a structure of chapters, sections, and articles. This structure served as a foundation for the U.S. Constitution. The Massachusetts Constitution also had substantial influence on the subsequent revisions of many of the other state constitutions. In particular, the preamble sets forth the document's purpose as creating a social compact the end of which is the common good.

The social compact theory of government allows individuals to band together in community, out of their state in nature, to form a structure for their common good and security. This creates a structure that then secures the rights of the individuals as the common good is pursued. This is an important distinction that explains why throughout late 18th-century political writings the common good was given precedence over the claims of individuals. This emphasis on the common good reveals the framers' understanding that individuals' rights are not absolute but are circumscribed directly and formally by the right of the people to self-government. The goal was to secure the peoples' collective well-being, their "common wealth," not supremely the rights of individuals. It is no coincidence that John Adams suggested that Massachusetts adopt the title of "Commonwealth" and placed in its constitution the goal of creating a government of laws for the common good. The constitution, with only minimal limitations, protected the right of the citizens of the commonwealth to make laws and set policies that affirmed the common good.

FURTHER READING

Handlin, Oscar, and Mary Flug Handlin. *The Popular Sources of Political Authority; Documents on the Massachusetts Constitution of 1780*. Cambridge, Mass.: Belknap Press of Harvard University Press, 1966.

Peters, Ronald M. *The Massachusetts Constitution of 1780: A Social Compact*. Amherst: University of Massachusetts Press, 1978.

U.S. Constitution: Fifth Amendment

- ***Document:*** The Fifth Amendment to the U.S. Constitution
- ***Date:*** December 15, 1791
- ***Where:*** Washington, D.C.
- ***Significance:*** The Fifth Amendment protects against abuse of government authority by a legal procedure.

DOCUMENT

United States Constitution

Amendment 5—Trial and Punishment, Compensation for Takings. Ratified 12/15/1791

No person shall be held to answer for a capital, or otherwise infamous crime, unless on a presentment or indictment of a Grand Jury, except in cases arising in the land or naval forces, or in the Militia, when in actual service in time of War or public danger; nor shall any person be subject for the same offense to be twice put in jeopardy of life or limb; nor shall be compelled in any criminal case to be a witness against himself, nor be deprived of life, liberty, or property, without due process of law; nor shall private property be taken for public use, without just compensation.

SOURCE: http://www.usconstitution.net/const.html#Am5

ANALYSIS

The language of the Fifth Amendment outlines basic constitutional limits on criminal procedures including: grand juries for capital crimes, a prohibition on double jeopardy, a prohibition against required self-incrimination, a guarantee that all criminal defendants will have a fair trial (due process), and a promise that the government will not seize private property without paying market value. While the Fifth Amendment originally only applied to federal courts, the U.S. Supreme Court has interpreted most of the Fifth Amendment's provisions as incorporated to the states through the due process clause of the Fourteenth Amendment. The grand jury indictment clause has not been incorporated by the Fourteenth Amendment. States are thus free to abolish grand juries and many have replaced them with preliminary hearings.

FURTHER READING

Levy, Leonard W. *Origins of the Fifth Amendment; The Right against Self-Incrimination*. New York: Oxford University Press, 1968.

DID YOU KNOW?

Alexander Hamilton, "Remarks on an Act for Regulating Elections," 1787

In an influential speech to the New York State Assembly in February 1787, Alexander Hamilton, one of the principal architects of the federal Constitution, speculated that only formal court proceedings could suspend rights, not laws passed in the legislature. Hamilton argued that the due process of law is largely based on the decisions of courts and should not be left up to the legislatures, which couldn't be trusted to exercise the prudence and respect that law requires: "It is there declared that, no man shall be disfranchised or deprived of any right, but by *due process of law,* or the judgment of his peers. The words '*due process*' have a precise technical import, and are only applicable to the process and proceedings of the courts of justice; they can never be referred to an act of legislature." New York requested that this principle of due process be added to the federal Constitution. In response to New York's proposal, James Madison drafted a due process clause for Congress that was included as the Fifth Amendment to the Bill of Rights. The Bill of Rights was ratified in 1791.

Luther Martin, Genuine Information

- ***Document:*** Luther Martin, Genuine Information
- ***Date:*** February 8, 1788
- ***Where:*** Philadelphia, Pennsylvania
- ***Significance:*** Luther Martin was an Anti-Federalist from Maryland who wrote about his opposition to the ratification of the federal Constitution.

DOCUMENT

Luther Martin, Genuine Information

1788 Storing 2.4.49–52

The seventh section of this article was also the subject of contest—It was thought by many members of the convention, that it was very wrong to confine the origination of all revenue bills to the house of representatives, since the members of the senate will be chosen by the people as well as the members of the house of delegates, if not immediately, yet mediately, being chosen by the members of the State legislature, which members are elected by the people, and that it makes no real difference whether we do a thing in person, or by a deputy, or agent, appointed by us for that purpose.

That no argument can be drawn from the House of Lords in the British constitution, since they are neither mediately nor immediately the representatives of the people, but are one of the three estates, composing that kingdom, having hereditary right and privileges, distinct from, and independent of, the people.

That it may, and probably will be a future source of dispute and controversy between the two branches, what are, or are not revenue bills, and the more so, as they are not defined in the constitution; which controversies may be difficult to settle, and may become serious in their consequences, [there] being no power in the constitution to decide upon, or authorised in cases of absolute necessity to terminate them by a prorogation or dissolution of either of the branches; a remedy provided in the British constitution, where the King has that power, which has been found necessary at times to be exercised in case of violent dissentions between the Lords and Commons on the subject of money bills.

That every regulation of commerce; every law relative to excises, stamps, the post-office, the imposing of taxes, and their collection, the creation of courts and offices; in fine, every law for the union, if enforced by any pecuniary sanctions, as they would tend to bring money into the continental treasury, might and no doubt would be considered a revenue act—That consequently the senate, the members of whom will it may be presumed, be the most select in their choice, and consist of men the most enlightened, and of the greatest abilities, who from the duration of their appointment and the permanency of their body, will probably be best acquainted with the common concerns of the States, and with the means of providing for them, will be rendered almost useless as a part of the legislature; and that they will have but little to do in that capacity, except patiently to wait the proceedings of the house of representatives, and afterwards examine and approve, or propose amendments.

SOURCE: http://press-pubs.uchicago.edu/founders/documents/a1_7_1s8.html

Luther Martin was a prominent Maryland attorney who stood firm in his Anti-Federalist views during the writing of the Constitution. He was concerned about the strong power of the newly formed central government. Later in his law career, Martin defended Samuel Chase and Aaron Burr in their high-profile court cases. (Library of Congress.)

ANALYSIS

Luther Martin was the attorney general of Maryland at the time of the founding and he also attended the Constitutional Convention. Luther Martin was adamantly opposed to the ratification of the Federal Constitution because he was opposed to slavery and direct taxation and he generally believed that the document placed too much power in the hands of the national government. In Genuine Information, Martin argues that Article IV, Section 3 of the Constitution prohibits the formation or erection of new breakaway states without the consent of parent states; these (larger) states will not provide their consent; domestic violence will likely ensue; and the smaller states will be forced to defend the larger states against domestic violence pursuant to the guarantee clause. The entirety of Martin's detailed discussion of Article IV, Section 3 makes clear that the would-be states of Franklin (Tennessee), Vermont, and Maine could be admitted into the Union as new breakaway states with the consent of their parent states and of Congress. In sum, Luther Martin believed that the second clause of Article IV, Section 3 was not a flat prohibition on new breakaway states. Martin played a significant role at the Convention, especially in his efforts to preserve the role of the smaller states.

FURTHER READING

Reynolds, William L., II. "Essay: Luther Martin, Maryland and the Constitution." *Maryland Law Review* 47 (1987): 291.

Debate at the Massachusetts Ratifying Convention

- ***Document:*** The Debate at the Massachusetts Ratifying Convention, Excerpt
- ***Date:*** January 30, 1788
- ***Where:*** Boston, Massachusetts
- ***Significance:*** The Massachusetts Convention was the first serious test for ratifying the Constitution, because of a concern about the election and the process of representation in Congress.

DOCUMENT

Debate in Massachusetts Ratifying Convention

30 Jan. 1788 Elliot 2:116–17

The Hon. Mr. King observed, that he believed gentlemen had not, in their objections to the Constitution, recollected that this article was a part of it; for many of the arguments of gentlemen were founded on the idea of future amendments being impracticable. The honorable gentleman observed on the superior excellence of the proposed Constitution in this particular, and called upon gentlemen to produce an instance, in any other national constitution, where the people had so fair an opportunity to correct any abuse which might take place in the future administration of the government under it.

Dr. Jarvis. Mr. President, I cannot suffer the present article to be passed, without rising to express my entire and perfect approbation of it. Whatever may have been my private opinion of any other part, or whatever faults or imperfections I have remarked, or fancied I have seen, in any other instance, here, sir, I have found complete satisfaction: this has been a resting place, on which I have reposed myself in the fullest security, whenever a doubt has occurred, in considering any other passage in the proposed Constitution. The honorable gentleman last speaking has called upon those persons who are opposed to our receiving the present system, to show another government, in which such a wise precaution has been taken to secure to the people the right of making such alterations and amendments, in a peaceable way, as experience shall have proved to be necessary. Allow me to say, sir, as far as the narrow limits of my own information extend, I know of no such example. In other countries, sir,—unhappily for mankind,—the history of their respective revolutions has been written in blood; and it is in this only that any great or important change in our political situation has been effected, without public commotions. When we shall have adopted the Constitution before us, we shall have in this article an adequate provision for all the purposes of political reformation. If, in the course of its operation, this government shall appear to be too severe, here are the means by which this severity may be assuaged and corrected. If, on the other hand, it shall become too languid in its movements, here, again, we have a method designated, by which a new portion of health and spirit may be infused into the Constitution.

There is, sir, another view, which I have long since taken of this subject, which has produced the fullest conviction, in my own mind, in favor of our receiving the government which we have now in contemplation. Should it be rejected, I beg gentlemen would observe, that a concurrence of all the states must be had before a new convention can be called to form another Constitution; but the present article provides, upon nine states' concurring in any alteration or amendment to be proposed either by Congress or any future convention, that this situation shall be a part of the Constitution, equally powerful and obligatory with any other part. If it be alleged that this union is not likely to happen, will it be more likely that a union of a greater number of concurring sentiments may be had, as must be, in case we reject the Constitution in hopes of a better? But that this is practicable, we may safely appeal to the history of this country as a proof, in the last twenty years. We have united against the British; we have united in calling the late federal Convention; and we may certainly unite again in such alterations as in reason shall appear to be important for the peace and happiness of America.

In the constitution of this state, the article providing for alterations is limited in its operation to a given time; but in the present Constitution, the article is perfectly at large, unconfined to any period, and may admit of measures being taken in any moment after it is adopted. In this point it has undoubtedly the advantage. I shall not sit down, sir, without repeating, that, as it is clearly more difficult for twelve states to agree to another convention, than for nine to unite in favor of amendments, so it is certainly better to receive the present Constitution, in the hope of its being amended, than it would be to reject it altogether, with, perhaps, the vain expectation of obtaining another more agreeable than the present. I see no fallacy in the argument, Mr. President; but, if there is, permit me to call upon any gentleman to point it out, in order that it may be corrected; for, at present, it seems to me of such force as to give me entire satisfaction.

SOURCE: http://press-pubs.uchicago.edu/founders/documents/a5s7.html

ANALYSIS

The Massachusetts Convention was the largest in terms of the number of delegates. These delegates included many prominent figures such as Caleb Strong, Rufus

King, and Nathaniel Gorham, who were all at the Philadelphia Convention. They were joined by Fisher Ames, James Bowdoin, Francis Dana, and Theophilus Parsons in defending and explaining the Constitution. Elbridge Gerry, a prominent Anti-Federalist was requested to attend by the delegates after the first week. Gerry had refused to sign the Constitution in Philadelphia and accepted an invitation to the Massachusetts Convention. He never made it to the floor of the convention and after January 19, he withdrew from view, leaving people with less prestige and experience to lead the opposition.

The delegates generally agreed with the Massachusetts public that the series of recent troubles, ranging from Congress's inability to pay the national debt to Shays's Rebellion in western Massachusetts, warranted a change in the Articles of Confederation. Within the convention, however, Anti-Federalists argued that the Constitution went too far in creating an overly powerful national government at the expense of state sovereignty and individual liberties. As Anti-Federalist delegates outnumbered Federalists, the Massachusetts Convention was the first serious threat to ratification. The constitutional provisions on representation formed the basis of much of this opposition. The Anti-Federalists' conceptualization of representation has been described through the metaphor of the mirror, in which the representative was expected to pursue those policies that reflected the interests of his constituents. Through mirroring the constituency's sentiments and values, a representative might best act as the voters' agent and pursue their localized interests. The Constitution's lack of constituent controls that had existed under the Articles of Confederation fueled Anti-Federalist worries that representation would no longer operate in this manner, thus reducing popular sovereignty and destroying liberty. In the end, though, these sentiments did not prevail, and Massachusetts ratified the Constitution. The ratifying document however included proposed amendments aimed at correcting perceived problems concerning representation in the Constitution. Allowing these amendments to be added to the document was a critical compromise that secured the victory for the proponents of the Constitution because approximately 10 delegates changed their mind to secure ratification by a 187–168 vote.

FURTHER READING

Ackerman, Bruce. *We the People: Foundations*. Cambridge, Mass.: Harvard University Press, 1991, 166–67.

Rutland, Robert Allen. *The Ordeal of the Constitution: The Antifederalists and the Ratification Struggle of 1787–1788*. Boston: Northeastern University Press, 1983, 66–70.

Federalist Paper #84

- ***Document:*** Federalist Paper #84: Certain General and Miscellaneous Objections to the Constitution Considered and Answered
- ***Date:*** May 28, 1788
- ***Where:*** New York
- ***Significance:*** Written by Alexander Hamilton under the pseudonym "Publius," Federalist #84 argued against the need for the Bill of Rights.

DOCUMENT

The Federalist Papers: No. 84; Certain General and Miscellaneous Objections to the Constitution Considered and Answered

To the People of the State of New York:

IN THE course of the foregoing review of the Constitution, I have taken notice of, and endeavored to answer most of the objections which have appeared against it. There, however, remain a few which either did not fall naturally under any particular head or were forgotten in their proper places. These shall now be discussed; but as the subject has been drawn into great length, I shall so far consult brevity as to comprise all my observations on these miscellaneous points in a single paper.

The most considerable of the remaining objections is that the plan of the convention contains no bill of rights. Among other answers given to this, it has been upon different occasions remarked that the constitutions of several of the States are in a similar predicament. I add that New York is of the number. And yet the opposers of the new system, in this State, who profess an unlimited admiration for its constitution, are among the most intemperate partisans of a bill of rights. To justify their zeal in this matter, they allege two things: one is that, though the constitution of New York has no bill of rights prefixed to it, yet it contains, in the body of it, various provisions in favor of particular privileges and rights, which, in substance amount to the same thing; the other is, that the Constitution adopts, in their full extent, the common and statute law of Great Britain, by which many other rights, not expressed in it, are equally secured.

To the first I answer, that the Constitution proposed by the convention contains, as well as the constitution of this State, a number of such provisions.

Independent of those which relate to the structure of the government, we find the following: Article 1, section 3, clause 7—"Judgment in cases of impeachment shall not extend further than to removal from office, and disqualification to hold and enjoy any office of honor, trust, or profit under the United States; but the party convicted shall, nevertheless, be liable and subject to indictment, trial, judgment, and punishment according to law." Section 9, of the same article, clause 2—"The privilege of the writ of habeas corpus shall not be suspended, unless when in cases of rebellion or invasion the public safety may require it." Clause 3—"No bill of attainder or ex-post-facto law shall be passed." Clause 7—"No title of nobility shall be granted by the United States; and no person holding any office of profit or trust under them, shall, without the consent of the Congress, accept of any present, emolument, office, or title of any kind whatever, from any king, prince, or foreign state." Article 3, section 2, clause 3—"The trial of all crimes, except in cases of impeachment, shall be by jury; and such trial shall be held in the State where the said crimes shall have been committed; but when not committed within any State, the trial shall be at such place or places as the Congress may by law have directed." Section 3, of the same article—"Treason against the United States shall consist only in levying war against them, or in adhering to their enemies, giving them aid and comfort. No person shall be convicted of treason, unless on the testimony of two witnesses to the same overt act, or on confession in open court." And clause 3, of the same section—"The Congress shall have power to declare the punishment of treason; but no attainder of treason shall work corruption of blood, or forfeiture, except during the life of the person attainted."

It may well be a question, whether these are not, upon the whole, of equal importance with any which are to be found in the constitution of this State. The establishment of the writ of *habeas corpus*, the prohibition of *ex post facto* laws, and of TITLES OF NOBILITY, *to which we have no corresponding provision in our Constitution*, are perhaps greater securities to liberty and republicanism than any it contains. The creation of crimes after the commission of the fact, or, in other words, the subjecting of men to punishment for things which, when they were done, were breaches of no law, and the practice of arbitrary imprisonments, have been, in all ages, the

DID YOU KNOW?

Thomas Jefferson to James Madison, July 31, 1788

Jefferson's letters to James Madison are very instructive as to the problems he believed existed with the Constitution. Troubled that the Constitution was lacking a bill of rights, Jefferson urged Madison in a July 1788 letter to add protections against the tyranny of the federal government. The Federalists opposed including a bill of rights on the ground that it was unnecessary. The Anti-Federalists were afraid of a strong centralized government and refused to support the Constitution without one. It would take four more years of intense debate before the new government's form would be resolved.

A number of scholars and historians believe that Jefferson played a role in persuading Madison to include a bill of rights. Jefferson's letters were also widely distributed and helped convince others of the importance of adding a bill of rights to the Constitution. Other scholars and historians argue that Madison changed his position because of a promise he had made during his heated campaign against James Monroe for election to the House of Representatives. Madison's opposition to a bill of rights had hurt him politically in Virginia, and he pledged to attach civil liberties amendments to the Constitution as soon as the new government was in operation.

The Bill of Rights, inspired by Jefferson and drafted by James Madison, was adopted, and in 1791 the Constitution's first 10 amendments became the law of the land.

Alexander Hamilton helped frame the U.S. Constitution and was a founding father of the new nation. (Library of Congress.)

favorite and most formidable instruments of tyranny. The observations of the judicious Blackstone, in reference to the latter, are well worthy of recital: "To bereave a man of life, [says he] or by violence to confiscate his estate, without accusation or trial, would be so gross and notorious an act of despotism, as must at once convey the alarm of tyranny throughout the whole nation; but confinement of the person, by secretly hurrying him to jail, where his sufferings are unknown or forgotten, is a less public, a less striking, and therefore *a more dangerous engine* of arbitrary government." And as a remedy for this fatal evil he is everywhere peculiarly emphatical in his encomiums on the *habeas corpus* act, which in one place he calls "the BULWARK of the British Constitution."

Nothing need be said to illustrate the importance of the prohibition of titles of nobility. This may truly be denominated the corner-stone of republican government; for so long as they are excluded, there can never be serious danger that the government will be any other than that of the people.

To the second that is, to the pretended establishment of the common and state law by the Constitution, I answer, that they are expressly made subject "to such alterations and provisions as the legislature shall from time to time make concerning the same." They are therefore at any moment liable to repeal by the ordinary legislative power, and of course have no constitutional sanction. The only use of the declaration was to recognize the ancient law and to remove doubts which might have been occasioned by the Revolution. This consequently can be considered as no part of a declaration of rights, which under our constitutions must be intended as limitations of the power of the government itself.

It has been several times truly remarked that bills of rights are, in their origin, stipulations between kings and their subjects, abridgements of prerogative in favor of privilege, reservations of rights not surrendered to the prince. Such was MAGNA CHARTA, obtained by the barons, sword in hand, from King John. Such were the subsequent confirmations of that charter by succeeding princes. Such was the *Petition of Right* assented to by Charles I., in the beginning of his reign. Such, also, was the Declaration of Right presented by the Lords and Commons to the Prince of Orange in 1688, and afterwards thrown into the form of an act of parliament called the Bill of Rights. It is evident, therefore, that, according to their primitive signification, they have no application to constitutions professedly founded upon the power of the people, and executed by their immediate representatives and servants. Here, in strictness, the people surrender nothing; and as they retain everything they have no need of particular reservations. "WE, THE PEOPLE of the United States, to secure the blessings of liberty to ourselves and our posterity, do *ordain* and *establish* this Constitution for the United States of America." Here is a better recognition of popular rights, than volumes of those aphorisms which make the principal figure in several of our State bills of rights, and which would sound much better in a treatise of ethics than in a constitution of government.

But a minute detail of particular rights is certainly far less applicable to a Constitution like that under consideration, which is merely intended to regulate the general political interests of the nation, than to a constitution which has the regulation of every species of personal and private concerns. If, therefore, the loud clamors against the plan of the convention, on this score, are well founded, no epithets of reprobation will be too strong for the constitution of this State. But the truth is, that both of them contain all which, in relation to their objects, is reasonably to be desired.

I go further, and affirm that bills of rights, in the sense and to the extent in which they are contended for, are not only unnecessary in the proposed Constitution, but would even be dangerous. They would contain various exceptions to powers not granted; and, on this very account, would afford a colorable pretext to claim more than were granted. For why declare that things shall not be done which there is no power to do? Why, for instance, should it be said that the liberty of the press shall not be restrained, when no power is given by which restrictions may be imposed? I will not contend that such a provision would confer a regulating power; but it is evident that it would furnish, to men disposed to usurp, a plausible pretense for claiming that power. They might urge with a semblance of reason, that the Constitution ought not to be charged with the absurdity of providing against the abuse of an authority which was not given, and that the provision against restraining the liberty of the press afforded a clear implication, that a power to prescribe proper regulations concerning it was intended to be vested in the national government. This may serve as a specimen of the numerous handles which would be given to the doctrine of constructive powers, by the indulgence of an injudicious zeal for bills of rights.

On the subject of the liberty of the press, as much as has been said, I cannot forbear adding a remark or two: in the first place, I observe, that there is not a syllable concerning it in the constitution of this State; in the next, I contend, that whatever has been said about it in that of any other State, amounts to nothing. What signifies a declaration, that "the liberty of the press shall be inviolably preserved"? What is the liberty of the press? Who can give it any definition which would not leave the utmost latitude for evasion? I hold it to be impracticable; and from this I infer, that its security, whatever fine declarations may be inserted in any constitution respecting it, must altogether depend on public opinion, and on the general spirit of the people and of the government. And here, after all, as is intimated upon another occasion, must we seek for the only solid basis of all our rights.

There remains but one other view of this matter to conclude the point. The truth is, after all the declamations we have heard, that the Constitution is itself, in every rational sense, and to every useful purpose, A BILL OF RIGHTS. The several bills of rights in Great Britain form its Constitution, and conversely the constitution of each State is its bill of rights. And the proposed Constitution, if adopted, will be the bill of rights of the Union. Is it one object of a bill of rights to declare and specify the political privileges of the citizens in the structure and administration of the government? This is done in the most ample and precise manner in the plan of the convention; comprehending various precautions for the public security, which are not to be found in any of the State constitutions. Is another object of a bill of rights to define certain immunities and modes of proceeding, which are relative to personal and private concerns? This we have seen has also been attended to, in a variety of cases, in the same plan. Adverting therefore to the substantial meaning of a bill of rights, it is absurd to allege that it is not to be found in the work of the convention. It may be said that it does not go far enough, though it will not be easy to make this appear; but it can with no propriety be contended that there is no such thing. It certainly must be immaterial what mode is observed as to the order of declaring the rights of the citizens, if they are to be found in any part of the instrument which establishes the government. And hence it must be apparent, that much of what has been said on this subject rests merely on verbal and nominal distinctions, entirely foreign from the substance of the thing.

PUBLIUS

SOURCE: http://avalon.law.yale.edu/18th_century/fed84.asp

ANALYSIS

Although they had been a defense of the federal Constitution, this particular Federalist Paper, written by Alexander Hamilton, took issue with the need for the Bill of Rights. Hamilton acknowledges that there are a number of objections to the Constitution that had not yet been discussed. The most important of the remaining objections is that the Constitution does not contain a bill of rights. Hamilton argues that there is no need for a bill of rights because there are many safeguards against the abuse of power which are built into the structure of the national government, such as the separation of powers and checks and balances. Hamilton also discusses six provisions of the Constitution designed to protect individual liberties including: the power to impeach, the writ of habeas corpus, the prohibition of bills of attainder and ex-post-facto laws, the prohibition against the granting of any title of nobility by the United States, the right to trial by jury in all criminal cases, and the clear distinction made between political dissent and treason.

Hamilton also felt that had a bill of rights been adopted, those who wished to take away the rights and liberties of the citizenry would view this list as finite, and should a need arise to circumvent this, the opportunity would be taken. Hamilton further argues that a bill of rights would not only be unnecessary but dangerous. A bill of rights would, for instance, attempt to limit certain governmental powers which are not even granted. For Hamilton, the Preamble of the Constitution is a superior recognition of popular rights because the Constitution is concerned with general political interest and rights, not with specific and minute details of every right.

FURTHER READING

Epstein, David F. *The Political Theory of the Federalist*. Chicago: University of Chicago Press, 1984.

White, Morton Gabriel. *Philosophy, The Federalist, and the Constitution*. New York: Oxford University Press, 1987.

William Rawle, *A View of the Constitution of the United States,* 1829

- ***Document:*** William Rawle, *A View of the Constitution of the United States*, 1829
- ***Date:*** 1829
- ***Where:*** London, England
- ***Significance:*** William Rawle examined the due process involved in writs of habeas corpus, acknowledging that the right to the writs, as written in the constitution, is a protection of citizens' rights, and there is no easy way for the federal government to get around it.

DOCUMENT

William Rawle, *A View of the Constitution of the United States,* 1829

States 117–19 (2d ed.)

Reasons will be given hereafter for considering many of the restrictions, contained in the amendments to the Constitution, as extending to the states as well as to the United States, but the nature of the writ of *habeas corpus* seems peculiarly to call for this construction. It is the great remedy of the citizen or subject against arbitrary or illegal imprisonment; it is the mode by which the judicial power speedily and effectually protects the personal liberty of every individual, and repels the injustice of unconstitutional laws or despotic governors. After erecting the distinct government which we are considering, and after declaring what should constitute the supreme law in every state in the Union, fearful minds might entertain jealousies of this great and all-controlling power, if some protection against its energies when misdirected, was not provided by itself.

The national code in which the writ of *habeas corpus* was originally found, is not expressly or directly incorporated into the Constitution.

DID YOU KNOW?

**Joseph Story,
Commentaries on the Constitution, 1833**

Joseph Story was a lawyer and judge who served on the Supreme Court of the United States from 1811 to 1845. His *Commentaries on the Constitution* contains very influential treatises on U.S. constitutional law and is still widely respected. One area of significance concerns Story's interpretation of the suspension clause and the importance of the writ of habeas corpus (3:§§ 1333–36, 1833). Story believed that the writ of habeas corpus is a great protection of personal liberty because it determines whether a person is rightfully confined or not. If the holder cannot give sufficient reason to continue the denial of liberty, the confined person is entitled to immediate release. The writ applies to every type of illegal restraint, whatever the reason or consequence. Echoing William Rawle, Story believed that, under the Constitution, the power is given exclusively to Congress to suspend the writ of habeas corpus in cases of rebellion or invasion. Story nevertheless disagreed with Rawle in concluding that Congress's decision to suspend the writ is not subject to judicial review. Story's writings concerning the suspension clause had a tremendous impact on U.S. jurisprudence.

If this provision had been omitted, the existing powers under the state governments, none of whom are without it, might be questioned, and a person imprisoned on a mandate of the president or other officer, under colour of lawful authority derived from the United States, might be denied relief. But the judicial authority, whether vested in a state judge, or a judge of the United States, is an integral and identified capacity; and if congress never made any provision for issuing writs of *habeas corpus*, either the state judges must issue them, or the individual be without redress. The Constitution seems to have secured this benefit to the citizen by the description of the writ, and in an unqualified manner admitting its efficacy, while it declares that *it shall not be suspended unless when, in case of rebellion or invasion, the public safety shall require it.* This writ is believed to be known only in countries governed by the common law, as it is established in England; but in that country the benefit of it may at any time be withheld by the authority of parliament, whereas we see that in this country it cannot be suspended even in cases of rebellion or invasion, unless the public safety shall require it. Of this necessity the Constitution probably intends, that the legislature of the United States shall be the judges. Charged as they are with the preservation of the United States from both those evils, and superseding the powers of the several states in the prosecution of the measures they may find it expedient to adopt, it seems not unreasonable that this control over the writ of *habeas corpus*, which ought only to be exercised on extraordinary occasions, should rest with them. It is at any rate certain, that congress, which has authorized the courts and judges of the United States to issue writs of *habeas corpus* in cases within their jurisdiction, can alone suspend their power, and that no state can prevent those courts and judges from exercising their regular functions, which are, however, confined to cases of imprisonment professed to be under the authority of the United States. But the state courts and judges possess the right of determining on the legality of imprisonment under either authority.

SOURCE: http://press-pubs.uchicago.edu/founders/documents/a1_9_2s15.html

ANALYSIS

Under the U.S. Constitution, the federal government can suspend the privilege of the writ of habeas corpus if the public safety requires it during times of rebellion or invasion. The question of which political branch has the power to suspend the privilege of the writ of habeas corpus is an important constitutional separation of powers question with important consequences for civil liberties. William Rawle is another early constitutional commentator who argued that Congress has the authority of whether the writ of habeas corpus should be suspended. Rawle, who was a strong supporter of states' rights, also believed that state courts have the authority to issue writs of habeas corpus to review the detention of prisoners held under state or federal authority, even if Congress suspended the writ under Article I, Section 9. This position concerning the power to suspend the writ and the jurisdiction of the judicial branch to hear such cases has been mimicked by a number of constitutional scholars and has continued to influence American jurisprudence.

FURTHER READING

Federman, Cary. *The Body and the State: Habeas Corpus and American Jurisprudence*. SUNY Series in American Constitutionalism. Albany: State University of New York Press, 2006.

Mian, Badshah K. *American Habeas Corpus: Law, History, and Politics*. San Francisco: Cosmos of Humanists Press, 1984.

President Lincoln's Suspension of the Writ of Habeas Corpus

- ***Document:*** Lincoln's "Domestic Intelligence: A Proclamation," Excerpt
- ***Date:*** May 27, 1862
- ***Where:*** Washington, D.C.
- ***Significance:*** During the Civil War, President Lincoln appropriated powers no previous president had used before; he suspended the writ of habeas corpus and imprisoned approximately 18,000 suspected Confederate sympathizers without trial.

DOCUMENT

Abraham Lincoln's "Domestic Intelligence: A Proclamation"

By the President of the United States of America:

Whereas, It has become necessary to call into service, not only volunteers, but also portions of the militia of the States by draft, in order to suppress the insurrection existing in the United States, and disloyal persons are not adequately restrained by the ordinary processes of law from hindering this measure, and from giving aid and comfort in various ways to the insurrection. Now, therefore, be it ordered, that during the existing insurrection, and as a necessary measure for suppressing the same, all rebels and insurgents, their aiders and abettors within the United States, and all persons discouraging volunteer enlistments, resisting militia drafts, or guilty of any disloyal practice affording aid and comfort to the rebels against the authority of the United States, shall be subject to martial law, and liable to trial and punishment by courts-martial or military commission. Second: That the writ of habeas corpus is suspended in respect to all persons arrested, or who are now, or hereafter during the rebellion shall be, imprisoned in any fort, camp, arsenal, military prisons, or other place of confinement, by any military authority, or by the sentence of any court-martial or military commission. . . .

SOURCE: http://www.thecivilwaromnibus.com/articles/94

ANALYSIS

The Constitution, in Section 9 of Article I, specifically authorizes the suspension of habeas corpus "when in cases or rebellion or invasion the public safety may require it." The federal government has only officially suspended habeas corpus twice in the history of the continental United States. President Abraham Lincoln suspended the writ, initially without congressional authorization, during the Civil War and President Ulysses S. Grant suspended the writ, pursuant to congressional authorization, during Reconstruction. The reason that Lincoln's actions were considered controversial is because the Constitution itself is silent as to whether the president or Congress has the exclusive right to exercise the power to suspend the writ of habeas corpus.

In 1861, right before the start of the Civil War, confederate sympathizers burned railroad bridges in and around Baltimore. The bridges were needed to move state militias into Washington, D.C., to protect the capital from confederate invasion. Lincoln believed that the war would be lost if the Confederates seized the capital, resulting in complete isolation, but he was reluctant to suspend the writ in part because Congress was not in session. In response to this threat, and also with the additional urging of his secretary of state, William H. Seward, Lincoln suspended habeas corpus between Washington and Philadelphia without congressional authorization.

Lincoln's unilateral suspension of habeas corpus is seen as instrumental in maintaining the communication lines to the nation's capital. However, this action raised an immediate question as to whether the president had the power to suspend habeas corpus under the Constitution. This suspension triggered one of the most intense and significant constitutional disputes of the Lincoln administration. Lincoln responded that his actions were not only justified but were required due to his oath to preserve, protect, and defend the Constitution of the United States. Congress eventually ratified the president's actions by passing the Habeas Corpus Act of 1863. These debates about the suspension clause are equally

DID YOU KNOW?

Aaron Burr and the Suspension of Habeas Corpus Debate, 1807

In January 1807 the U.S. House of Representatives debated the constitutionality of the suspension of habeas corpus in order to deal with a crisis created by a series of events involving former vice president Aaron Burr. In the House's debate, members explored the dangers of suspending rights in time of crisis, arriving at the conclusion that the prospect of rebellion wasn't a sufficient reason to suspend constitutionally guaranteed rights. Since the Congress is allowed to suspend the writ only in such cases, the Congress is left to determine the circumstances severe enough to suspend habeas corpus.

Suspension of the writ of habeas corpus became the subject of debate in the House as a result of the infamous alleged "Burr Conspiracy." Aaron Burr, who served as vice president during Thomas Jefferson's first term as president (and who had tied Jefferson in electoral votes in the election of 1800) had been under investigation for treason, based on evidence that he was trying to incite rebellion in the western part of the country. Jefferson, who had come to detest and distrust Burr, conducted an investigation of the charges, but he largely excluded Congress from his findings. In an effort to pursue the matter, Congress requested that the president update them on his efforts. The problems with habeas corpus arose when detained co-conspirators were granted writs and then released for lack of evidence. The Senate and the House contemplated suspending habeas corpus to allow the president to deal with the crisis quickly. Yet when the matter came up before the House for debate, members openly questioned the need, looking first to history by examining the Roman tradition of suspending rights in times of crisis and then debating the question of what constituted a rebellion. Striking down the measure, the House concluded that suspension of the writ was not necessary, on the grounds that the situation was not dangerous enough to warrant being labeled a "rebellion." In fact, no rebellion occurred.

relevant today concerning the war on terror and will be discussed in more detail in chapter 6.

FURTHER READING

Fehrenbacher, Don E. (ed.). *Abraham Lincoln: Speeches and Writings, 1859–1865*. New York: Library of America, 1989, 456–57.

Neely, Jr., Mark E. *The Fate of Liberty: Abraham Lincoln and Civil Liberties*. Oxford: Oxford University Press, 1991.

The Habeas Corpus Act of 1863

Document: The Habeas Corpus Act, 1863
Date: March 3, 1863
Where: Washington, D.C.
Significance: The Habeas Corpus Act of 1863 legitimized Lincoln's suspension of habeas corpus and approved future suspensions throughout the duration of the Civil War.

DOCUMENT

United States Statutes at Large, Vol. 12, 37th Cong., Sess. III, p. 755–758

An Act relating to Habeas Corpus, and regulating Judicial Proceedings in Certain Cases.

Be it enacted by the Senate and House of Representatives of the United States of America in Congress assembled, That, during the present rebellion, the President of the United States, whenever, in his judgment, the public safety may require it, is authorized to suspend the privilege of the writ of habeas corpus in any case throughout the United States, or any part thereof. And whenever and wherever the said privilege shall be suspended, as aforesaid, no military or other officer shall be compelled, in answer to any writ of habeas corpus, to return the body of any person or persons detained by him by authority of the President; but upon the certificate, under oath, of the officer having charge of any one so detained that such person is detained by him as a prisoner under authority of the President, further proceedings under the writ of habeas corpus shall be suspended by the judge or court having issued the said writ, so long as said suspension by the President shall remain in force, and said rebellion continue.

Sec. 2. And be it further enacted, That the Secretary of State and the Secretary of War be, and they are hereby, directed, as soon as may be practicable, to furnish to

Confederate prisoners at a Chattanooga railroad depot, Tennessee, ca. 1864. The Union Army retained control of Chattanooga after the battle in November 1863, and the following year the strategic transportation center was used as the base for Major General William T. Sherman's Atlanta Campaign. (Library of Congress.)

the judges of the circuit and district courts of the United States and of the District of Columbia a list of the names of all persons, citizens of states in which the administration of the laws has continued unimpaired in the said Federal courts, who are now, or may hereafter be, held as prisoners of the United States, by order or authority of the President of the United States or either of said Secretaries, in any fort, arsenal, or other place, as state or political prisoners, or otherwise than as prisoners of war; the said list to contain the names of all those who reside in the respective jurisdictions of said judges, or who may be deemed by the said Secretaries, or either of them, to have violated any law of the United States in any of said jurisdictions, and also the date of each arrest; the Secretary of State to furnish a list of such persons as are imprisoned by the order or authority of the President, acting through the State Department, and the Secretary of War a list of such as are imprisoned by the order or authority of the President, acting through the Department of War. And in all cases where a grand jury, having attended any of said courts having jurisdiction in the premises, after the passage of this act, and after the furnishing of said list, as aforesaid has terminated its session without finding an indictment or presentment, or other proceeding against any such person, it shall be the duty of the judge of said court forthwith to make an order that any such prisoner desiring a discharge from said imprisonment be brought before him to be discharged; and every officer of the United States having custody of such prisoner is hereby directed immediately to obey and execute said judge's order; and in case he shall delay or refuse so to do, he shall be subject to indictment for a misdemeanor, and be punished by a fine of not less than five hundred dollars and imprisonment in the common jail for a period not less than six months, in the discretion of the court: Provided however, That no person shall be discharged by virtue of the provisions of this act until after he or she shall have taken an oath of allegiance to the Government of the United States, and to support the Constitution thereof; and that he or she will not hereafter in any way encourage or give aid and comfort to the present rebellion, or the supporters thereof: And provided, also, That the judge or court before whom such person may be brought, before discharging him or her from imprisonment, shall have power, on examination of the case, and, if the public safety shall require it, shall be required to cause him or her to enter into recognizance, with or without surety, in a sum to be fixed by said judge or court, to keep the peace and be of good behavior towards the United States and its citizens, and from time to time, and at such times as such judge or court may direct, appear before said judge or court to be further dealt with, according to law, as the circumstances may require. And it shall be the duty of the district attorney of the United States to attend such examination before the judge.

Sec. 3. And be it further enacted, That in case any of such prisoners shall be under indictment or presentment for any offence against the laws of the United States, and by existing laws bail or a recognizance may be taken for the appearance for trial of such person, it shall be the duty of said judge at once to discharge such person upon bail or recognizance for trial as aforesaid. And in case the said Secretaries of State and Was shall for any reason refuse or omit to furnish the said list of persons held as prisoners as aforesaid at the time of the passage of this act within twenty days thereafter, and of such persons as hereafter maybe arrested within twenty days from the time of the arrest, any citizen may, after a grand jury shall have terminated its session without finding an indictment or presentment, as provided in the second section of this act, by a petition alleging the facts aforesaid touching any of the persons so as aforesaid imprisoned, supported by the oath of such petitioner or any other credible person, obtain and be entitled to have the said judge's order to discharge such prisoner on the same terms and conditions prescribed in the second section of this act: Provided, however, That the said judge shall be satisfied such allegations are true.

Sec. 4. And be it further enacted, That any order of the President, or under his authority, made at any time during the existence of the present rebellion, shall be a defence in all courts to any action or prosecution, civil or criminal, pending, or to be commenced, for any search, seizure, arrest, or imprisonment, made, done, or committed, or acts omitted to be done, under and by virtue of such order, or under color of any law of Congress, and such defence may be made by special plea, or under the general issue.

Sec. 5. And be it further enacted, That if any suit or prosecution, civil or criminal, has been or shall be commenced in any state court against any officer, civil or military, or against any other person, for any arrest of imprisonment made, or other trespasses or wrongs done or committed, or any act omitted to be done, at anytime during the present rebellion, by virtue or under color of any authority derived from or exercised by or under the President of the United States, or any act of Congress, and the defendant shall, at the time of entering his appearance in such court, or if such appearance shall have been entered before the passage of this act, then at the next session of the court in which such suit or prosecution is pending, file a petition, stating the facts and verified by affidavit, for the removal of the cause for trial at the next circuit court of the United States, to be holden in the district where the suit is pending, and offer good and sufficient surety for his filing in such court, on the first day of its session, copies of such process and other proceedings against him, and also for his appearing in such court and entering special bail in the cause, if special bail was originally required therein. It shall then be the duty of the state court to accept the surety and proceed no further in the cause or prosecution, and the bail that shall have been originally taken shall be discharged. And such copies being filed as aforesaid in such court of the United States, the cause shall proceed therein in the same manner as if it had been brought in said court by original process, whatever may be the amount in dispute or the damages claimed, or whatever the citizenship of the parties, any former law to the contrary notwithstanding. And any attachment of the goods or estate of the defendant by the original process shall hold the goods or estate so attached to answer the final judgment in the same manner as by the laws of such state they would have been holden to answer final judgment had it been rendered in the court in which the suit or prosecution was commenced. And it shall be lawful in any such action or prosecution which may be now pending, or hereafter commenced, before any state court whatever, for any cause aforesaid, after final judgment, for either party to remove and transfer, by appeal, such case during the session or terms of said court at which the same shall have taken place, from such court to the next circuit court of the United States to be held in the district in which such appeal shall be taken, in manner aforesaid. And it shall be duty of the person taking such appeal to produce and file in the said circuit court attested copies of the process, proceedings, and judgment in such cause; and it shall also be competent for either party, within six months after the rendition of a judgment in any such cause, by writ of error or other process, to remove the same to the circuit court of the United States of that district in which such judgment shall have been rendered; and the said circuit court shall thereupon proceed to try and determine the facts and the law in such action, in the same manner as if the same had been there originally commenced, the judgment, in such case notwithstanding. And any bail which may have been taken, or property attached, shall be holden on the final judgment of the said circuit court in such action, in the same manner as if no such removal and transfer had been made, aforesaid. And the state court, from which any such action, civil or criminal, may be removed and transferred as aforesaid, upon the parties giving good and sufficient security for the prosecution thereof, shall allow the same to be removed and transferred, and proceed no further in the case: Provided, however, That if the party aforesaid shall fail duly to enter the removal and transfer, as aforesaid, in the circuit court of the United States, agreeably to this act, state court, by which judgment shall have been rendered, and from which the transfer and removal shall have been made, as aforesaid, shall be authorized, on motion for that purpose, to issue execution, and to carry into effect any such judgment, the same as if no such removal and transfer had been made. And provided also, That no such appeal or writ of error shall be allowed in any criminal action or prosecution where final judgment shall have been rendered in favor of the defendant or respondent by the state court. And if in any suit hereafter commenced the plaintiff is nonsuited or judgment pass against him, the defendant shall recover double costs.

Sec. 6. And be it further enacted, That any suit or prosecution described in this act, in which final judgment may be rendered in the circuit court, may be carried by writ of error to the supreme court, whatever may be the amount of said judgment.

Sec. 7. And be it further enacted, That no suit or prosecution, civil or criminal, shall be maintained for any arrest or imprisonment made, or other trespasses or wrongs done or committed, or act omitted to be done, at any time during the present rebellion, by virtue or under color of any authority derived from or exercised by or under the President of the United States, or by or under any act of Congress, unless the same shall have been commenced within two years next after such arrest, imprisonment, trespass, or wrong may have been done or committed or act may have been omitted to be done: Provided, That in no case shall the limitation herein provided commence to run until the passage of this act, so that no party shall, by virtue of this act, be debarred of his remedy by suit or prosecution until two years from and after the passage of this act. Approved, March 3, 1863.

SOURCE: http://web.ebscohost.com/ehost/detail?vid=1&hid=6&sid=948ba806-a1ec-45af-9085–62d32753d62c%40sessionmgr10&bdata=JnNpdGU9ZWhvc3QtbGl2ZQ%3d%3d#db=a2h&AN=21212276

ANALYSIS

The Habeas Corpus Act of 1863 codified the suspension of the writ of habeas corpus proclaimed by President Lincoln in 1861 at the start of the Civil War. On September 15, 1863, Lincoln proclaimed the suspension of the privilege throughout the United States for the war's duration, for the first time acting under statutory authority. It authorized suspensions throughout the war and enabled the government to detain persons suspected of disloyalty to the Union. Congress built a number of safeguards into the act to protect against possible abuses of authority. Section 2 of the act required that a list of all those arrested under military or civilian authority would have their names forwarded to federal judges within the district of the arrest. A grand jury was to assemble and indict the detainee. If the grand jury failed to bring back an indictment, the person would be released immediately. It also authorized removal of these suits to federal courts and stipulated that any order made under authority of the president was a defense against such suits. To ensure the safety of the judicial process, federal judges were given the power under this act of Congress to supervise the indictment process. If any lower court failed to release the detainee, having not obtained an indictment, federal judges were empowered to try and convict any officer refusing to follow the law under this act. Section 5 of the act afforded protection to federal officials who were sued in state court for arresting and detaining civilians and for acts performed while enforcing federal conscription and emancipation policies. This greatly expanded the jurisdiction and oversight of the federal courts.

FURTHER READING

Hyman, Harold M., and Wiecek, William M. *Equal Justice Under Law: Constitutional Development, 1835–1875*. New York: Harper and Row, 1982.

The Fourteenth Amendment

- ***Document:*** U.S. Constitution: The Fourteenth Amendment
- ***Date:*** Ratified July 9, 1868
- ***Where:*** Washington, D.C.
- ***Significance:*** The Fourteenth Amendment was originally designed to grant citizenship to and protect the civil liberties of recently freed slaves. It did this by prohibiting states from denying or abridging the privileges or immunities of citizens of the United States, depriving any person of his life, liberty, or property without due process of law, or denying to any person within their jurisdiction the equal protection of the laws. The Fourteenth Amendment has had extensive impacts on the laws and culture of the United States since its ratification.

DOCUMENT

Fourteenth Amendment, 1868

Amendment XIV

Section 1. All persons born or naturalized in the United States, and subject to the jurisdiction thereof, are citizens of the United States and of the state wherein they reside. No state shall make or enforce any law which shall abridge the privileges or immunities of citizens of the United States; nor shall any state deprive any person of life, liberty, or property, without due process of law; nor deny to any person within its jurisdiction the equal protection of the laws.

Section 2. Representatives shall be apportioned among the several states according to their respective numbers, counting the whole number of persons in each state, excluding Indians not taxed. But when the right to vote at any election for the choice of electors for President and Vice President of the United States, Representatives in Congress, the executive and judicial officers of a state, or the members of the legislature thereof, is denied to any of the male inhabitants of such state, being twenty-one years of age, and citizens of the United States, or in any way abridged, except for participation in rebellion, or other crime, the basis of representation therein shall be reduced in the proportion which the number of such male citizens shall bear to the whole number of male citizens twenty-one years of age in such state.

Section 3. No person shall be a Senator or Representative in Congress, or elector of President and Vice President, or hold any office, civil or military, under the United States, or under any state, who, having previously taken an oath, as a member of Congress, or as an officer of the United States, or as a member of any state legislature, or as an executive or judicial officer of any state, to support the Constitution of the United States, shall have engaged in insurrection or rebellion against the same, or given aid or comfort to the enemies thereof. But Congress may by a vote of two-thirds of each House, remove such disability.

Section 4. The validity of the public debt of the United States, authorized by law, including debts incurred for payment of pensions and bounties for services in suppressing insurrection or rebellion, shall not be questioned. But neither the United States nor any state shall assume or pay any debt or obligation incurred in aid of insurrection or rebellion against the United States, or any claim for the loss or emancipation of any slave; but all such debts, obligations and claims shall be held illegal and void.

Section 5. The Congress shall have power to enforce, by appropriate legislation, the provisions of this article.

SOURCE: http://www.law.cornell.edu/constitution/constitution.amendmentxiv.html

DID YOU KNOW?

Declaration of Independence, 1776

The Declaration of Independence, chiefly written by Thomas Jefferson, was a formal statement adopted by the Second Continental Congress on July 4, 1776, announcing that the 13 American colonies were now independent states and therefore no longer parts of the British Empire. The importance of the principles underlying the Declaration of Independence has not diminished since its adoption. Although its initial importance, as a formal declaration of freedom, was limited, its ringing philosophical assertion that "We hold these truths to be self-evident, that all men are created equal, that they are endowed by their Creator with certain unalienable Rights, that among these are Life, Liberty and the pursuit of Happiness" has served as an enduring and inspiring expression of freedom and equality. At the time it was formulated, however, "equality" only extended to white male property owners. This changed with the adoption of the Thirteenth, Fourteenth, and Fifteenth Amendments after the conclusion of the Civil War. The underlying principles of the Declaration of Independence served as a basis for the due process and equal protection clauses of the Fourteenth Amendment.

ANALYSIS

The Fourteenth Amendment to the U.S. Constitution was ratified in 1868 in the aftermath of the Civil War. It is part of the "Reconstruction Amendments," along with the Thirteenth Amendment, which freed the slaves, and the Fifteenth Amendment, which granted freed male slaves the right to vote. The Fourteenth Amendment is fundamental to protection against discrimination on grounds of race, religion, or sex, and to safeguarding fundamental rights, such as freedom of speech and the right to marry.

Section 1 of the Fourteenth Amendment was designed to end the denial of those fundamental rights that belong to all citizens of the United States by virtue of citizenship under Article IV, Section 2 of the U.S. Constitution wherever they traveled within the Union. Under the original Constitution, citizens of the United States were required to be first a citizen of some state—something newly emancipated citizens could not claim. This is why it was essential for the first section to start with a definition of citizenship so that no state could decline recognition of newly freed slaves as U.S. citizens by withholding the right to protection of the laws in life, liberty, or property in the courts as enjoyed by white citizens.

Sections 2 through 5 deal almost exclusively with the Confederacy and its officials. Some of these sections seem anachronistic today because they reflect the immediate concerns of the Union's political leadership following the North's victory over the South in the Civil War. Section 2, for instance, penalized any state that attempted to abridge the voting rights of its black male residents by reducing the state's representation in Congress. Section 3 prohibited from holding state or federal office any person who engaged in "insurrection or rebellion" or otherwise gave "aid or comfort to the enemies" during the Civil War. Section 4 reaffirmed the United States' promise to pay its Civil War debt, while pronouncing all debts and obligations incurred by the Confederate government "illegal and void." Section 5 enabled, and continues to enable, Congress to pass "appropriate legislation" to enforce the provisions of the Fourteenth Amendment such as the Civil Rights Act of 1964 or the Americans with Disabilities Act of 1990.

Prior to the adoption of the Fourteenth Amendment, the protections in the Bill of Rights limited only the actions of the federal government, unless the provision specifically declared it otherwise. The Supreme Court has used the due process clause as the basis to selectively incorporate the Bill of Rights to the states and has also been used to recognize: (1) substantive due process rights, such as parental and marriage rights; and (2) procedural due process rights requiring that certain steps, such as a hearing, be followed before a person's life, liberty, or property can be taken away. This has meant that the Fourteenth Amendment has been used more frequently in modern court cases than any other constitutional provision.

Although the Declaration of Independence declared that all men were created equal, many persons living in our early republic, including Native Americans, African American slaves, and women were denied fundamental rights and liberties such as the right to vote, own property, and freely travel. The equal protection clause of the Fourteenth Amendment—along with the power of Congress to enforce it, incorporated the Declaration's ideal into the Constitution. The equal protection clause limits the ability of states to discriminate against people based on their race, national origin, gender, or other status. The amendment's equal protection clause requires states to provide equal protection under the law to all people within their jurisdictions. This clause later became the basis for *Brown v. Board of Education* (1954), the Supreme Court decision which was the impetuous to the dismantling of racial segregation in the United States. The clause has also been used to guarantee voting rights, the rights of women and minorities to equal employment opportunities, and the rights of immigrants to attend public school. The extensive history of litigation under the equal protection clause in fact mirrors the struggle for civil rights of all Americans and limits arbitrary state action.

FURTHER READING

Bond, James Edward. *No Easy Walk to Freedom: Reconstruction and the Ratification of the Fourteenth Amendment*. Westport, Conn.: Praeger, 1997.

Curtis, Michael Kent. *No State Shall Abridge: The Fourteenth Amendment and the Bill of Rights*. Durham, N.C.: Duke University Press, 1986.

Montesquieu and the Importance of Free Speech

- ***Document:*** **Montesquieu, *Spirit of Laws*, bk. 12, CHS. 12–13**
- ***Date:*** 1748
- ***Where:*** France
- ***Significance:*** The *Spirit of Laws* had a tremendous impact on the thoughts, ideas, and philosophies which were integrated into the Constitution. One area of influence concerns the ability of an individual to speak or write against the government without being tried for treason.

DOCUMENT

Montesquieu, Spirit of Laws, bk. 12, CHS. 12–13

12.—Of indiscreet Speeches

Nothing renders the crime of high treason more arbitrary than declaring people guilty of it for indiscreet speeches. Speech is so subject to interpretation; there is so great a difference between indiscretion and malice; and frequently so little is there of the latter in the freedom of expression, that the law can hardly subject people to a capital punishment for words unless it expressly declares what words they are.

Words do not constitute an overt act; they remain only in idea. When considered by themselves, they have generally no determinate signification; for this depends on the tone in which they are uttered. It often happens that in repeating the same words they have not the same meaning; this depends on their connection with other things, and sometimes more is signified by silence than by any expression whatever. Since there can be nothing so equivocal and ambiguous as all this, how is it possible to convert it into a crime of high treason? Wherever this law is established, there is an end not only of liberty, but even of its very shadow.

> **DID YOU KNOW?**
>
> **The Licensing Act: Censorship for Pay, 1662**
>
> England's Act for Preventing Abuses in Printing Seditious, Treasonable and Unlicensed Books and Pamphlets, and for Regulating Printing and Printing Presses (14 Chas. 2, c. 33, 1662), commonly known as the Licensing Act, set out a comprehensive set of provisions concerning both the licensing of the press and the regulation and management of the book trade. The act required that all printing presses be registered with the Stationers' Company, and it set out severe penalties of fine and imprisonment for offenders. It was the last of series of English censorship acts.

In the manifesto of the late Czarina against the family of the D'Olgoruckys, one of those princes is condemned to death for having uttered some indecent words concerning her person: another, for having maliciously interpreted her imperial laws, and for having offended her sacred person by disrespectful expressions.

Not that I pretend to diminish the just indignation of the public against those who presume to stain the glory of their sovereign; what I mean is, that if despotic princes are willing to moderate their power, a milder chastisement would be more proper on those occasions than the charge of high treason—a thing always terrible even to innocence itself.

Overt acts do not happen every day; they are exposed to the eye of the public; and a false charge with regard to matters of fact may be easily detected. Words carried into action assume the nature of that action. Thus a man who goes into a public market-place to incite the subject to revolt incurs the guilt of high treason, because the words are joined to the action, and partake of its nature. It is not the words that are punished, but an action in which words are employed. They do not become criminal, but when they are annexed to a criminal action: everything is confounded if words are construed into a capital crime, instead of considering them only as a mark of that crime.

The Emperors Theodosius, Arcadius, and Honorius wrote thus to Rufinus, who was praefectus praetorio: "Though a man should happen to speak amiss of our person or government, we do not intend to punish him: if he has spoken through levity, we must despise him; if through folly, we must pity him; and if he wrongs us, we must forgive him. Therefore, leaving things as they are, you are to inform us accordingly, that we may be able to judge of words by persons, and that we may duly consider whether we ought to punish or overlook them."

13.—Of Writings

In writings there is something more permanent than in words, but when they are in no way preparative to high treason they cannot amount to that charge.

And yet Augustus and Tiberius subjected satirical writers to the same punishment as for having violated the law of majesty. Augustus, because of some libels that had been written against persons of the first quality; Tiberius, because of those which he suspected to have been written against himself. Nothing was more fatal to Roman liberty. Cremutius Cordus was accused of having called Cassius in his annals the last of the Romans.

Satirical writings are hardly known in despotic governments, where dejection of mind on the one hand, and ignorance on the other, afford neither abilities nor will to write. In democracies they are not hindered, for the very same reason which causes them to be prohibited in monarchies; being generally levelled against men of power and authority, they flatter the malignancy of the people, who are the governing party. In monarchies they are forbidden, but rather as a subject of civil animadversion than as a capital crime. They may amuse the general malevolence, please the malcontents, diminish the envy against public employments, give the people patience to suffer, and make them laugh at their sufferings.

But no government is so averse to satirical writings as the aristocratic. There the magistrates are petty sovereigns, but not great enough to despise affronts. If in a monarchy a satirical stroke is designed against the prince, he is placed on such an eminence that it does not reach him; but an aristocratic lord is pierced to the very heart. Hence the decemvirs, who formed an aristocracy, punished satirical writings with death.

SOURCE: http://press-pubs.uchicago.edu/founders/documents/amendI_speechs3.html

The Baron de Montesquieu was a French political philosopher whose most famous work, *The Spirit of the Laws,* was one of the most influential texts of the 18th century. (Library of Congress.)

ANALYSIS

Montesquieu went to great lengths to distinguish opinion from action. In particular, Montesquieu expressed well the framers' interests in not punishing someone for their mere thoughts or "indiscreet speeches." Montesquieu believed that words were not the same as actions and that expression could be interpreted in many different ways. Even though irreverent writings are more permanent than words, unless accompanied by action, they should not be sufficient to put the author on trial for treason. These underlying principles were taken by the founders when they drafted the constitution. The framers wanted to make sure that one would only be tried for treason if one's spoken or written words were "joined" to some sort of action. In constructing Article III, Section 3 of the Constitution, the framers combined known precedent from English law, French philosophy, and even religion, and finally agreed upon the requirement of two witnesses to the same overt act. Similar to Montesquieu, the framers wanted to ensure that a person would not be tried for treason unless he or she committed an act that breached his or her allegiance to the United States. What the framers did not clarify, and thereby left the Courts to have to decide, was what exactly constituted an overt act.

FURTHER READING

Plamenatz, John P. *Man and Society: Political and Social Theory*, vol. 2. New York: McGraw-Hill, 1963.

Shackleton, Robert. *Montesquieu: A Critical Biography*. London: Oxford University Press, 1961.

The First Amendment of the United States Constitution

- ***Document:*** U.S. Constitution: The First Amendment
- ***Date:*** December 15, 1791
- ***Where:*** Washington, D.C.
- ***Significance:*** The First Amendment provides protection from the government concerning the creation of a state religion, the exercise of religion, the freedom of speech and the press, the right of assembly, and the right to petition the government.

DOCUMENT

Article I

Congress shall make no law respecting an establishment of religion, or prohibiting the free exercise thereof; or abridging the freedom of speech, or of the press; or the right of the people peaceably to assemble, and to petition the Government for a redress of grievances.

SOURCE: http://topics.law.cornell.edu/constitution/billofrights

ANALYSIS

The First Amendment has been at the front lines for protecting individuals against arbitrary state action. Even though the Supreme Court has determined that the First Amendment is not absolute as it relates to speech and expression, the trend has been to protect an individual's right to dissent. In particular, political speech or speech which criticizes the government in some way has been determined to receive the greatest protection under the First Amendment. Over time, a number of justices on the Supreme Court have advocated for a number of theories concerning the limits of the First Amendment. There are three approaches which have been adopted including the absolutist approach, the categorical approach, and finally the balancing approach.

The absolutist approach is most frequently connected with Justice Black, who held that the First Amendment meant exactly what it says: that Congress shall make NO law abridging the freedom of speech. Under this approach, the only issue is whether the action in conduct is truly "speech" and therefore protected or exclusively "conduct" and therefore subject to reasonable governmental regulation. The categorical approach would protect or not protect speech based on the label that is attached to the speech in question. Certain categories of speech are seen as falling completely outside of First Amendment protection, whereas most other categories of speech are either highly protected or protected absolutely. Several of the unprotected categories include libel, slander, and obscenity. The balancing approach rejects the absolutist approach as impracticable and the categorical approach as artificial. The balancing approach is used to weigh the individual's interest in free expression in opposition to the government's interest in restricting the speech in question. Under this theory, the presumption is usually determined to be in favor of free expression. This third approach is what dominates the courts analysis concerning the First Amendment. In cases where the state interest concerns national security, the Court has been more willing to defer to the legislature in those cases at the expense of liberty.

FURTHER READING

Friendly, Fred W., and Martha J. H. Elliott. *The Constitution, That Delicate Balance*. New York: Random House, 1984.

Levy, Leonard W. *Origins of the Bill of Rights*. Contemporary Law Series. New Haven, Conn.: Yale University Press, 1999.

Government Controlling Speech during Times of Crisis

- ***Document:*** Sedition Act, 1798
- ***Date:*** 1798
- ***Where:*** Washington, D.C.
- ***Significance:*** Passed by a Federalist-controlled Congress, the Sedition Act of 1798 reflected growing national panic over the possibility of war with France. In an effort to silence the opposition press and opposition Democratic-Republican Party, the act provided that those who criticized Congress or the president could be fined or imprisoned.

DOCUMENT

Sedition Act of 1798

U.S. Statutes at Large, Volume I, pp. 596–7

An Act in addition to the act, entitled "An act for the punishment of certain crimes against the United States."

SEC. I Be it enacted . . . , That if any persons shall unlawfully combine or conspire together, with intent to oppose any measure or measures of the government of the United States, which are or shall be directed by proper authority, or to impede the operation of any law of the United States, or to intimidate or prevent any person holding a place or office in or under the government of the United States, from undertaking, performing or executing his trust or duty; and if any person or persons, with intent as aforesaid, shall counsel, advise or attempt to procure any insurrection, riot. unlawful assembly, or combination, whether such conspiracy, threatening, counsel, advice, or attempt shall have the proposed effect or not, he or they shall be deemed guilty of a high misdemeanor, and on conviction, before any court of the United States having jurisdiction thereof, shall be punished by a fine not exceeding five thousand dollars, and by imprisonment during a term not less than six months nor exceeding five years; and further, at the discretion of the court may be holden to find sureties for his good behaviour in such sum, and for such time, as the said court may direct.

SEC. 2. That if any person shall write, print, utter. Or publish, or shall cause or procure to be written, printed, uttered or published, or shall knowingly and willingly assist or aid in writing, printing, uttering or publishing any false, scandalous and malicious writing or writings against the government of the United States, or either house of the Congress of the United States, or the President of the United States, with intent to defame the said government, or either house of the said Congress, or the said President, or to bring them. or either of them, into contempt or disrepute; or to excite against them, or either or any of them, the hatred of the good people of the United States, or to excite any unlawful combinations therein, for opposing or resisting any law of the United States, or any act of the President of the United States, done in pursuance of any such law, or of the powers in him vested by the constitution of the United States, or to resist, oppose, or defeat any such law or act, or to aid, encourage or abet any hostile designs of any foreign nation against the United States, their people or government, then such person, being thereof convicted before any court of the United States having jurisdiction thereof, shall be punished by a fine not exceeding two thousand dollars, and by imprisonment not exceeding two years.

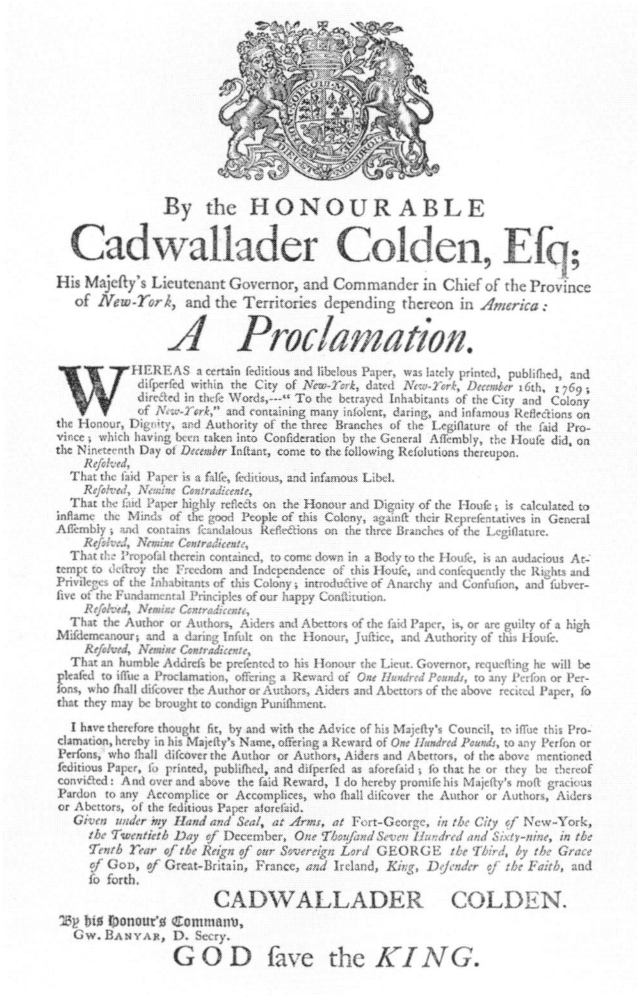

By the HONOURABLE

Cadwallader Colden, Eſq;

His Majeſty's Lieutenant Governor, and Commander in Chief of the Province of *New-York*, and the Territories depending thereon in *America*:

A Proclamation.

WHEREAS a certain ſeditious and libelous Paper, was lately printed, publiſhed, and diſperſed within the City of *New-York*, dated *New-York, December* 16th, 1769; directed in theſe Words,---" To the betrayed Inhabitants of the City and Colony of *New-York*," and containing many inſolent, daring, and infamous Reflections on the Honour, Dignity, and Authority of the three Branches of the Legiſlature of the ſaid Province; which having been taken into Conſideration by the General Aſſembly, the Houſe did, on the Nineteenth Day of *December* Inſtant, come to the following Reſolutions thereupon.

Reſolved,

That the ſaid Paper is a falſe, ſeditious, and infamous Libel.

Reſolved, Nemine Contradicente,

That the ſaid Paper highly reflects on the Honour and Dignity of the Houſe; is calculated to inflame the Minds of the good People of this Colony, againſt their Repreſentatives in General Aſſembly; and contains ſcandalous Reflections on the three Branches of the Legiſlature.

Reſolved, Nemine Contradicente,

That the Propoſal therein contained, to come down in a Body to the Houſe, is an audacious Attempt to deſtroy the Freedom and Independence of this Houſe, and conſequently the Rights and Privileges of the Inhabitants of this Colony; introductive of Anarchy and Confuſion, and ſubverſive of the Fundamental Principles of our happy Conſtitution.

Reſolved, Nemine Contradicente,

That the Author or Authors, Aiders and Abettors of the ſaid Paper, is, or are guilty of a high Miſdemeanour; and a daring Inſult on the Honour, Juſtice, and Authority of this Houſe.

Reſolved, Nemine Contradicente,

That an humble Addreſs be preſented to his Honour the Lieut. Governor, requeſting he will be pleaſed to iſſue a Proclamation, offering a Reward of *One Hundred Pounds*, to any Perſon or Perſons, who ſhall diſcover the Author or Authors, Aiders and Abettors of the above recited Paper, ſo that they may be brought to condign Puniſhment.

I have therefore thought fit, by and with the Advice of his Majeſty's Council, to iſſue this Proclamation, hereby in his Majeſty's Name, offering a Reward of *One Hundred Pounds*, to any Perſon or Perſons, who ſhall diſcover the Author or Authors, Aiders and Abettors, of the above mentioned ſeditious Paper, ſo printed, publiſhed, and diſperſed as aforeſaid; ſo that he or they be thereof convicted: And over and above the ſaid Reward, I do hereby promiſe his Majeſty's moſt gracious Pardon to any Accomplice or Accomplices, who ſhall diſcover the Author or Authors, Aiders or Abettors, of the ſeditious Paper aforeſaid.

Given under my Hand and Seal, at Arms, at Fort-George, *in the City of* New-York, *the Twentieth Day of* December, *One Thouſand Seven Hundred and Sixty-nine, in the Tenth Year of the Reign of our Sovereign Lord* GEORGE *the Third, by the Grace of* GOD, *of* Great-Britain, France, *and* Ireland, *King, Defender of the Faith*, and ſo forth.

CADWALLADER COLDEN.

By his Honour's Command,
GW. BANYAR, D. Secry.

GOD ſave the *KING*.

This type of proclamation was quite typical under the Sedition Act which was passed by the Federalists to prosecute editors of Democratic-Republican newspapers. The Sedition Act trials led to criticism against the Federalists and contributed to their defeat in the election of 1800. (Library of Congress.)

SEC. 3. That if any person shall be prosecuted under this act, for the writing or publishing any libel aforesaid, it shall be lawful for the defendant, upon the trial of the cause, to give in evidence in his defence, the truth of the matter contained in the publication charged as a libel. And the jury who shall try the cause, shall have a right to determine the law and the fact, under the direction of the court, as in other cases.

SEC. 4. That this act shall continue to be in force until March 3, 1801, and no longer.

SOURCE: http://www.constitution.org/rf/sedition_1798.htm

ANALYSIS

In 1794, President Washington negotiated a treaty with England to settle outstanding differences between the two countries. The resulting improvement in American-English relations angered the revolutionary French leaders, who were enemies of the English. In the election of 1796, Federalist John Adams won the most electoral votes to become president. Republican Thomas Jefferson came in second, which made him vice president. Shortly after becoming president, Adams sent diplomats to France to smooth over the bad feelings. But three French representatives—dubbed X, Y, and

Z—met secretly with the U.S. diplomats and demanded $10 million in bribes to the French government to begin negotiations. When the Americans refused, Mr. X threatened the United States with the "power and violence of France." News of the "XYZ Affair" enraged most Americans and increased hostilities with France.

In 1798 the United States was on the brink of war with France. The Federalists believed that Democratic-Republican criticism of Federalist policies was disloyal and feared that aliens living in the United States would sympathize with the French during a war. As a result, a Federalist-controlled Congress passed four laws, known collectively as the Alien and Sedition Acts. In particular, the Sedition Act made it a high misdemeanor, punishable by fine, imprisonment, or both, for citizens or aliens (1) to oppose the execution of federal laws; (2) to prevent a federal officer from performing his or her duties; (3) to aid any insurrection, riot, unlawful assembly, or combination; or (4) to make any defamatory statement about the federal government or the president. The laws were directed against Democratic-Republicans, the party typically favored by new citizens, and the only journalists prosecuted under the Sedition Act were editors of Democratic-Republican newspapers. Approximately 25 individuals were arrested under the Sedition Act. Fifteen were indicted; 10 cases went to trial and all 10 resulted in convictions.

For many years, English and American courts had prosecuted individuals for this kind of seditious libel using the common law—a collection of court precedents and traditions—rather than acts of a legislature. Some doubted that the federal courts had jurisdiction over common law crimes, so the Sedition Act provided the statutory authority for federal prosecution of seditious libel. Although early drafts included drastic penalties for even general criticisms of the government, the act incorporated recent liberalizations in American and English practice, such as permitting the truth as a defense and allowing juries to determine whether the law properly applied to the case. Federalist supporters argued that the act embodied a broadly accepted understanding of the freedom of speech, which was necessarily balanced by individual responsibility for false statements. Republicans in Congress responded to the proposed Sedition Act with the most sweeping defense of free speech yet articulated in the United States. They argued that in a representative government, citizens needed to have unrestricted access to a full range of political opinions if they were to make knowledgeable choices in elections.

The Sedition Act trials, along with the Senate's use of its contempt powers to suppress dissent, set off a firestorm of criticism against the Federalists and contributed to their defeat in the election of 1800. The validity of the Sedition Act was never tested in the Supreme Court before it expired in 1801. But Congress later passed a law that repaid all fines collected under it, and Jefferson, after becoming president in 1801, pardoned all those convicted under the act. The controversies surrounding them, however, provided for some of the first test of the limits of freedom of speech and press.

FURTHER READING

Sharpe, James Rogers. *American Politics in the Early Republic: The New Nation in Crisis*. New Haven, Conn.: Yale University Press, 1993.

Smith, James Morton. *Freedom's Fetters: The Alien and Sedition Laws and American Civil Liberties*. Ithaca, N.Y.: Cornell University Press, 1956.

Stone, Geoffrey R. *Perilous Times: Free Speech in Wartime From the Sedition Act of 1798 to the War on Terrorism*. New York: W. W. Norton, 2004.

The Rights of Noncitizens during Times of Crisis

- ***Document:*** The Alien Enemies Act
- ***Date:*** July 6, 1798
- ***Where:*** Washington, D.C.
- ***Significance:*** Passed by a Federalist-controlled Congress, the Alien Enemies Act of 1798 reflected a growing national panic over the possibility of war with France. In an effort to restrict the movement of aliens, the act provided for the expulsion or imprisonment of aliens deemed dangerous during wartime.

DOCUMENT

The Alien Enemies Act

An Act Respecting Alien Enemies

SECTION 1.

Be it enacted by the Senate and House of Representatives of the United States of America in Congress assembled, That whenever there shall be a declared war between the United States and any foreign nation or government, or any invasion or predatory incursion shall be perpetrated, attempted, or threatened against the territory of the United States, by any foreign nation or government, and the President of the United States shall make public proclamation of the event, all natives, citizens, denizens, or subjects of the hostile nation or government, being males of the age of fourteen years and upwards, who shall be within the United States, and not actually naturalized, shall be liable to be apprehended, restrained, secured and removed, as alien enemies. And the President of the United States shall be, and he is hereby authorized, in any event, as aforesaid, by his proclamation thereof, or other public act, to direct the conduct to be observed, on the part of the United States, towards the aliens who shall become liable, as aforesaid; the manner and degree of the restraint to which they shall be subject, and in what cases, and upon what security their residence shall be permitted, and to provide for the removal of those, who, not being permitted to reside within the United States, shall refuse or neglect to depart therefrom; and to establish any other regulations which shall be found necessary in the premises and for the public safety: Provided, that aliens resident within the United States, who shall become liable as enemies, in the manner aforesaid, and who shall not be chargeable with actual hostility, or other crime against the public safety, shall be allowed, for the recovery, disposal, and removal of their goods and effects, and for their departure, the full time which is, or shall be stipulated by any treaty, where any shall have been between the United States, and the hostile nation or government, of which they shall be natives, citizens, denizens or subjects: and where no such treaty shall have existed, the President of the United States may ascertain and declare such reasonable time as may be consistent with the public safety, and according to the dictates of humanity and national hospitality.

SEC. 2.

And be it further enacted, That after any proclamation shall be made as aforesaid, it shall be the duty of the several courts of the United States, and of each state, having criminal jurisdiction, and of the several judges and justices of the courts of the United States, and they shall be, and are hereby respectively, authorized upon complaint, against any alien or alien enemies, as aforesaid, who shall be resident and at large within such jurisdiction or district, to the danger of the public peace or safety, and contrary to the tenor or intent of such proclamation, or other regulations which the President of the United States shall and may establish in the premises, to cause such alien or aliens to be duly apprehended and convened before such court, judge or justice; and after a full examination and hearing on such complaint and sufficient cause therefor appearing, shall and may order such alien or aliens to be removed out of the territory of the United States, or to give sureties of their good behaviour, or to be otherwise restrained, conformably to the proclamation or regulations which shall and may be established as aforesaid, and may imprison, or otherwise secure such alien or aliens, until the order which shall and may be made, as aforesaid, shall be performed.

SEC. 3.

And be it further enacted, That it shall be the duty of the marshal of the district in which any alien enemy shall be apprehended, who by the President of the United States, or by order of any court, judge or justice, as aforesaid, shall be required to depart, and to be removed, as aforesaid, to provide therefor, and to execute such order, by himself or his deputy, or other discreet person or persons to be employed by him, by causing a removal of such alien out of the territory of the United States; and for such removal the marshal shall have the warrant of the President of the United States, or of the court, judge or justice ordering the same, as the case may be.

APPROVED, July 6, 1798.

SOURCE: http://www.pbs.org/wgbh/amex/adams/filmmore/ps_alien.html

ANALYSIS

In 1794, President Washington negotiated a treaty with England to settle outstanding differences between the two countries. The resulting improvement in American-English relations angered the revolutionary French leaders, who were enemies of the English. In the election of 1796, Federalist John Adams won the most electoral votes to become president. Republican Thomas Jefferson came in second, which made him vice president. Shortly after becoming president, Adams sent diplomats to France to smooth over the bad feelings. But three French representatives called "X, Y, and Z" met secretly with the United States diplomats and demanded $10 million in bribes to the French government to begin negotiations. When the Americans refused, Mr. X threatened the United States with the "power and violence of France." News of the "XYZ Affair" enraged most Americans and increased hostilities with France.

In 1798, the United States was on the brink of war with France. The Federalists believed that Democratic-Republican criticism of Federalist policies was disloyal and feared that aliens living in the United States would sympathize with the French during a war. As a result, a Federalist-controlled Congress passed four laws, known collectively as the Alien and Sedition Acts. In particular, the Alien Enemies Act authorized the president to apprehend and deport resident aliens if their home countries were at war with the United States of America. The act did not have a sunset provision and is still in full effect.

The Alien Enemy Act explicitly conditions its sweeping delegation of authority to the president on the formality of Congress having previously declared war or on the existence of an actual or imminent foreign invasion. Where there has been no formal declaration of war—as in the cases of the wars that the United States fought in Korea, Vietnam, and Iraq—the president cannot use the act to summarily arrest, intern, and deport enemy aliens. Accordingly, none of the presidents who served during those recent wars attempted to exercise the extraordinary powers specified in the act. The formality of declaring war, with its accompanying high transaction costs, provides what may be the only significant safeguard in the Alien Enemy Act for protecting individual liberty, for the decision to terminate its delegation of powers rests, in practical terms, with the president himself, and the limited judicial review available under the act does not extend to claims that the president has abused his discretion.

FURTHER READING

Smith, James Morton. *Freedom's Fetters: The Alien and Sedition Laws and American Civil Liberties*. Ithaca, N.Y.: Cornell University Press, 1956.

The Right to Privacy in America

- ***Document:*** Excerpt, "The Right to Privacy" by Warren and Brandeis
- ***Date:*** December 15, 1890
- ***Where:*** Boston, Massachusetts
- ***Significance:*** Warren and Brandeis's article is almost universally regarded as the origin of the four invasion of privacy torts including: (1) unreasonable intrusion upon the seclusion of another; (2) appropriation of the other's name or likeness; (3) unreasonable publicity given to the other's private life; and (4) publicity that unreasonably places the other in a false light before the public. The article has also been widely recognized by scholars and judges as a seminal force in the development of a right to privacy in American jurisprudence.

DOCUMENT

The Right to Privacy by Samuel D. Warren and Louis D. Brandeis

Harvard Law Review. Vol. IV December 15, 1890 No. 5

That the individual shall have full protection in person and in property is a principle as old as the common law; but it has been found necessary from time to time to define anew the exact nature and extent of such protection. Political, social, and economic changes entail the recognition of new rights, and the common law, in its eternal youth, grows to meet the new demands of society.

Thus, in very early times, the law gave a remedy only for physical interference with life and property, for trespasses vi et armis. Then the "right to life" served only to protect the subject from battery in its various forms; liberty meant freedom from actual restraint; and the right to property secured to the individual his lands and his cattle. Later, there came a recognition of man's spiritual nature, of his feelings and his intellect. Gradually the scope of these legal rights broadened; and now the right to life has come to mean the right to enjoy life,—the right to be let alone; the right to liberty secures the exercise of extensive civil privileges; and the term "property" has grown to comprise every form of possession—intangible, as well as tangible.

Thus, with the recognition of the legal value of sensations, the protection against actual bodily injury was extended to prohibit mere attempts to do such injury; that is, the putting another in fear of such injury. From the action of battery grew that of assault. Much later there came a qualified protection of the individual against offensive noises and odors, against dust and smoke, and excessive vibration. The law of nuisance was developed. So regard for human emotions soon extended the scope of personal immunity beyond the body of the individual. His reputation, the standing among his fellow-men, was considered, and the law of slander and libel arose. Man's family relations became a part of the legal conception of his life, and the alienation of a wife's affections was held remediable. Occasionally the law halted, as in its refusal to recognize the intrusion by seduction upon the honor of the family. But even here the demands of society were met. A mean fiction, the action per quod servitium amisit, was resorted to, and by allowing damages for injury to the parents' feelings, an adequate remedy was ordinarily afforded. Similar to the expansion of the right to life was the growth of the legal conception of property. From corporeal property arose the incorporeal rights issuing out of it; and then there opened the wide realm of intangible property, in the products and processes of the mind, as works of literature and art, goodwill, trade secrets, and trademarks.

This development of the law was inevitable. The intense intellectual and emotional life, and the heightening of sensations which came with the advance of civilization, made it clear to men that only a part of the pain, pleasure, and profit of life lay in physical things. Thoughts, emotions, and sensations demanded legal recognition, and the beautiful capacity for growth which characterizes the common law enabled the judges to afford the requisite protection, without the interposition of the legislature.

Recent inventions and business methods call attention to the next step which must be taken for the protection of the person, and for securing to the individual what Judge Cooley calls the right "to be let alone" Instantaneous photographs and newspaper enterprise have invaded the sacred precincts of private and domestic life; and numerous mechanical devices threaten to make good the prediction that "what is whispered in the closet shall be proclaimed from the house-tops." For years there has been a feeling that the law must afford some remedy for the unauthorized circulation of portraits of private persons; and the evil of invasion of privacy by the newspapers, long keenly felt, has been but recently discussed by an able writer. The alleged facts of a somewhat notorious case brought before an inferior tribunal in New York a few months ago, directly involved the consideration of the right of circulating portraits; and the question whether our law will recognize and protect the right to privacy in this and in other respects must soon come before our courts for consideration.

Of the desirability—indeed of the necessity—of some such protection, there can, it is believed, be no doubt. The press is overstepping in every direction the obvious bounds of propriety and of decency. Gossip is no longer the resource of the idle and of the vicious, but has become a trade, which is pursued with industry as well as effrontery. To satisfy a prurient taste the details of sexual relations are spread broadcast in the columns of the daily papers. To occupy the indolent, column upon column is filled with idle gossip, which can only be procured by intrusion upon the domestic circle. The intensity and complexity of life, attendant upon advancing civilization, have rendered necessary some retreat from the world, and man, under the refining influence of culture, has become more sensitive to publicity, so that solitude and privacy have become more essential to the individual; but modern enterprise and invention have, through invasions upon his privacy, subjected him to mental pain and distress, far greater than could be inflicted by mere bodily injury. Nor is the harm wrought by such invasions confined to the suffering of those who may be the subjects of journalistic or other enterprise. In this, as in other branches of commerce, the supply creates the demand. Each crop of unseemly gossip, thus harvested, becomes the seed of more, and, in direct proportion to its circulation, results in the lowering of social standards and of morality. Even gossip apparently harmless, when widely and persistently circulated, is potent for evil. It both belittles and perverts. It belittles by inverting the relative importance of things, thus dwarfing the thoughts and aspirations of a people. When personal gossip attains the dignity of print, and crowds the space available for matters of real interest to the community, what wonder that the ignorant and thoughtless mistake its relative importance. Easy of comprehension, appealing to that weak side of human nature which is never wholly cast down by the misfortunes and frailties of our neighbors, no one can be surprised that it usurps the place of interest in brains capable of other things. Triviality destroys at once robustness of thought and delicacy of feeling. No enthusiasm can flourish, no generous impulse can survive under its blighting influence.

It is our purpose to consider whether the existing law affords a principle which can properly be invoked to protect the privacy of the individual; and, if it does, what the nature and extent of such protection is.

Owing to the nature of the instruments by which privacy is invaded, the injury inflicted bears a superficial resemblance to the wrongs dealt with by the law of slander and of libel, while a legal remedy for such injury seems to involve the treatment of mere wounded feelings, as a substantive cause of action. The principle on which the law of defamation rests, covers, however, a radically different class of effects from those for which attention is now asked. It deals only with damage to reputation, with the injury done to the individual in his external relations to the community, by lowering him in the estimation of his fellows. The matter published of him, however widely circulated, and however unsuited to publicity, must, in order to be actionable, have a direct tendency to injure him in his intercourse with others, and even if in writing or in print, must subject him to the hatred, ridicule, or contempt of his fellowmen,—the effect of the publication upon his estimate of himself and upon his own feelings nor forming an essential element in the cause of action. In short, the wrongs and correlative rights recognized by the law of slander and libel are in their nature material rather than spiritual. That branch of the law simply extends the protection surrounding physical property to certain of the conditions necessary or helpful to worldly prosperity. On the other hand, our law recognizes no principle upon which compensation can be granted for mere injury to the feelings. However painful the mental effects upon another of an act, though purely wanton or even malicious, yet if the act itself is otherwise lawful, the suffering inflicted is dannum absque injuria. Injury of feelings may indeed be taken account of in ascertaining the amount of damages when attending what is recognized as a legal injury; but our system, unlike the Roman law, does not afford a remedy even for mental suffering which results from mere contumely and insult, but from an intentional and unwarranted violation of the "honor" of another.

It is not however necessary, in order to sustain the view that the common law recognizes and upholds a principle applicable to cases of invasion of privacy, to invoke the analogy, which is but superficial, to injuries sustained, either by an attack upon reputation or by what the civilians called a violation of honor; for the legal doctrines relating to infractions of what is ordinarily termed the common-law right to intellectual and artistic property are, it is believed, but instances and applications of a general right to privacy, which properly understood afford a remedy for the evils under consideration.

The common law secures to each individual the right of determining, ordinarily, to what extent his thoughts, sentiments, and emotions shall be communicated to others. Under our system of government, he can never be compelled to express them (except when upon the witness stand); and even if he has chosen to give them expression, he generally retains the power to fix the limits of the publicity which shall be given them. The existence of this right does not depend upon the particular method of expression adopted. It is immaterial whether it be by word or by signs, in painting, by sculpture, or in music. Neither does the existence of the right depend upon the nature or value of the thought or emotions, nor upon the excellence of the means of expression. The same protection is accorded to a casual letter or an entry in a diary and to the most valuable poem or essay, to a botch or daub and to a masterpiece. In every such case the individual is entitled to decide whether that which is his shall be given to the public. No other has the right to publish his productions in any form, without his consent. This right is wholly independent of the material on which, the thought, sentiment, or emotions is expressed. It may exist independently of any corporeal being, as in words spoken, a song sung, a drama acted....

If the invasion of privacy constitutes a legal injuria, the elements for demanding redress exist, since already the value of mental suffering, caused by an act wrongful in itself, is recognized as a basis for compensation.

The right of one who has remained a private individual, to prevent his public portraiture, presents the simplest case for such extension; the right to protect one's self from pen portraiture, from a discussion by the press of one's private affairs, would be a more important and far-reaching one. If casual and unimportant statements in a letter, if handiwork, however inartistic and valueless, if possessions of all sorts are protected not only against reproduction, but also against description and enumeration, how much more should the acts and sayings of a man in his social and domestic relations be guarded from ruthless publicity. If you may not reproduce a woman's face photographically without her consent, how much less should be tolerated the reproduction of her face, her form, and her actions, by graphic descriptions colored to suit a gross and depraved imagination.

It remains to consider what are the limitations of this right to privacy, and what remedies may be granted for the enforcement of the right. To determine in advance of experience the exact line at which the dignity and convenience of the individual must yield to the demands of the public welfare or of private justice would be a difficult task; but the more general rules are furnished by the legal analogies already developed in the law of slander and libel, and in the law of literary and artistic property.

1. The right to privacy does not prohibit any publication of matter which is of public or general interest. In determining the scope of this rule, aid would be afforded by the analogy, in the law of libel and slander, of cases which deal with the qualified privilege of comment and criticism on matters of public and general interest. There are of course difficulties in applying such a rule; but they are inherent in the subject-matter, and are certainly no greater than those which exist in many other branches of the law,—for instance, in that large class of cases in which the reasonableness or unreasonableness of an act is made the test of liability. The design of the law must be to protect those persons with whose affairs the community has no legitimate concern, from being dragged into an undesirable and undesired publicity and to protect all persons, whatsoever; their position or station, from having matters which they may properly prefer to keep private, made public against their will. It is the unwarranted invasion of individual privacy which is reprehended, and to be, so far as possible, prevented. The distinction, however, noted in the above statement is obvious and fundamental. There are persons who may reasonably claim as a right, protection from the notoriety entailed by being made the victims of journalistic enterprise. There are others who, in varying degrees, have renounced the right to live their lives screened from public observation. Matters which men of the first class may justly contend, concern themselves alone, may in those of the second be the subject of legitimate interest to their fellow-citizens. Peculiarities of manner and person, which in the ordinary individual should be free from comment, may acquire a public importance, if found in a candidate for public office. Some further discrimination is necessary, therefore, than to class facts or deeds as public or private according to a standard to be applied to the fact or deed per se. To publish of a modest and retiring individual that he suffers from an impediment in his speech or that he cannot spell correctly, is an unwarranted, if not an unexampled, infringement of his rights, while to state and comment on the same characteristics found in a would-be congressman could not be regarded as beyond the pale of propriety.

The general object in view is to protect the privacy of private life, and to whatever degree and in whatever connection a man's life has ceased to be private, before the publication under consideration has been made, to that extent the protection is likely to be withdrawn.[43] Since, then, the propriety of publishing the very same facts may depend wholly upon the person concerning whom they are published, no fixed formula can be used to prohibit obnoxious publications. Any rule of liability adopted must have in it an elasticity which shall take account of the varying circumstances of each case,—a necessity which unfortunately renders such a doctrine not only more difficult of application, but also to a certain extent uncertain in its operation and easily rendered abortive. Besides, it is only the more flagrant breaches of decency and propriety that could in practice be reached, and it is not perhaps desirable even to attempt to repress everything which the nicest taste and keenest sense of the respect due to private life would condemn.

In general, then, the matters of which the publication should be repressed may be described as those which concern the private life, habits, acts, and relations of an individual, and have no legitimate connection with his fitness for a public office which he seeks or for which he is suggested, or for any public or quasi public position which he seeks or for which he is suggested, and have no legitimate relation to or bearing upon any act done by him in a public or quasi public capacity. The foregoing is not designed as a wholly accurate or exhaustive definition, since that which must ultimately in a vast number of cases become a question of individual judgment and opinion is incapable of such definition; but it is an attempt to indicate broadly the class of matters referred to. Some things all men alike are entitled to keep from popular curiosity, whether in public life or not, while others are only private because the persons concerned have not assumed a position which makes their doings legitimate matters of public investigation.

2. The right to privacy does not prohibit the communication of any matter, though in its nature private, when the publication is made under circumstances which would render it a privileged communication according to the law of slander and libel. Under this rule, the right to privacy is not invaded by any publication made in a court of justice, in legislative bodies, or the committees of those bodies; in municipal assemblies, or the committees of such assemblies, or practically by any communication in any other public body, municipal or parochial, or in any body quasi public, like the large voluntary associations formed for almost every purpose of benevolence, business, or other general interest; and (at least in many jurisdictions) reports of any such proceedings would in some measure be accorded a like privilege. Nor would the rule prohibit any publication made by one in the discharge of some public or private duty, whether legal or moral, or in conduct of one's own affairs, in matters where his own interest is concerned.

3. The law would probably not grant any redress for the invasion of privacy by oral publication in the absence of special damage. The same reasons exist for distinguishing between oral and written publications of private matters, as is afforded in the law of defamation by the restricted liability for slander as compared with the liability for libel. The injury resulting from such oral communications would ordinarily be so trifling that the law might well, in the interest of free speech, disregard it altogether.

4. The right to privacy ceases upon the publication of the facts by the individual, or with his consent.

This is but another application of the rule which has become familiar in the law of literary and artistic property. The cases there decided establish also what should be deemed a publication,—the important principle in this connection being that a private communication of circulation for a restricted purpose is not a publication within the meaning of the law.

5. The truth of the matter published does not afford a defence. Obviously this branch of the law should have no concern with the truth or falsehood of the matters published. It is not for injury to the individual's character that redress or prevention is sought, but for injury to the right of privacy. For the former, the law of slander and libel provides perhaps a sufficient safeguard. The latter implies the right not merely to prevent inaccurate portrayal of private life, but to prevent its being depicted at all.

6. The absence of "malice" in the publisher does not afford a defence. Personal ill-will is not an ingredient of the offence, any more than in an ordinary case of trespass to person or to property. Such malice is never necessary to be shown in an action for libel or slander at common law, except in rebuttal of some defence, e.g., that the occasion rendered the communication privileged, or, under the statutes in this State and elsewhere, that the statement complained of was true. The invasion of the privacy that is to be protected is equally complete and equally injurious, whether the motives by which the speaker or writer was actuated are taken by themselves, culpable or not; just as the damage to character, and to some extent the tendency

to provoke a breach of the peace, is equally the result of defamation without regard to motives leading to its publication. Viewed as a wrong to the individual, this rule is the same pervading the whole law of torts, by which one is held responsible for his intentional acts, even thought they care committed with no sinister intent; and viewed as a wrong to society, it is the same principle adopted in a large category of statutory offences.

It would doubtless be desirable that the privacy of the individual should receive the added protection of the criminal law, but for this, legislation would be required. Perhaps it would be deemed proper to bring the criminal liability for such publication within narrower limits; but that the community has an interest in preventing such invasions of privacy, sufficiently strong to justify the introduction of such a remedy, cannot be doubted. Still, the protection of society must come mainly through a recognition of the rights of the individual. Each man is responsible for his own acts and omissions only. If he condones what he reprobates, with a weapon at hand equal to his defence, he is responsible for the results. If he resists, public opinion will rally to his support. Has he then such a weapon? It is believed that the common law provides him with one, forged in the slow fire of the centuries, and to-day fitly tempered to his hand. The common law has always recognized a man's house as his castle, impregnable, often, even to his own officers engaged in the execution of its command. Shall the courts thus close the front entrance to constituted authority, and open wide the back door to idle or prurient curiosity?

Samuel D. Warren,
Louis D. Brandeis.
BOSTON, December, 1890.

SOURCE: http://groups.csail.mit.edu/mac/classes/6.805/articles/privacy/Privacy_brand_warr2.html

ANALYSIS

Warren and Brandeis's article identified privacy as an implicit concept running throughout Anglo-American common law. At the time, there was no constitutional right to privacy, and even if one could discern such a right in the Fourth or Ninth Amendments, the Bill of Rights did not apply to the states. The conventional wisdom is that Warren and Brandeis constructed a right to privacy out of a very modest body of law. In particular, Warren and Brandeis framed their article around the intersection of the news media and new technology. The newspaper industry was going through an incredible growth during the second half of the 19th century. Between 1850 and 1890, the number of readers grew from approximately 800,000 to more than 8 million. Warren and Brandeis complained that journalism had become sensationalistic and were overstepping the bounds of common decency. Given the increasing capacity of government, the press, and other agencies and institutions to invade previously inaccessible aspects of personal activity, they argued that the law must evolve in response to technological change.

Warren and Brandeis were particularly concerned about the new technology of instant photography. In 1884, the Eastman Kodak Company produced the "snap camera," a small inexpensive camera that the general public could afford en masse.

Before the snap camera, cameras had been expensive and heavy; they had to be set up and people would have to pose to have pictures taken. The snap camera enabled people to take candid pictures and created an obsession for amateur photography by thousands of people who had previously not been able to afford a camera. These developments prompted Warren and Brandeis to search for a legal right to protect individual privacy. "It is our purpose," the authors wrote, "to consider whether the existing law affords a principle which can properly be invoked to protect the privacy of the individual; and, if it does, what the nature and extent of such protection is." Warren and Brandeis contended that the law currently did not provide sufficient protection to privacy, but they demonstrated how a right to privacy could be derived using common law reasoning.

Warren and Brandeis adopted the "right to be let alone" language from Cooley's 1888 treatise *The Law of Torts*. Cooley's "right to be let alone" was a passing observation in a discussion of why tort law protected against not only batteries but also assaults where there was no physical contact. Cooley observed that in assaults, victims endured "a shock to the nerves, and the peace and quiet of the individual is disturbed for a period of greater or lesser duration." Warren and Brandeis utilized Cooley's recognition of psychological injury as a basis for tort recovery. In essence, they suggested a new tort that allowed people to recover damages for unwarranted intrusion into their private affairs. This essay is widely acknowledged as one of the first and most significant ever written in defense of a distinctive identifiable right to privacy. The essay significantly influenced American law and jurisprudence.

FURTHER READING

Breckenridge Carlyle, Adam. *The Right to Privacy*. Lincoln: University of Nebraska Press, 1970.

Glenn, Richard A. *The Right to Privacy: Rights and Liberties under the Law*. Santa Barbara, Calif.: ABC-CLIO, 2003.

2

EARLY COURT RULINGS ON DUE PROCESS, EQUAL PROTECTION, FIRST AMENDMENT, AND PRIVACY

The Appeal of Richard Chambers and the Writ of Habeas Corpus

- ***Document:*** The Chambers Case, Excerpt
- ***Date:*** July 2, 1629
- ***Where:*** England
- ***Significance:*** This case concerns a writ of habeas corpus from a merchant who was imprisoned for speaking against taxes or "tonnage and poundage" imposed by King Charles I on imported goods.

DOCUMENT

Chambers's Case

79 Eng. Rep. 746 K.B. 1629

Chambers was brought by a *habeas corpus* out of the Fleet, and returned, that he was "committed to the Fleet by virtue of a decree in the Star Chamber, by reason of certain words he used at the council table, viz. that the merchants of England were screwed up here in England more than in Turkey." And for these and other words of defamation of the Government, he was censured to be committed to the Fleet, and to be there imprisoned until he made his submission at the council table, and to pay a fine of two thousand pounds.

And now at the Bar he prayed to be delivered, because this sentence is not warranted by any law or statute; for the statute of 3 Hen. 7. c. 1. which is the foundation of the Court of Star Chamber, doth not give them any authority to punish for words only.

But all the Court informed him, that the Court of Star Chamber was not erected by the 3 Hen. 7. c. 1. but was a Court many years before, and one of the most high and honourable Courts of Justice; and to deliver one who was committed by the decree of one of the Courts of Justice, was not the usage of this Court. And therefore he was remanded.

SOURCE: http://press-pubs.uchicago.edu/founders/documents/a1_9_2s1.html

ANALYSIS

Richard Chambers was a silk merchant who was part of a tax strike against King Charles I for refusing to pay "tonnage" and "poundage" on imported goods. He was called before the Privy Council at which time he stated "that the merchants are in no part of the world so screwed and wrung as in England; that in Turkey they have more encouragement." Chambers was held in contempt and ordered to pay a fine of 2,000 pounds and imprisoned until he admitted that his statements were wrong. Chambers applied to the Court of King's Bench for a writ of habeas corpus. For the first time the judges were called upon to exercise authority granted to them by the Petition of Right. The Petition of Right is a major English constitutional document, which sets out specific liberties of the subject that the king is prohibited from infringing. The Petition of Right was passed by Parliament in May, 1628, and given the royal assent by Charles I in June of that year. The Petition is most notable for its confirmation of the principles that taxes can be levied only by Parliament and that prisoners must be able to challenge the legitimacy of their detentions through the writ of habeas corpus. Chambers sought redress through a writ of habeas corpus arguing that the Star Chamber had no authority to punish him for words only. But the Court of King's Bench refused to release him, saying that the Star Chamber was one of the most high and honorable Courts of Justice. Chambers remained in prison for six years.

FURTHER READING

Popofsky, Linda. "The Crisis over Tonnage and Poundage in Parliament in 1629." *Past and Present* 126 (February 1990): 44–75.

DID YOU KNOW?

Brass Crosby's Case, 1771

The British House of Commons charged the Lord Mayor of London, Brass Crosby, with contempt after he refused to punish a newspaper printer (J. Miller) who published the proceedings of Parliament in the *London Evening Post.* Up until this point, parliamentary debates had been published under fake titles, and fictitious names were given to the Members of Parliament (MPs). Miller's newspaper, however, named the MPs, infuriating many of them. As part of the legal dispute, a messenger was dispatched with a warrant to arrest the printer, and he was brought before Brass Crosby for sentencing. Crosby, a lawyer and former MP, refused to punish Miller, asserting that British citizens had the right to know what those who represented them and made their laws were saying and doing.

Crosby was subsequently ordered to appear before the House of Commons to explain his actions. He argued that London Charters gave him the responsibility to protect the rights of the people, and that he was therefore bound to uphold these rights. Crosby was sentenced by the House of Commons to imprisonment in the Tower of London, by a vote of 202 to 39. Contending that the House of Commons had no right to imprison him for contempt of their authority, Crosby filed a writ of habeas corpus. He was twice brought up on a writ of habeas corpus, but in both cases the judges refused to interfere, and Crosby was remanded back to the Tower. While he was imprisoned, unruly rallies were held in his support, not only throughout London but around the country. Effigies of leading members of Parliament were burned, and cups were inscribed with slogans demanding his release. Crosby was released six weeks after his imprisonment, at the end of the parliamentary session, to a rousing hero's welcome. Since this case, no further attempts have been made to prevent the publication of parliamentary debates.

The Status of Slavery Is Changed by the Sommersett Case

- ***Document:*** *Ex Parte Sommersett*, Excerpt
- ***Date:*** 1772
- ***Where:*** England
- ***Significance:*** This decision is significant because the judgment of the English Court of King's Bench strongly impacted the constitutional status of slavery in England and in the United States after independence by recognizing that slavery did not exist where it was not established by positive law.

DOCUMENT

The Sommersett Case

Howell's State Trials, vol. 20, cols 1–6, 79–82 548. The Case of JAMES SOMMERSETT, a Negro, on a Habeas Corpus,* King's-Bench: 12 GEORGE III. A.D. 1771–72.

. . . .

Lord Mansfield.—The question is, if the owner had a right to detain the slave, for the sending of him over to be sold in Jamaica. In five or six cases of this nature, I have known it to be accommodated by agreement between the parties: on its first coming before me, I strongly recommended it here. But if the parties will have it decided, we must give our opinion. Compassion will not, on the one hand, nor inconvenience on the other, be to decide; but the law: in which the difficulty will be principally from the inconvenience on both sides. Contract for sale of a slave is good here; the sale is a matter to which the law properly and readily attaches, and will maintain the price according to the agreement. But here the person of the slave himself is immediately the object of enquiry; which makes a very material difference. The now question is, Whether any dominion, authority or coercion can be exercised in this country, on a slave according to the American laws? The difficulty of adopting the relation, without adopting it in all its consequences, is indeed extreme; and yet, many of those consequences are absolutely contrary to the municipal law of England. We have no authority to regulate the conditions in which law shall operate. On the other hand, should we think the coercive power cannot be exercised: it is now about 50 years since the opinion given by two of the greatest men of their own or any times, (since which no contract has been brought to trial, between the masters and slaves;) the service performed by the slaves without wages, is a clear indication they did not think themselves free by coming hither. The setting 14,000 or 15,000 men at once loose by a solemn opinion, is very disagreeable in the effects it threatens. There is a case in Hobart, (Coventry and Woodfall) where a man had contracted to go as a mariner: but the now case will not come within that decision. Mr. Steuart advances no claims on contract; he rests his whole demand on a right to the negro as slave, and mentions the purpose of detainure to be the sending of him over to be sold in Jamaica. If the parties will have judgment, 'fiat justitia, ruat coelum;' let justice be done whatever be the consequence. 50l. a-head may not be a high price; then a loss follows to the proprietors of above 700,000l. sterling. How would the law stand with respect to their settlement; their wages? How many actions for any slight coercion by the master? We cannot in any of these points direct the law; the law must rule us. In these particulars, it may be matter of weighty consideration, what provisions are made or set by law. Mr. Steuart may end the question, by discharging or giving freedom to the negro. I did think at first to put the matter to a more solemn way of argument: but if my brothers agree, there seems no occasion. I do not imagine, after the point has been discussed on both sides so extremely well, any new light could be thrown on the subject. If the parties chuse to refer it to the Common Pleas, they can give themselves that satisfaction whenever they think fit. An application to parliament, if the merchants think the question of great commercial concern, is the best, and perhaps the only method of settling the point for the future. The Court is greatly obliged to the gentlemen of the bar who have spoke on the subject; and by whose care and abilities so much has been effected, that the rule of decision will be reduced to a very easy compass. I cannot omit to express particular happiness in seeing young men, just called to the bar, have been able so much to profit by their reading. I think it is right the matter should stand over; and if we are called on for a decision, proper notice shall be given

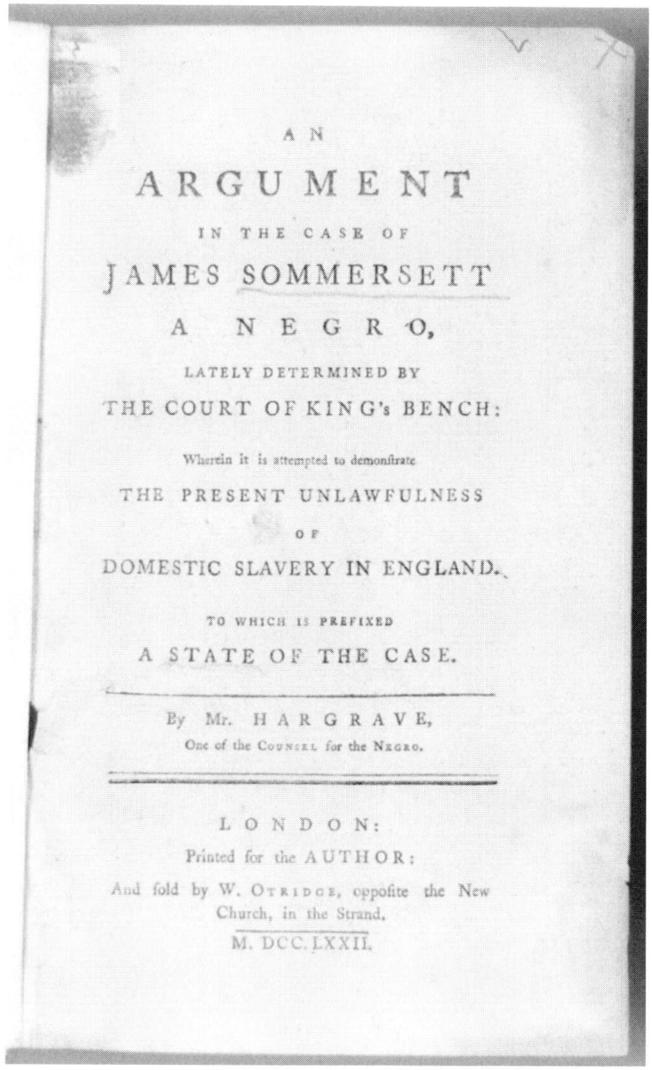
AN
ARGUMENT
IN THE CASE OF
JAMES SOMMERSETT
A NEGRO,
LATELY DETERMINED BY
THE COURT OF KING's BENCH:
Wherein it is attempted to demonstrate
THE PRESENT UNLAWFULNESS
OF
DOMESTIC SLAVERY IN ENGLAND.
TO WHICH IS PREFIXED
A STATE OF THE CASE.

By Mr. HARGRAVE,
One of the COUNSEL for the NEGRO.

LONDON:
Printed for the AUTHOR:
And sold by W. OTRIDGE, opposite the New
Church, in the Strand.
M. DCC. LXXII.

The case of James Sommersett in 1772 determined that slavery was illegal in England. (Library of Congress.)

Trinity Term, June 22, 1772.

Lord Mansfield.—On the part of Sommersett, the case which we gave notice should be decided this day, the Court now proceeds to give its opinion. I shall recite the return to the writ of Habeas Corpus, as the ground of our determination; omitting only words of form. The captain of the ship on board of which the negro was taken, makes his return to the writ in terms signifying that there have been, and still are, slaves to a great number in Africa; and that the trade in them is authorized by the laws and opinions of Virginia and Jamaica; that they are goods and chattels; and, as such, saleable and sold. That James Sommersett is a negro of Africa, and long before the return of the king's writ was brought to be sold, and was sold to Charles Steuart, esq. then in Jamaica, and has not been manumitted since; that Mr. Steuart, having occasion to transact business, came over hither, with an intention to return; and brought Sommersett to attend and abide with him, and to carry him back as soon as the business should be transacted. That such intention has been, and still continues; and that the negro did remain till the time of his departure in the service of his master Mr. Steuart, and quitted it without his consent; and thereupon, before the return of the king's writ, the said Charles Steuart did commit the slave on board the Anne and Mary, to safe custody, to be kept till he should set sail, and then to be taken with him to Jamaica, and there sold as a slave. And this is the cause why he, captain Knowles, who was then and now is, commander of the above vessel, then and now lying in the river of Thames, did the said negro, committed to his custody, detain; and on which he now renders him to the orders of the Court. We pay all due attention to the opinion of sir Philip Yorke, and lord chancellor Talbot, whereby they pledged themselves to the British planters, for all the legal consequences of slaves coming over to this kingdom or being baptized, recognized by lord Hardwicke, sitting as chancellor on the 19th of October, 1749, that trover would lie: that a notion had prevailed, if a negro came over, or became a Christian, he was emancipated, but no ground in law: that he and lord Talbot, when attorney and solicitor-general, were of opinion, that no such claim for freedom was valid; that though the statute of tenures had abolished villeins regardant to a manor, yet he did not conceive but that a man might still become a villein in gross, by confessing himself such in open court. We are so well agreed, that we think there is no occasion of having it argued (as I intimated an intention at first,) before all the judges, as is usual, for obvious reasons, on a return to Habeas Corpus. The only question before us is, whether the cause on the return is sufficient? If it is, the negro must be remanded; if it is not, he must be discharged. Accordingly, the return states, that the slave departed and refused to serve; whereupon he was kept, to be sold abroad. So high an act of dominion must be recognized by the law of the country where it is used. The power of a master over his slave has been extremely different, in different countries. The state of slavery is of such a nature, that it is incapable of being introduced on any reasons, moral or political, but only by positive law, which preserves its force long after the reasons, occasion, and time itself from whence it was created, is erased from memory. It is so odious, that nothing can be suffered to support it, but positive law. Whatever inconveniences, therefore, may follow from the decision, I cannot say this case is allowed or approved by the law of England; and therefore the black must be discharged.

SOURCE: http://www.nationalarchives.gov.uk/pathways/blackhistory/rights/transcripts/somerset_case.htm

ANALYSIS

James Sommersett (or Somersett) had been born in Africa and brought to Virginia by a slave trader in 1749 at which time Charles Steuart, a Scots merchant living in

Norfolk, purchased him. Steuart moved to Boston as a high official in the customs service. In 1769, Steuart went to England on business, taking Sommersett with him as his personal servant, but in 1771 Sommersett escaped. He was recaptured and was delivered to Captain John Knowles of the ship *Ann and Mary* bound for the British colony of Jamaica to be sold. Interested parties, acting as Sommersett's godparents, but most likely British abolitionists, intervened. On the strength of their affidavits, a writ of habeas corpus was granted on November 28, 1772, and Captain Knowles was ordered to produce Sommersett before the Court of King's Bench, to determine whether Sommersett's imprisonment was legal. British abolitionist Granville Sharp agreed to help Sommersett's legal defense.

On behalf of Sommersett, it was argued that while colonial laws might permit slavery, neither the common law of England nor any law made by Parliament recognized the existence of slavery, and slavery was therefore illegal. Moreover, English contract law did not allow for any person to enslave himself, nor could any contract be binding without the individual's consent. When the two lawyers for Charles Steuart put their case, they argued that property was paramount and that it would be dangerous to free all the black people in England.

Explaining the result, Chief Justice Lord Mansfield recognized that slavery existed in various parts of the British Empire and conceded that contracts for the sale of overseas slaves had been recognized as valid in England, but found that there was no "positive law," that is, no statute, confirming the existence of slavery in England. So an answer to the question of its legality had to be sought in the common law. Utilizing the common law method, Mansfield searched for an analogy but could not find one. Without an analogous case, the common law provided no law to justify Sommersett's confinement. Lord Mansfield held that a master could not seize slaves in England and hold them against their will for the purpose of selling them outside of England. The case therefore made a writ of habeas corpus available to slaves, preventing them from being held against their will. This meant that a vital right had been extended to a black man, said to be a slave, in opposition to his supposed owner. Even though this case did not formally abolish slavery in England or America, it was interpreted to mean that slavery did not exist where it was not established by positive law.[1]

FURTHER READING

Davis, David B. *The Problem of Slavery in the Age of Revolution, 1770–1823*. Ithaca, N.Y.: Cornell University Press, 1975.

Paley, Ruth. "After *Somerset:* Mansfield, Slavery and the Law in England, 1772–1830." In *Law, Crime and English Society, 1660–1830*, edited by Norma Landau, 184. New York: Cambridge University Press, 2002.

NOTE

1. William M. Wiecek, *The Sources of Antislavery Constitutionalism in America, 1769–1848* (Ithaca, N.Y.: Cornell University Press, 1977), 20.

The Supreme Court and the Writ of Habeas Corpus

- ***Document:*** The Supreme Court case *Ex parte Bollman & Swartwout*, Excerpt
- ***Date:*** February, 1807
- ***Where:*** Washington, D.C.
- ***Significance:*** This holding established that the Supreme Court had the power to order that a writ of habeas corpus be issued to release individuals from prison because the Constitution grants that power to federal courts unless Congress suspends it.

DOCUMENT

Ex parte Bollman & Swartwout, 8 U.S. 75 (1807)

John Marshall delivered the opinion of the court, as follows:

As preliminary to any investigation of the merits of this motion, this court deems it proper to declare that it disclaims all jurisdiction not given by the constitution, or by the laws of the United States.

Courts which originate in the common law possess a jurisdiction which must be regulated by their common law, until some statute shall change their established principles; but courts which are created by written law, and whose jurisdiction is defined by written law, cannot transcend that jurisdiction. It is unnecessary to state the reasoning on which this opinion is founded, because it has been repeatedly given by this court; and with the decisions heretofore rendered on this point, no member of the bench has, even for an instant, been dissatisfied. The reasoning from the bar, in relation to it, may be answered by the single observation, that for the meaning of the term habeas corpus, resort may unquestionably be had to the common law; but the power to award the writ by any of the courts of the United States, must be given by written law.

This opinion is not to be considered as abridging the power of courts over their own officers, or to protect themselves, and their members, from being disturbed in the exercise of their functions. It extends only to the power of taking cognizance of any question between individuals, or between the government and individuals.

To enable the court to decide on such question, the power to determine it must be given by written law. The inquiry therefore on this motion will be, whether by any statute, compatible with the constitution of the United States, the power to award a writ of habeas corpus, in such a case as that of Erick Bollman and Samuel Swartwout, has been given to this court.

The 14th section of the judicial act (Laws U.S. vol. 1. p. 58) has been considered as containing a substantive grant of this power. It is in these words: "That all the before mentioned courts of the United States shall have power to issue writs of scire facias, habeas corpus, and all other writs, not specially provided for by statute, which may be necessary for the exercise of their respective jurisdictions, and agreeable to the principles and usages of law. And that either of the justices of the supreme court, as well as judges of the district courts, shall have power to grant writs of habeas corpus, for the purpose of an inquiry into the cause of commitment. Provided, that writs of habeas corpus shall in no case extend to prisoners in gaol, unless where they are in custody under or by colour of the authority of the United States, or are committed for trial before some court of the same, or are necessary to be brought into court to testify."

The only doubt of which this section can be susceptible is, whether the restrictive words of the first sentence limit the power to the award of such writs of habeas corpus as are necessary to enable the courts of the United States to exercise their respective jurisdictions in some cause which they are capable of finally deciding.

It has been urged, that in strict grammatical construction, these words refer to the last antecedent, which is, "all other writs not specially provided for by statute."

This criticism may be correct, and is not entirely without its influence; but the sound construction which the court thinks it safer to adopt, is, that the true sense of the words is to be determined by the nature of the provision, and by the context.

It may be worthy of remark, that this act was passed by the first congress of the United States, sitting under a constitution which had declared "that the privilege of the writ of habeas corpus should not be suspended, unless when, in cases of rebellion or invasion, the public safety might require it."

Acting under the immediate influence of this injunction, they must have felt, with peculiar force, the obligation of providing efficient means by which this great constitutional privilege should receive life and activity; for if the means be not in existence, the privilege itself would be lost, although no law for its suspension should be enacted. Under the impression of this obligation, they give, to all the courts, the power of awarding writs of habeas corpus. It has been truly said, that this is a generic term, and includes every species of that writ. To this it may be added, that when used singly—when we say the writ of habeas corpus, without addition, we most generally mean that great writ which is now applied for; and in that sense it is used in the constitution.

The section proceeds to say, that "either of the justices of the supreme court, as well as judges of the district courts, shall have power to grant writs of habeas corpus for the purpose of an inquiry into the cause of commitment."

It has been argued that congress could never intend to give a power of this kind to one of the judges of this court, which is refused to all of them when assembled. There is certainly much force in this argument, and it receives additional strength from the consideration, that if the power be denied to this court, it is denied to every other court of the United States, the right to grant this important writ is given, in this sentence, to every judge of the circuit, or district court, but can neither be exercised by the circuit nor district court. It would be strange if the judge, sitting on the bench, should be unable to hear a motion for this writ where it might be openly made, and openly discussed, and might yet retire to his chamber, and in private receive and decide upon the motion. This is not consistent with the genius of our legislation, nor with the course of our judicial proceedings. It would be much more consonant with both, that the power of the judge at his chambers should be suspended during his term, than that it should be exercised only in secret.

Whatever motives might induce the legislature to withhold from the supreme court the power to award the great writ of habeas corpus, there could be none which would induce them to withhold it from every court in the United States: and as it is granted to all in the same sentence and by the same words, the sound construction would seem to be, that the first sentence vests this power in all the courts of the United States; but as those courts are not always in session, the second sentence vests it in every justice or judge of the United States. The doubt which has been raised on this subject may be further explained by examining the character of the various writs of habeas corpus, and selecting those to which this general grant of power must be restricted, if taken in the limited sense of being merely used to enable the court to exercise its jurisdiction in causes which it is enabled to decide finally.

If the party should be confined by process from a state court, there are many additional reasons against the use of this writ in such a case. The state courts are not, in any sense of the word, inferior courts, except in the particular cases in which an appeal lies from their judgment to this court; and in these cases the mode of proceeding is particularly prescribed, and is not by habeas corpus. They are not inferior courts because they emanate from a different authority, and are the creatures of a distinct government.

It would not be difficult to demonstrate that the writ of habeas corpus cum causa cannot be the particular writ contemplated by the legislature in the section under consideration; but it will be sufficient to observe generally that the same act prescribes a different mode for bringing into the courts of the United States suits brought in a state court against a person having a right to claim the jurisdiction of the courts of the United States. He may, on his first appearance, file his petition and authenticate the fact, upon which the cause is ipso facto removed into the courts of the United States.

The only power then, which on this limited construction would be granted by the section under consideration, would be that of issuing writs of habeas corpus ad testificandum. The section itself proves that this was not the intention of the legislature.

This proviso extends to the whole section. It limits the powers previously granted to the courts, because it specifies a case in which it is particularly applicable to the use of the power by courts:—where the person is necessary to be brought into court to testify. That construction cannot be a fair one which would make the legislature except from the operation of a proviso, limiting the express grant of a power, the whole power intended to be granted.

From this review of the extent of the power of awarding writs of habeas corpus, if the section be construed in its restricted sense; from a comparison of the nature of the writ which the courts of the United States would, on that view of the subject, be enabled to issue; from a comparison of the power so granted with the other parts of the section, it is apparent that this limited sense of the term cannot be that which was contemplated by the legislature.

If, by the sound construction of the act of congress, the power to award writs of habeas corpus in order to examine into the cause of commitment is given to this court, it remains to inquire whether this be a case in which the writ ought to be granted.

If the act of congress gives this court the power to award a writ of habeas corpus in the present case, it remains to inquire whether that act be compatible with the constitution.

In the mandamus case, (Marbury v. Madison) it was decided that this court would not exercise original jurisdiction except so far as that jurisdiction was given by the constitution. But so far as that case has distinguished between original and appellate jurisdiction, that which the court is now asked to exercise is clearly appellate. It is the revision of a decision of an inferior court, by which a citizen has been committed to jail.

It has been demonstrated at the bar, that the question brought forward on a habeas corpus, is always distinct from that which is involved in the cause itself. The question whether the individual shall be imprisoned is always distinct from the question whether he shall be convicted or acquitted of the charge on which he is to be tried, and therefore these questions are separated, and may be decided in different courts.

The decision that the individual shall be imprisoned must always precede the application for a writ of habeas corpus, and this writ must always be for the purpose of revising that decision, and therefore appellate in its nature. If at any time the public safety should require the suspension of the powers vested by this act in the courts of the United States, it is for the legislature to say so. That question depends on political considerations, on which the legislature is to decide. Until the legislative will be expressed, this court can only see its duty, and must obey the laws.

The motion, therefore, must be granted.

SOURCE: http://press-pubs.uchicago.edu/founders/documents/a1_9_2s14.html

---

ANALYSIS

This case came before the Supreme Court after the arrest of former Vice President Aaron Burr and his accomplices as part of their attempt to seize a portion of the newly acquired Louisiana Territory with the intentions of creating an independent nation. Bollman and Swartwout were implicated in Aaron Burr's plot and had been jailed by a District of Columbia court to await trial on charges of treason. They filed a petition for habeas corpus in the Supreme Court. The Court granted their petitions.

Chief Justice Marshall writing for the court held that although habeas corpus is a constitutional right under the suspension clause, this right is not self-executing and instead requires a congressional statute to effectuate it. The majority stated that Section 14 of the Judiciary Act of 1789 provided circuit courts with power to issue writs of habeas corpus and that the justices of the Supreme Court, as well as judges of the district court's jurisdiction, had the power to grant writs of habeas corpus for the purpose of an inquiry into the cause of commitment. The Court determined that such writs were issuable under the court's appellate jurisdiction and were therefore distinguishable from the writ asked for in *Marbury v. Madison*, which was not reviewable because it was an exercise of original jurisdiction. *Bollman* has been criticized because of the holding's dependency upon statutorily granted habeas corpus jurisdiction, rather than constitutionally conferred jurisdiction. This decision to grant habeas corpus under statutory authority provides a tremendous power to Congress at the expense of individual liberty.

FURTHER READING

Freedman, Eric M. "Milestones in Habeas Corpus: Part I Just Because John Marshall Said It, Doesn't Make it So: Ex Parte Bollman and the Illusory Prohibition on the Federal Writ of Habeas Corpus for State Prisoners in the Judiciary Act of 1789." *Alabama Law Review* 51 (2000): 531.

Executive Authority and the Suspension Clause of the United States Constitution

- ***Document:*** The Supreme Court case *Ex parte Merryman*, Excerpt
- ***Date:*** April, 1861
- ***Where:*** Washington, D.C.
- ***Significance:*** The Supreme Court held that President Lincoln's suspension of habeas corpus during the beginning of the Civil War was unconstitutional.

DOCUMENT

Ex parte Merryman, 17 F. Cas. 144 (1861)

R. B. Taney, Chief Justice
April, 1861

Before the Chief Justice of the Supreme Court of the United States, at Chambers.

The application in this case for a writ of *habeas corpus* is made to me under the 14th section of the Judiciary Act of 1789, which renders effectual for the citizen the constitutional privilege of the *habeas corpus*....

The case, then, is simply this: A military officer residing in Pennsylvania issues an order to arrest a citizen of Maryland, upon vague and indefinite charges, without any proof, so far as appears. Under this order his house is entered in the night; he is seized as a prisoner, and conveyed to Fort McHenry, and there kept in close confinement. And when a *habeas corpus* is served on the commanding officer, requiring him to produce the prisoner before a Justice of the Supreme Court, in order that he may examine into the legality of the imprisonment, the answer of the officer is that he is authorized by the President to suspend the writ of *habeas corpus* at his discretion, and, in the exercise of that discretion, suspends it in this case, and on that ground refuses obedience to the writ.

DID YOU KNOW?

The Constitutionality of U.S. Military Tribunals during the Civil War: *Ex parte Milligan,* 1866

On September 15, 1863, President Abraham Lincoln imposed congressionally authorized martial law. The authorizing act allowed the president to suspend habeas corpus throughout the United States. In 1864 the Union Army arrested Lambdin Milligan in Indiana and charged him with conspiracy, inciting insurrection, disloyal practices, and violations of the laws of war. He was tried by a military commission and sentenced to death by hanging. Milligan appealed for his release under the 1863 Habeas Corpus Act.

In December 1866, the Supreme Court in *Ex parte Milligan* (71 U.S. 2, 1866) unanimously invalidated Milligan's conviction based on the U.S. Constitution, in the opinion of the majority of five, or on the basis of the federal Habeas Corpus Act of 1863, in the opinion of the concurring four justices. The Court decided that the suspension of habeas corpus was lawful but that military tribunals did not apply to citizens in states that had upheld the authority of the Constitution and where civilian courts were still operating. It observed further that during the suspension of the writ of habeas corpus, citizens may only be held without charges—not tried, and certainly not executed by military tribunals. Thus the Court decided that martial law could not supersede the civil courts in areas where the civil courts and government remained open and operational. Indiana had remained within the Union, and its regular government and courts had functioned throughout the war. In such a situation, the military courts had no jurisdiction over civilians. Milligan was released from prison, and he was never convicted by a civilian court.

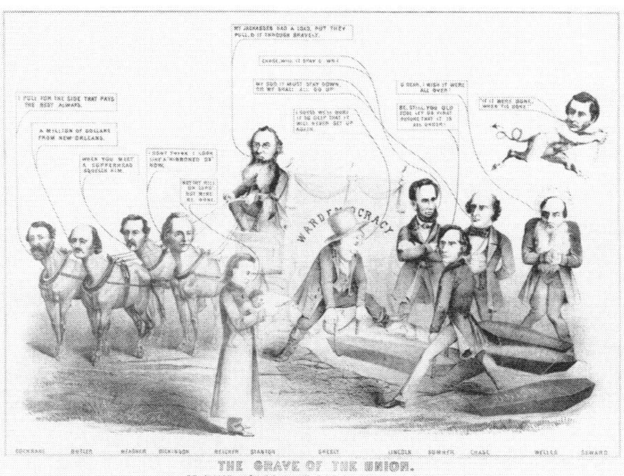

The first in a series of four harsh anti-Lincoln satires published by Bromley & Co. in New York. Political caricature. No. 1, The grave of the Union. Or Major Jack Downing's dream, drawn by Zeke. Published by Bromley & Co., New York, 1864. (Library of Congress.)

As the case comes before me, therefore, I understand that the President not only claims the right to suspend the writ of *habeas corpus* himself, at his discretion, but to delegate that discretionary power to a military officer, and to leave it to him to determine whether he will or will not obey judicial process that may be served upon him.

No official notice has been given to the courts of justice, or to the public, by proclamation or otherwise, that the President claimed this power, and had exercised it in the manner stated in the return. And I certainly listened to it with some surprise, for I had supposed it to be one of those points of constitutional law upon which there is no difference of opinion, and that it was admitted on all hands that the privilege of the writ could not be suspended except by act of Congress.

When the conspiracy of which Aaron Burr was the head became so formidable, and was so extensively ramified to justify, in Mr. Jefferson's opinion, the suspension of the writ, he claimed, on his part, no power to suspend it, but communicated his opinion to Congress, with all the proofs in his possession, in order that Congress might exercise its discretion upon the subject, and determine whether the public safety required it. And in the debate which took place upon the subject, no one suggested that Mr. Jefferson might exercise the power himself, if, in his opinion, the public safety demanded it.

Having, therefore, regarded the question as too plain and too well settled to be open to dispute, if the commanding officer had stated that upon his own responsibility, and in the exercise of his own discretion, he refused obedience to the writ, I should have contented myself with referring to the clause in the Constitution, and to the construction it received from every jurist and statesman of that day, when the case of Burr was before them. But being thus officially notified that the privilege of the writ has been suspended under the orders and by the authority of the President, and believing as I do that the President has exercised a power which he does not possess under the Constitution, a proper respect for the high office he fills requires me to state plainly and fully the grounds of my opinion, in order to show that I have not ventured to question the legality of this act without a careful and deliberate examination of the whole subject.

The clause in the Constitution which authorizes the suspension of the privilege of the writ of *habeas corpus* is in the ninth section of the first article.

This article is devoted to the Legislative Department of the United States, and has not the slightest reference to the Executive Department. It begins by providing "that all legislative powers therein granted shall be vested in a Congress of the United States, which shall consist of a Senate and House of Representatives." And after prescribing the manner in which these two branches of the legislative department shall be chosen, it proceeds to enumerate specifically the legislative powers which it thereby grants, and legislative powers which it expressly prohibits, and, at the conclusion of this specification, a clause is inserted giving Congress "the power to make all laws which may be necessary and proper for carrying into execution the foregoing powers, and all other powers vested by this Constitution in the Government of the United States or in any department or office thereof."

The power of legislation granted by this latter clause is by its word carefully confined to the specific objects before enumerated. But as this limitation was unavoidably somewhat indefinite, it was deemed necessary to guard more effectually certain great cardinal principles essential to the liberty of the citizen and to the rights and equality of the States by denying to Congress, in express terms, any power of legislation over them. It was apprehended, it seems, that such legislation might be attempted under the pretext that it was necessary and proper to carry into execution the powers granted; and it was determined that there should be no room to doubt, where rights of such vital importance were concerned, and, accordingly this clause is immediately followed by an enumeration of certain subjects to which the powers of legislation shall not extend; and the great importance which the framers of the Constitution attached to the privilege of the writ of *habeas corpus*, to protect the liberty of the citizen, is proved by the fact that its suspension, except in cases of invasion and rebellion, is first in the list of prohibited powers; and even in these cases the power is denied and its exercise prohibited unless the public safety shall require it. It is true that in the cases mentioned Congress is of necessity the judge of whether the public safety does or does not require it; and its judgment is conclusive. But the introduction of these words is a standing admonition to the legislative body of the danger of suspending it and of the extreme caution they should exercise before they give the Government of the United States such power over the liberty of a citizen.

It is the second article of the Constitution that provides for the organization of the Executive Department, and enumerates the powers conferred on it, and prescribes its duties. And if the high power over the liberty of the citizens now claimed was intended to be conferred on the President, it would undoubtedly be found in plain words in this article. But there is not a word in it that can furnish the slightest ground to justify the exercise of the power.

The article begins by declaring that the Executive power shall be vested in a President of the United States of America, to hold his office during the term of four years, and then proceeds to prescribe the mode of election, and to specify in precise and plain words the powers delegated to him and the duties imposed upon him. And the short term for which he is elected, and the narrow limits to which his power is confined, show the jealousy and apprehensions of future danger which the framers of the Constitution felt in relation to that department of the Government, and how carefully they withheld from it many of the powers belonging to the executive branch of the English Government which were considered as dangerous to the liberty of the subject, and conferred (as that in clear and specific terms) those powers only which were deemed essential to secure the successful operation of the Government.

He is elected, as I have already said, for the brief term of four years, and is made personally responsible, by impeachment, for malfeasance in office. He is, from necessity, and the nature of his duties, the Commander-in-Chief of the army and navy, and of the militia, when called into actual service. But no appropriation for the support of the army can be made by Congress for a longer term than two years, so that it is in the power of the succeeding House of Representatives to withhold the appropriation for its support, and thus disband it, if, in their judgment, the President used or designed to use it for improper purposes. And although the militia, when in actual service, are under his command, yet the appointment of the officers is reserved to the States, as a security against the use of the military power for purposes dangerous to the liberties of the people, or the rights of the States.

So, too, his powers in relation to the civil duties and authority necessarily conferred on him are carefully restricted, as well as those belonging to his military character. He cannot appoint the ordinary officers of Government, nor make a treaty with a foreign nation or Indian tribe without the advice and consent of the Senate, and cannot appoint even inferior officers unless he is authorized by an act of Congress to do so. He is not empowered to arrest any one charged with an offence against the United States, and whom he may, from the evidence before him, believe to be guilty; nor can he authorize any officer, civil or military, to exercise this power, for the fifth article of the amendments to the Constitution expressly provides that no person "shall be deprived of life, liberty, or property without due process of law;" that is, judicial process. And even if the privilege of the writ of *habeas corpus* was suspended by act of Congress, and a party not subject to the rules and articles of war was afterwards arrested and imprisoned by regular judicial process, he could not be detained in prison or brought to trial before a military tribunal, for the article in the Amendments to the Constitution immediately following the one above referred to that is, the sixth article provides that, "In all criminal prosecutions, the accused shall enjoy the right to a speedy and public trial by an impartial jury of the State and district wherein the crime shall have been committed, which district shall have been previously ascertained by law; and to be informed of the nature and cause of the accusation; to be confronted with the witnesses against him; to have compulsory process for obtaining witnesses in his favor, and to have the assistance of counsel for his defence."

And the only power, therefore, which the President possesses, where the "life, liberty, or property" of a private citizen is concerned, is the power and duty prescribed in the third section of the second article, which requires "that he shall take care that the laws be faithfully executed." He is not authorized to execute them himself, or through agents or officers, civil or military, appointed by himself, but he is to take care that they be faithfully carried into execution as they are expounded and adjudged by the coordinate branch of the Government to which that duty is assigned by the Constitution. It is thus made his duty to come in aid of the judicial authority, if it shall be resisted by a force too strong to be overcome without the assistance of the Executive arm. But in exercising this power, he acts in subordination to judicial authority, assisting it to execute its process and enforce its judgments.

With such provisions in the Constitution, expressed in language too clear to be misunderstood by any one, I can see no ground whatever for supposing that the President, in any emergency or in any state of things, can authorize the suspension of the privilege of the writ of *habeas corpus*, or arrest a citizen, except in aid of the judicial power. He certainly does not faithfully execute the laws if he takes upon himself legislative power by suspending the writ of *habeas corpus* and the judicial power, also, by arresting and imprisoning a person without due process of law. Nor can any argument be drawn from the nature of sovereignty, or the necessities of government for self-defense, in times of tumult and danger. The Government of the United States is one of delegated and limited powers. It derives it existence and authority altogether from the Constitution, and neither of its branches executive, legislative or judicial can exercise any of the powers of government beyond those specified and granted. For the tenth article of the amendments to the Constitution, in express terms, provides that "the powers not delegated to the United States by the Constitution, nor prohibited by it to the States, are reserved to the States, respectively, or to the people."

Indeed, the security against imprisonment by Executive authority, provided for in the fifth article of the Amendments of the Constitution, which I have before quoted, is nothing more than a copy of a like provision in the English constitution, which had been firmly established before the Declaration of Independence.

And the people of the United Colonies, who had themselves lived under its protection while they were British subjects, were well aware of the necessity of this safeguard for their personal liberty. And no one can believe that in framing the Government intended to guard still more efficiently the rights and the liberties of the citizens against executive encroachment and oppression, they would have conferred on the President a power which the history of England had proved to be dangerous and oppressive in the hands of the Crown, and which the people of England had compelled it to surrender after a long and obstinate struggle on the part of the English Executive to usurp and retain it.

The right of the subject to the benefit of the writ of *habeas corpus*, it must be recollected, was one of the great points in controversy during the long struggle in England between arbitrary government and free institutions, and must therefore have strongly attracted the attention of statesmen engaged in framing a new and, as they supposed, a freer government than the one which they had thrown off by the Revolution. For, from the earliest history of the common law, if a person was imprisoned no matter by what authority he had a right to the writ of *habeas corpus*, to bring his case before the King's Bench, and, if no specific offence was charged against him in the warrant of commitment, he was entitled to be forthwith discharged; and if an offence was charged which was bailable in its character the court was bound to set him at liberty on bail. And the most exciting contests between the Crown and the people of England from the time of *Magna Charta* were in relation to the privilege of this writ, and they continued until the passage of the statute of 31st Charles 2d, commonly known as the great *habeas corpus* act.

This statute put an end to the struggle, and finally and firmly secured the liberty of the subject against the usurpation and oppression of the executive branch of the Government. It nevertheless conferred no new right upon the subject, but only secured a right already existing; for, although the right could not justly be denied, there was often no effectual remedy against its violation. Until the statute of 13 William III., the Judges held their offices at the pleasure of the King, and the influence which he exercised over timid, time-serving and partisan judges, often induced them, upon some pretext or other, to refuse to discharge the party, although entitled by law to his discharge, or delayed their decision, from time to time, so as to prolong the imprisonment of persons who were obnoxious to the King for their political opinions, or had incurred his resentment in any other way.

The great and inestimable value of the *habeas corpus* act of the 31st Charles II is that it contains provisions which compel courts and judges, and all parties concerned, to perform their duties promptly, in the manner specified in the statute.

But the documents before me show that the military authority in this case has gone far beyond the mere suspension of the privilege of the writ of *habeas corpus*. It has, by force of arms, thrust aside the judicial authorities and officers to whom the Constitution has confided the power and duty of interpreting and administering the laws, and substituted a military government in its place, to be administered and executed by military officers. For at the time these proceedings were had against John Merryman, the District Judge of Maryland the commissioner appointed under the act of Congress the District Attorney and the Marshal, all resided in the city of Baltimore, a few miles only from the home of the prisoner. Up to that time there had never been the slightest resistance or obstruction to the process of any Court or judicial officer of the United States in Maryland, except by the military authority. And if a military officer, or any other person, had reason to believe that the prisoner had committed any offence against the laws of the United States, it was his duty to give information of the fact and the evidence to support it to the District Attorney, and it would then have become the duty of that officer to bring the matter before the District Judge or Commissioner, and if there was sufficient legal evidence to justify his arrest, the Judge or Commissioner would have issued his warrant to the Marshal to arrest him, and, upon the hearing of the party, would have held him to bail, or committed him for trial, according to the character of the offense as it appeared in the testimony, or would have discharged him immediately if there was not sufficient evidence to support the accusation. There was no danger of any obstruction or resistance to the action of the civil authorities, and therefore no reason whatever for the interposition of the military. And yet, under these circumstances, a military officer, stationed in Pennsylvania, without giving any information to the District Attorney, and without any application to the judicial authorities, assumes to himself the judicial power in the District of Maryland; undertakes to decide what constitutes the crime of treason or rebellion; what evidence (if, indeed, he required any) is sufficient to support the accusation and justify the commitment; and commits the party, without having a hearing even before himself, to close custody in a strongly garrisoned fort, to be there held, it would seem, during the pleasure of those who committed him.

The Constitution provides, as I have before said, that "no person shall be deprived of life, liberty, or property, without due process of law." It declares that "the right of the people to be secure in their persons, houses, papers, and effects against unreasonable searches and seizures shall not be violated, and no warrant shall issue but upon probable cause, supported by oath or affirmation, and particularly describing the place to be searched and the persons or things to be seized." It provides that the party accused shall be entitled to a speedy trial in a court of justice.

And these great and fundamental laws, which Congress itself could not suspend, have been disregarded and suspended, like the writ of *habeas corpus*, by a military order, supported by force of arms. Such is the case now before me; and I can only say that if the authority which the Constitution has confided to the judiciary department and judicial officers may thus upon any pretext or under any circumstances be usurped by the military power at its discretion, the people of the United States are no longer living under a Government of laws, but every citizen holds life, liberty, and property at the will and pleasure of the army officer in whose military district he may happen to be found.

In such a case my duty was too plain to be mistaken. I have exercised all the power which the Constitution and laws confer on me, but that power has been resisted by a force too strong for me to overcome. It is possible that the officer who has incurred this grave responsibility may have misunderstood his instructions, and exceeded the authority intended to be given him. I shall, therefore, order all the proceedings in this case, with my opinion, to be filed and recorded in the Circuit Court of the United States for the District of Maryland, and direct the clerk to transmit a copy, under seal, to the President of the United States. It will then remain for that high officer, in fulfilment of his constitutional obligation to "take care that the laws be faithfully executed," to determine what measures he will take to cause the civil process of the United States to be respected and enforced.

R. B. Taney, Chief Justice of the Supreme Court of the United States

SOURCE: http://teachingamericanhistory.org/library/index.asp?document=442

ANALYSIS

Following the inauguration of President Lincoln on March 4, 1861, the security of the nation's capital depended on holding Maryland in the Union. This was because after Virginia voted to secede, federal troops and supplies could only reach the capital through Maryland. When a Massachusetts regiment passed through Baltimore on the way to Washington on April 19, a mob attacked the Northern troops. After this violence, Maryland governor Thomas Hicks authorized the destruction of railroad bridges connecting Baltimore to Northern states. Merryman was one of the Maryland militia officers who had helped to blow up the railroad bridges between Washington, D.C., and the North, and was also training secessionist troops. At the same time, secessionist allies destroyed telegraph lines and severed communications with Washington. On April 27, 1861, President Lincoln ordered Winfield Scott, then head of the nation's military, to arrest anyone between Washington and Philadelphia suspected of subversive acts or speech, and his order specifically authorized suspension of the writ of habeas corpus.

On May 25, 1861, John Merryman was woken from his bed in Baltimore County by federal soldiers and imprisoned in Fort McHenry without a warrant. Within hours of his detention, Merryman contacted lawyers who drafted a petition for a writ of habeas corpus on the grounds that no warrant authorized his arrest and that no legal process held him in custody. The petition was addressed to Chief Justice Roger Taney, who also sat as a judge on the Federal Circuit Court for Maryland, and delivered to him at his home in Washington, D.C. Taney left the capital to convene a Sunday court session in Baltimore and to consider the petition. The resulting case, *Ex parte Merryman*, was the first judicial opinion to address the issue of whether the President could suspend habeas corpus without a grant of congressional power.

Chief Justice Taney held that President Lincoln did not have the authority under the constitution to suspend the writ of habeas corpus. First, Taney directly challenges Lincoln's claim that his duty to faithfully execute the nation's laws justifies the suspension of habeas corpus. The clause that requires the president to "faithfully execute" the laws, Taney argues, does not permit him to "execute them himself, or through agents or officers, civil or military." Instead, the president's duty is to assure that no outside force interferes with the government's execution of the laws. Therefore, he must help the judicial branch if some outside force threatens the judiciary's power; he does not have the right to utilize the military to usurp judicial authority.

Second, Taney argues that it defies common sense to believe the framers would have trusted the executive with the right to suspend habeas corpus. They had just broken away from a powerful, despotic English monarch. Therefore, they distrusted a powerful executive, especially one who could arrest citizens and hold them indefinitely without trial. Taney therefore noted that the clause prohibiting the suspension of habeas corpus was found among the enumerated powers of Congress in Article I, rather than the Article II powers of the president. As additional evidence, Taney cites the strict limits Article 2 places on the executive, such as the requirement for congressional approval of treaties with foreign nations and his short term of office.

Taney also analyzed the manner in which presidents had historically treated the right of habeas corpus. As an example, he cites a major crisis during Thomas Jefferson's presidency. Aaron Burr, Jefferson's vice president, led a conspiracy to seize territory around New Orleans to form a new country. During this time, Jefferson actually *wanted* to suspend the writ, but wrote that he lacked the authority. Instead, he suggested that Congress exercise its power to suspend habeas corpus. Taney also expressed a belief that the Supreme Court's opinion in *Ex parte Bollman* which resulted from this crisis, clearly established that Congress is the only branch entitled to suspend the writ. *Ex parte Merryman* was an important early precedent sharply delineating the respective powers of the President and Congress. Ironically, *Ex parte Merryman's* ringing endorsement of the pre-eminence of Congress in the field of habeas corpus had little practical effect because Congress ratified President Lincoln's suspension of habeas corpus two years later. The *Merryman* decision is still among the best-known Civil War–era court cases, and was recently restated by the Supreme Court in *Hamdi v. Rumsfeld* (2004).

FURTHER READING

Halbert, Sherrill. "The Suspension of the Writ of Habeas Corpus by President Lincoln." *American Journal of Legal History* 2 (1958): 95–114.

Long, Joseph C. "Ex parte Merryman: The Showdown Between Two Great Antagonists: Lincoln and Taney." *South Dakota Law Review* 14 (1969): 208–34.

Paulsen, Michael Stokes. "The Merryman Power and the Dilemma of Autonomous Executive Branch Interpretation." *Cardozo Law Review* 15 (1993): 88–99.

The Sedition Act Trials

- ***Document:*** The Trial of James Thompson Callender, Excerpt
- ***Date:*** 1800
- ***Where:*** Virginia
- ***Significance:*** The prosecutions like that of James Callender and Matthew Lyon under the Sedition Act of 1798 provoked debates on the significance of a free press and the rights of the political opposition. As the first federal trials to attract widespread public attention, the Sedition Act trials also encouraged consideration of the political influence of life-tenured judges and of the proper relationship between the judiciary and the elected branches of the federal government.

DOCUMENT

Trial of James Thompson Callender, 25 F.Cas. 239, Whart.St.Tr. 688 (1800)

Circuit Court, D. Virginia.

Indictment against James Thompson Callender for a seditious libel against the president of the United States.

Judge CHASE then proceeded. I will assign my reasons why I will not permit the counsel for the traverser to offer arguments to the jury, to urge them to do what the constitution and law of this country will not permit; and which, if I should allow, I should, in my judgment, violate my duty, disregard the constitution and law, and surrender up the judicial power of the United States, that is, the power intrusted by the constitution to the federal courts, to a petit jury, in direct breach of my oath of office. The indictment charges that the traverser, on the 1st day of February, 1800, designing and intending to defame the president of the United States, and to bring him into contempt and disrepute, and to excite the hatred of the good people of the United States against him, did wickedly and maliciously write, print, utter, and publish (or did cause or procure to be printed and published), a false, scandalous, and malicious writing, against the said president of the United States, of the tenor and effect stated in the indictment. On examining the indictment, it appears, that twenty separate and distinct sets of words are set forth therein, as allegations or charges against the traverser. He has plead "not guilty" to all of them. To support this indictment on behalf of the government of the United States, it must be proved to the jury; first, that the traverser did write, print, utter or publish, or did cause or procure to be printed or published, a false and scandalous writing against the president of the United States; secondly, that the said writing is false, scandalous, and malicious; and thirdly, that it was published with intent to defame the president, &c., as stated in the statute and charged in the indictment. It these three facts shall be established to the satisfaction of the jury, they must find the traverser guilty, generally, unless he can prove to them the truth of the matter contained in the publication, in which case, the statute on which the traverser is indicted excuses him. If all the twenty sets of words, stated in the indictment as charges against the traverser, shall not be proved against him; or if he can prove that any of them are true, the jury will acquit him of such of them as shall not be established against him, and also of such of them as he can prove to be true; and they will find him guilty of the residue.

These inquiries, on behalf of the government of the United States, and on the part of the traverser, are proper for, and within the jurisdiction and the terms of the oath of the petit jury, who have been sworn "that they will well and truly try the issue joined between the United States and the traverser at the bar, and a true verdict give according to their evidence." The issue joined, therefore, is, whether the traverser is guilty of the several offences charged in the indictment; and to this issue no evidence is admissible (on the part of the government, or of the traverser) but what is pertinent of applicable to it. The petit jury, to discharge their duty, must first inquire, whether the traverser committed all or any of the facts alleged in the indictment to have been done by him, some time before the indictment. If they find that he did commit all or any of the said facts, their next inquiry is, whether the doing such facts have been made criminal and punishable by the statute of the United States, on which the traverser is indicted. For this purpose, they must peruse the statute, and carefully examine whether the facts charged and proved are within the provisions of it. If the words that create the offence are plain and intelligible, they must then determine whether the offence proved is of the species of criminality charged in the indictment; but if the words are ambiguous or doubtful, all construction should be rejected. The statute, on which the traverser is indicted, enacts "that the jury who shall try the cause shall have a right to determine the law and the fact, under the direction of the court, as in other cases." By this provision, I understand that a right is given to the jury to determine what the law is in the case before them; and not to decide whether a statute of the United States produced to them, is a law or not, or whether it is void, under an opinion that it is unconstitutional, that is, contrary to the constitution of the United States. I admit that the jury are to compare the statute with the facts proved, and then to decide whether the acts done are prohibited by the law; and whether they amount to the offence described in the indictment. This power the jury necessarily possesses, in order to enable them to decide on the guilt or innocence of the person accused. It is one thing to decide what the law is, on the facts proved, and another and a very different thing, to determine that the statute produced is no law. To decide what the law is on the facts, is an admission that the law exists. If there be no law in the case, there can be no comparison between it and the facts; and it is unnecessary to establish facts before it is ascertained that there is a law to punish the commission of them.

The existence of the law is a previous inquiry, and the inquiry into facts is altogether unnecessary, if there is no law to which the facts can apply. By this right to decide what the law is in any case arising under the statute. I cannot conceive that a right is given to the petit jury to determine whether the statute (under which they claim this right) is constitutional or not. To determine the validity of the statute, the constitution of the United States must necessarily be resorted to and considered, and its provisions inquired into. It must be determined whether the statute alleged to be void, because contrary to the constitution, is prohibited by it expressly, or by necessary implication. Was it ever intended, by the framers of the constitution, or by the people of America, that it should ever be submitted to the examination of a jury, to decide what restrictions are expressly or impliedly imposed by it on the national legislature? I cannot possibly believe that congress intended, by the statute, to grant a right to a petit jury to declare a statute void. The man who maintains this position must have a most contemptible opinion of the understanding of that body; but I believe the defect lies with himself. If any one can be so weak in intellect as to entertain this opinion of congress, he must give up the exercise of the power, when he is informed that congress had no authority to vest it in any body whatsoever; because, by the constitution, (as I will hereafter show,) this right is expressly granted to the judicial power of the United States, and is recognized by congress by a perpetual statute. If the statute should be held void by a jury, it would seem that they could not claim a right to such decision under an act that they themselves consider as mere waste paper. Their right must, therefore, be derived from some other source.

It appears to me that all the rights, powers, and duties of the petit jury, sworn in this cause, can only be derived from the constitution, or statutes of the United States made agreeably to it; or from some statute of this commonwealth not contrary to the federal constitution or statutes of congress; or from the common law, which was adopted by the federal constitution in the case of trials by jury in criminal cases. It never was pretended, as I ever heard, before this time, that a petit jury in England (from whence our common law is derived,) or in any part of the United States ever exercised such power. If a petit jury can rightfully exercise this power over one statute of congress, they must have an equal right and power over any other statute, and indeed over all the statutes; for no line can be drawn, no restriction imposed on the exercise of such power; it must rest in discretion only. If this power be once admitted, petit jurors will be superior to the national legislature, and its laws will be subject to their control. The power to abrogate or to make laws nugatory, is equal to the authority of making them. The evident consequences of this right in juries will be, that a law of congress will be in operation in one state and not in another. A law to impose taxes will be obeyed in one state, and not in another, unless force be employed to compel submission. The doing certain acts will be held criminal, and punished in one state, and similar acts may be held innocent, and even approved and applauded in another. The effects of the exercise of this power by petit jurors may be readily conceived. It appears to me that the right now claimed has a direct tendency to dissolve the union of the United States, on which, under Divine Providence, our political safety, happiness, and prosperity depend.

No citizen of knowledge and information, unless under the influence of passion or prejudice, will believe, without very strong and indubitable proof, that congress will, intentionally, make any law in violation of the federal constitution, and their sacred trust. I admit that the constitution contemplates that congress may, from inattention or error in judgment, pass a law prohibited by the constitution; and, therefore, it has provided a peaceable, safe, and adequate remedy. If such a case should happen, the mode of redress is pointed out in the constitution, and no other mode can be adopted without a manifest infraction of it. Every man must admit that the power of deciding the constitutionality of any law of the United States, or of any particular state, is one of the greatest and most important powers the people could grant. Such power is restrictive of the legislative power of the Union, and also of the several states; not absolute and unlimited, but confined to such cases only where the law in question shall clearly appear to have been prohibited by the federal constitution, and not in any doubtful case. On referring to the ninth section of the first article of the constitution, there may be seen many restrictions imposed on the powers of the national legislature, and also on the powers of the several state legislatures. Among the special exceptions to their authority, is the power to make ex post facto laws, to lay any capitation, or other direct tax, unless in proportion to the census; to lay any tax or duty on articles exported from any state, &c. &c. It should be remembered that the judicial power of the United States is co-existent, co-extensive, and co-ordinate with, and altogether independent of, the federal legislature, or the executive. By the sixth article of the constitution, among other things, it is declared that the constitution shall be the supreme law of the land. By the third article, it is established "that the judicial power of the United States shall be vested in one supreme court, and in such other inferior courts as congress may from time to time ordain and establish; and that the judicial power shall extend to all cases in law and equity, arising under the constitution and laws of the United States."

Among the cases which may arise under the constitution, are all the restrictions on the authority of congress, and of the state legislatures. It is very clear, that the present case arises under the constitution, and also under a law of the United States, and therefore it is the very case to which the constitution declares the judicial powers of the United States shall extend. It is incontrovertible that the constitution is the supreme law, and therefore, it must be the rule by which the federal and state judges are bound to regulate their decisions. By the sixth article of the constitution, it is provided (among other things) that all members of congress, and of the several state legislatures, and all judicial officers of the United States, and of the several states, shall be bound by an oath or affirmation to support the constitution. By this provision, I understand that every person, so sworn or affirmed, promises that he will preserve the constitution as established, and the distribution of powers thereby granted; and that he will not assent to any amendment or alteration thereof, but in the mode prescribed in the fifth article; and that he will not consent to any usurpation by any one branch of the legislature upon the other, or upon the executive, or by the executive upon either branch, or by any department or officer of government, of the power granted to another; or that the power granted to either shall be exercised by others. I also understand by this engagement, that the person taking it, promises also that he will oppose by his example, argument, advice, and persuasion, and by all other means in his power, force only excepted, any design, advice or attempt to impair or destroy the constitution. If this exposition of this solemn obligation is substantially correct, I cannot believe that any person having the same understanding of it, will maintain that a petit jury can rightfully exercise the power granted by the constitution to the federal judiciary.

From these considerations I draw this conclusion, that the judicial power of the United States is the only proper and competent authority to decide whether any statute made by congress (or any of the state legislatures) is contrary to, or in violation of, the federal constitution. . . .

The decision of courts of justice will not be influenced by political and local principles, and prejudices. If inferior courts commit error, it may be rectified; but if juries make mistakes, there can be no revision or control over their verdicts, and therefore, there can be no mode to obtain uniformity in their decisions. Besides, petit juries are under no obligation by the terms fo their oath, to decide the constitutionality of any law; their determination, therefore, will be extra judicial. I should also imagine, that no jury would wish to have a right to determine such great, important, and difficult questions; and I hope no jury can be found, who will exercise the power desired over the statutes of congress, against the opinion of the federal courts.

I have consulted with my brother, Judge GRIFFIN, and I now deliver the opinion of the court, "That the petit jury have no right to decide on the constitutionality of

Congress Hall, Philadelphia, February 15, 1798. (Library of Congress.)

the statute on which the traverser is indicted; and that, if the jury should exercise that power, they would thereby usurp the authority entrusted by the constitution of the United States to this court." Governed by this opinion, the court will not allow the counsel for the traverser to argue before the petit jury, that they have a right to decide on the constitutionality of the statute, on which the traverser stands indicted. If the counsel for the traverser had offered sufficient arguments to the court, to show that the petit jury had this right, the court, on being convinced that the opinion delivered was erroneous, would have changed it; for they hold it a much greater reproach for a judge to continue in his error, than to retract. The gentlemen of the profession know, that questions have sometimes occurred in the state courts, whether acts of assembly had expired, or had been repealed; but no one will say that such questions were ever submitted to a jury. If the constitution of the United States had not given to the judiciary a right to decide on the constitutionality of federal laws—yet, if such power could be exercised, it could not be by a juror, from this consideration—it is a maxim of law in all the states, that the courts have the exclusive right to decide every question, as to the admissibility of evidence in every case, civil or criminal, whether the evidence be by act of assembly, or by deed, or other writing, or by witnesses.

Judge CHASE concluded with observing, that, if he knew himself, the opinion he had delivered and the reasons offered in its support, flowed not from political motives, or reasons of state, with which he had no concern, and which he conceived never ought to enter courts of justice; but from a deliberate conviction of what the constitution and the law of the land required. "I hold myself equally bound," said he, "to support the rights of the jury, as the rights of the court." I consider it of the greatest consequence to the administration of justice, that the powers of the court, and the powers of the petit jury, should be kept distinct and separate. I have uniformly delivered the opinion, "that the petit jury have a right to decide the law as well as the fact, in criminal cases;" but it never entered into my mind that they, therefore, had a right to determine the constitutionality of any statute of the United States. It is my duty to execute the laws of the United States with justice and impartiality, with firmness and decision, and I will endeavour to discharge this duty with the assistance of the Fountain of Wisdom, and the Giver of all human reason and understanding.

After two hours, the jury returned with a verdict of guilty, upon which the court sentenced the traverser to a fine of two hundred dollars, and an imprisonment of nine months.

SOURCE: http://www.uniset.ca/other/cs5/25FCas239.html

ANALYSIS

In 1794, President Washington negotiated a treaty with England to settle outstanding differences between the two countries. The resulting improvement in American-English relations angered the revolutionary French leaders, who were enemies of the English. In the election of 1796, Federalist John Adams won the most electoral votes to become president. Republican Thomas Jefferson came in second, which made him vice president. Shortly after becoming president, Adams sent diplomats to France to smooth over the bad feelings. But three French representatives—dubbed X,

Y, and Z—met secretly with the U.S. diplomats and demanded $10 million in bribes to the French government to begin negotiations. When the Americans refused, Mr. X threatened the United States with the "power and violence of France." News of the "XYZ Affair" enraged most Americans and increased hostilities with France.

In 1798 the United States was on the brink of war with France. The Federalists believed that Democratic-Republican criticism of Federalist policies was disloyal and feared that aliens living in the United States would sympathize with the French during a war. As a result, a Federalist-controlled Congress passed four laws, known collectively as the Alien and Sedition Acts. In particular, the Sedition Act made it a high misdemeanor, punishable by fine, imprisonment, or both, for citizens or aliens (1) to oppose the execution of federal laws; (2) to prevent a federal officer from performing his or her duties; (3) to aid any insurrection, riot, unlawful assembly, or combination; or (4) to make any defamatory statement about the federal government or the president. The laws were directed against Democratic-Republicans, the party typically favored by new citizens, and the only journalists prosecuted under the Sedition Act were editors of Democratic-Republican newspapers. Approximately 25 individuals were arrested under the Sedition Act. Fifteen were indicted; 10 cases went to trial and all 10 resulted in convictions until its expiration, by its own terms, on March 3, 1801. The most notable Sedition Act trials were those of Matthew Lyon and James Thompson Callender.

One of the first persons to be indicted and tried under the Sedition Act was a Democratic Republican member of Congress. Representative Matthew Lyon of Vermont was campaigning for reelection when a grand jury in October 1798 indicted him for publishing letters with the "intent and design" to defame the government and President Adams. The first count of the indictment cited a published letter that Lyon wrote before passage of the Sedition Act. In this critique of the Adams administration, Lyon asserted that he had seen "every consideration of public welfare swallowed up in a continual grasp for power, in an unbounded thirst for ridiculous pomp, foolish adulation, or selfish avarice." Two other counts accused Lyon of further promoting sedition through his role in publicizing a letter in which the poet Joel Barlow blamed Adams and the Senate for the diplomatic crisis with France. Supreme Court Justice William Paterson presided over the trial and instructed the jury that its deliberations should not consider the constitutionality or unconstitutionality of the sedition law. He instructed the jury that the only issue they should consider is whether Lyon published the letters and whether his intent was to stir up sedition. Paterson also announced that the fact of publication was certain, so the jury had only to decide if the language could be interpreted as anything other than seditious. Within an hour, the jury returned a verdict of guilty. Lyon was convicted under the act and Justice Paterson sentenced him to four months of imprisonment and fined him $1,000.

A second high-profile case and the subject of the document above was the trial of James Thompson Callender. James Callender was the author of *The Prospect before Us*, whose subject was the pervasiveness of political corruption, particularly among Federalists and the Adams administration. In June 1800, in retaliation for his writings, Callender was prosecuted under the Sedition Act by the Adams administration. His trial was presided over by Supreme Court Justice Samuel Chase, who was later impeached, in part due to his handling of the Callender trial. Chase devoted most of his lengthy instructions to the jury to a sweeping rejection of the argument that a jury might consider the constitutionality of a law. The jury returned a guilty verdict, and Chase sentenced Callender to nine months' imprisonment and a $400 fine.

The Sedition Act trials, along with the Senate's use of its contempt powers to suppress dissent, set off a firestorm of criticism against the Federalists and contributed to their defeat in the election of 1800. The validity of the Sedition Act was never tested in the Supreme Court before it expired. But Congress later passed a law that repaid all fines collected under it, and Jefferson, after becoming president in 1801, pardoned all those convicted under the Sedition Act. The controversies surrounding these cases, however, provided for the first assessment on the limits of freedom of speech and press.

FURTHER READING

Durey, Michael. *"With the Hammer of Truth": James Thomas Callender and America's Early National Heroes*. Charlottesville: University Press of Virginia, 1990.

Preyer, Kathryn. "*United States v. Callender:* Judge and Jury in a Republican Society." In *Origins of the Federal Judiciary: Essays on the Judiciary Act of 1789*, edited by Maeva Marcus, 173–95. New York: Oxford University Press, 1992.

The Right to Be Let Alone

- ***Document:*** The Supreme Court case *Wheaton v. Peters*, Excerpt
- ***Date:*** 1834
- ***Where:*** Washington, D.C.
- ***Significance:*** As part of the Supreme Court decision to uphold the power of Congress to make a grant of copyright protection and rejecting the doctrine of a common law copyright, the opinion includes language later used to describe the right to privacy.

DOCUMENT

Wheaton v. Peters, 8 Pet. 591 (1834)

Mr. Justice M'Lean delivered the opinion of the court.

. . . .

This last act provides, section 1, that the author, 'before he shall be entitled to the benefit, &c. shall,' in addition to the requisites enjoined in the third and fourth sections of said act, &c. 'give information, by causing the copy of the record, &c. to be inserted at full length in the title page, & c.'

It thus makes those clauses which had before been of doubtful name, requisites. It requires him to perform them, not as preliminary to forfeiture or penalty, which are only particular provisions of parts of the act, but as preliminary to the benefit of the act itself. He, therefore, in terms, is denied its advantages, unless he perform the conditions precedent. These, agreeably to a well known rule, are to be construed strictly, and the party who omits to bring himself within them can claim no right whatever. The statute becomes a unit; all its benefits are yielded or withheld, exactly as all its requisites have been fulfilled or disregarded.

Requisite it aptly defined by the American lexicographer, Noah Webster, to be 'so needful that it cannot be dispensed with; something indispensable.' An author must show that he has complied with these affirmative requisitions, or they will not be presumed for him.

There are familiar analogies which will fully sustain this position. Take the statute which regulates distresses for rent. Certain provisions are made which justify a landlord for acts which would otherwise amount to a trespass. But he must show that he has performed them strictly, or, as the law at first stood in England, and does still in Pennsylvania, he is a trespasser ab initio; and the statute of George II. only so far alters the rule, as to leave the party to his remedy action on the case for the recovery of the actual damages that may have been sustained.

If notice be required by statute, as, for example, preparatory to a suit against a magistrate for misconduct in office, not only is it never presumed, but nothing can supply its proof; not even knowledge of the design to sue, which might be substantially the same thing. In such case, knowledge is not notice.

There is nothing against our construction in the principle which requires a strict interpretation of certain statutes. If the act be penal, we are not endeavouring to enforce the penalty. There is nothing penal as to the author claiming the copyright. All the penalties are against other persons. It is to be construed strictly when it is to be enforced against them. He claims the benefit of his copyright, which is a grant to be obtained only on conditions precedent and well defined. He attempts to enforce with rigour, if not the penal forfeitures, at least the penal prohibitions of the law against the defendant, whom he alleges to be a wrong doer. Against the defendant, thus, without (if it be without) bringing himself under the provisions of the law, the alleged proprietor denounces awful consequences. The defendant asks nothing—wants nothing, but to be let alone until it can be shown that he has violated the rights of another.....

SOURCE: http://caselaw.lp.findlaw.com/scripts/getcase.pl?court=US&vol=33&invol=591

ANALYSIS

One of the most effective ways to safeguard our liberty interests in privacy vis-à-vis the government is to rely on the decisions of the federal judiciary. The Supreme Court is in the best position to act as a check against government tyranny especially in a time of crisis because it is the branch that is most independent of the political system. The Court also holds an important position in our federal system as the final arbiter of the Constitution and its decisions have the force of law which impacts the entire country. The famous phrase, the right "to be let alone" has a long history related to privacy. And even though the *Wheaton* case is not directly dealing with the right of privacy, the language is used to explain that before an individual is accused of breaking the law and subject to a state prosecution, the individual should be protected against intrusion. This notion of privacy will become more prominent and further developed in the later part of the 19th century.

FURTHER READING

Gertz, Janet Dean. "Comment, The Purloined Personality: Consumer Profiling in Financial Services." *San Diego Law Review* 39 (2002): 943, 968.

3

20TH-CENTURY STATEMENTS AND ENACTMENTS

Executive Order to Intern Japanese Americans

- ***Document:*** President Franklin Delano Roosevelt's United States Executive Order 9066
- ***Date:*** February 19, 1942
- ***Where:*** Washington, D.C.
- ***Significance:*** Executive Order 9066 provided for the internment of Japanese Americans during World War II.

DOCUMENT

Executive Order 9066

February 19, 1942

AUTHORIZING THE SECRETARY OF WAR TO PRESCRIBE MILITARY AREAS WHEREAS the successful prosecution of the war requires every possible protection against espionage and against sabotage to national-defense material, national-defense premises, and national-defense utilities as defined in Section 4, Act of April 20, 1918, 40 Stat. 533, as amended by the Act of November 30, 1940, 54 Stat. 1220, and the Act of August 21, 1941, 55 Stat. 655 (U.S.C., Title 50, Sec. 104):

NOW, THEREFORE, by virtue of the authority vested in me as President of the United States, and Commander in Chief of the Army and Navy, I hereby authorize and direct the Secretary of War and the Military Commanders whom he may from time to time designate, whenever he or any designated Commander deems such action necessary or desirable, to prescribe military areas in such places and of such extent as he or the appropriate Military Commander may determine, from which any or all persons may be excluded, and with respect to which, the right of any person to enter, remain in, or leave shall be subject to whatever restrictions the Secretary of War or the appropriate Military Commander may impose in his discretion. The Secretary of war is hereby authorized to provide for residents of any such area who are excluded therefrom, such transportation, food, shelter, and other accommodations as may be necessary, in the judgment of the Secretary of War or the said Military Commander, and until other arrangements are made, to accomplish the purpose of this order. The designation of military areas in any region or locality shall supersede designations of prohibited and restricted areas by the Attorney General under the Proclamations of December 7 and 8, 1941, and shall supersede the responsibility and authority of the Attorney General under the said Proclamations in respect of such prohibited and restricted areas.

U.S. Army medical corps members assist a Japanese woman after she collapsed during the evacuation of more than 300 Japanese from Bainbridge Island, April 1, 1942. (AP Photo.)

I hereby further authorize and direct the secretary of War and the said Military Commanders to take such other steps as he or the appropriate Military Commander may deem advisable to enforce compliance with the restrictions applicable to each Military area hereinabove authorized to be designated, including the use of Federal troops and other Federal Agencies, with authority to accept assistance of state and local agencies.

I hereby further authorize and direct all Executive Departments, independent establishments and other Federal Agencies, to assist the Secretary of War or the said Military Commanders in carrying out this Executive Order, including the furnishing of medical aid, hospitalization, food, clothing, transportation, use of land, shelter, and other supplies, equipment, utilities, facilities, and services.

This order shall not be construed as modifying or limiting in any way the authority heretofore granted under Executive Order No. 8972, dated December 12, 1941, nor shall it be construed as limiting or modifying the duty and responsibility of the Federal Bureau of Investigation, with respect to the investigation of alleged acts of sabotage or the duty and responsibility of the Attorney General and the department of Justice under the Proclamations of December 7 and 8, 1941, prescribing regulations for the conduct and control of alien enemies, except as such duty and responsibility is superseded by the designation of military areas hereunder.

Franklin D. Roosevelt

February 19, 1942

SOURCE: http://docs.fdrlibrary.marist.edu/od9066t.html

ANALYSIS

After the bombing of Pearl Harbor by the Japanese in 1941, Roosevelt came under increasing pressure by military and political advisors to address the nation's fears of further Japanese attack or sabotage, particularly on the West Coast, where naval ports, commercial shipping, and agriculture were most vulnerable. On February 19, 1942, President Roosevelt signed Executive Order 9066 which gave the military broad powers to ban any citizen from a 50- to 60-mile-wide coastal area stretching from Washington State to California and extending inland into southern Arizona. This order authorized the secretary of war and his designated military commanders to exclude certain individuals from military areas as they deemed it necessary. Although the executive order was developed with Japanese nationals and citizens in mind to exclude them from most of the West Coast of the United States, the executive order was drafted broadly to authorize the military to exclude any individual from any military area. While 9066 also affected Italian and German Americans, the largest numbers of detainees were by far Japanese. For example, 3,200 resident aliens of Italian background were arrested and more than 300 of them were interned. Approximately 11,000 German residents including some naturalized citizens were arrested and more than 5,000 were interned. Even though these individuals suffered serious violations of their civil liberties, the wartime measures applied to Japanese Americans were worse and more far-reaching, displacing whole communities and pursuing citizens as well as resident aliens.

Japanese immigrants and their descendants, regardless of American citizenship status or length of residence, were systematically rounded up and placed in detention centers. "Evacuees," as they were sometimes called, could take only as many possessions as they could carry and were housed in crude, cramped quarters. In the western states, camps on remote and barren sites accommodated thousands of families whose lives were interrupted and in some cases destroyed by Executive Order 9066. Many lost businesses, farms and loved ones as a result. During the war, the U.S. Supreme Court heard two cases challenging the constitutionality of Executive Order 9066, upholding it both times. Finally, on February 19, 1976, decades after the war, Gerald Ford signed an order prohibiting the executive branch from reinstituting the notorious and tragic World War II order. In 1988, President Ronald Reagan issued a public apology on behalf of the government and authorized reparations for former Japanese internees or their descendants.

FURTHER READING

DeWitt, J. L. *Final Report: Japanese Evacuation from the West Coast, 1942.* Washington, D.C.: U.S. Government Printing Office, 1943, 34.

Robinson, Greg. *By Order of the President: FDR and the Internment of Japanese Americans.* Cambridge, Mass.: Harvard University Press, 2001.

Executive Order 9835

- ***Document:*** President Harry Truman's United States Executive Order 9835, also called "The Loyalty Order"
- ***Date:*** March 21, 1947
- ***Where:*** Washington, D.C.
- ***Significance:*** Executive Order 9835 established the first general loyalty program in the United States, which was designed to root out Communist influence within the various agencies and departments of the federal government.

DOCUMENT

Executive Order 9835—Prescribing Procedures for the Administration of an Employees Loyalty Program in the Executive Branch of the Government

March 21, 1947

WHEREAS each employee of the Government of the United States is endowed with a measure of trusteeship over the democratic processes which are the heart and sinew of the United States; and

WHEREAS it is of vital importance that persons employed in the Federal service be of complete and unswerving loyalty to the United States; and

WHEREAS, although the loyalty of by far the overwhelming majority of all Government employees is beyond question, the presence within the Government service of any disloyal or subversive person constitutes a threat to our democratic processes; and

WHEREAS maximum protection must be afforded the United States against infiltration of disloyal persons into the ranks of its employees, and equal protection

Whittaker Chambers (right), senior editor for *Time* magazine, takes the stand before the House Un-American Activities Committee on August 25, 1948. In his testimony, Chambers identified Alger Hiss, a State Department official, as a member of the American Communist Party assigned to infiltrate the U.S. government. (Library of Congress.)

from unfounded accusations of disloyalty must be afforded the loyal employees of the Government:

NOW, Therefore, by virtue of the authority vested in me by the Constitution and statutes of the United States, including the Civil Service Act of 1883 (22 Stat. 403), as amended, and section 9A of the act approved August 2, 1939 (18 U.S.C. 61i), and as President and Chief Executive of the United States, it is hereby, in the interest of the internal management of the Government, ordered as follows:

PART I—INVESTIGATION OF APPLICANTS

1. There shall be a loyalty investigation of every person entering the civilian employment of any department or agency of the executive branch of the Federal Government.

   a. Investigations of persons entering the competitive service shall be conducted by the Civil Service Commission, except in such cases as are covered by a special agreement between the Commission and any given department or agency.

b. Investigations of persons other than those entering the competitive service shall be conducted by the employing department or agency. Departments and agencies without investigative organizations shall utilize the investigative facilities of the Civil Service Commission.

2. The investigations of persons entering the employ of the executive branch may be conducted after any such person enters upon actual employment therein, but in any such case the appointment of such person shall be conditioned upon a favorable determination with respect to his loyalty.

   a. Investigations of persons entering the competitive service shall be conducted as expeditiously as possible; provided, however, that if any such investigation is not completed within 18 months from the date on which a person enters actual employment, the condition that his employment is subject to investigation shall expire, except in a case in which the Civil Service Commission has made an initial adjudication of disloyalty and the case continues to be active by reason of an appeal, and it shall then be the responsibility of the employing department or agency to conclude such investigation and make a final determination concerning the loyalty of such person.

> **DID YOU KNOW?**
>
> **Antiterrorism and Effective Death Penalty Act of 1996 (AEDPA)**
>
> Prior to 9/11, the United States pursued several legislative avenues in an effort to deal effectively with international terrorist threats. The AEDPA had a tremendous impact on the use of habeas corpus to challenge criminal convictions because the law limits the scope of the writ both procedurally and substantively. Procedurally, it bans successive petitions by the same person, requiring defendants to combine all of their claims into a single appeal. Substantively, it narrows the grounds on which successful habeas claims can be made, allowing claims to succeed only when the convictions were contrary to "clearly established federal law" or when a conviction was based on an "unreasonable determination of the facts in light of the evidence."
>
> Soon after it was enacted, the constitutionality of AEDPA was tested in the U.S. Supreme Court. The basis of the challenge was that the provisions limiting the ability of persons to file successive habeas petitions violated Article I, Section 9, Clause 2 of the U.S. Constitution, the Suspension Clause. In *Felker v. Turpin,* 518 U.S. 651 (1997), however, the Supreme Court held unanimously that these limitations did not unconstitutionally suspend the writ.

3. An investigation shall be made of all applicants at all available pertinent sources of information and shall include reference to:

   a. Federal Bureau of Investigation files.
   b. Civil Service Commission files.
   c. Military and naval intelligence files.
   d. The files of any other appropriate government investigative or intelligence agency.
   e. House Committee on un-American Activities files.
   f. Local law-enforcement files at the place of residence and employment of the applicant, including municipal, county, and State law-enforcement files.
   g. Schools and colleges attended by applicant.
   h. Former employers of applicant.
   i. References given by applicant.
   j. Any other appropriate source.

4. Whenever derogatory information with respect to loyalty of an applicant is revealed a full investigation shall be conducted. A full field

investigation shall also be conducted of those applicants, or of applicants for particular positions, as may be designated by the head of the employing department or agency, such designations to be based on the determination by any such head of the best interests of national security.

PART II—INVESTIGATION OF EMPLOYEES

1. The head of each department and agency in the executive branch of the Government shall be personally responsible for an effective program to assure that disloyal civilian officers or employees are not retained in employment in his department or agency.

   a. He shall be responsible for prescribing and supervising the loyalty determination procedures of his department or agency, in accordance with the provisions of this order, which shall be considered as providing minimum requirements.
   b. The head of a department or agency which does not have an investigative organization shall utilize the investigative facilities of the Civil Service Commission.

2. The head of each department and agency shall appoint one or more loyalty boards, each composed of not less than three representatives of the department or agency concerned, for the purpose of hearing loyalty cases arising within such department or agency and making recommendations with respect to the removal of any officer or employee of such department or agency on grounds relating to loyalty, and he shall prescribe regulations for the conduct of the proceedings before such boards.

   a. An officer or employee who is charged with being disloyal shall have a right to an administrative hearing before a loyalty board in the employing department or agency. He may appear before such board personally, accompanied by counsel or representative of his own choosing, and present evidence on his own behalf, through witnesses or by affidavit.
   b. The officer or employee shall be served with a written notice of such hearing in sufficient time, and shall be informed therein of the nature of the charges against him in sufficient detail, so that he will be enabled to prepare his defense. The charges shall be stated as specifically and completely as, in the discretion of the employing department or agency, security considerations permit, and the officer or employee shall be informed in the notice (1) of his right to reply to such charges in writing within a specified reasonable period of time, (2) of his right to an administrative hearing on such charges before a loyalty board, and (3) of his right to appear before such board personally, to be accompanied by counsel or representative of his own choosing, and to present evidence on his behalf, through witness or by affidavit.

3. A recommendation of removal by a loyalty board shall be subject to appeal by the officer or employee affected, prior to his removal, to the head of the employing department or agency or to such person or persons as may be designated by such head, under such regulations as may be prescribed by him, and the decision of the department or agency concerned shall be subject to appeal to the Civil Service Commission's Loyalty Review Board, hereinafter provided for, for an advisory recommendation.
4. The rights of hearing, notice thereof, and appeal therefrom shall be accorded to every officer or employee prior to his removal on grounds of disloyalty, irrespective of tenure, or of manner, method, or nature of appointment, but the head of the employing department or agency may suspend any officer or employee at any time pending a determination with respect to loyalty.
5. The loyalty boards of the various departments and agencies shall furnish to the Loyalty Review Board, hereinafter provided for, such reports as may be requested concerning the operation of the loyalty program in any such department or agency.

PART III—RESPONSIBILITIES OF CIVIL SERVICE COMMISSION

1. There shall be established in the Civil Service Commission a Loyalty Review Board of not less than three impartial persons, the members of which shall be officers or employees of the Commission.

   a. The Board shall have authority to review cases involving persons recommended for dismissal on grounds relating to loyalty by the loyalty board of any department or agency and to make advisory recommendations thereon to the head of the employing department or agency. Such cases may be referred to the Board either by the employing department or agency, or by the officer or employee concerned.
   b. The Board shall make rules and regulations, not inconsistent with the provisions of this order, deemed necessary to implement statutes and Executive orders relating to employee loyalty.
   c. The Loyalty Review Board shall also:

      1. Advise all departments and agencies on all problems relating to employee loyalty.
      2. Disseminate information pertinent to employee loyalty programs.
      3. Coordinate the employee loyalty policies and procedures of the several departments and agencies.
      4. Make reports and submit recommendations to the Civil Service Commission for transmission to the President from time to time as may be necessary to the maintenance of the employee loyalty program.

2. There shall also be established and maintained in the Civil Service Commission a central master index covering all persons on whom loyalty investigations have been made by any department or agency since September 1, 1939. Such master index shall contain the name of each person investigated, adequate identifying information concerning each such person, and a reference to each department and agency which has conducted a loyalty investigation concerning the person involved.
   a. All executive departments and agencies are directed to furnish to the Civil Service Commission all information appropriate for the establishment and maintenance of the central master index.
   b. The reports and other investigative material and information developed by the investigating department or agency shall be retained by such department or agency in each case.
3. The loyalty Review Board shall currently be furnished by the Department of Justice the name of each foreign or domestic organization, association, movement, group or combination of persons which the Attorney General, after appropriate investigation and determination, designates as totalitarian, fascist, communist or subversive, or as having adopted a policy of advocating or approving the commission of acts of force or violence to deny others their rights under the Constitution of the United States, or as seeking to alter the form of government of the United States by unconstitutional means.
   a. The Loyalty Review Board shall disseminate such information to all departments and agencies.

PART IV—SECURITY MEASURES IN INVESTIGATIONS

1. At the request of the head of any department or agency of the executive branch an investigative agency shall make available to such head, personally, all investigative material and information collected by the investigative agency concerning any employee or prospective employee of the requesting department or agency, or shall make such material and information available to any officer or officers designated by such head and approved by the investigative agency.
2. Notwithstanding the foregoing requirement, however, the investigative agency may refuse to disclose the names of confidential informants, provided it furnishes sufficient information about such informants on the basis of which the requesting department or agency can make an adequate evaluation of the information furnished by them, and provided it advises the requesting department or agency in writing that it is essential to the protection of the informants or to the investigation of other cases that the identity of the informants not be revealed. Investigative agencies shall not use this discretion to decline to reveal sources of information where such action is not essential.

3. Each department and agency of the executive branch should develop and maintain, for the collection and analysis of information relating to the loyalty of its employees and prospective employees, a staff specially trained in security techniques, and an effective security control system for protecting such information generally and for protecting confidential sources of such information particularly.

PART V—STANDARDS

1. The standard for the refusal of employment or the removal from employment in an executive department or agency on grounds relating to loyalty shall be that, on all the evidence, reasonable grounds exist for belief that the person involved is disloyal to the Government of the United States.
2. Activities and associations of an applicant or employee which may be considered in connection with the determination of disloyalty may include one or more of the following:

    a. Sabotage, espionage, or attempts or preparations therefor, or knowingly associating with spies or saboteurs;
    b. Treason or sedition or advocacy thereof;
    c. Advocacy of revolution or force or violence to alter the constitutional form of government of the United States;
    d. Intentional, unauthorized disclosure to any person, under circumstances which may indicate disloyalty to the United States, of documents or information of a confidential or non-public character obtained by the person making the disclosure as a result of his employment by the Government of the United States;
    e. Performing or attempting to perform his duties, or otherwise acting, so as to serve the interests of another government in preference to the interests of the United States.
    f. Membership in, affiliation with or sympathetic association with any foreign or domestic organization, association, movement, group or combination of persons, designated by the Attorney General as totalitarian, fascist, communist, or subversive, or as having adopted a policy of advocating or approving the commission of acts of force or violence to deny other persons their rights under the Constitution of the United States, or as seeking to alter the form of government of the United States by unconstitutional means.

PART VI—MISCELLANEOUS

1. Each department and agency of the executive branch, to the extent that it has not already done so, shall submit, to the Federal Bureau of Investigation of the Department of Justice, either directly or through the Civil Service Commission, the names (and such other necessary identifying

material as the Federal Bureau of Investigation may require) of all of its incumbent employees.

a. The Federal Bureau of Investigation shall check such names against its records of persons concerning whom there is substantial evidence of being within the purview of paragraph 2 of Part V hereof, and shall notify each department and agency of such information.
b. Upon receipt of the above-mentioned information from the Federal Bureau of Investigation, each department and agency shall make, or cause to be made by the Civil Service Commission, such investigation of those employees as the head of the department or agency shall deem advisable.

2. The Security Advisory Board of the State-War-Navy Coordinating Committee shall draft rules applicable to the handling and transmission of confidential documents and other documents and information which should not be publicly disclosed, and upon approval by the President such rules shall constitute the minimum standards for the handling and transmission of such documents and information, and shall be applicable to all departments and agencies of the executive branch.
3. The provisions of this order shall not be applicable to persons summarily removed under the provisions of section 3 of the act of December 17, 1942, 56 Stat. 1053, of the act of July 5, 1946, 60 Stat. 453, or of any other statute conferring the power of summary removal.
4. The Secretary of War and the Secretary of the Navy, and the Secretary of the Treasury with respect to the Coast Guard, are hereby directed to continue to enforce and maintain the highest standards of loyalty within the armed services, pursuant to the applicable statutes, the Articles of War, and the Articles for the Government of the Navy.
5. This order shall be effective immediately, but compliance with such of its provisions as require the expenditure of funds shall be deferred pending the appropriation of such funds.

Executive Order No. 9300 of February 5, 1943, is hereby revoked
Harry S. Truman

SOURCE: http://www.presidency.ucsb.edu/ws/index.php?pid=75524

ANALYSIS

On March 21, 1947, President Truman issued Executive Order 9835, which provided that the head of each department and agency in the executive branch would be held personally accountable for a successful program to guarantee that disloyal civilian officers or employees are not retained. It directed the establishment within each department or agency of one or more loyalty boards for the purpose of hearing loyalty cases arising within such department or agency and making recommendations with respect to the removal of any employees on grounds relating to loyalty. The order also provided for the establishment of a central Loyalty Review Board in the Civil Service Commission. The board, in addition to various supervisory functions, was authorized to review cases involving persons recommended for dismissal by the loyalty board of any department or agency. The standard for removal prescribed by the order was whether, "on all the evidence, reasonable grounds exist for belief that the person involved is disloyal to the Government of the United States." As a quasi-criminal law that did not call for criminal penalties, it did not require the customary proof of guilt beyond a reasonable doubt. The objective of the program, however, was the removal of civilian employees of the federal government whenever a loyalty board found reasonable grounds to believe they were disloyal to the government.

Dismissal from employment carried with it the stigma of not only disloyalty, but also destruction of reputation, family, personal associations, and professional careers. Usually, dismissal entailed serious economic consequences because a person dismissed under these circumstances could hardly expect to resume his career anywhere in this country. Yet, the law provided no protection for the innocent. Although it allowed for a hearing of sorts before an executive loyalty board—not a court of law—little, if any, due process was provided. There was no presumption of innocence and the government had no burden of proof to establish disloyalty. On the contrary, the burden of proof to establish innocence was firmly fixed on the accused. Of the 3 million government employees who were investigated, 308 were fired as security risks. The president's loyalty order was challenged before the U.S. Supreme Court by discharged employees in *Peters v. Hobby*, 349 U.S. 331 (1955) and *Cole v. Young*, 351 U.S. 536 (1956). Even though the Court ruled in each instance that the employees were unlawfully discharged, it confined its examination to whether statutory guidelines had been followed and not the constitutionality of the orders.

FURTHER READING

Anderson, Leanna M. "Executive Orders, 'The Very Definition of Tyranny,' and the Congressional Solution, and the Separation of Powers Restoration Act." *Hastings Constitutional Law Quarterly* 29 (Spring 2002): 589–611.

Ostrow, Steven. "Enforcing Executive Orders: Judicial Review of Agency Action under the Administrative Procedure Act." *George Washington Law Review* 55 (1987).

Registration of Communist Organizations

- ***Document:*** The McCarran Internal Security Act, also known as the Subversive Activities Control Act of 1950, Excerpt
- ***Date:*** September 23, 1950
- ***Where:*** Washington, D.C.
- ***Significance:*** The Subversive Activities Control Act of 1950 required the registration of Communist organizations with the U.S. Attorney General and established the Subversive Activities Control Board to investigate individuals suspected of engaging in subversive activities or otherwise promoting Communist ideologies.

DOCUMENT

McCarran Internal Security Act

September 23, 1950

(Public Law 831, 81st Congress)

AN ACT

To protect the United States against certain un-American and subversive activities by requiring registration of Communist organizations, and for other purposes.

SEC. 2. As a result of evidence adduced before various committees of the Senate and House of Representatives, the Congress hereby finds that-

(1) There exists a world Communist movement which, in its origins, its development, and its present practice, is a world-wide revolutionary movement whose purpose it is, by treachery, deceit, infiltration into other groups (governmental and otherwise), espionage, sabotage, terrorism, and any other means deemed necessary, to establish a Communist totalitarian dictatorship in the countries throughout the world through the medium of a world-wide Communist organization....

(4) The direction and control of the world Communist movement is vested in and exercised by the Communist dictatorship of a foreign country.

(15) The Communist movement in the United States is an organization numbering thousands of adherents, rigidly and ruthlessly disciplined. Awaiting and seeking to advance a moment when the United States may be so far extended by foreign engagements, so far divided in counsel, or so far in industrial or financial straits, that overthrow of the Government of the United States by force and violence may seem possible of achievement, it seeks converts far and wide by an extensive system of schooling and indoctrination. Such preparations by Communist organizations in other countries have aided in supplanting existing governments. The Communist organization in the United States, pursuing its stated objectives, the recent successes of Communist methods in other countries, and the nature and control of the world Communist movement itself, present a clear and present danger to the security of the United States and to the existence of free American institutions, and make it necessary that Congress, in order to provide for the common defense, to preserve the sovereignty of the United States as an independent nation, and to guarantee to each State a republican form of government, enact appropriate legislation recognizing the existence of such World-wide conspiracy and design to prevent it from accomplishing its purpose in the United States....

SEC. 4. (a) It shall be unlawful for any person knowingly to combine, conspire, or agree with any other person to perform any act which would substantially contribute to the establishment within the United States of a totalitarian dictatorship, as defined in paragraph (15) of section 3 of this title, the direction and control of which is to be vested in, or exercised by or under the domination or control of, any foreign government, foreign organization, or foreign individual: Provided, however, That this subsection shall not apply to the proposal of a constitutional amendment....

(f) Neither the holding of office nor membership in any Communist organization by any person shall constitute per se a violation of subsection (a) or subsection (c) of this section or of any other criminal statute. The fact of the registration of any person under section 7 or 8 of this title as an officer or member of any Communist organization shall not be received in evidence against such person in any prosecution for any alleged violation of subsection (a) or subsection (c) of this section or for any alleged violation of any other criminal statute....

SEC. 7. (a) Each Communist-action organization (including any organization required, by a final order or the Board, to register as a Communist-action organization) shall, within the time specified in subsection (c) of this section, register with the Attorney General, on a form prescribed by him by regulations, as a Communist-action organization.

(b) Each Communist-front organization...shall...register with the Attorney General, on a form prescribed by him by regulations, as a Communist-front organization....

(d) Upon the registration of each Communist organization under the provisions of this title, the Attorney General shall publish in the Federal Register the fact that such organization has registered as a Communist-action organization, or as a Communist-front organization, as the case may be, and the publication thereof shall constitute notice to all members of such organization that such organization has so registered....

SEC. 12. (a) There is hereby established a board, to be known as the Subversive Activities Control Board, which shall be composed of five members, who shall be appointed by the President, by and with the advice and consent of the Senate. Not more than three member of the Board shall be members of the same political party. Two of the original members shall be appointed for a term of one year, two for a term of two years, and one for a term of three years, but their successors shall be appointed for terms of three years each, except that any individual chosen to fill a vacancy shall be appointed only for the unexpired term of the member whom he shall succeed. The Presidents hall designate one member to serve as Chairman of the Board. Any member of the Board may be removed by the President, upon notice and hearing, for neglect of duty or malfeasance in office, but for no other cause....

(e) It shall be the duty of the Board-

(1) upon application made by the Attorney General under section 13 (a) of this title, or by any organization under section 13 (b) of this title, to determine whether any organization is a communist-action organization within the meaning of paragraph (3) of section 3 of this title, or a Communist-front organization within the meaning of paragraph (4) of section 3 of this title; and

(2) upon application made by the Attorney General under section 13 (a) of this title, or by any individual under section 13 (b) of this title, to determine whether any individual is a member of any Communist-action organization registered, or by final order of the Board required to be registered, under section 7 (a) of this title....

SEC. 22. This Act of October 16, 1918...is hereby amended to read as follows: That any alien who is a member of any one of the following classes shall be excluded from admission into the United States:

(1) Aliens who seek to enter the Unites States whether solely, principally, or incidentally, to engage in activities which would be prejudicial to the public interest, or would endanger the welfare or safety of the Unites States;

(2) Aliens who, at any time, shall be or shall have been members of any of the following classes:

(A) Aliens who are anarchists;

(B) Aliens who advocate or teach, or who are members of or affiliated with any organization that advocates or teaches, opposition to all organized government;

(C) Aliens who are members of or affiliated with (i) the Communist Party of the United States, (ii) any other totalitarian party of the United States, (iii) the Communist Political Association, (iv) the Communists or other totalitarian party of any State of the United States, of any foreign state, or of any political or geographical subdivision of any foreign state; (v) any section, subsidiary, branch, affiliate, or subdivision of any such association or party; or (vi) the direct predecessors or successors of any such association or party, regardless of what name such group or organization may have used, may now bear, or may hereafter adopt;

(D) Aliens not within any of the other provisions of this paragraph (2) who advocate the economic, international, and governmental doctrines of world communism or the economic and governmental doctrines of any other form of totalitarianism, or who are members of or affiliated with any organization that advocates the economic, international, and government doctrines of world communism, or the economic and governmental doctrines of any other form of totalitarianism, either through its own utterances or through any written or printed publications issued or published by or with the permission or consent of or under the authority of such organization or paid for by the funds of such organization....

(F) Aliens who advocate or teach or who are members of or affiliated with any organization that advocates or teaches (i) the overthrow by force or violence or other unconstitutional means of the Government of the United States or of all forms of law; or (ii) the duty, necessity, or propriety of the unlawful assaulting or killing of any officer or officers (either of specific individuals or of officers generally) of the Government of the United States or of any other organized government, because of his or their official character; or (iii) the unlawful damage, injury, or destruction of property; or (iv) sabotage;

(G) Aliens who write or publish, or cause to be written or published, or who knowingly circulate, distribute, print, or display, or knowingly cause to be circulated, or displayed, or who knowingly have in their possession for the purpose of circulation, publication, or display any written or printed matter, advocating or teaching opposition to a âll organized government, or advocating (i) the overthrow by force or violence or other unconstitutional means of the Government of the United States or of all forms of law; or (ii) the duty, necessity, or propriety of the unlawful assaulting or killing of any officer or officers (either of specific individuals or officers generally) of the Government of the United States or of any other organized government; or (iii) the unlawful damage, injury, or destruction of property; or (iv) sabotage; or (v) the economic, international, and governmental doctrines of world communism or the economic and governmental doctrines of any other form of totalitarianism. . . .

SEC. 102. (a) In the event of any one of the following:

(1) Invasion of the territory of the Unites States or its possessions,

(2) Declaration of war by Congress, or

(3) Insurrection within the United States in aid of a foreign enemy, and if, upon the occurrence of one or more of the above, the President shall find that the proclamation of an emergency pursuant to this section is essential to the preservation, protection and defense of the Constitution, and to the common defense and safety of the territory and people of the United States, the President is authorized to make public proclamation of the existence of an Internal Security Emergency. (b) A state of Internal Security Emergency (hereinafter referred to as the Òemergency so declared shall continue in existence until terminated by proclamation of the President or by concurrent resolution of the Congress. . . .

SEC. 103. (a) Whenever there shall be in existence such an emergency, the President, acting through the Attorney General, is hereby authorized to apprehend and by order detain, pursuant to the provisions of this title, each person as to whom there is reasonable ground to believe that such person probably will engage in, or probably will conspire with others to engage in, acts of espionage or of sabotage.

SOURCE: http://wadsworth.com/history_d/special_features/ilrn_legacy/wawc2c01c/content/wciv2/readings/mccarr1.html

ANALYSIS

Due to the increased tensions concerning the Cold War and domestic security, and in response to increased anti-Communism during the Red Scare, Congress passed the McCarran Act. It was designed to fight both the larger threat of international hostility by Communist nations as well as the chance of internal insurrection domestically. The McCarran Act created a Subversive Activities Control Board to register members of a "Communist-action organization or a Communist-front organization." The act also included an Emergency Detention statute, which gave the president authority during times of internal security emergency, to apprehend and detain individuals who might likely engage in, or probably will conspire with others to engage in, acts of espionage or sabotage. The McCarran Internal Security Act was the most comprehensive and severe piece of anti-Communist legislation signed into law during the post-1945 Red Scare.

The McCarran Act is one of the most significant pieces of anti-Communist legislation passed during the McCarthy era and one that is hardly examined. The McCarran Act characterizes the atmosphere of the McCarthy era, calling for the registration of all Communists and any other individuals associated with Communism, in order to fully expose the "perceived" threat to the United States. The conflict between the conflicting needs of national security and civil liberties has occurred throughout much of American history and will continue to transpire. Both national security and civil liberties require a government with strong powers, but differ in how this power should be used. Those who advocate for national security sometimes believe that no limits should be placed on the national government when security issues are involved, while advocates of civil liberties believe in stringent Constitutional protections for the rights of citizens. A successful democracy demands that both these needs be satisfied; it requires a citizenry that is safe and secure from both external threats and from its own government. The McCarran Act raised important questions regarding the constitutionality of internal security legislation and the debate over internal security and civil liberties.

FURTHER READING

Forman, James D. *Anarchism: Political Innocence or Social Violence?* New York: Franklin Watts, 1975.

Haynes, John E. *Red Scare or Red Menace? American Communism and Anticommunism in the Cold War Era*. Chicago, Ill.: Ivan R. Dee Publishers, 1996.

Morgan, Ted. *Reds: McCarthyism in Twentieth-Century America*. New York: Random House, 2003.

Outlawing the Communist Party in America

- ***Document:*** The Communist Control Act of 1954
- ***Date:*** August 24, 1954
- ***Where:*** Washington, D.C.
- ***Significance:*** The Communist Control Act of 1954 outlawed the Communist Party of the United States and criminalized membership in, or support for, the Party.

DOCUMENT

The Communist Control Act of 1954

AN ACT

To outlaw the Communist Party, to prohibit members of Communist organizations from serving in certain representative capacities, and for other purposes. Be it enacted by the Senate and House of Representatives of the United States of America in Congress assembled, That this Act may be cited as the "Communist Control Act of 1954". Findings of Fact

Sec. 2. The Congress hereby finds and declares that the Communist Party of the United States, although purportedly a political party, is in fact an instrumentality of a conspiracy to overthrow the Government of the United States. It constitutes an authoritarian dictatorship within a republic, demanding for itself the rights and privileges accorded to political parties, but denying to all others the liberties guaranteed by the Constitution. Unlike political parties, which evolve their policies and programs through public means, by the reconciliation of a wide variety of individual views, and submit those policies and programs to the electorate at large for approval or disapproval, the policies and programs of the Communist Party are secretly prescribed for it by the foreign leaders of the world Communist movement. Its members have no part in determining its goals, and are not permitted to voice

dissent to party objectives. Unlike members of political parties, members of the Communist Party are recruited for indoctrination with respect to its objectives and methods, and are organized, instructed, and disciplined to carry into action slavishly the assignments given them by their hierarchical chieftains. Unlike political parties, the Communist Party acknowledges no constitutional or statutory limitations upon its conduct or upon that of its members. The Communist Party is relatively small numerically, and gives scant indication of capacity ever to attain its ends by lawful political means. The peril inherent in its operation arises not from its numbers, but from its failure to acknowledge any limitation as to the nature of its activities, and its dedication to the proposition that the present constitutional Government of the United States ultimately must be brought to ruin by any available means, including resort to force and violence. Holding that doctrine, its role as the agency of a hostile foreign power renders its existence a clear present and continuing danger to the security of the United States. It is the means whereby individuals are seduced into the service of the world Communist movement, trained to do its bidding, and directed and controlled in the conspiratorial performance of their revolutionary services. Therefore, the Communist Party should be outlawed.
Proscribed Organizations

Sec. 3. The Communist Party of the United States, or any successors of such party regardless of the assumed name, whose object or purpose is to overthrow the Government of the United States, or the government of any State, Territory, District, or possession thereof, or the government of any political subdivision therein by force and violence, are not entitled to any of the rights, privileges, and immunities attendant upon legal bodies created under the jurisdiction of the laws of the United States or any political subdivision thereof; and whatever rights, privileges, and immunities which have heretofore been granted to said party or any subsidiary organization by reason of the laws of the United States or any political subdivision thereof, are hereby terminated: Provided, however, That nothing in this section shall be construed as amending the Internal Security Act of 1950, as amended.

Sec. 4. Whoever knowingly and willfully becomes or remains a member of (1) the Communist Party, or (2) any other organization having for one of its purposes or objectives the establishment, control conduct, seizure, or overthrow of the Government of the United States, or the government of any State or political subdivision thereof, by the use of force or violence, with knowledge of the purpose or objective of such organization shall be subject to all the provisions and penalties of the Internal Security Act of 1950, as amended, as a member of a "Communist-action" organization. (b) For the purposes of this section, the term "Communist Party" means the organization now known as the Communist Party of the United States of America, the Communist Party of any State or subdivision thereof, and any unit or subdivision of any such organization, whether or not any change is hereafter made in the name thereof.

Sec. 5. In determining membership or participation in the Communist Party or any other organization defined in this Act, or knowledge of the purpose or objective of such party or organization, the jury, under instructions from the court, shall consider evidence, if presented, as to whether the accused person: (1) Has been listed to his knowledge as a member in any book or any of the lists, records, correspondence, or any other document of the organization; (2) Has made financial contribution to the organization in dues, assessments, loans, or in any other form; (3) Has made himself subject to the discipline of the organization in any form whatsoever; (4) Has executed orders, plans, or directives of any kind of the organization; (5) Has acted as an agent, courier, messenger, correspondent, organizer, or in any other capacity in behalf of the organization; (6) Has conferred with officers or other members of the organization in behalf of any plan or enterprise of the organization; (7) Has been accepted to his knowledge as an officer or member of the organization or as one to be called upon for services by other officers or members of the organization; (8) Has written, spoken or in any other way communicated by signal, semaphore, sign, or in any other form of communication orders, directives, or plans of the organization; (9) Has prepared documents, pamphlets, leaflets, books, or any other type of publication in behalf of the objectives and purposes of the organization; (10) Has mailed, shipped, circulated, distributed, delivered, or in any other way sent or delivered to others material or propaganda of any kind in behalf of the organization; (11) Has advised, counseled or in any other way imparted information, suggestions, recommendations to officers or members of the organization or to anyone else in behalf of the objectives of the organization; (12) Has indicated by word, action, conduct, writing or in any other way a willingness to carry out in any manner and to any degree the plans, designs, objectives, or purposes of the organization; (13) Has in any other way participated in the activities, planning, actions, objectives, or purposes of the organization; (14) The enumeration of the above subjects of evidence on membership or participation in the Communist Party or any other organization as above defined, shall not limit the inquiry into and consideration of any other subject of evidence on membership and participation as herein stated.

Sec. 6. Subsection 5 (a) (1) of the Subversive Activities Control Act of 1950 (50 U.S.C. 784) is amended by striking out the period at the end thereof and inserting lieu thereof a semicolon and the following: "or "(E) to hold office or employment with any labor organization, as that term is defined in section 2 (5) of the National Labor Relations Act, as amended (29 U.S. C. 152), or to represent any employer in any matter or proceeding arising or pending under that Act." Communist-Infiltrated Organizations

Sec. 7. (a) Section 3 of the Subversive Activities Control Act of 1950 (50 U.S. C. 782) is amended by inserting, immediately after paragraph (4) thereof, the following new paragraph: "(4A) The term 'Communist-infiltrated organization' means any organization in the United States

(other than a Communist-action organization or a Communist-front organization) which (A) is substantially directed, dominated, or controlled by an individual or individuals who are, or who within three years have been actively engaged in, giving aid or support to a Communist-action organization, a Communist foreign government, or the world Communist movement referred to in section 2 of this title, and (B) is serving, or within three years has served, as a means for (i) the giving of aid or support to any such organization, government, or movement, or (ii) the impairment of the military strength of the United States or its industrial capacity to furnish logistical or other material support required by its Armed Forces: Provided, however, That any labor organization which is an affiliate in good standing of a national federation or other labor organization whose policies and activities have been directed to opposing Communist organizations, any Communist foreign government, or the world Communist movement, shall be presumed prima facie not to be a

'Communist-infiltrated organization'." (b) Paragraph (5) of such section is amended to read as follows: "(5) The term 'Communist organization' means any Communist-action organization, Communist-front organization, or Communist-infiltrated organization." (c) Subsections 5 (c) and 6 (c) of such Act are repealed.

Sec. 8. (a) Section 10 of such Act (50 U.S. C. 789) is amended by inserting, immediately after the words "final order of the Board requiring it to register under section 7", the words "or determining that it is a Communist-infiltrated organization". (b) Subsections (a) and (b) of section 11 of such Act (50 U.S. C. 790) are amended by inserting immediately preceding the period at the end of each such subsection, the following: "or determining that it is a Communist-infiltrated organization".

Sec. 9. (a) Subsection 12 (e) of such Act (50 U.S. C. 791) is amended by- (1) striking out the period at the end thereof and inserting in lieu thereof a semicolon and the word "and"; and (2) inserting at the end thereof the following new paragraph: "(3) upon any application made under subsection (a) or subsection (b) of section 13A of this title, to determine whether any organization is a Communist-infiltrated organization." (b) The section caption to section 13 of such Act (50 U.S. C. 792) is amended to read as follows: "Registration Proceedings before the Board".

Sec. 10. Such Act is amended by inserting, immediately after section 13 thereof, the following new section: "Proceedings with Respect to Communist-Infiltrated Organizations", Sec. 13A. (a)

Whenever the Attorney General has reason to believe that any organization is a Communist-infiltrated organization, he may file with the Board and serve upon such organization a petition for a determination that such organization is a Communist-infiltrated organization. In any proceeding so instituted, two or more affiliated organizations may be named as joint respondents. Whenever any such petition is accompanied by a certificate of the Attorney General to the effect that the proceeding so instituted is one of exceptional public importance, such proceeding shall be set for hearing at the earliest possible time and all proceedings therein before the Board or any court shall be expedited to the greatest practicable extent. "(b) Any organization which has been determined under this section to be a Communist-infiltrated organization may, within six months after such determination, file with the Board and serve upon the Attorney General a petition for a determination that such organization no longer is a Communist-infiltrated organization. "(c) Each such petition shall be verified under oath, and shall contain a statement of the facts relied upon in support thereof. Upon the filing of any such petition, the Board shall serve upon each party to such proceeding a notice specifying the time and place for hearing upon such petition. No such hearing shall be conducted within twenty days after the service of such notice.

"(d) The provisions of subsections (c) and (d) of section 13 shall apply to hearings conducted under this section, except that upon the failure of any organization named as a party in any petition filed by or duly served upon it pursuant to this section to appear at any hearing upon such petition, the Board may conduct such hearing in the absence of such organization and may enter such order under this section as the Board shall determine to be warranted by evidence presented at such hearing. "(e) In determining whether any organization is a Communist-infiltrated organization, the Board shall consider- "(1) to what extent, if any, the effective management of the affairs of such organization is conducted by one or more individuals who are, or within two years have been, (A) members, agents, or representatives of any Communist organization, and Communist foreign government, or the world Communist movement referred to in section 2 of this title, with knowledge of the nature and purpose thereof, or (B) engaged in giving aid or support to any such organization, government, or movement with knowledge of the nature and purpose thereof; "(2) to what extent, if any, the policies of such organization are, or within three years have been, formulated and carried out pursuant to the direction or advice of any member, agent or representative of any such organization, government, or movement; "(3) to what extent, if any, the personnel and resources of such organization are, or within three years have been, used to further or promote the objectives of any such Communist organization, government, or movement; "(4) to what extent, if any, such organization within three years has received from, or furnished to or for the use of, any such Communist organization, government, or movement any funds or other material assistance; "(5) to what extent, if any, such organization is, or within three years has been, affiliated in any way with any such Communist organization, government, or movement; "(6) to what extent, if any, the affiliation of such organization, or of any individual or individuals who are members thereof or who manage its affairs, with any such Communist organization, government, or movement is concealed from or is not disclosed to the membership of such organization; and "(7) to what extent, if any, such organization or any of its members or managers are, or within three years have been, knowingly engaged- "(A) in any conduct punishable under section 4 or 15 of this Act or under chapter 37, 105, or 115 of title 18 of the United States Code; or "(B) with intent to impair the military strength of the United States or its industrial capacity to furnish logistical or other support required by its armed forces, in any activity resulting in or contributing to any such impairment. "(f) After hearing upon any petition filed under this section, the Board shall (1) make a support in writing in which it shall state its findings as to the facts and its conclusions with respect to the issues presented by such petition, (2) enter its order granting or denying the determination sought by such petition, and (3) serve upon each party to the proceeding a copy of such order. Any order granting any determination on the question whether any organization is a Communist-infiltrated organization shall become final as provided in section 14 (b) of this Act. "(g) When any order has been entered by the Board under this section with respect to any labor organization or employer (as these terms are defined by section 2 of the National Labor Relations Act, as amended, and which are organizations within the meaning of section 3 of the Subversive Activities Control Act of 1950), the Board shall serve a true and correct copy of such order upon the National Labor Relations Board and shall publish in the Federal Register a statement of the substance of such order and its effective date. "(h) When there is in effect a final order of the Board determining that any such labor organization is a Communist-action organization, a Communist-front organization, or a Communist-infiltrated organization, such labor organization shall be ineligible to- "(1) act as representative of any employee within the meaning or for the purposes of section 7 of the National Labor Relations Act, as amended (29 U.S.C. 157); "(2) serve as an exclusive representative of employees of any bargaining unit under section 9 of such Act, as amended (29 U.S.C. 159); "(3) make, or obtain any hearing upon, any charge under section 10 of such Act (29 U.S.C. 160); or "(4) exercise any other right or privilege, or receive any other benefit, substantive or procedural, provided by such Act for labor organizations. "(i) When an order of the Board determining that any such labor organization is a Communist-infiltrated organization has become final, and such labor organization theretofore has been certified under the National Labor Relations Act, as amended, as a representative of employees in any bargaining unit- "(1) a question of representation affecting commerce, within the meaning of section 9 (c) of such Act, shall be deemed to exist with respect to such bargaining unit; and "(2) the National Labor Relations Board, upon petition of not less than 20 per centum of the employees in such bargaining unit or any person or persons acting in their behalf, shall under section 9 of such Act (notwithstanding any limitation of time contained therein) direct elections in such bargaining unit or any subdivision thereof (A) for the selection of a representative thereof for collective bargaining purposes, and (B) to determine whether the employees thereof desire to rescind any authority previously granted to such labor organization to enter into any agreement with their employer pursuant to section 8 (a) (3) (ii) of such Act. "(j) When there is in effect a final order of the Board determining that any such employer is a Communist-infiltrated organization, such employer shall be ineligible to- "(1) file any petition for an election under section 9 of the National Labor Relations Act, as amended (29 U.S.C. 157), or participate in any proceeding under such section; or "(2) make or obtain any hearing upon any charge under section 10 of such Act (29 U.S.C. 160); or "(3) exercise any other right or privilege or receive any other benefit, substantive or procedural, provided by such Act for employers."

Sec. 11. Subsections (a) and (b) of section 14 of such Act (50 U.S.C. 793) are amended by inserting in each such subsection, immediately after the words "section 13", a comma and the following: "or subsection (f) of section 13A".

Sec. 12. If any provision of this title or the application thereof to any person or circumstances is held invalid, the remainder of the title, and the application of such provisions to other persons or circumstances, shall not be affected thereby.

Approved August 24, 1954, 9:40 a.m., M.S.T.

SOURCE: http://www-rohan.sdsu.edu/dept/polsciwb/brianl/docs/1954CommunistControlAct.pdf

ANALYSIS

Similar to the Subversive Activities Control Act, the Communist Control Act was a law that was passed in order to protect America from the potential threat posed by the international Communists. In 1954, the Second Red Scare still raged in the United States even though Senator Joseph McCarthy had been disgraced earlier in 1954 when he attempted to demonstrate that Communists were in the U.S. Army. However, many Americans still believed that Communists were working in this country. Responding to this fear, Congress passed the Communist Control Act which stated that the Communist Party within the United States was a subversive organization attempting to overthrow the government. The act went on to argue that the party was a continuing threat to national security and should therefore be outlawed. In the years after its enactment, the Communist Party of the United States continued to survive, even though the federal government used these anti-Communist pieces of legislation to harass and arrest Communist Party members. The government also used such acts to investigate and harass a number of other organizations that were considered to have Communist leanings and sympathies. These included groups such as the American Civil Liberties Union, labor unions, and the NAACP.

As the Supreme Court of the United States has not ruled on its constitutionality, the act has become dead letter. In 1968, Congress removed the registration obligation under the Subversive Activities Control Act. Instead, the Subversive Activities Control Board was authorized to keep records, open to public inspection, of the names and addresses of Communist organizations and their members. But in 1969 and 1970 the courts held that mere membership in the party was protected by the First Amendment, and the board was disbanded in 1973. In 1993 Congress repealed all the other provisions as they related to the Communist Party. By this time, the Soviet Union, and with it the world Communist movement, had collapsed, the Cold War had ended, and the Communist Party of the United States had diminished almost entirely away.

FURTHER READING

Barber, Kathleen L. "The Legal Status of the American Communist Party: 1965." *Journal of Public Law* 15 (1966): 94–121. Atlanta: Emory University Law School.

Rohr, Marc. "Communists and the First Amendment: The Shaping of Freedom of Advocacy in the Cold War Era." *San Diego Law Review* 28, No. 1 (1991): 1–116.

The Impact of World War I on Speech Rights: The Espionage Act of 1917

- ***Document:*** The Espionage Act of 1917, Excerpt
- ***Date:*** June 15, 1917
- ***Where:*** Washington, D.C.
- ***Significance:*** The purpose of the act was to prevent citizens from spying or interfering with military actions during World War I.

DOCUMENT

The Espionage Act of 1917

Title I—ESPIONAGE

Section 1

That:

(a) whoever, for the purpose of obtaining information respecting the national defence with intent or reason to believe that the information to be obtained is to be used to the injury of the United States, or to the advantage of any foreign nation, goes upon, enters, flies over, or otherwise obtains information, concerning any vessel, aircraft, work of defence, navy yard, naval station, submarine base, coaling station, fort, battery, torpedo station, dockyard, canal, railroad, arsenal, camp, factory, mine, telegraph, telephone, wireless, or signal station, building, office, or other place connected with the national defence, owned or constructed, or in progress of construction by the United States or under the control or the United States, or of any of its officers or agents, or within the exclusive jurisdiction of the United States, or any place in which any vessel, aircraft, arms, munitions, or other materials or instruments for use in time of war are being made, prepared, repaired. or stored, under any contract or agreement with the United States, or with any person on behalf of the United States, or otherwise on behalf of the United States, or any prohibited place within the meaning of section six of this title; or

(b) whoever for the purpose aforesaid, and with like intent or reason to believe, copies, takes, makes, or obtains, or attempts, or induces or aids another to copy, take, make, or obtain, any sketch, photograph, photographic negative, blue print, plan, map, model, instrument, appliance, document, writing or note of anything connected with the national defence; or

(c) whoever, for the purpose aforesaid, receives or obtains or agrees or attempts or induces or aids another to receive or obtain from any other person, or from any source whatever, any document, writing, code book, signal book, sketch, photograph, photographic negative, blue print, plan, map, model, instrument, appliance, or note, of anything connected with the national defence, knowing or having reason to believe, at the time he receives or obtains, or agrees or attempts or induces or aids another to receive or obtain it, that it has been or will be obtained, taken, made or disposed of by any person contrary to the provisions of this title; or

(d) whoever, lawfully or unlawfully having possession of, access to, control over, or being entrusted with any document, writing, code book, signal book, sketch, photograph, photographic negative, blue print, plan, map, model, instrument, appliance, or note relating to the national defence, wilfully communicates or transmits or attempts to communicate or transmit the same and fails to deliver it on demand to the officer or employee of the United States entitled to receive it; or

Political cartoon criticizing the Espionage Act of 1917. (Library of Congress.)

(e) whoever, being entrusted with or having lawful possession or control of any document, writing, code book, signal book, sketch, photograph, photographic negative, blue print, plan, map, model, note, or information, relating to the national defence, through gross negligence permits the same to be removed from its proper place of custody or delivered to anyone in violation of his trust, or to be list, stolen, abstracted, or destroyed, shall be punished by a fine of not more than $10,000, or by imprisonment for not more than two years, or both.

Section 2

Whoever, with intent or reason to believe that it is to be used to the injury or the United States or to the advantage of a foreign nation, communicated, delivers, or transmits, or attempts to, or aids, or induces another to, communicate, deliver or transmit, to any foreign government, or to any faction or party or military or naval force within a foreign country, whether recognized or unrecognized by the United States, or to any representative, officer, agent, employee, subject, or citizen thereof, either directly or indirectly and document, writing, code book, signal book, sketch, photograph, photographic negative, blue print, plan, map, model, note, instrument, appliance, or information relating to the national defence, shall be punished by imprisonment for not more than twenty years: Provided, That whoever shall violate the provisions of subsection:

(a) of this section in time of war shall be punished by death or by imprisonment for not more than thirty years; and

(b) whoever, in time of war, with intent that the same shall be communicated to the enemy, shall collect, record, publish or communicate, or attempt to elicit any information with respect to the movement, numbers, description, condition, or disposition of any of the armed forces, ships, aircraft, or war materials of the United States, or with respect to the plans or conduct, or supposed plans or conduct of any naval of military operations, or with respect to any works or measures undertaken for or connected with, or intended for the fortification of any place, or any other information relating to the public defence, which might be useful to the enemy, shall be punished by death or by imprisonment for not more than thirty years.

Section 3

Whoever, when the United States is at war, shall wilfully make or convey false reports or false statements with intent to interfere with the operation or success of the military or naval forces of the United States or to promote the success of its enemies and whoever when the United States is at war, shall wilfully cause or attempt to cause insubordination, disloyalty, mutiny, refusal of duty, in the military or naval forces of the United States, or shall wilfully obstruct the recruiting or enlistment service of the United States, to the injury of the service or of the United States, shall be punished by a fine of not more than $10,000 or imprisonment for not more than twenty years, or both.

Section 4

If two or more persons conspire to violate the provisions of section two or three of this title, and one or more of such persons does any act to effect the object of the conspiracy, each of the parties to such conspiracy shall be punished as in said sections provided in the case of the doing of the act the accomplishment of which is the object of such conspiracy. Except as above provided conspiracies to commit offences under this title shall be punished as provided by section thirty-seven of the Act to codify, revise, and amend the penal laws of the United States approved March fourth, nineteen hundred and nine.

Section 5

Whoever harbours or conceals any person who he knows, or has reasonable grounds to believe or suspect, has committed, or is about to commit, an offence under this title shall be punished by a fine of not more than $10,000 or by imprisonment for not more than two years, or both.

Section 6

The President in time of war or in case of national emergency may by proclamation designate any place other than those set forth in subsection: (a) of section one hereof in which anything for the use of the Army or Navy is being prepared or constructed or stored as a prohibited place for the purpose of this title: Provided, That he shall determine that information with respect thereto would be prejudicial to the national defence.

Section 7

Nothing contained in this title shall be deemed to limit the jurisdiction of the general courts-martial, military commissions, or naval courts-martial under sections thirteen hundred and forty-two, thirteen hundred and forty-three, and sixteen hundred and twenty-four of the Revised Statutes as amended.

Section 8

The provisions of this title shall extend to all Territories, possessions, and places subject to the jurisdiction of the United States whether or not contiguous thereto, and offences under this title, when committed upon the high seas or elsewhere within the admiralty and maritime jurisdiction of the United States and outside the territorial limits thereof shall be punishable hereunder.

Section 9

The Act entitles "An Act to prevent the disclosure of national defence secrets," approved March third, nineteen hundred and eleven, is hereby repealed.

SOURCE: http://www.firstworldwar.com/source/espionageact.htm

ANALYSIS

The Espionage Act was passed by Congress in 1917 after the United States entered the First World War. The legislation was passed at the urging of President Woodrow Wilson, who feared any widespread dissent in time of war constituted a real threat to an American victory. It prescribed a $10,000 fine and 20 years in prison for interfering with the recruiting of troops or the disclosure of information dealing with national defense. Additional penalties were included for the refusal to perform military duty, and use of the United States mail for material urging treason or resistance was also prohibited. As a result of the this provision of the act, about 75 newspapers either lost their mailing privileges or were pressured to print nothing more about World War I between June 1917 and May 1918. Additionally, the editor of the *Milwaukee Leader* was sentenced to 20 years imprisonment after being convicted on a charge of conspiracy to violate the Espionage Act. While most of the Espionage Act was straightforward and noncontroversial, parts of this legislation curtailed freedom of speech in such a way as to draw an outcry from civil libertarians. This curtailment of speech rights led to approximately 900 people being convicted under the Espionage Act. This measure was quickly challenged in the courts but the law was upheld by the Supreme Court in *Schenck v. United States* (1919).

FURTHER READING

Kohn, Stephen M. *American Political Prisoners: Prosecutions under the Espionage and Sedition Acts*. Westport, Conn.: Praeger, 1994.

Murphy, Paul L. *World War I and the Origin of Civil Liberties in the United States*. New York: W.W. Norton, 1979.

The Impact of World War I on Speech Rights: The Sedition Act of 1918

- ***Document:*** The Sedition Act of 1918, Excerpt
- ***Date:*** May 16, 1918
- ***Where:*** Washington, D.C.
- ***Significance:*** This legislation was a set of amendments to the Espionage Act of 1917 that made it a felony for individuals who interfered with the draft, but also those individuals who publicly criticized the government including negative comments about the flag, military, or Constitution.

DOCUMENT

Sedition Act, 1918

Sec. 3. Whoever, when the United States is at war, shall willfully make or convey false reports or false statements with intent to interfere with the operation or success of the military or naval forces of the United States, or to promote the success of its enemies, or shall willfully make or convey false reports or false statements, or say or do anything except by way of bona fide and not disloyal advice to an investor or investors, with intent to obstruct the sale by the United States of bonds or other securities of the United States or the making of loans by or to the United States, and whoever when the United States is at war, shall willfully cause or attempt to cause, or incite or attempt to incite, insubordination, disloyalty, mutiny, or refusal of duty, in the military or naval forces of the United States, or shall willfully obstruct or attempt to obstruct the recruiting or enlistment services of the United States, and whoever, when the United States is at war, shall willfully utter, print, write or publish any disloyal, profane, scurrilous, or abusive language about the form of government of the United States or the Constitution of the United States, or the military or naval forces of the United States, or the flag of the United States, or the uniform of the Army or Navy of the United States into contempt, scorn, contumely, or disrepute, or shall willfully utter, print, write, or publish any language intended to incite, provoke, or encourage resistance to the United States, or to promote the cause of its enemies, or shall willfully display the flag of any foreign enemy, or shall willfully by utterance, writing, printing, publication, or language spoken, urge, incite, or advocate any curtailment of production in this country of any thing or things, product or products, necessary or essential to the prosecution of the war in which the United States may be engaged, with intent by such curtailment to cripple or hinder the United States in the prosecution of war, and whoever shall willfully advocate, teach, defend, or suggest the doing of any of the acts or things in this section enumerated, and whoever shall by word or act support or favor the cause of any country with which the United States is at war or by word or act oppose the cause of the United States therein, shall be punished by a fine of not more than $10,000 or the imprisonment for not more than twenty years, or both: Provided, That any employee or official of the United States Government who commits any disloyal act or utters any unpatriotic or disloyal language, or who, in an abusive and violent manner criticizes the Army or Navy or the flag of the United States shall be at once dismissed from the service. . . .

Sec. 4. When the United States is at war, the Postmaster General may, upon evidence satisfactory to him that any person or concern is using the mails in violation of any of the provisions of this Act, instruct the postmaster at any post office at which mail is received addressed to such person or concern to return to the postmaster at the office at which they were originally mailed all letters or other matter so addressed, with the words 'Mail to this address undeliverable under Espionage Act' plainly written or stamped upon the outside thereof, and all such letters or other matter so returned to such postmasters shall be by them returned to the senders thereof under such regulations as the Postmaster General may prescribe.

Approved, May 16, 1918.

SOURCE: http://www.gwpda.org/1918/usspy.html

ANALYSIS

During World War I, a small but vocal resistance movement gained ground. Congress passed the Sedition Act of 1918 in order to silence criticism of the United States during World War I, restricting freedom of speech in the interest of national security. It was not the first time that speech had been restricted for this reason, nor would it be the last. The act made it a felony (1) to convey false statements interfering with American war efforts; (2) to willfully employ "disloyal, profane, scurrilous, or abusive language" about the United States form of government, the Constitution, the flag, or United States military or naval forces; (3) to urge the curtailed production of necessary war materials; or (4) to advocate, teach, defend, or suggest the doing of any such acts. Violations were punishable by fine, imprisonment, or both. The Sedition Act was meant to do what the Espionage Act had not done—criminalize speech intended to undermine citizens' faith in their government and in its efforts to prosecute the war. The law was aimed at curbing political dissent expressed by Socialists, anarchists, pacifists, and certain labor leaders. The Sedition Act was repealed in 1921.

FURTHER READING

Kohn, Stephen M., *American Political Prisoners: Prosecutions under the Espionage and Sedition Acts*. Westport, Conn.: Praeger, 1994.

Murphy, Paul L. *World War I and the Origin of Civil Liberties in the United States*. New York: W. W. Norton, 1979.

Alien Registration Act

- ***Document:*** The Alien Registration Act, also known as the Smith Act
- ***Date:*** February 19, 1940
- ***Where:*** Washington, D.C.
- ***Significance:*** The act made it illegal for anyone in the United States to advocate, abet, or teach the desirability of overthrowing the government, and it required all alien residents in the United States over 14 years of age to register, be finger printed, and file a comprehensive statement of their personal and occupational status and a record of their political beliefs.

DOCUMENT

Alien Registration Act of 1940

U.S. Statutes at Large (76th Cong., 3rd Sess., 670–676)

AN ACT

To prohibit certain subversive activities; to amend certain provisions of law with respect to the admission and deportation of aliens; to require the fingerprinting and registration of aliens; and for other purposes.

Be it enacted by the Senate and House of Representatives of the United States of America in Congress assembled,

TITLE I

Section 1. (a) It shall be unlawful for any person, with intent to interfere with, impair, or influence the loyalty, morale, or discipline of the military or naval forces of the United States—

(1) to advise, counsel, urge, or in any manner cause insubordination, disloyalty, mutiny, or refusal of duty by any member of the military or naval forces of the United States; or

(2) to distribute any written or printed matter which advises, counsels, or urges insubordination, disloyalty, mutiny, or refusal of duty by any member of the military or naval forces of the United States.

(b) For the purposes of this section, the term "military or naval forces of the United States" includes the Army of the United States, as defined in section 1 of the National Defense Act of June 3, 1916, as amended (48 Stat. 153; U.S.C., title 10, sec. 2), the Navy, Marine Corps, Coast Guard, Naval Reserve, and Marine Corps Reserve of the United States; and, when any merchant vessel is commissioned in the Navy or is in the service of the Army or the Navy, includes the master, officers, and crew of such vessel.

Sec. 2. (a) It shall be unlawful for any person—

(1) to knowingly or willfully advocate, abet, advise, or teach the duty, necessity, desirability, or propriety of overthrowing or destroying any government in the United States by force or violence, or by the assassination of any officer of any such government;

(2) with the intent to cause the overthrow or destruction of any government in the United States, to print, publish, edit, issue, circulate, sell, distribute, or publicly display any written or printed matter advocating, advising, or teaching the duty, necessity, desirability, or propriety of overthrowing or destroying any government in the United States by force or violence.

(3) to organize or help to organize any society, group, or assembly of persons who teach, advocate, or encourage the overthrow or destruction of any government in the United States by force or violence; or to be or become a member of, or affiliate with, any such society, group, or assembly of persons, knowing the purposes thereof.

(b) For the purposes of this section, the term "government in the United States" means the Government of the United States, the government of any State, Territory, or possession of the United States, the government of the District of Columbia, or the government of any political subdivision of any of them.

Sec. 3. It shall be unlawful for any person to attempt to commit, or to conspire to commit, any of the acts prohibited by the provisions of this title.

Sec. 4. Any written or printed matter of the character described in section 1 or section 2 of this Act, which is intended for use in violation of this Act, may be taken from any house or other place in which it may be found, or from any person in whose possession it may be, under a search warrant issued pursuant to the provisions of title XI of the Act entitled "An Act to punish acts of interference with the foreign relations, the neutrality and the foreign commerce of the United States, to punish espionage, and better to enforce the criminal laws of the United States, and for other purposes", approved June 15, 1917 (40 Stat. 228; U.S.C., title 18, ch. 18).

Sec. 5. (a) Any person who violates any of the provisions of this title shall, upon conviction thereof, be fined not more than $10,000 or imprisoned for not more than ten years, or both.

(b) No person convicted of violating any of the provisions of this title shall, during the five years next following his conviction, be eligible for employment by the United States, or by any department or agency thereof (including any corporation the Stock of which is wholly owned by the United States).

TITLE II

Sec. 20. Section 19 of the Immigration Act of February 5, 1917 (39 Stat. 889; U.S.C., title 8, sec. 155), as amended, is amended by inserting, after "Sec. 19.", the letter "(a)", and by adding at the end of such section the following new subsections:

"(b) Any alien of any of the classes specified in this subsection, in addition to aliens who are deportable under other provisions of law, shall, upon warrant of the Attorney General, be taken into custody and deported:

"(1) Any alien who, at any time within five years after entry, shall have, knowingly and for gain, encouraged, induced, assisted, abetted, or aided any other alien to enter or to try to enter the United States in violation of law.

"(2) Any alien who, at any time after entry, shall have on more than one occasion, knowingly and for gain, encouraged, induced, assisted, abetted, or aided any other alien or aliens to enter or to try to enter the United States in violation of law.

"(3) Any alien who, at any time after entry, shall have been convicted of possessing or carrying in violation of any law any weapon which shoots or is designed to shoot automatically or semi-automatically more than one shot without manual reloading, by a single function of the trigger, or a weapon commonly called a sawed-off shotgun.

"(4) Any alien who, at any time within five years after entry, shall have been convicted of violating the provisions of title I of the Alien Registration Act, 1940.

"(5) Any alien who, at any time after entry, shall have been convicted more than once of violating the provisions of title I of the Alien Registration Act, 1940.

"No alien who is deportable under the provisions of paragraph (3), (4), or (5) of this subsection shall be deported until the termination of his imprisonment or the entry of an order releasing him on probation or parole.

"(c) In the same of any alien (other than one to whom subsection (d) is applicable) who is deportable under any law of the United States and who has proved good moral character for the preceding five years, the Attorney General may (1) permit such alien to depart the United States to any country of his choice at his own expense, in lieu of deportation, or (2) suspend deportation of such alien if not racially inadmissible or ineligible to naturalization in the United States if he finds that such deportation would result in serious economic detriment to a citizen or legally resident alien who is the spouse, parent, or minor child of such deportable alien. If the deportation of any alien is suspended under the provisions of this subsection for more than six months, all of the facts and pertinent provisions of law in the case shall be reported to the Congress within ten days after the beginning of its next regular session, with the reasons for such suspension. The Clerk of the House shall have such report printed as a public document. If during that session the two Houses pass a concurrent resolution stating in substance that the Congress does not favor the suspension of such deportation, the Attorney General shall thereupon deport such alien in the manner provided by law. If during the session the two Houses do not pass such a resolution, the Attorney General shall cancel deportation proceedings upon the termination of such session, except that such proceedings shall not be canceled in the case of any alien who was not legally admitted for permanent residence at the time of his last entry into the United States, unless such alien pays to the Commissioner of Immigration and Naturalization a fee of $18 (which fee shall be deposited in the Treasury of the United States as miscellaneous receipts). Upon the cancelation of such proceedings in any case in which such fee has been paid, the Commissioner shall record the alien's admission for permanent residence as of the date of his last entry into the United States and the Secretary of State shall, if the alien was a quota immigrant at the time of entry and was not charged to the appropriate quota, reduce by one the immigration quota of the country of the alien's nationality as defined in section 12 of the Act of May 26, 1924 (U.S. C., title 8, sec. 212), for the fiscal year then current or next following.

"(d) The provisions of subsection (c) shall not be applicable in the case of any alien who is deportable under (1) the Act of October 16, 1918 (40 Stat. 1008; U.S. C., title 8, sec. 137), entitled 'An Act to exclude and expel from the United States aliens who are members of the anarchist and similar classes', as amended; (2) the Act of May 26, 1922, entitled 'An Act to amend the Act entitled "An Act to prohibit the importation and use of opium for other than medicinal purposes", approved February 9, 1909, as amended' (42 Stat. 596; U.S. C., title 21, sec. 175); (3) the Act of February 18, 1931, entitled 'An Act to provide for the deportation of aliens convicted and sentenced for violation of any law regulating traffic in narcotics', as amended (46 Stat. 1171; U.S. C., title 8, sec. 156a); (4) any of the provisions of so much of subsection (a) of this section as relates to criminals, prostitutes, procurers, or other immoral persons, the mentally and physically deficient, anarchists, and similar classes; or (5) subsection (b) of this section."

Sec. 21. The Act entitled "An Act to provide for the deportation of aliens convicted and sentenced for violation of any law regulating traffic in narcotics", approved February 18, 1931, is amended—

(1) By striking out the words "and sentenced";

(2) By inserting after the words "any statute of the United States" the following: "or of any State, Territory, possession, or of the District of Columbia,"; and

(3) By inserting after the word "heroin" a comma and the word "marihuana".

Sec. 22. No alien shall be deportable by reason of the amendments made by section 20 or 21 on account of any act committed prior to the date of enactment of this Act.

Sec. 23. (a) The first paragraph of section 1 of the Act entitled "An Act to exclude and expel from the United States aliens who are members of the anarchistic and similar classes", approved October 16, 1918, as amended, is amended to read as follows:

"That any alien who, at any time, shall be or shall have been a member of any one of the following classes shall be excluded from admission into the United States:".

(b) Section 2 of such Act of October 16, 1918, as amended, is amended to read as follows:

"Sec. 2. Any alien who was at the time of entering the United States, or has been at any time thereafter, a member of any one of the classes of aliens enumerated in section 1 of this Act, shall, upon the warrant of the Attorney General, be taken into custody and deported in the manner provided in the Immigration Act of February 5, 1917. The provisions of this section shall be applicable to the classes of aliens mentioned in this Act, irrespective of the time of their entry into the United States."

TITLE III

Sec. 30. No visa shall hereafter be issued to any alien seeking to enter the United States unless said alien has been registered and fingerprinted in duplicate. One copy of the registration and fingerprint record shall be retained by the consul. The second copy shall be attached to the alien's visa and shall be taken up by the examining immigrant inspector at the port of arrival of the alien in the United States and forwarded to the Department of Justice, at Washington, District of Columbia.

Any alien seeking to enter the United States who does not present a visa (except in emergency cases defined by the Secretary of State), a reentry permit, or a border-crossing identification card shall be excluded from admission to the United States.

Sec. 31. (a) It shall be the duty of every alien now or hereafter in the United States, who (1) is fourteen years of age or older, (2) has not been registered and fingerprinted under section 30, and (3) remains in the United States for thirty days or longer, to apply for registration and to be fingerprinted before the expiration of such thirty days.

(b) It shall be the duty of every parent or legal guardian of any alien now or hereafter in the United States, who (1) is less than fourteen years of age, (2) has not been registered under section 30, and (3) remains in the United States for thirty days or longer, to apply for the registration of such alien before the expiration of such thirty days. Whenever any alien attains his fourteenth birthday in the United States he shall, within thirty days thereafter, apply in person for registration and to be fingerprinted.

Sec. 32. Notwithstanding the provisions of sections 30 and 31—

(a) The application for the registration and fingerprinting, or for the registration, of any alien who is in the United States on the effective date of such sections may be made at any time within four months after such date.

(b) No foreign government official, or member of his family, shall be required to be registered or fingerprinted under this title.

(c) The Commissioner is authorized to prescribe, with the approval of the Attorney General, special regulations for the registration and fingerprinting of (1) alien seamen, (2) holders of border-crossing identification cards, (3) aliens confined in institutions within the United States, (4) aliens under order or deportation, and (5) aliens of any other class not lawfully admitted to the United States for permanent residence.

Sec. 33. (a) All applications for registration and fingerprinting under section 31 shall be made at post offices or such other places as may be designated by the Commissioner.

(b) It shall be the duty of every postmaster, with such assistance as shall be provided by the Commissioner, to register and fingerprint any applicant for registration and fingerprinting under such section, and for such purposes to designate appropriate space in the local post office for such registration and fingerprinting. Every postmaster shall forward promptly to the Department of Justice, at Washington, District of Columbia, the registration and fingerprint record of every alien registered and fingerprinted by him. The Commissioner may designate such other places for registration and fingerprinting as may be necessary for carrying out the provisions of this Act, and provide for registration and fingerprinting of aliens at such places by officers or employees of the Immigration and Naturalization Service designated by the Commissioner. The duties imposed upon any postmaster under this Act shall also be performed by any employees at the post office of such postmaster who are designated by the postmaster for such purpose.

Sec. 34. (a) The Commissioner is authorized and directed to prepare forms for the registration and fingerprinting of aliens under this title. Such forms shall contain inquiries with respect to (1) the date and place of entry of the alien into the United States; (2) activities in which he has been and intends to be engaged; (3) the length of time he expects to remain in the United States; (4) the criminal record, if any, of such alien; and (5) such additional matters as may be prescribed by the Commissioner, with the approval of the Attorney General.

(b) All registration and fingerprint records made under the provisions of this title shall be secret and confidential, and shall be made available only to such persons or agencies as may be designated by the Commissioner, with the approval of the Attorney General.

(c) Every person required to apply for the registration of himself or another under this title shall submit under oath the information required for such registration. Any person authorized to register aliens under this title shall be authorized to administer oaths for such purpose.

Sec. 35. Any alien required to be registered under this title who is a resident of the United States shall notify the Commissioner in writing of each change of residence and new address within five days from the date of such change. Any other alien required to be registered under this title shall notify the Commissioner in writing of his address at the expiration of each three months' period of residence in the United States. In the case of an alien for whom a parent or legal guardian is required to apply for registration, the notices required by this section shall be given by such parent or legal guardian.

Sec. 36. (a) Any alien required to apply for registration and to be fingerprinted who willfully fails to refuses to make such application or to be fingerprinted, and any parent or legal guardian required to apply for the registration of any alien who willfully fails or refuses to file application for the registration of such alien shall, upon conviction thereof be fined not to exceed $1,000 or be imprisoned not more than six months, or both.

(b) Any alien, or any parent or legal guardian of any alien, who fails to give written notice to the Commissioner of change of address as required by section 35 of this Act shall, upon conviction thereof, be fined not to exceed $100, or be imprisoned not more than thirty days, or both.

(c) Any alien or any parent or legal guardian of any alien, who files an application for registration containing statements known by him to be false, or who procures or attempts to procure registration of himself or another person through fraud, shall, upon conviction thereof, be fined not to exceed $1,000, or be imprisoned not more than six months, or both; and any alien so convicted within five years after entry into the United States shall, upon the warrant of the Attorney General, be taken into custody and be deported in the manner provided in sections 19 and 20 of the Immigration Act of February 5, 1917, as amended.

Sec. 37. (a) The Commissioner, with the approval of the Attorney General, is authorized and empowered to make the prescribe, and from time to time to change and amend, such rules and regulations not in conflict with this Act as he may deem necessary and proper in aid of the administration and enforcement of this title (including provisions for the identification of aliens registered under this title); except that all such rules and regulations, insofar as they relate to the performance of functions by consular officers or officers or employees in the Postal Service, shall be prescribed by the Secretary of State and the Postmaster General, respectively, upon recommendation of the Attorney General. The powers conferred upon the Attorney

General by this Act and all other powers of the Attorney General relating to the administration of the Immigration and Naturalization Service may be exercised by the Attorney General through such officers of the Department of Justice, including officers of the Immigration and Naturalization Service, attorneys, special attorneys, and special assistants to the Attorney General, as he may designate specifically for such purposes.

(b) The Commissioner is authorized to make such expenditures, to employ such additional temporary and permanent employees, and to rent such quarters outside the District of Columbia as may be necessary for carrying out the provisions of this title.

Sec. 38. (a) For the purposes of this title—

(1) the term "United States", when used in a geographical sense, means the States, the Territories of Alaska and Hawaii, the District of Columbia, Puerto Rico, and the Virgin Islands;

(2) the term "Commissioner" means the Commissioner of Immigration and Naturalization.

(b) The provisions of this title shall take effect upon the date of enactment of this Act; except that sections 30 and 31 shall take effect sixty days after the date of its enactment.

Sec. 39. The President is authorized to provide, by Executive order, for the registration and fingerprinting, in a manner as nearly similar to that provided in this title as he deems practicable, of aliens in the Panama Canal Zone.

Approved, June 28, 1940.

SOURCE: http://tucnak.fsv.cuni.cz/~calda/Documents/1940s/Alien%20Registration%20Act%20of%201940.html

ANALYSIS

The Alien Registration Act of 1940 was proposed by Congressman Howard Smith of Virginia, a poll tax supporter and a leader of the antilabor bloc in Congress, and is generally referred to as the Smith Act. Signed into law by President Franklin Roosevelt, it was the first statute since the Alien and Sedition Acts of 1798 to make mere advocacy of ideas a federal crime. In particular, it was illegal to print, publish, or circulate printed matter advocating, or teaching the overthrow of the U.S. government. The act also required all aliens living within the United States to register with the government, be fingerprinted, carry identification cards, and report annually. Individuals found to have ties to "subversive organizations" could be deported. By acquiring a detailed work history of aliens, the government sought to identify potential problems before they occurred. The other primary objective of the Alien Registration Act was to identify elements of the American Communist Party or other Socialist organizations. The government successfully prosecuted under the law when it showed that teachings by a political organization could have led to the overthrow of the government in a timely manner.

Although 5 million aliens were registered and fingerprinted following its passage, its antisubversive sections were not used until 1943, when a small group of Minneapolis Trotskyites were convicted. When the Cold War intensified, following 1947, the Truman administration began a series of dramatic prosecutions of Communist Party leaders. These and subsequent prosecutions eventually forced the Supreme Court to clarify the act's terms and reach. In *Dennis v. United States*, 341 U.S. 494 (1951), the Court considered the convictions of eleven Communist Party leaders on charges of conspiracy to violate the advocacy and organizing sections of the statute. Chief Justice Vinson's plurality opinion for the Court held that there was a distinction between the mere teaching of communist philosophies and active advocacy of those ideas. The Court applied a revised clear and present danger test and concluded that the evil sought to be prevented by the federal government was serious enough to justify suppression of speech.

FURTHER READING

Fried, Albert. *McCarthyism: The Great American Red Scare: A Documentary History*. Oxford: Oxford University Press, 1996.

President Dwight D. Eisenhower's Executive Order 10450

- ***Document:*** President Dwight D. Eisenhower's United States Executive Order 10450
- ***Date:*** April 27, 1953
- ***Where:*** Washington, D.C.
- ***Significance:*** Executive Order 10450 mandated the firing of all federal employees who were determined to be homosexual.

DOCUMENT

Executive Order 10450—Security Requirements for Government Employment

April 27, 1953

WHEREAS the interests of the national security require that all persons privileged to be employed in the departments and agencies of the Government, shall be reliable, trustworthy, of good conduct and character, and of complete and unswerving loyalty to the United States; and

WHEREAS the American tradition that all persons should receive fair, impartial, and equitable treatment at the hands of the Government requires that all persons seeking the privilege of employment or privileged to be employed in the departments and agencies of the Government be adjudged by mutually consistent and no less than minimum standards and procedures among the departments and agencies governing the employment and retention in employment of persons in the Federal service:

NOW, THEREFORE, by virtue of the authority vested in me by the Constitution and statutes of the United States, including section 1753 of the Revised Statutes of the United States (5 U.S.C. 631); the Civil Service Act of 1883 (22 Stat. 403; 5 U.S.C. 632, et seq.); section 9A of the act of August 2, 1939, 53 Stat. 1148 (5 U.S.C. 118j); and the act of August 26, 1950, 64 Stat. 476 (5 U.S.C. 22–1, et seq.), and as President of the United States, and deeming such action necessary in the best interests of the national security, it is hereby ordered as follows:

Sec. 1. In addition to the departments and agencies specified in the said act of August 26, 1950, and Executive Order No. 10237 of April 26, 1951, the provisions of that act shall apply to all other departments and agencies of the Government.

Sec. 2. The head of each department and agency of the Government shall be responsible for establishing and maintaining within his department or agency an effective program to insure that the employment and retention in employment of any civilian officer or employee within the department or agency is clearly consistent with the interests of the national security.

Sec. 3. (a) The appointment of each civilian officer or employee in any department or agency of the Government shall be made subject to investigation. The scope of the investigation shall be determined in the first instance according to the degree of adverse effect the occupant of the position sought to be filled could bring about, by virtue of the nature of the position, on the national security, but in no event shall the investigation include less than a national agency check (including a check of the fingerprint files of the Federal Bureau of Investigation), and written inquiries to appropriate local law-enforcement agencies, former employers and supervisors, references, and schools attended by the person under investigation: *Provided*, that upon request of the head of the department or agency concerned, the Office of Personnel Management may, in its discretion, authorize such less investigation as may meet the requirements of the national security with respect to per-diem, intermittent, temporary, or seasonal employees, or aliens employed outside the United States. Should there develop at any stage of investigation information indicating that the employment of any such person may not be clearly consistent with the interests of the national security, there shall be conducted with respect to such person a full field investigation, or such less investigation as shall be sufficient to enable the head of the department or agency concerned to determine whether retention of such person is clearly consistent with the interests of the national security.

(b) The head of any department or agency shall designate, or cause to be designated, any position within his department or agency the occupant of which could bring about, by virtue of the nature of the position, a material adverse effect on the national security as a sensitive position. Any position so designated shall be filled or occupied only by a person with respect to whom a full field investigation has been conducted: *Provided*, that a person occupying a sensitive position at the time it is designated as such may continue to occupy such position pending the completion of a full field investigation, subject to the other provisions of this order: *And provided further*, that in case of emergency a sensitive position may be filled for a limited period by a person with respect to whom a full field pre-appointment investigation has not been completed if the head of the department or agency concerned finds that such action is necessary in the national interest, which finding shall be made a part of the records of such department or agency.

[Sec. 3 amended by EO 12107 of Dec. 28, 1978, 44 FR 1055, 3 CFR, 1978 Comp., p. 264]

Sec. 4. The head of each department and agency shall review, or cause to be reviewed, the cases of all civilian officers and employees with respect to whom there has been conducted a full field investigation under Executive Order No. 9835 of March 21, 1947, and, after such further investigation as may be appropriate, shall re-adjudicate, or cause to be re-adjudicated, in accordance with the said act of August 26, 1950, such of those cases as have not been adjudicated under a security standard commensurate with that established under this order.

Sec. 5. Whenever there is developed or received by any department or agency information indicating that the retention in employment of any officer or employee of the Government may not be clearly consistent with the interests of the national security, such information shall be forwarded to the head of the employing department or agency or his representative, who, after such investigation as may be appropriate, shall review, or cause to be reviewed, and, where necessary, re-adjudicate, or cause to be re-adjudicated, in accordance with the said act of August 26, 1950, the case of such officer or employee.

Sec. 6. Should there develop at any stage of investigation information indicating that the employment of any officer or employee of the Government may not be clearly consistent with the interests of the national security, the head of the department or agency concerned or his representative shall immediately suspend the employment of the person involved if he deems such suspension necessary in the interests of the national security and, following such investigation and review as he deems necessary, the head of the department or agency concerned shall terminate the employment of such suspended officer or employee whenever he shall determine such termination necessary or advisable in the interests of the national security, in accordance with the said act of August 26, 1950.

Sec. 7. Any person whose employment is suspended or terminated under the authority granted to heads of departments and agencies by or in accordance with the said act of August 26, 1950, or pursuant to the said Executive Order No. 9835 or any other security or loyalty program relating to officers or employees of the Government, shall not be reinstated or restored to duty or reemployed in the same department or agency and shall not be reemployed in any other department or agency, unless the head of the department or agency concerned finds that such reinstatement, restoration, or reemployment is clearly consistent with the interests of the national security, which finding shall be made a part of the records of such department or agency: *Provided,* that no person whose employment has been terminated under such authority thereafter may be employed by any other department or agency except after a determination by the Office of Personnel Management that such person is eligible for such employment.

[Sec. 7 amended by EO 12107 of Dec. 28, 1978, 44 FR 1055, 3 CFR, 1978 Comp., p. 264]

Sec. 8. (a) The investigations conducted pursuant to this order shall be designed to develop information as to whether the employment or retention in employment in the Federal service of the person being investigated is clearly consistent with the interests of the national security. Such information shall relate, but shall not be limited, to the following:

(1) Depending on the relation of the Government employment to the national security:

(i) Any behavior, activities, or associations which tend to show that the individual is not reliable or trustworthy.

(ii) Any deliberate misrepresentations, falsifications, or omissions of material facts.
(iii) Any criminal, infamous, dishonest, immoral, or notoriously disgraceful conduct, habitual use of intoxicants to excess, drug addiction, sexual perversion.
(iv) Any illness, including any mental condition, of a nature which in the opinion of competent medical authority may cause significant defect in the judgment or reliability of the employee, with due regard to the transient or continuing effect of the illness and the medical findings in such case.
(v) Any facts which furnish reason to believe that the individual may be subjected to coercion, influence, or pressure which may cause him to act contrary to the best interests of the national security.

(2) Commission of any act of sabotage, espionage, treason, or sedition, or attempts thereat or preparation therefore, or conspiring with, or aiding or abetting, another to commit or attempt to commit any act of sabotage, espionage, treason, or sedition.
(3) Establishing or continuing a sympathetic association with a saboteur, spy, traitor, seditionist, anarchist, or revolutionist, or with an espionage or other secret agent or representative of a foreign nation, or any representative of a foreign nation whose interests may be inimical to the interests of the United States, or with any person who advocates the use of force or violence to overthrow the government of the United States or the alteration of the form of government of the United States by unconstitutional means.
(4) Advocacy of use of force or violence to overthrow the government of the United States, or of the alteration of the form of government of the United States by unconstitutional means.
(5) Knowing membership with the specific intent of furthering the aims of, or adherence to and active participation in, any foreign or domestic organization, association, movement, group, or combination of persons (hereinafter referred to as organizations) which unlawfully advocates or practices the commission of acts of force or violence to prevent others from exercising their rights under the Constitution or laws of the United States or of any State, or which seeks to overthrow the Government of the United States or any State or subdivision thereof by unlawful means.
(6) Intentional, unauthorized disclosure to any person of security information, or of other information disclosure of which is prohibited by law, or willful violation or disregard of security regulations.
(7) Performing or attempting to perform his duties, or otherwise acting, so as to serve the interests of another government in preference to the interests of the United States.
(8) Refusal by the individual, upon the ground of constitutional privilege against self-incrimination, to testify before a congressional committee regarding charges of his alleged disloyalty or other misconduct.

(b) The investigation of persons entering or employed in the competitive service shall primarily be the responsibility of the Office of Personnel Management, except in cases in which the head of a department or agency assumes that responsibility pursuant to law or by agreement with the Office. The Office shall furnish a full investigative report to the department or agency concerned.

(c) The investigation of persons (including consultants, however employed), entering employment of, or employed by, the Government other than in the competitive service shall primarily be the responsibility of the employing department or agency. Departments and agencies without investigative facilities may use the investigative facilities of the Office of Personnel Management, and other departments and agencies may use such facilities under agreement with the Office.

(d) There shall be referred promptly to the Federal Bureau of Investigation all investigations being conducted by any other agencies which develop information indicating that an individual may have been subjected to coercion, influence, or pressure to act contrary to the interests of the national security, or information relating to any of the matters described in subdivisions (2) through (8) of subsection (a) of this section. In cases so referred to it, the Federal Bureau of Investigation shall make a full field investigation.

Sec. 9. (a) There shall be established and maintained in the Office of Personnel Management a security-investigations index covering all persons as to whom security investigations have been conducted by any department or agency of the Government under this order. The central index established and maintained by the Office under Executive Order No. 9835 of March 21, 1947, shall be made a part of the security-investigations index. The security-investigations index shall contain the name of each person investigated, adequate identifying information concerning each such person, and a reference to each department and agency which has conducted an investigation concerning the person involved or has suspended or terminated the employment of such person under the authority granted to heads of departments and agencies by or in accordance with the said act of August 26, 1950.

(b) The heads of all departments and agencies shall furnish promptly to the Office of Personnel Management information appropriate for the establishment and maintenance of the security-investigations index.

(c) The reports and other investigative material and information developed by investigations conducted pursuant to any statute, order, or program described in section 7 of this order shall remain the property of the investigative agencies conducting the investigations, but may, subject to considerations of the national security, be retained by the department or agency concerned. Such reports and other investigative material and information shall be maintained in confidence, and no access shall be given thereto except, with the consent of the investigative agency concerned, to other departments and agencies conducting security programs under the authority granted by or in accordance with the said act of August 26, 1950, as may be required for the efficient conduct of Government business.

Sec. 10. Nothing in this order shall be construed as eliminating or modifying in any way the requirement for any investigation or any determination as to security which may be required by law.

Sec. 11. On and after the effective date of this order the Loyalty Review Board established by Executive Order No. 9835 of March 21, 1947, shall not accept agency findings for review, upon appeal or otherwise. Appeals pending before the Loyalty Review Board on such date shall be heard to final determination in accordance with the provisions of the said Executive Order No. 9835, as amended.

Agency determinations favorable to the officer or employee concerned pending before the Loyalty Review Board on such date shall be acted upon by such Board, and whenever the Board is not in agreement with such favorable determination the case shall be remanded to the department or agency concerned for determination in accordance with the standards and procedures established pursuant to this order. Cases pending before the regional loyalty boards of the Office of Personnel Management on which hearings have not been initiated on such date shall be referred to the department or agency concerned. Cases being heard by regional loyalty boards on such date shall be heard to conclusion and the determination of the board shall be forwarded to the head of the department or agency concerned: *Provided,* that if no specific department or agency is involved, the case shall be dismissed without prejudice to the applicant. Investigations pending in the Federal Bureau of Investigation or the Office of Personnel Management on such date shall be completed, and the reports thereon shall be made to the appropriate department or agency.

Sec. 12. Executive Order No. 9835 of March 21, 1947, as amended, is hereby revoked.

[Sec. 12 amended by EO 11785 of June 4, 1974, 39 FR 20053, 3 CFR, 1971–1975 Comp., p. 874]

Sec. 13. The Attorney General is requested to render to the heads of departments and agencies such advice as may be requisite to enable them to establish and maintain an appropriate employee-security program.

Sec. 14. (a) The Office of Personnel Management, with the continuing advice and collaboration of representatives of such departments and agencies as the National Security Council may designate, shall make a continuing study of the manner in which this order is being implemented by the departments and agencies of the Government for the purpose of determining:

(1) Deficiencies in the department and agency security programs established under this order which are inconsistent with the interests of, or directly or indirectly weaken, the national security.

(2) Tendencies in such programs to deny to individual employees fair, impartial, and equitable treatment at the hands of the Government, or rights under the Constitution and laws of the United States or this order.

Information affecting any department or agency developed or received during the course of such continuing study shall be furnished immediately to the head of the department or agency concerned. The Office of Personnel Management shall report to the National Security Council, at least semiannually, on the results of such study, shall recommend means to correct any such deficiencies or tendencies, and shall inform the National Security Council immediately of any deficiency which is deemed to be of major importance.

(b) All departments and agencies of the Government are directed to cooperate with the Office of Personnel Management to facilitate the accomplishment of the responsibilities assigned to it by subsection (a) of this section.

(c) To assist the Office of Personnel Management in discharging its responsibilities under this order, the head of each department and agency shall, as soon as possible and in no event later than ninety days after receipt of the final investigative report on a civilian officer or employee subject to a full field investigation under the provisions of this order, advise the Office as to the action taken with respect to such officer or employee. The information furnished by the heads of departments and agencies pursuant to this section shall be included in the reports which the Office of Personnel Management is required to submit to the National Security Council in accordance with subsection (a) of this section. Such reports shall set forth any deficiencies on the part of the heads of departments and agencies in taking timely action under this order, and shall mention specifically any instances of noncompliance with this subsection.

Sec. 15. This order shall become effective thirty days after the date hereof.

SOURCE: http://www.presidency.ucsb.edu/ws/index.php?pid=60589

ANALYSIS

On April 27, 1953, President Dwight D. Eisenhower signed Executive Order 10450: Security Requirements for Government Employment. The order listed "sexual perversion" as a condition for firing a federal employee and for denying employment to potential applicants. The three categories included homosexuality, moral perversion, and Communism—all listed as national security threats. This order stemmed from the public investigation of Republican senator Joseph McCarthy concerning the issue of gay federal employees. Capitalizing on news reports about the connection between morality and Communism, McCarthy claimed that there was a "homosexual underground" which was aiding the Communist conspiracy threat.

In June of 1950, a congressional subcommittee was formed to study the effects of the Truman administration's employment policy concerning homosexuals. After the hearings, the senators argued that homosexuals were a security risk due to the potential blackmail and threat of exposure. The committee concluded that the federal bureaucracy had inadequate procedures to prevent homosexuals from resigning from one federal job and taking up employment in another part of the government. The Civil Service Commission, in response to the committee's recommendations, instructed federal agencies to document the reasons why employees left or lost their federal jobs, including any moral issues that could affect employees' suitability for re-employment. President Eisenhower's order not only made it much more difficult for gays and lesbians to obtain and hold federal employment but also affected civilian government contractors.

The order barred gays and lesbians from 20 percent of the nation's jobs and led to the firing of 1,500 and the resignation of 6,000 federal employees. Many business owners and bureaucrats were so afraid of being accused of protecting "subversives" that they began to quickly dismiss homosexual employees. From 1947 to 1950, dismissals of homosexuals averaged about five per month in civilian government jobs. In 1950, there were 720 dismissals, and in 1955, there were 837 dismissals. Through the late 1950s and 1960s, dismissals lowered to an average of 25 per year. In 1998, President Bill Clinton signed Executive Order 13087, which prohibits discrimination based on sexual orientation in federal employment.

FURTHER READING

Brown, Ralph S., Jr. *Loyalty and Security: Employment Tests in the United States*. New Haven, Conn.: Yale University Press, 1958.

D'Emilio, John. *Sexual Politics, Sexual Communities: The Making of a Homosexual Minority in the United States, 1940–1970*. 1983. 2nd ed. Chicago: University of Chicago Press, 1998.

The Privacy Act of 1974

- ***Document:*** The Privacy Act of 1974, Excerpt
- ***Date:*** December 31, 1974
- ***Where:*** Washington, D.C.
- ***Significance:*** The Privacy Act of 1974 was passed out of the need to protect individuals from illegal surveillance and investigation by federal agencies, a necessity demonstrated by the Watergate scandal. The Watergate scandal uncovered the Nixon administration's use of federal agencies to illegally investigate individuals for political purposes. Not only were records being accessed, but agencies were using illegal surveillance as well.

DOCUMENT

The Privacy Act of 1974

5 U.S.C. § 552a

Conditions of disclosure

No agency shall disclose any record which is contained in a system of records by any means of communication to any person, or to another agency, except pursuant to a written request by, or with the prior written consent of, the individual to whom the record pertains, unless disclosure of the record would be—

(1) to those officers and employees of the agency which maintains the record who have a need for the record in the performance of their duties;
(2) required under section 552 of this title;
(3) for a routine use as defined in subsection (a)(7) of this section and described under subsection (e)(4)(D) of this section;
(4) to the Bureau of the Census for purposes of planning or carrying out a census or survey or related activity pursuant to the provisions of Title 13;

DID YOU KNOW?

President Lyndon B. Johnson Moves to Protect Privacy, 1967

President Johnson included privacy issues in his January 10, 1967, Annual Message to the Congress on the State of the Union. It was significant that a sitting president included the issue of privacy in his annual State of the Union address (which signals an issue as an administration priority), and still more remarkable that Congress should take action to outlaw such practices by the federal government. President Johnson was responding to *Olmstead v. United States,* 277 U.S. 438 (1928), in which Justice Louis D. Brandeis dissented from an opinion upholding the warrantless wiretapping of private telephone conversations. Johnson pushed for a federal law that would ban all wiretapping and electronic eavesdropping, public and private, except in instances in which national security was at stake.

Before he left office, President Johnson signed the Omnibus Crime Control and Safe Streets Act of 1968, which included a ban on all wiretapping and eavesdropping by private parties and also prohibited the sale and distribution of "listening-in" devices in interstate commerce. Johnson was concerned about technological advances that would make it easier for the federal government to watch Americans in their most private domains, such as their homes. Johnson's own comprehensive privacy law never made it to the floor of Congress, but the issue of privacy reemerged years later due to the Watergate scandal.

(5) to a recipient who has provided the agency with advance adequate written assurance that the record will be used solely as a statistical research or reporting record, and the record is to be transferred in a form that is not individually identifiable;

(6) to the National Archives and Records Administration as a record which has sufficient historical or other value to warrant its continued preservation by the United States Government, or for evaluation by the Archivist of the United States or the designee of the Archivist to determine whether the record has such value;

(7) to another agency or to an instrumentality of any governmental jurisdiction within or under the control of the United States for a civil or criminal law enforcement activity if the activity is authorized by law, and if the head of the agency or instrumentality has made a written request to the agency which maintains the record specifying the particular portion desired and the law enforcement activity for which the record is sought;

(8) to a person pursuant to a showing of compelling circumstances affecting the health or safety of an individual if upon such disclosure notification is transmitted to the last known address of such individual;

(9) to either House of Congress, or, to the extent of matter within its jurisdiction, any committee or subcommittee thereof, any joint committee of Congress or subcommittee of any such joint committee;

(10) to the Comptroller General, or any of his authorized representatives, in the course of the performance of the duties of the General Accounting Office;

(11) pursuant to the order of a court of competent jurisdiction; or

(12) to a consumer reporting agency in accordance with section 3711(e) of Title 31.

Accounting of Certain Disclosures

Each agency, with respect to each system of records under its control, shall—

(1) except for disclosures made under subsections (b)(1) or (b)(2) of this section, keep an accurate accounting of—

(A) the date, nature, and purpose of each disclosure of a record to any person or to another agency made under subsection (b) of this section; and

(B) the name and address of the person or agency to whom the disclosure is made;

(2) retain the accounting made under paragraph (1) of this subsection for at least five years or the life of the record, whichever is longer, after the disclosure for which the accounting is made;
(3) except for disclosures made under subsection (b)(7) of this section, make the accounting made under paragraph (1) of this subsection available to the individual named in the record at his request; and
(4) inform any person or other agency about any correction or notation of dispute made by the agency in accordance with subsection (d) of this section of any record that has been disclosed to the person or agency if an accounting of the disclosure was made.

Access to records

Each agency that maintains a system of records shall—

(1) upon request by any individual to gain access to his record or to any information pertaining to him which is contained in the system, permit him and upon his request, a person of his own choosing to accompany him, to review the record and have a copy made of all or any portion thereof in a form comprehensible to him, except that the agency may require the individual to furnish a written statement authorizing discussion of that individual's record in the accompanying person's presence;
(2) permit the individual to request amendment of a record pertaining to him and—

(A) not later than 10 days (excluding Saturdays, Sundays, and legal public holidays) after the date of receipt of such request, acknowledge in writing such receipt; and
(B) promptly, either—

(i) make any correction of any portion thereof which the individual believes is not accurate, relevant, timely, or complete; or
(ii) inform the individual of its refusal to amend the record in accordance with his request, the reason for the refusal, the procedures established by the agency for the individual to request a review of that refusal by the head of the agency or an officer designated by the head of the agency, and the name and business address of that official;

(3) permit the individual who disagrees with the refusal of the agency to amend his record to request a review of such refusal, and not later than 30 days (excluding Saturdays, Sundays, and legal public holidays) from the date on which the individual requests such review, complete such review and make a final determination unless, for good cause shown, the head of the agency extends such 30-day period; and if, after his review, the reviewing official also refuses to amend the record in accordance with the request, permit the individual to file with the agency a concise statement setting forth the reasons for his disagreement with the refusal of the agency, and notify the individual of the provisions for judicial review of the reviewing official's determination under subsection (g)(1)(A) of this section;

(4) in any disclosure, containing information about which the individual has filed a statement of disagreement, occurring after the filing of the statement under paragraph (3) of this subsection, clearly note any portion of the record which is disputed and provide copies of the statement and, if the agency deems it appropriate, copies of a concise statement of the reasons of the agency for not making the amendments requested, to persons or other agencies to whom the disputed record has been disclosed; and
(5) nothing in this section shall allow an individual access to any information compiled in reasonable anticipation of a civil action or proceeding.

Agency requirements

Each agency that maintains a system of records shall—

(1) maintain in its records only such information about an individual as is relevant and necessary to accomplish a purpose of the agency required to be accomplished by statute or by Executive order of the President;
(2) collect information to the greatest extent practicable directly from the subject individual when the information may result in adverse determinations about an individual's rights, benefits, and privileges under Federal programs;
(3) inform each individual whom it asks to supply information, on the form which it uses to collect the information or on a separate form that can be retained by the individual—

   (A) the authority (whether granted by statute, or by Executive order of the President) which authorizes the solicitation of the information and whether disclosure of such information is mandatory or voluntary;
   (B) the principal purpose or purposes for which the information is intended to be used;
   (C) the routine uses which may be made of the information, as published pursuant to paragraph (4)(D) of this subsection; and
   (D) the effects on him, if any, of not providing all or any part of the requested information;

(4) subject to the provisions of paragraph (11) of this subsection, publish in the Federal Register upon establishment or revision a notice of the existence and character of the system of records, which notice shall include—

   (A) the name and location of the system;
   (B) the categories of individuals on whom records are maintained in the system;
   (C) the categories of records maintained in the system;
   (D) each routine use of the records contained in the system, including the categories of users and the purpose of such use;
   (E) the policies and practices of the agency regarding storage, retrievability, access controls, retention, and disposal of the records;
   (F) the title and business address of the agency official who is responsible for the system of records;
   (G) the agency procedures whereby an individual can be notified at his request if the system of records contains a record pertaining to him;

(H) the agency procedures whereby an individual can be notified at his request how he can gain access to any record pertaining to him contained in the system of records, and how he can contest its content; and
(I) the categories of sources of records in the system;

(5) maintain all records which are used by the agency in making any determination about any individual with such accuracy, relevance, timeliness, and completeness as is reasonably necessary to assure fairness to the individual in the determination;
(6) prior to disseminating any record about an individual to any person other than an agency, unless the dissemination is made pursuant to subsection (b)(2) of this section, make reasonable efforts to assure that such records are accurate, complete, timely, and relevant for agency purposes;
(7) maintain no record describing how any individual exercises rights guaranteed by the First Amendment unless expressly authorized by statute or by the individual about whom the record is maintained or unless pertinent to and within the scope of an authorized law enforcement activity;
(8) make reasonable efforts to serve notice on an individual when any record on such individual is made available to any person under compulsory legal process when such process becomes a matter of public record;
(9) establish rules of conduct for persons involved in the design, development, operation, or maintenance of any system of records, or in maintaining any record, and instruct each such person with respect to such rules and the requirements of this section, including any other rules and procedures adopted pursuant to this section and the penalties for noncompliance;
(10) establish appropriate administrative, technical and physical safeguards to insure the security and confidentiality of records and to protect against any anticipated threats or hazards to their security or integrity which could result in substantial harm, embarrassment, inconvenience, or unfairness to any individual on whom information is maintained;
(11) at least 30 days prior to publication of information under paragraph (4)(D) of this subsection, publish in the Federal Register notice of any new use or intended use of the information in the system, and provide an opportunity for interested persons to submit written data, views, or arguments to the agency; and
(12) if such agency is a recipient agency or a source agency in a matching program with a non-Federal agency, with respect to any establishment or revision of a matching program, at least 30 days prior to conducting such program, publish in the Federal Register notice of such establishment or revision.

Agency rules

In order to carry out the provisions of this section, each agency that maintains a system of records shall promulgate rules, in accordance with the requirements (including general notice) of section 553 of this title, which shall—

(1) establish procedures whereby an individual can be notified in response to his request if any system of records named by the individual contains a record pertaining to him;

(2) define reasonable times, places, and requirements for identifying an individual who requests his record or information pertaining to him before the agency shall make the record or information available to the individual;
(3) establish procedures for the disclosure to an individual upon his request of his record or information pertaining to him, including special procedure, if deemed necessary, for the disclosure to an individual of medical records, including psychological records, pertaining to him;
(4) establish procedures for reviewing a request from an individual concerning the amendment of any record or information pertaining to the individual, for making a determination on the request, for an appeal within the agency of an initial adverse agency determination, and for whatever additional means may be necessary for each individual to be able to exercise fully his rights under this section; and
(5) establish fees to be charged, if any, to any individual for making copies of his record, excluding the cost of any search for and review of the record.

The Office of the Federal Register shall biennially compile and publish the rules promulgated under this subsection and agency notices published under subsection (e)(4) of this section in a form available to the public at low cost.

SOURCE: http://privacy.defense.gov/files/pa1974.pdf

ANALYSIS

There are three primary sources of privacy protection in the United States. They include the common law of torts, federal and state statutes, and constitutions. The common law is based on judicial precedents from the 12th and 13th centuries in England that are applied to present-day legal conflicts. State constitutions vary in their protections of privacy and only apply to residents of their home states. Federal and state legislatures have adopted an "ad hoc" approach to safeguarding privacy, partially because the federal Constitution does not explicitly guarantee this right. Even though the Court has since held that a right to privacy is implicit in the Bill of Rights, the absence of a concrete, broad privacy right has led to continued government abuse.

Federal and state laws addressing privacy are a hodgepodge of unsystematic and inconsistent protections; they are usually codified after a crisis or public outcry leads to broad bipartisan support. One problem with a fragmented legislative response from both the state and federal level is that it may require continual updates to be enacted each time a new technology is enhanced or developed. A second problem involves the loopholes provided in the language of the laws. For example, the Privacy Act of 1974 requires federal agencies to collect information only from the individuals implicated, to maintain complete records, provide access for review and correction, and to establish procedures to ensure the privacy and accuracy of the information. A system of records is defined as a group of records under the control of an agency from which information is retrieved by the name of the individual or by some identifier assigned to the individual.

The effectiveness of the act is diminished because it allows for disclosure of any data requested by another government agency for "routine use." In a closely related exception, information can also be given out to other parties without prior consent if used in conjunction with law enforcement. This would also relate to terrorist activities broadly defined by the government. These broad exceptions diminish the impact of the act and highlight the fundamental problems associated with legislative responses to information privacy. The act was passed in response to the Watergate scandal and the fear that the executive branch was expanding its power beyond what was proscribed by the Constitution and yet has been unable to prevent the current administration from expanding surveillance programs against its own citizens.

The Freedom of Information Act (FOIA) extended the protection provided by the Privacy Act of 1974 by controlling the dissemination of information stored in federal data banks. The FOIA applies to documents held by government agencies within the executive branch of the federal government, including the Executive Office of the President, and independent regulatory agencies such as the Federal Commissions and the Securities Exchange Commission. The FOIA makes agency records available to the general public upon request and shifts the burden of nondisclosure to the government. However, similar to the Privacy Act, the FOIA does not include records maintained by state or local government, by the courts or by Congress. FOIA also has nine related statutory exemptions that agencies can use to deny requests or redact portions of documents, including privileged or confidential trade secrets or commercial or financial information. The Privacy Act does not generally apply to records maintained by state and local governments or private companies or organizations. This is why the absence of a concrete, broad privacy right has led to continued government abuse.

FURTHER READING

Alderman, Ellen, and Caroline Kennedy, *The Right to Privacy*. New York: Vintage Books, 1995.

Gavison, Ruth, "Privacy and the Limits of Law." *Yale Law Journal* 89 (1980).

Westin, Alan, *Privacy and Freedom*. New York: Atheneum, 1967.

The Foreign Intelligence Surveillance Act of 1978

- ***Document:*** The Foreign Intelligence Surveillance Act of 1978, Excerpt
- ***Date:*** October 25, 1978
- ***Where:*** Washington, D.C.
- ***Significance:*** This act prescribes procedures for requesting judicial authorization for electronic surveillance and physical search of persons engaged in espionage or international terrorism against the United States on behalf of a foreign power.

DOCUMENT

The Foreign Intelligence Surveillance Act of 1978

An Act

To authorize electronic surveillance to obtain foreign intelligence information.

Be it enacted by the Senate and House of Representatives of the United States of America in Congress assembled

Title 50—Electronic Surveillance Within The United States For Foreign Intelligence Purposes

Sec. 1802. Authorization for Electronic Surveillance for Foreign Intelligence Purposes.

(a)(1) Notwithstanding any other law, the President, through the Attorney General, may authorize electronic surveillance without a court order under this title to acquire foreign intelligence information for periods of up to one year if the Attorney General certifies in writing under oath that—

(A) the electronic surveillance is solely directed at—

(i) the acquisition of the contents of communications transmitted by means of communications used exclusively between or among foreign powers, as defined in section 101(a)(1), (2), or (3); or

(ii) the acquisition of technical intelligence, other than the spoken communications of individuals, from property or premises under the open and exclusive control of a foreign power, as defined in section 101(a)(1), (2), or (3);

(B) there is no substantial likelihood that the surveillance will acquire the contents of any communication to which a United States person is a party; and

(C) the proposed minimization procedures with respect to such surveillance meet the definition of minimization procedures under section 101(h); and

if the Attorney General reports such minimization procedures and any changes thereto to the House Permanent Select Committee on Intelligence and the Senate Select Committee on Intelligence at least thirty days prior to their effective date, unless the Attorney General determines immediate action is required and notifies the committees immediately of such minimization procedures and the reason for their becoming effective immediately.

(2) An electronic surveillance authorized by this subsection may be conducted only in accordance with the Attorney General's certification and the minimization procedures adopted by him. The Attorney General shall assess compliance with such procedures and shall report such assessments to the House Permanent Select Committee on Intelligence and the Senate Select Committee on Intelligence under the provisions of section 108(a).

(3) The Attorney General shall immediately transmit under seal to the court established under section 103(a) a copy of his certification. Such certification shall be maintained under security

DID YOU KNOW?

The Second Restatement of Torts 1977

A tort is a civil wrong for which an action for damages may be brought. Restatements of the Law provide a clear and concise account of the rules of common law in various legal fields such as contracts and torts. They are written by eminent legal scholars to summarize and restate the common law. Restatements are often cited by the courts and therefore can be cited to, with care, for their persuasive value.

This second restatement includes the four common law privacy torts including: intrusion upon seclusion, appropriation of another's name or likeness, unreasonable publicity given to the other's private life, and publicity that unreasonably places the other in a false light before the public. The common law reflects the longstanding historical usages and customs that have protected individuals and their property in our society. These common law privacy torts are remedies that can only be applied to a private actor. However, these torts have been used in a limited fashion against companies that release information to law enforcement. Even this usage is limited because these torts are not accepted use in every state making it difficult for individuals to utilize these protections in any organized way.

Second, three of these four privacy torts require publication of some allegedly private matter to give rise to a cause of action. The intrusion upon seclusion tort, however, does not require a publication to be actionable and is most relevant to this inquiry concerning privacy and security. The Restatement (Second) of Torts § 652B defines the tort of intrusion upon seclusion in the following manner: One who intentionally intrudes, physically or otherwise, upon the solitude or seclusion of another or his private affairs or concerns, is subject to liability to the other for invasion of his privacy, if the intrusion would be highly offensive to a reasonable person. The FBI and other law enforcement officials might not be violating the Restatement by gathering information on terrorist suspects as long as their activity is deemed reasonable. This makes it difficult to assert that actions of the FBI are unreasonable when they are tracking down potential terrorists and working for the greater security and protection of all Americans. These common law actions have been used with limited success when relating to information privacy.

measures established by the Chief Justice with the concurrence of the Attorney General, in consultation with the Director of Central Intelligence, and shall remain sealed unless—

(A) an application for a court order with respect to the surveillance is made under sections 101(h)(4) and 104; or
(B) the certification is necessary to determine the legality of the surveillance under section 106(f).

(4) With respect to electronic surveillance authorized by this subsection, the Attorney General may direct a specified communication common carrier to—

(A) furnish all information, facilities, or technical assistance necessary to accomplish the electronic surveillance in such a manner as will protect its secrecy and produce a minimum of interference with the services that such carrier is providing its customers; and
(B) maintain under security procedures approved by the Attorney General and the Director of Central Intelligence any records concerning the surveillance or the aid furnished which such carrier wishes to retain.

The Government shall compensate, at the prevailing rate, such carrier for furnishing such aid.

(b) Applications for a court order under this title are authorized if the President has, by written authorization, empowered the Attorney General to approve applications to the court having jurisdiction under section 103, and a judge to whom an application is made may, notwithstanding any other law, grant an order, in conformity with section 105, approving electronic surveillance of a foreign power or an agent of a foreign power for the purpose of obtaining foreign intelligence information, except that the court shall not have jurisdiction to grant any order approving electronic surveillance directed solely as described in paragraph (1)(A) of subsection (a) unless such surveillance may involve the acquisition of communications of any United States person.

Sec. 1803. Designation of Judges.

(a) The Chief Justice of the United States shall publicly designate seven district court judges from seven of the United States judicial circuits who shall constitute a court which shall have jurisdiction to hear applications for and grant orders approving electronic surveillance anywhere within the United States under the procedures set forth in this Act, except that no judge designated under this subsection shall hear the same application for electronic surveillance under this Act which has been denied previously by another judge designated under this subsection. If any judge so designated denies an application for an order authorizing electronic surveillance under this Act, such judge shall provide immediately for the record a written statement of each reason of his decision and, on motion of the United States, the record shall be transmitted, under seal, to the court of review established in subsection (b).

(b) The Chief Justice shall publicly designate three judges, one of whom shall be publicly designated as the presiding judge, from the United States district courts or courts of appeals who together shall comprise a court of review which shall have jurisdiction to review the denial of any application made under this Act. If such court determines that the application was properly denied, the court shall immediately provide for the record a written statement of each reason for its decision and, on petition of the United States for a writ of certiorari, the record shall be transmitted under seal to the Supreme Court, which shall have jurisdiction to review such decision.

(c) Proceedings under this Act shall be conducted as expeditiously as possible. The record of proceedings under this Act, including applications made and orders granted, shall be maintained under security measures established by the Chief Justice in consultation with the Attorney General and the Director of Central Intelligence.

(d) Each judge designated under this section shall so serve for a maximum of seven years and shall not be eligible for redesignation, except that the judges first designated under subsection (a) shall be designated for terms of from one to seven years so that one term expires each year, and that judges first designated under subsection (b) shall be designated for terms of three, five, and seven years.

Sec. 1804. Application for an Order.

(a) Each application for an order approving electronic surveillance under this title shall be made by a Federal officer in writing upon oath or affirmation to a judge having jurisdiction under section 103. Each application shall require the approval of the Attorney General based upon his finding that it satisfies the criteria and requirements of such application as set forth in this title. It shall include—

(1) the identity of the Federal officer making the application;

(2) the authority conferred on the Attorney General by the President of the United States and the approval of the Attorney General to make the application;

(3) the identity, if known, or a description of the specific target of the electronic surveillance;

(4) a statement of the facts and circumstances relied upon by the applicant to justify his belief that—

(A) the target of the electronic surveillance is a foreign power or an agent of a foreign power; and

(B) each of the facilities or places at which the electronic surveillance is directed is being used, or is about to be used, by a foreign power or an agent of a foreign power;

(5) a statement of the proposed minimization procedures;

(6) a detailed description of the nature of the information sought and the type of communications or activities to be subjected to the surveillance;

(7) a certification or certifications by the Assistant to the President for National Security Affairs or an executive branch official or officials designated by the President from among those executive officers employed in the area of national security or defense and appointed by the President with the advice and consent of the Senate—

(A) that the certifying official deems the information sought to be foreign intelligence information;

(B) that a significant purpose of the surveillance is to obtain foreign intelligence information;

(C) that such information cannot reasonably be obtained by normal investigative techniques;

(D) that designates the type of foreign intelligence information being sought according to the categories described in section 101(e); and

(E) including a statement of the basis for the certification that—

(i) the information sought is the type of foreign intelligence information designated; and

(ii) such information cannot reasonably be obtained by normal investigative techniques;

(8) a statement of the means by which the surveillance will be effected and a statement whether physical entry is required to effect the surveillance;

(9) a statement of the facts concerning all previous applications that have been made to any judge under this title involving any of the persons, facilities, or places specified in the application, and the action taken on each previous application;

(10) a statement of the period of time for which the electronic surveillance is required to be maintained, and if the nature of the intelligence gathering is such that the approval of the use of electronic surveillance under this title should not automatically terminate when the described type of information has first been obtained, a description of facts supporting the belief that additional information of the same type will be obtained thereafter; and

(11) whenever more than one electronic, mechanical or other surveillance device is to be used with respect to a particular proposed electronic surveillance, the coverage of the devices involved and what minimization procedures apply to information acquired by each device.

(b) Whenever the target of the electronic surveillance is a foreign power, as defined in section 101 (a)(1), (2), or (3), and each of the facilities or places at which the surveillance is directed is owned, leased, or exclusively used by that foreign power, the application need not contain the information required by paragraphs (6), (7)(E), (8), and (11) of subsection (a), but shall state whether physical entry is required to effect the surveillance and shall contain such information about the surveillance techniques and communications or other information concerning United States persons likely to be obtained as may be necessary to assess the proposed minimization procedures.

(c) The Attorney General may require any other affidavit or certification from any other officer in connection with the application.

(d) The judge may require the applicant to furnish such other information as may be necessary to make the determinations required by section 105.

Sec. 1805. Issuance of an Order.

(a) Upon an application made pursuant to section 104, the judge shall enter an ex parte order as requested or as modified approving the electronic surveillance if he finds that—

(1) the President has authorized the Attorney General to approve applications for electronic surveillance for foreign intelligence information;

(2) the application has been made by a Federal officer and approved by the Attorney General;

(3) on the basis of the facts submitted by the applicant there is probable cause to believe that—

(A) the target of the electronic surveillance is a foreign power or an agent of a foreign power: *Provided,* That no United States person may be considered a foreign power or an agent of a foreign power solely upon the basis of activities protected by the first amendment to the Constitution of the United States; and

(B) each of the facilities or places at which the electronic surveillance is directed is being used, or is about to be used, by a foreign power or an agent of a foreign power;

(4) the proposed minimization procedures meet the definition of minimization procedures under section 101(h); and

(5) the application which has been filed contains all statements and certifications required by section 104 and, if the target is a United States person, the certification or certifications are not clearly erroneous on the basis of the statement made under section 104(a)(7)(E) and any other information furnished under section 104(d).

(b) An order approving an electronic surveillance under this section shall—

(1) specify—

(A) the identity, if known, or a description of the specific target of the electronic surveillance;

(B) the nature and location of each of the facilities or places at which the electronic surveillance will be directed;

(C) the type of information sought to be acquired and the type of communications or activities to be subjected to the surveillance;
(D) the means by which the electronic surveillance will be effected and whether physical entry will be used to effect the surveillance;
(E) the period of time during which the electronic surveillance is approved; and
(F) whenever more than one electronic, mechanical, or other surveillance device is to be used under the order, the authorized coverage of the devices involved and what minimization procedures shall apply to information subject to acquisition by each device; and

(2) direct—

(A) that the minimization procedures be followed;
(B) that, upon the request of the applicant, a specified communication or other common carrier, landlord, custodian, or other specified person furnish the applicant forthwith all information, facilities, or technical assistance necessary to accomplish the electronic surveillance in such a manner as will protect its secrecy and produce a minimum of interference with the services that such carrier, landlord, custodian, or other person is providing that target of electronic surveillance;
(C) that such carrier, landlord, custodian, or other person maintain under security procedures approved by the Attorney General and the Director of Central Intelligence any records concerning the surveillance or the aid furnished that such person wishes to retain; and
(D) that the applicant compensate, at the prevailing rate, such carrier, landlord, custodian, or other person for furnishing such aid.

(c) Whenever the target of the electronic surveillance is a foreign power, as defined in section 101(a)(1), (2), or (3), and each of the facilities or places at which the surveillance is directed is owned, leased, or exclusively used by that foreign power, the order need not contain the information required by subparagraphs (C), (D), and (F) of subsection (b)(1), but shall generally describe the information sought, the communications or activities to be subjected to the surveillance, and the type of electronic surveillance involved, including whether physical entry is required.

(d) (1) An order issued under this section may approve an electronic surveillance for the period necessary to achieve its purpose, or for ninety days, whichever is less, except that an order under this section shall approve an electronic surveillance targeted against a foreign power, as defined in section 101(a)(1), (2), or (3), for the period specified in the application or for one year, whichever is less.
(2) Extensions of an order issued under this title may be granted on the same basis as an original order upon an application for an extension and new findings made in the same manner as required for an

original order, except that an extension of an order under this Act for a surveillance targeted against a foreign power, as defined in section 101(a)(5) or (6), or against a foreign power as defined in section 101(a)(4) that is not a United States person, may be for a period not to exceed one year if the judge finds probable cause to believe that no communication of any individual United States person will be acquired during the period.

(3) At or before the end of the period of time for which electronic surveillance is approved by an order or an extension, the judge may assess compliance with the minimization procedures by reviewing the circumstances under which information concerning United States persons was acquired, retained, or disseminated.

(e) Notwithstanding any other provision of this title, when the Attorney General reasonably determines that—

(1) an emergency situation exists with respect to the employment of electronic surveillance to obtain foreign intelligence information before an order authorizing such surveillance can with due diligence be obtained; and

(2) the factual basis for issuance of an order under this subchapter to approve such surveillance exists;

he may authorize the emergency employment of electronic surveillance if a judge having jurisdiction under section 108 is informed by the Attorney General or his designee at the time of such authorization that the decision has been made to employ emergency electronic surveillance and if an application in accordance with this title is made to that judge as soon as practicable, but not more than twenty-four hours after the Attorney General authorizes such surveillance. If the Attorney General authorizes such emergency employment of electronic surveillance, he shall require that the minimization procedures required by this title for the issuance of a judicial order be followed. In the absence of a judicial order approving such electronic surveillance, the surveillance shall terminate when the information sought is obtained, when the application for the order is denied, or after the expiration of twenty-four hours from the time of authorization by the Attorney General, whichever is earliest. In the event that such application for approval is denied, or in any other case where the electronic surveillance is terminated and no order is issued approving the surveillance, no information obtained or evidence derived from such surveillance shall be received in evidence or otherwise disclosed in any trial, hearing, or other proceeding in or before any court, grand jury, department, office, agency, regulatory body, legislative committee, or other authority of the United States, a State, or political subdivision thereof, and no information concerning any United States person acquired from such surveillance shall subsequently be used or disclosed in any other manner by Federal officers or employees without the consent of such person, except with the approval of the Attorney General if the information indicates a threat of death or serious bodily harm to any person. A denial of the application made under this subsection may be reviewed as provided in section 103.

(f) Notwithstanding any other provision of this subchapter, officers, employees, or agents of the United States are authorized in the normal course of their official duties to conduct electronic surveillance not targeted against the communications of any particular person or persons, under procedures approved by the Attorney General, solely to—

(1) test the capability of electronic equipment, if—

(A) it is not reasonable to obtain the consent of the persons incidentally subjected to the surveillance;
(B) the test is limited in extent and duration to that necessary to determine the capability of the equipment;
(C) the contents of any communication acquired are retained and used only for the purpose of determining the capability of the equipment, are disclosed only to test personnel, and are destroyed before or immediately upon completion of the test; and:
(D) *Provided*, That the test may exceed ninety days only with the prior approval of the Attorney General;

(2) determine the existence and capability of electronic surveillance equipment being used by persons not authorized to conduct electronic surveillance, if—

(A) it is not reasonable to obtain the consent of persons incidentally subjected to the surveillance;
(B) such electronic surveillance is limited in extent and duration to that necessary to determine the existence and capability of such equipment; and
(C) any information acquired by such surveillance is used only to enforce chapter 119 of title 18, United States Code, or section 605 of the Communications Act of 1934, or to protect information from unauthorized surveillance; or

(3) train intelligence personnel in the use of electronic surveillance equipment, if—

(A) it is not reasonable to—

(i) obtain the consent of the persons incidentally subjected to the surveillance;
(ii) train persons in the course of surveillances otherwise authorized by this title; or
(iii) train persons in the use of such equipment without engaging in electronic surveillance;

(B) such electronic surveillance is limited in extent and duration to that necessary to train the personnel in the use of the equipment; and

(C) no contents of any communication acquired are retained or disseminated for any purpose, but are destroyed as soon as reasonably possible.

(g) Certifications made by the Attorney General pursuant to section 102(a) and applications made and orders granted under this title shall be retained for a period of at least ten years from the date of the certification or application.

Sec. 1806. Use of Information.

(a) Information acquired from an electronic surveillance conducted pursuant to this title concerning any United States person may be used and disclosed by Federal officers and employees without the consent of the United States person only in accordance with the minimization procedures required by this title. No otherwise privileged communication obtained in accordance with, or in violation of, the provisions of this title shall lose its privileged character. No information acquired from an electronic surveillance pursuant to this title may be used or disclosed by Federal officers or employees except for lawful purposes.

(b) No information acquired pursuant to this title shall be disclosed for law enforcement purposes unless such disclosure is accompanied by a statement that such information, or any information derived therefrom, may only be used in a criminal proceeding with the advance authorization of the Attorney General.

(c) Whenever the Government intends to enter into evidence or otherwise use or disclose in any trial, hearing, or other proceeding in or before any court, department, officer, agency, regulatory body, or other authority of the United States, against an aggrieved person, any information obtained or derived from an electronic surveillance of that aggrieved person pursuant to the authority of this title, the Government shall, prior to the trial, hearing, or other proceeding or at a reasonable time prior to an effort to so disclose or so use that information or submit it in evidence, notify the aggrieved person and the court or other authority in which the information is to be disclosed or used that the Government intends to so disclose or so use such information.

(d) Whenever any State or political subdivision thereof intends to enter into evidence or otherwise use or disclose in any trial, hearing, or other proceeding in or before any court, department, officer, agency, regulatory body, or other authority of a State or a political subdivision thereof, against an aggrieved person any information obtained or derived from an electronic surveillance of that aggrieved person pursuant to the authority of this title, the State or political subdivision thereof shall notify the aggrieved person, the court or other authority in which the information is to be disclosed or used, and the Attorney General that the State or political subdivision thereof intends to so disclose or so use such information.

(e) Any person against whom evidence obtained or derived from an electronic surveillance to which he is an aggrieved person is to be, or has been, introduced or otherwise used or disclosed in any trial, hearing, or other proceeding in or before any court, department, officer, agency, regulatory body, or other authority of the United States, a State, or a political subdivision thereof, may move to suppress the evidence obtained or derived from such electronic surveillance on the grounds that—

(1) the information was unlawfully acquired; or
(2) the surveillance was not made in conformity with an order of authorization or approval.

Such a motion shall be made before the trial, hearing, or other proceeding unless there was no opportunity to make such a motion or the person was not aware of the grounds of the motion.

(f) Whenever a court or other authority is notified pursuant to subsection (c) or (d) of this section, or whenever a motion is made pursuant to subsection (e), or whenever any motion or request is made by an aggrieved person pursuant to any other statute or rule of the United States or any State before any court or other authority of the United States or any State to discover or obtain applications or orders or other materials relating to electronic surveillance or to discover, obtain, or suppress evidence or information obtained or derived from electronic surveillance under this Act, the United States district court or, where the motion is made before another authority, the United States district court in the same district as the authority, shall, notwithstanding any other law, if the Attorney General files an affidavit under oath that disclosure or an adversary hearing would harm the national security of the United States, review in camera and ex parte the application, order, and such other materials relating to the surveillance as may be necessary to determine whether the surveillance of the aggrieved person was lawfully authorized and conducted. In making this determination, the court may disclose to the aggrieved person, under appropriate security procedures and protective orders, portions of the application, order, or other materials relating to the surveillance only where such disclosure is necessary to make an accurate determination of the legality of the surveillance.

(g) If the United States district court pursuant to subsection (f) determines that the surveillance was not lawfully authorized or conducted, it shall, in accordance with the requirements of law, suppress the evidence which was unlawfully obtained or derived from electronic surveillance of the aggrieved person or otherwise grant the motion of the aggrieved person. If the court determines that the surveillance was lawfully authorized and conducted, it shall deny the motion of the aggrieved person except to the extent that due process requires discovery or disclosure.

(h) Orders granting motions or requests under subsection (g), decisions under this section that electronic surveillance was not lawfully authorized or conducted, and orders of the United States district court requiring review or granting disclosure of applications, orders, or other materials relating to a surveillance shall be final orders and binding upon all courts of the United States and the several States except a United States court of appeals and the Supreme Court.

(i) In circumstances involving the unintentional acquisition by an electronic, mechanical, or other surveillance device of the contents of any radio communication, under circumstances in which a person has a reasonable expectation of privacy and a warrant would be required for law enforcement purposes, and if both the sender and all intended recipients are located within the United States, such contents shall be destroyed upon recognition, unless the Attorney General determines that the contents indicate a threat of death or serious bodily harm to any person.

(j) If an emergency employment of electronic surveillance is authorized under section 105(e) [1] and a subsequent order approving the surveillance is not obtained, the judge shall cause to be served on any United States person named in the application and on such other United States persons subject to electronic surveillance as the judge may determine in his discretion it is in the interest of justice to serve, notice of—

  (1) the fact of the application;
  (2) the period of the surveillance; and
  (3) the fact that during the period information was or was not obtained.

  On an ex parte showing of good cause to the judge the serving of the notice required by this subsection may be postponed or suspended for a period not to exceed ninety days. Thereafter, on a further ex parte showing of good cause, the court shall forego ordering the serving of the notice required under this subsection.

Sec. 1807. Report of Electronic Surveillance.

In April of each year, the Attorney General shall transmit to the Administrative Office of the United States Court and to Congress a report setting forth with respect to the preceding calendar year—

(a) the total number of applications made for orders and extensions of orders approving electronic surveillance under this title; and
(b) the total number of such orders and extensions either granted, modified, or denied.

Sec. 1808. Congressional Oversight.

(a) On a semiannual basis the Attorney General shall fully inform the House Permanent Select Committee on Intelligence and the Senate Select Committee on Intelligence, and the Committee on the Judiciary of the Senate, concerning all electronic surveillance under this title. Nothing in this title shall be deemed to limit the authority and responsibility of the appropriate committees of each House of Congress to obtain such information as they may need to carry out their respective functions and duties.

(b) On or before one year after the effective date of this Act and on the same day each year for four years thereafter, the Permanent Select Committee on Intelligence and the Senate Select Committee on Intelligence shall report respectively to the House of Representatives and the Senate, concerning the implementation of this Act. Said reports shall include but not be limited to an analysis and recommendations concerning whether this chapter should be

(1) amended,
(2) repealed, or
(3) permitted to continue in effect without amendment.

Sec. 1809. Criminal Sanctions.

(a) OFFENSE.—

A person is guilty of an offense if he intentionally—

(1) engages in electronic surveillance under color of law except as authorized by statute; or
(2) discloses or uses information obtained under color of law by electronic surveillance, knowing or having reason to know that the information was obtained through electronic surveillance not authorized by statute.

(b) DEFENSE.—

It is a defense to a prosecution under subsection (a) that the defendant was a law enforcement or investigative officer engaged in the course of his official duties and the electronic surveillance was authorized by and conducted pursuant to a search warrant or court order of a court of competent jurisdiction.

(c) PENALTY.—

An offense described in this section is punishable by a fine of not more than $10,000 or imprisonment for not more than five years, or both.

(d) JURISDICTION.—

There is Federal jurisdiction over an offense under this section if the person committing the offense was an officer or employee of the United States at the time the offense was committed.

Sec. 1810. Civil Liability.

CIVIL ACTION.—

An aggrieved person, other than a foreign power or an agent of a foreign power, as defined in section 101(a) or (b)(1)(A), respectively, who has been subjected to an electronic surveillance or about whom information obtained by electronic surveillance of such person has been disclosed or used in violation of section 109 shall have a cause of action against any person who committed such violation and shall be entitled to recover—

(a) actual damages, but not less than liquidated damages of $1,000 or $100 per day for each day of violation, whichever is greater;
(b) punitive damages; and
(c) reasonable attorney's fees and other investigation and litigation costs reasonably incurred.

Sec. 1811. Authorization During Time of War.
Notwithstanding any other law, the President, through the Attorney General, may authorize electronic surveillance without a court order under this title to acquire foreign intelligence information for a period not to exceed fifteen calendar days following a declaration of war by the Congress.

Approved October 25, 1978.

SOURCE: http://www.law.cornell.edu/uscode/html/uscode50/usc_sec_50_00001802----000-.html

---

ANALYSIS

The Foreign Intelligence Surveillance Act (FISA) as passed in 1978, provided a statutory framework for the use of electronic surveillance in the context of foreign intelligence gathering. FISA created two courts with special jurisdiction: the Foreign Intelligence Surveillance Court (FISC) and the Foreign Intelligence Surveillance Court of Review (FISCR). Until 2002, the FISC had never published an opinion, and the FICSR had never convened. Under (FISA), the National Security Agency (NSA) is limited to targeting communications of a person within the United States if a federal judge finds probable cause to believe that the individual is an agent of a foreign power. For example, a judge may determine that an American citizen is an agent of a foreign power only if there is information supporting a finding that the individual is a terrorist or someone who aids and abets terrorists.

The act also allowed the Federal Bureau of Investigations (FBI) to conduct surveillance and secret searches to gather foreign intelligence information without probable cause that an individual was engaged in criminal activity. To obtain a FISA warrant, law enforcement had to demonstrate that the primary purpose of an investigation was to collect foreign intelligence. A provision of the PATRIOT Act exempts a number of searches conducted pursuant to the "war on terror" from the probable cause requirement. It gives the government leeway to intercept, without warrants, communications between foreigners that are routed through equipment in the United States, provided that "foreign intelligence information" is at stake. Normally, the Fourth Amendment prohibits the government from conducting searches without probable cause to believe that an individual is engaged in criminal activity or possesses evidence of a crime. The PATRIOT Act waives that requirement when the government demonstrates the investigation has a "significant" foreign intelligence purpose. These vague guidelines effectively allowed the FBI to circumvent the Fourth Amendment's requirement that warrants be issued upon probable cause. The Bush administration was criticized as a result.

Subsequent legislation expanded federal laws dealing with foreign intelligence gathering to address physical searches, pen registers, trap and trace devices, and access to certain business records. The USA PATRIOT Act made significant changes to some of these provisions. This law removes some surveillance from the limited FISA court review, allows the government to create more surveillance programs with limited judicial review, and immunizes telecommunications companies who participate in these programs from lawsuits. The PATRIOT Act also allows the use of a pen register and trap and trace orders to Internet-based communications. Applications for the installation and use of such devices must be made by the attorney general or a designated attorney for the government and must include the applicant's certification that the information likely to be produced through the use is relevant to an ongoing investigation to protect against international terrorism or clandestine intelligence activities. This new authority extends not only to the tracking of telephone calls but also to the tracking of any form of electronic communication, such as e-mails. The government does not need to establish probable cause and judges are required to approve all reasonable requests. The law also provides a legal framework for much of the surveillance without warrants that was being conducted in secret by the NSA and initiated by the Bush administration.

FISA has since its enactment been a bold and productive tool in this country's fight against the efforts of foreign governments and their agents to engage in intelligence gathering aimed at the U.S. government, either to ascertain its future policy or to effect its current policy, to acquire proprietary information not publicly available, or to engage in disinformation efforts. With the enactment of the USA PATRIOT Act FISA has been expanded and broadened to make it a useful tool in exposing and combating foreign terrorist groups' efforts to target the United States but this might further undermine our civil liberties.

FURTHER READING

Birkenstock, Gregory E. "The Foreign Intelligence Surveillance Act and Standards of Probable Cause: An Alternative Analysis." *Georgetown Law Journal* 80 (February 1992): 843–71.

Chiarella, Louis A., and Michael A. Newton. "'So Judge, How Do I Get That FISA Warrant?': The Policy and Procedure for Conducting Electronic Surveillance." *Army Lawyer* (October 1997): 25–36.

The Communications Assistance for Law Enforcement Act, 1994

- ***Document:*** The Communications Assistance for Law Enforcement Act (CALEA)
- ***Date:*** October 25, 1994
- ***Where:*** Washington, D.C.
- ***Significance:*** CALEA was passed to preserve the ability of law enforcement agencies to conduct electronic surveillance by requiring that telecommunications carriers and manufacturers of telecommunications equipment modify and design their equipment, facilities, and services to ensure that they have the necessary surveillance capabilities to continue to protect national security.

DOCUMENT

Communications Assistance for Law Enforcement Act.

47 USC §1001, CALEA §102 Sec. 1001. Definitions

For purposes of this chapter—

(1) The terms defined in section 2510 of title 18 have, respectively, the meanings stated in that section.
(2) The term "call-identifying information" means dialing or signaling information that identifies the origin, direction, destination, or termination of each communication generated or received by a subscriber by means of any equipment, facility, or service of a telecommunications carrier.
(3) The term "Commission" means the Federal Communications Commission.
(4) The term "electronic messaging services" means software-based services that enable the sharing of data, images, sound, writing, or other information among computing devices controlled by the senders or recipients of the messages.

(5) The term "government" means the government of the United States and any agency or instrumentality thereof, the District of Columbia, any commonwealth, territory, or possession of the United States, and any State or political subdivision thereof authorized by law to conduct electronic surveillance.

(6) The term "information services"—

 (A) means the offering of a capability for generating, acquiring, storing, transforming, processing, retrieving, utilizing, or making available information via telecommunications; and

 (B) includes—

  (i) a service that permits a customer to retrieve stored information from, or file information for storage in, information storage facilities;

  (ii) electronic publishing; and

  (iii) electronic messaging services; but

 (C) does not include any capability for a telecommunications carrier's internal management, control, or operation of its telecommunications network.

(7) The term "telecommunications support services" means a product, software, or service used by a telecommunications carrier for the internal signaling or switching functions of its telecommunications network.

(8) The term "telecommunications carrier"—

 (A) means a person or entity engaged in the transmission or switching of wire or electronic communications as a common carrier for hire; and

 (B) includes—

  (i) a person or entity engaged in providing commercial mobile service (as defined in section 332(d) of this title); or

  (ii) a person or entity engaged in providing wire or electronic communication switching or transmission service to the extent that the Commission finds that such service is a replacement for a substantial portion of the local telephone exchange service and that it is in the public interest to deem such a person or entity to be a telecommunications carrier for purposes of this chapter; but

 (C) does not include—

  (i) persons or entities insofar as they are engaged in providing information services; and

  (ii) any class or category of telecommunications carriers that the Commission exempts by rule after consultation with the Attorney General.

Sec. 1002. Assistance capability requirements

(a) Capability requirements

Except as provided in subsections (b), (c), and (d) of this section and sections 1007(a) and 1008(b) and (d) of this title, a telecommunications carrier shall ensure that its equipment, facilities, or services that provide a customer or subscriber with the ability to originate, terminate, or direct communications are capable of—

(1) expeditiously isolating and enabling the government, pursuant to a court order or other lawful authorization, to intercept, to the exclusion of any other communications, all wire and electronic communications carried by the carrier within a service area to or from equipment, facilities, or services of a subscriber of such carrier concurrently with their transmission to or from the subscriber's equipment, facility, or service, or at such later time as may be acceptable to the government;

(2) expeditiously isolating and enabling the government, pursuant to a court order or other lawful authorization, to access call-identifying information that is reasonably available to the carrier—

(A) before, during, or immediately after the transmission of a wire or electronic communication (or at such later time as may be acceptable to the government); and

(B) in a manner that allows it to be associated with the communication to which it pertains, except that, with regard to information acquired solely pursuant to the authority for pen registers and trap and trace devices (as defined in section 3127 of title 18), such call-identifying information shall not include any information that may disclose the physical location of the subscriber (except to the extent that the location may be determined from the telephone number);

(3) delivering intercepted communications and call-identifying information to the government, pursuant to a court order or other lawful authorization, in a format such that they may be transmitted by means of equipment, facilities, or services procured by the government to a location other than the premises of the carrier; and

(4) facilitating authorized communications interceptions and access to call-identifying information unobtrusively and with a minimum of interference with any subscriber's telecommunications service and in a manner that protects—

(A) the privacy and security of communications and call-identifying information not authorized to be intercepted; and

(B) information regarding the government's interception of communications and access to call-identifying information.

(b) Limitations

(1) Design of features and systems configurations

This chapter does not authorize any law enforcement agency or officer—

(A) to require any specific design of equipment, facilities, services, features, or system configurations to be adopted by any provider of a wire or electronic communication service, any manufacturer of telecommunications equipment, or any provider of telecommunications support services; or

(B) to prohibit the adoption of any equipment, facility, service, or feature by any provider of a wire or electronic communication service, any manufacturer of telecommunications equipment, or any provider of telecommunications support services.

(2) Information services; private networks and interconnection services and facilities

The requirements of subsection (a) of this section do not apply to—

(A) information services; or
(B) equipment, facilities, or services that support the transport or switching of communications for private networks or for the sole purpose of interconnecting telecommunications carriers.

(3) Encryption

A telecommunications carrier shall not be responsible for decrypting, or ensuring the government's ability to decrypt, any communication encrypted by a subscriber or customer, unless the encryption was provided by the carrier and the carrier possesses the information necessary to decrypt the communication.

(c) Emergency or exigent circumstances

In emergency or exigent circumstances (including those described in sections 2518(7) or (11)(b) and 3125 of title 18 and section 1805(e) of title 50), a carrier at its discretion may comply with subsection (a)(3) of this section by allowing monitoring at its premises if that is the only means of accomplishing the interception or access.

(d) Mobile service assistance requirements

A telecommunications carrier that is a provider of commercial mobile service (as defined in section 332(d) of this title) offering a feature or service that allows subscribers to redirect, hand off, or assign their wire or electronic communications to another service area or another service provider or to utilize facilities in another service area or of another service provider shall ensure that, when the carrier that had been providing assistance for the interception of wire or electronic communications or access to call-identifying information pursuant to a court order or lawful authorization no longer has access to the content of such communications or call-identifying information within the service area in which interception has been occurring as a result of the subscriber's use of such a feature or service, information is made available to the government (before, during, or immediately after the transfer of such communications) identifying the provider of a wire or electronic communication service that has acquired access to the communications.

Sec. 1003. Notices of capacity requirements

(a) Notices of maximum and actual capacity requirements

(1) In general

Not later than 1 year after October 25, 1994, after consulting with State and local law enforcement agencies, telecommunications carriers, providers of telecommunications support services, and manufacturers of telecommunications equipment, and after notice and comment, the Attorney General shall publish in the Federal Register and provide to appropriate telecommunications industry associations and standard-setting organizations—

(A) notice of the actual number of communication interceptions, pen registers, and trap and trace devices, representing a portion of the maximum capacity set forth under subparagraph (B), that the Attorney General estimates that government agencies authorized to conduct electronic surveillance may conduct and use simultaneously by the date that is 4 years after October 25, 1994; and

(B) notice of the maximum capacity required to accommodate all of the communication interceptions, pen registers, and trap and trace devices that the Attorney General estimates that government agencies authorized to conduct electronic surveillance may conduct and use simultaneously after the date that is 4 years after October 25, 1994.

(2) Basis of notices

The notices issued under paragraph (1)—

(A) may be based upon the type of equipment, type of service, number of subscribers, type or size or carrier, nature of service area, or any other measure; and

(B) shall identify, to the maximum extent practicable, the capacity required at specific geographic locations.

(b) Compliance with capacity notices

(1) Initial capacity

Within 3 years after the publication by the Attorney General of a notice of capacity requirements or within 4 years after October 25, 1994, whichever is longer, a telecommunications carrier shall, subject to subsection (e) of this section, ensure that its systems are capable of—

(A) accommodating simultaneously the number of interceptions, pen registers, and trap and trace devices set forth in the notice under subsection (a)(1)(A) of this section; and

(B) expanding to the maximum capacity set forth in the notice under subsection (a)(1)(B) of this section.

(2) Expansion to maximum capacity

After the date described in paragraph (1), a telecommunications carrier shall, subject to subsection (e) of this section, ensure that it can accommodate expeditiously any increase in the actual number of communication interceptions, pen registers, and trap and trace devices that authorized agencies may seek to conduct and use, up to the maximum capacity requirement set forth in the notice under subsection (a)(1)(B) of this section.

(c) Notices of increased maximum capacity requirements

(1) Notice

The Attorney General shall periodically publish in the Federal Register, after notice and comment, notice of any necessary increases in the maximum capacity requirement set forth in the notice under subsection (a)(1)(B) of this section.

(2) Compliance

Within 3 years after notice of increased maximum capacity requirements is published under paragraph (1), or within such longer time period as the Attorney General may specify, a telecommunications carrier shall, subject to subsection (e) of this section, ensure that its systems are capable of expanding to the increased maximum capacity set forth in the notice.

(d) Carrier statement
Within 180 days after the publication by the Attorney General of a notice of capacity requirements pursuant to subsection (a) or (c) of this section, a telecommunications carrier shall submit to the Attorney General a statement identifying any of its systems or services that do not have the capacity to accommodate simultaneously the number of interceptions, pen registers, and trap and trace devices set forth in the notice under such subsection.

(e) Reimbursement required for compliance
The Attorney General shall review the statements submitted under subsection (d) of this section and may, subject to the availability of appropriations, agree to reimburse a telecommunications carrier for costs directly associated with modifications to attain such capacity requirement that are determined to be reasonable in accordance with section 1008(e) of this title. Until the Attorney General agrees to reimburse such carrier for such modification, such carrier shall be considered to be in compliance with the capacity notices under subsection (a) or (c) of this section.

Sec. 1004. Systems security and integrity

A telecommunications carrier shall ensure that any interception of communications or access to call-identifying information effected within its switching premises can be activated only in accordance with a court order or other lawful authorization and with the affirmative intervention of an individual officer or employee of the carrier acting in accordance with regulations prescribed by the Commission.

Sec. 1005. Cooperation of equipment manufacturers and providers of telecommunications support services

(a) Consultation
A telecommunications carrier shall consult, as necessary, in a timely fashion with manufacturers of its telecommunications transmission and switching equipment and its providers of telecommunications support services for the purpose of ensuring that current and planned equipment,

facilities, and services comply with the capability requirements of section 1002 of this title and the capacity requirements identified by the Attorney General under section 1003 of this title.

(b) Cooperation Subject to sections 1003(e), 1007(a), and 1008(b) and (d) of this title, a manufacturer of telecommunications transmission or switching equipment and a provider of telecommunications support services shall, on a reasonably timely basis and at a reasonable charge, make available to the telecommunications carriers using its equipment, facilities, or services such features or modifications as are necessary to permit such carriers to comply with the capability requirements of section 1002 of this title and the capacity requirements identified by the Attorney General under section 1003 of this title.

Sec. 1006. Technical requirements and standards; extension of compliance date

(a) Safe harbor

(1) Consultation
To ensure the efficient and industry-wide implementation of the assistance capability requirements under section 1002 of this title, the Attorney General, in coordination with other Federal, State, and local law enforcement agencies, shall consult with appropriate associations and standard-setting organizations of the telecommunications industry, with representatives of users of telecommunications equipment, facilities, and services, and with State utility commissions.

(2) Compliance under accepted standards
A telecommunications carrier shall be found to be in compliance with the assistance capability requirements under section 1002 of this title, and a manufacturer of telecommunications transmission or switching equipment or a provider of telecommunications support services shall be found to be in compliance with section 1005 of this title, if the carrier, manufacturer, or support service provider is in compliance with publicly available technical requirements or standards adopted by an industry association or standard-setting organization, or by the Commission under subsection (b) of this section, to meet the requirements of section 1002 of this title.

(3) Absence of standards The absence of technical requirements or standards for implementing the assistance capability requirements of section 1002 of this title shall not—

(A) preclude a telecommunications carrier, manufacturer, or telecommunications support services provider from deploying a technology or service; or
(B) relieve a carrier, manufacturer, or telecommunications support services provider of the obligations imposed by section 1002 or 1005 of this title, as applicable.

(b) Commission authority If industry associations or standard-setting organizations fail to issue technical requirements or standards or if a Government agency or any other person believes that such requirements or standards are deficient, the agency or person may petition the Commission to establish, by rule, technical requirements or standards that—

(1) meet the assistance capability requirements of section 1002 of this title by cost-effective methods;
(2) protect the privacy and security of communications not authorized to be intercepted;
(3) minimize the cost of such compliance on residential ratepayers;
(4) serve the policy of the United States to encourage the provision of new technologies and services to the public; and
(5) provide a reasonable time and conditions for compliance with and the transition to any new standard, including defining the obligations of telecommunications carriers under section 1002 of this title during any transition period.

(c) Extension of compliance date for equipment, facilities, and services

(1) Petition
A telecommunications carrier proposing to install or deploy, or having installed or deployed, any equipment, facility, or service prior to the effective date of section 1002 of this title may petition the Commission for 1 or more extensions of the deadline for complying with the assistance capability requirements under section 1002 of this title.
(2) Grounds for extension The Commission may, after consultation with the Attorney General, grant an extension under this subsection, if the Commission determines that compliance with the assistance capability requirements under section 1002 of this title is not reasonably achievable through application of technology available within the compliance period.
(3) Length of extension An extension under this subsection shall extend for no longer than the earlier of—

(A) the date determined by the Commission as necessary for the carrier to comply with the assistance capability requirements under section 1002 of this title; or
(B) the date that is 2 years after the date on which the extension is granted.

(4) Applicability of extension An extension under this subsection shall apply to only that part of the carrier's business on which the new equipment, facility, or service is used.

Sec. 1007. Enforcement orders

(a) Grounds for issuance
A court shall issue an order enforcing this chapter under section 2522 of title 18 only if the court finds that—

(1) alternative technologies or capabilities or the facilities of another carrier are not reasonably available to law enforcement for implementing

the interception of communications or access to call-identifying information; and

(2) compliance with the requirements of this chapter is reasonably achievable through the application of available technology to the equipment, facility, or service at issue or would have been reasonably achievable if timely action had been taken.

(b) Time for compliance Upon issuing an order enforcing this chapter, the court shall specify a reasonable time and conditions for complying with its order, considering the good faith efforts to comply in a timely manner, any effect on the carrier's, manufacturer's, or service provider's ability to continue to do business, the degree of culpability or delay in undertaking efforts to comply, and such other matters as justice may require.

(c) Limitations An order enforcing this chapter may not—

(1) require a telecommunications carrier to meet the Government's demand for interception of communications and acquisition of call-identifying information to any extent in excess of the capacity for which the Attorney General has agreed to reimburse such carrier;

(2) require any telecommunications carrier to comply with assistance capability requirement of section 1002 of this title if the Commission has determined (pursuant to section 1008(b)(1) of this title) that compliance is not reasonably achievable, unless the Attorney General has agreed (pursuant to section 1008(b)(2) of this title) to pay the costs described in section 1008(b)(2)(A) of this title; or

(3) require a telecommunications carrier to modify, for the purpose of complying with the assistance capability requirements of section 1002 of this title, any equipment, facility, or service deployed on or before January 1, 1995, unless—(A) the Attorney General has agreed to pay the telecommunications carrier for all reasonable costs directly associated with modifications necessary to bring the equipment, facility, or service into compliance with those requirements; or (B) the equipment, facility, or service has been replaced or significantly upgraded or otherwise undergoes major modification.

Sec. 1008. Payment of costs of telecommunications carriers to comply with capability requirements

(a) Equipment, facilities, and services deployed on or before January 1, 1995

The Attorney General may, subject to the availability of appropriations, agree to pay telecommunications carriers for all reasonable costs directly associated with the modifications performed by carriers in connection with equipment, facilities, and services installed or deployed on or before January 1, 1995, to establish the capabilities necessary to comply with section 1002 of this title.

(b) Equipment, facilities, and services deployed after January 1, 1995

(1) Determinations of reasonably achievable

The Commission, on petition from a telecommunications carrier or any other interested person, and after notice to the Attorney General, shall determine whether compliance with the assistance capability requirements of section 1002 of this title is reasonably achievable with respect to any equipment, facility, or service installed or deployed after January 1, 1995. The Commission shall make such determination within 1 year after the date such petition is filed. In making such determination, the Commission shall determine whether compliance would impose significant difficulty or expense on the carrier or on the users of the carrier's systems and shall consider the following factors:

(A) The effect on public safety and national security.
(B) The effect on rates for basic residential telephone service.
(C) The need to protect the privacy and security of communications not authorized to be intercepted.
(D) The need to achieve the capability assistance requirements of section 1002 of this title by cost-effective methods.
(E) The effect on the nature and cost of the equipment, facility, or service at issue.
(F) The effect on the operation of the equipment, facility, or service at issue.
(G) The policy of the United States to encourage the provision of new technologies and services to the public.
(H) The financial resources of the telecommunications carrier.
(I) The effect on competition in the provision of telecommunications services.
(J) The extent to which the design and development of the equipment, facility, or service was initiated before January 1, 1995.
(K) Such other factors as the Commission determines are appropriate.

(2) Compensation If compliance with the assistance capability requirements of section 1002 of this title is not reasonably achievable with respect to equipment, facilities, or services deployed after January 1, 1995—

(A) the Attorney General, on application of a telecommunications carrier, may agree, subject to the availability of appropriations, to pay the telecommunications carrier for the additional reasonable costs of making compliance with such assistance capability requirements reasonably achievable; and
(B) if the Attorney General does not agree to pay such costs, the telecommunications carrier shall be deemed to be in compliance with such capability requirements.

(c) Allocation of funds for payment The Attorney General shall allocate funds appropriated to carry out this chapter in accordance with law enforcement priorities determined by the Attorney General.
(d) Failure to make payment with respect to equipment, facilities, and services deployed on or before January 1, 1995

If a carrier has requested payment in accordance with procedures promulgated pursuant to subsection (e) of this section, and the Attorney General has not agreed to pay the telecommunications carrier for all reasonable costs directly associated with modifications necessary to bring any equipment, facility, or service deployed on or before January 1, 1995, into compliance with the assistance capability requirements of section 1002 of this title, such equipment, facility, or service shall be considered to be in compliance with the assistance capability requirements of section 1002 of this title until the equipment, facility, or service is replaced or significantly upgraded or otherwise undergoes major modification.

(e) Cost control regulations

(1) In general
The Attorney General shall, after notice and comment, establish regulations necessary to effectuate timely and cost-efficient payment to telecommunications carriers under this chapter, under chapters 119 and 121 of title 18, and under the Foreign Intelligence Surveillance Act of 1978 (50 U.S.C. 1801 et seq.).

(2) Contents of regulations
The Attorney General, after consultation with the Commission, shall prescribe regulations for purposes of determining reasonable costs under this chapter. Such regulations shall seek to minimize the cost to the Federal Government and shall—

(A) permit recovery from the Federal Government of—

(i) the direct costs of developing the modifications described in subsection (a) of this section, of providing the capabilities requested under subsection (b)(2) of this section, or of providing the capacities requested under section 1003(e) of this title, but only to the extent that such costs have not been recovered from any other governmental or nongovernmental entity;
(ii) the costs of training personnel in the use of such capabilities or capacities; and
(iii) the direct costs of deploying or installing such capabilities or capacities;

(B) in the case of any modification that may be used for any purpose other than lawfully authorized electronic surveillance by a law enforcement agency of a government, permit recovery of only the incremental cost of making the modification suitable for such law enforcement purposes; and
(C) maintain the confidentiality of trade secrets.

(3) Submission of claims Such regulations shall require any telecommunications carrier that the Attorney General has agreed to pay for modifications pursuant to this section and that has installed or deployed such modification to submit to the Attorney General a claim for payment that contains or is accompanied by such information as the Attorney General may require.

Sec. 1009. Authorization of appropriations

There are authorized to be appropriated to carry out this chapter a total of $500,000,000 for fiscal years 1995, 1996, 1997, and 1998. Such sums are authorized to remain available until expended.

Sec. 1010. Reports

(a) Reports by Attorney General

(1) In general On or before November 30, 1995, and on or before November 30 of each year thereafter, the Attorney General shall submit to Congress and make available to the public a report on the amounts paid during the preceding fiscal year to telecommunications carriers under sections 1003(e) and 1008 of this title.

(2) Contents

A report under paragraph (1) shall include—

(A) a detailed accounting of the amounts paid to each carrier and the equipment, facility, or service for which the amounts were paid; and

(B) projections of the amounts expected to be paid in the current fiscal year, the carriers to which payment is expected to be made, and the equipment, facilities, or services for which payment is expected to be made.

(b) Reports by Comptroller General

(1) Payments for modifications

On or before April 1, 1996, and every 2 years thereafter, the Comptroller General of the United States, after consultation with the Attorney General and the telecommunications industry, shall submit to the Congress a report—

(A) describing the type of equipment, facilities, and services that have been brought into compliance under this chapter; and

(B) reflecting its analysis of the reasonableness and cost-effectiveness of the payments made by the Attorney General to telecommunications carriers for modifications necessary to ensure compliance with this chapter.

(2) Compliance cost estimates

A report under paragraph (1) shall include the findings and conclusions of the Comptroller General on the costs to be incurred by telecommunications carriers to comply with the assistance capability requirements of section 1002 of this title after the effective date of such section 1002 of this title, including projections of the amounts expected to be incurred and a description of the equipment, facilities, or services for which they are expected to be incurred.

(Pub. L. 103–414, title I, Sec. 112, Oct. 25, 1994, 108 Stat. 4288.)

SOURCE: http://www.techlawjournal.com/agencies/calea/47usc1001.htm

---

ANALYSIS

The Communications Assistance for Law Enforcement Act (CALEA) codifies the government's ability to obtain government access to communications systems.

The objective of CALEA implementation is to preserve law enforcement's ability to conduct lawfully authorized electronic surveillance while preserving public safety, the public's right to privacy, and the telecommunications industry's competitiveness. The original reason for adopting CALEA was the FBI's worry that increasing use of digital telephone exchange switches would make tapping phones at the phone company's central office harder and slower to execute, or in some cases impossible. Congress wrote CALEA to extend and clarify the previous obligations of telecommunications service providers to assist law enforcement with electronic surveillance orders. CALEA not only preserved the government's existing rights to circuit-switched telecommunications intercept, it also extended law enforcement's intercept rights to digital and wireless telephony.

FURTHER READING

Park, Gene D. "Internet Wiretaps: Applying the Communications Assistance for Law Enforcement Act to Broadband Services." *A Journal of Law and Policy for the Information Society* 2 (2006): 599.

4

20TH-CENTURY COURT RULINGS

Executive Power to Establish Military Commissions during World War II

- ***Document:*** The Supreme Court case *Ex parte Quirin*, Excerpt
- ***Date:*** 1942
- ***Where:*** Washington, D.C.
- ***Significance:*** This case was significant because the majority opinion upheld the use of military commissions to try violations for the laws of war and for the refusal to recognize a right to trial by jury.

DOCUMENT

Ex parte Quirin et al., 317 U.S. 1 (1942)

Ex parte Haupt, Ex parte Kerling, Ex parte Burger, Ex parte Heinck, Ex parte Thiel, Ex parte Neubauer.

Nos.—Original and Nos. 1, 2, 3, 4, 5, 6 and 7-July Special Term, 1942.

Argued July 29, 30, 1942.

Decided July 31, 1942.

Extended opinion filed Oct. 29, 1942.

Per Curiam

In these causes motions for leave to file petitions for habeas corpus were presented to the United States District Court for the District of Columbia, which entered orders denying the motions. Motions for leave to file petitions for habeas corpus were then presented to this Court, and the merits of the applications were fully argued at the Special Term of Court convened on July 29, 1942....

Mr. Chief Justice Stone delivered the opinion of the Court.

These cases are brought here by petitioners' several applications for leave to file petitions for habeas corpus in this Court ... The question for decision is whether the detention of petitioners by respondent for trial by Military Commission, appointed by Order of the President of July 2, 1942, on charges preferred against them purporting to set out their violations of the law of war and of the Articles of War, is in conformity to the laws and Constitution of the United States.

In view of the public importance of the questions raised by their petitions and of the duty which rests on the courts, in time of war as well as in time of peace, to preserve unimpaired the constitutional safeguards of civil liberty, and because in our opinion the public interest required that we consider and decide those questions without any avoidable delay, we directed that petitioners' applications be set down for full oral argument at a special term of this Court, convened on July 29, 1942. The applications for leave to file the petitions were presented in open court on that day and were heard on the petitions, the answers to them of respondent, a stipulation of facts by counsel, and the record of the testimony given before the Commission....

The President, as President and Commander in Chief of the Army and Navy, by Order of July 2, 1942, appointed a Military Commission and directed it to try petitioners for offenses against the law of war and the Articles of War, and prescribed regulations for the procedure on the trial and for review of the record of the trial and of any judgment or sentence of the Commission. On the same day, by Proclamation, the President declared that 'all persons who are subjects, citizens or residents of any nation at war with the United States or who give obedience to or act under the direction of any such nation, and who during time of war enter or attempt to enter the United States ... through coastal or boundary defenses, and are charged with committing or attempting or preparing to commit sabotage, espionage, hostile or warlike acts, or violations of the law of war, shall be subject to the law of war and to the jurisdiction of military tribunals'. The Proclamation also stated in terms that all such persons were denied access to the courts.

On July 3, 1942, the Judge Advocate General's Department of the Army prepared and lodged with the Commission the following charges against petitioners, supported by specifications:

1. Violation of the law of war.
2. Violation of Article 81 of the Articles of War, defining the offense of relieving or attempting to relieve, or corresponding with or giving intelligence to, the enemy.
3. Violation of Article 82, defining the offense of spying.
4. Conspiracy to commit the offenses alleged in charges 1, 2 and 3.

Petitioners' main contention is that the President is without any statutory or constitutional authority to order the petitioners to be tried by military tribunal for

DID YOU KNOW?

Military Tribunals and the "Yamashita Standard," 1946

The U.S. Supreme Court ruled in *In Re Yamashita,* 327 U.S. 1 (1946) that a foreign enemy can be held and tried by a U.S. military tribunal convened abroad. The Court's holding has become known as the "Yamashita Standard." It provides a strict standard of responsibility for military commanders concerning the actions of their subordinates. The Court recognized that international law, through the laws of war, assumes that violations of the laws of war are to be prevented by commanders, who are responsible for their subordinates. The Court believed that absent such a duty upon commanders, nothing would stop occupying forces from committing atrocities upon civilians. The Court held that General Yamashita was, by virtue of his position as commander of the Japanese forces in the Philippines, under an "affirmative duty to take such measures as were within his power and appropriate in the circumstances to protect prisoners of war and the civilian population." General Yamashita's writ of habeas corpus was denied, and he was executed by hanging by the United States military.

offenses with which they are charged; that in consequence they are entitled to be tried in the civil courts with the safeguards, including trial by jury, which the Fifth and Sixth Amendments guarantee to all persons charged in such courts with criminal offenses. In any case it is urged that the President's Order, in prescribing the procedure of the Commission and the method for review of its findings and sentence, and the proceedings of the Commission under the Order, conflict with Articles of War adopted by Congress—particularly Articles 38, 43, 46, 50½ and 70—and are illegal and void.

The Government challenges each of these propositions. But regardless of their merits, it also insists that petitioners must be denied access to the courts, both because they are enemy aliens or have entered our territory as enemy belligerents, and because the President's Proclamation undertakes in terms to deny such access to the class of persons defined by the Proclamation, which aptly describes the character and conduct of petitioners. It is urged that if they are enemy aliens or if the Proclamation has force no court may afford the petitioners a hearing. But there is certainly nothing in the Proclamation to preclude access to the courts for determining its applicability to the particular case. And neither the Proclamation nor the fact that they are enemy aliens forecloses consideration by the courts of petitioners' contentions that the Constitution and laws of the United States constitutionally enacted forbid their trial by military commission.

As announced in our per curiam opinion we have resolved those questions by our conclusion that the Commission has jurisdiction to try the charge preferred against petitioners. There is therefore no occasion to decide contentions of the parties unrelated to this issue. We pass at once to the consideration of the basis of the Commission's authority.

Congress and the President, like the courts, possess no power not derived from the Constitution.

The Constitution thus invests the President as Commander in Chief with the power to wage war which Congress has declared, and to carry into effect all laws passed by Congress for the conduct of war and for the government and regulation of the Armed Forces, and all laws defining and punishing offences against the law of nations, including those which pertain to the conduct of war.

By the Articles of War, Congress has provided rules for the government of the Army. It has provided for the trial and punishment, by courts martial, of violations of the Articles by members of the armed forces and by specified classes of persons associated or serving with the Army. But the Articles also recognize the 'military commission' appointed by military command as an appropriate tribunal for the trial and punishment of offenses against the law of war not ordinarily tried by court martial. Articles 38 and 46 authorize the President, with certain limitations, to prescribe the procedure for military commissions. Articles 81 and 82 authorize trial, either by court martial or military commission, of those charged with relieving, harboring or corresponding with the enemy and those charged with spying. And Article 15 declares that 'the provisions of these articles conferring jurisdiction upon courts-martial shall not be construed as depriving military commissions . . . or other military tribunals of concurrent jurisdiction in respect of offenders or offenses that by statute or by the law of war may be triable by such military commissions . . . or other military tribunals'. Article 2 includes among those persons subject to military law the personnel of our own military establishment. But this, as Article 12 provides, does not exclude from that class 'any other person who by the law of war is subject to trial by military tribunals' and who under Article 12 may be tried by court martial or under Article 15 by military commission....

From the very beginning of its history this Court has recognized and applied the law of war as including that part of the law of nations which prescribes, for the conduct of war, the status, rights and duties of enemy nations as well as of enemy individuals. By the Articles of War, and especially Article 15, Congress has explicitly provided, so far as it may constitutionally do so, that military tribunals shall have jurisdiction to try offenders or offenses against the law of war in appropriate cases. Congress, in addition to making rules for the government of our Armed Forces, has thus exercised its authority to define and punish offenses against the law of nations by sanctioning, within constitutional limitations, the jurisdiction of military commissions to try persons for offenses which, according to the rules and precepts of the law of nations, and more particularly the law of war, are cognizable by such tribunals. And the President, as Commander in Chief, by his Proclamation in time of war his invoked that law. By his Order creating the present Commission he has undertaken to exercise the authority conferred upon him by Congress, and also such authority as the Constitution itself gives the Commander in Chief, to direct the performance of those functions which may constitutionally be performed by the military arm of the nation in time of war.

An important incident to the conduct of war is the adoption of measures by the military command not only to repel and defeat the enemy, but to seize and subject to disciplinary measures those enemies who in their attempt to thwart or impede our military effort have violated the law of war. It is unnecessary for present purposes to determine to what extent the President as Commander in Chief has constitutional power to create military commissions without the support of Congressional legislation. For here Congress has authorized trial of offenses against the law of war before such commissions. We are concerned only with the question whether it is within the constitutional power of the national government to place petitioners upon trial before a military commission for the offenses with which they are charged.

We must therefore first inquire whether any of the acts charged is an offense against the law of war cognizable before a military tribunal, and if so whether the Constitution prohibits the trial. We may assume that there are acts regarded in other countries, or by some writers on international law, as offenses against the law of war which would not be triable by military tribunal here, either because they are not recognized by our courts as violations of the law of war or because they are of that class of offenses constitutionally triable only by a jury. It was upon such grounds that the Court denied the right to proceed by military tribunal in Ex parte Milligan, supra. But as we shall show, these petitioners were charged with an offense against the law of war which the Constitution does not require to be tried by jury.

It is no objection that Congress in providing for the trial of such offenses has not itself undertaken to codify that branch of international law or to mark its precise boundaries, or to enumerate or define by statute all the acts which that law condemns.... Congress had the choice of crystallizing in permanent form and in minute detail every offense against the law of war, or of adopting the system of common law applied by military tribunals so far as it should be recognized and deemed applicable by the courts. It chose the latter course.

By universal agreement and practice the law of war draws a distinction between the armed forces and the peaceful populations of belligerent nations and also between those who are lawful and unlawful combatants. Lawful combatants are subject to capture and detention as prisoners of war by opposing military forces. Unlawful combatants are likewise subject to capture and detention, but in addition they are subject to trial and punishment by military tribunals for acts which render their belligerency unlawful. The spy who secretly and without uniform passes the military lines of a belligerent in time of war, seeking to gather military information and communicate it to the enemy, or an enemy combatant who without uniform comes secretly through the lines for the purpose of waging war by destruction of life or property, are familiar examples of belligerents who are generally deemed not to be entitled to the status of prisoners of war, but to be offenders against the law of war subject to trial and punishment by military tribunals. Such was the practice of our own military authorities before the adoption of the Constitution, and during the Mexican and Civil Wars....

By a long course of practical administrative construction by its military authorities, our Government has recognized that those who during time of war pass surreptitiously from enemy territory into our own, discarding their uniforms upon entry, for the commission of hostile acts involving destruction of life or property, have the status of unlawful combatants punishable as such by military commission. This precept of the law of war has been so recognized in practice both here and abroad, and has so generally been accepted as valid by authorities on international law that we think it must be regarded as a rule or principle of the law of war recognized by this Government by its enactment of the Fifteenth Article of War.

Specification 1 of the First charge is sufficient to charge all the petitioners with the offense of unlawful belligerency, trial of which is within the jurisdiction of the Commission, and the admitted facts affirmatively show that the charge is not merely colorable or without foundation.

This specification so plainly alleges violation of the law of war as to require but brief discussion of petitioners' contentions. As we have seen, entry upon our territory in time of war by enemy belligerents, including those acting under the direction of the armed forces of the enemy, for the purpose of destroying property used or useful in prosecuting the war, is a hostile and war-like act. It subjects those who participate in it without uniform to the punishment prescribed by the law of war for unlawful belligerents. It is without significance that petitioners were not alleged to have borne conventional weapons or that their proposed hostile acts did not necessarily contemplate collision with the Armed Forces of the United States....

Citizenship in the United States of an enemy belligerent does not relieve him from the consequences of a belligerency which is unlawful because in violation of the law of war. Citizens who associate themselves with the military arm of the enemy government, and with its aid, guidance and direction enter this country bent on hostile acts are enemy belligerents within the meaning of the Hague Convention and the law of war. It is as an enemy belligerent that petitioner Haupt is charged with entering the United States, and unlawful belligerency is the gravamen of the offense of which he is accused.

Nor are petitioners any the less belligerents if, as they argue, they have not actually committed or attempted to commit any act of depredation or entered the theatre or zone of active military operations. The argument leaves out of account the nature of the offense which the Government charges and which the Act of Congress, by incorporating the law of war, punishes. It is that each petitioner, in circumstances which gave him the status of an enemy belligerent, passed our military and naval lines and defenses or went behind those lines, in civilian dress and with hostile purpose. The offense was complete when with that purpose they entered-or, having so entered, they remained upon-our territory in time of war without uniform or other appropriate means of identification. For that reason, even when committed by a citizen, the offense is distinct from the crime of treason defined in Article III, 3 of the Constitution, since the absence of uniform essential to one is irrelevant to the other.

But petitioners insist that even if the offenses with which they are charged are offenses against the law of war, their trial is subject to the requirement of the Fifth Amendment that no person shall be held to answer for a capital or otherwise infamous crime unless on a presentment or indictment of a grand jury, and that such trials must be by jury in a civil court . . . In the light of this long-continued and consistent interpretation we must conclude that Section 2 of Article III and the Fifth and Sixth Amendments cannot be taken to have extended the right to demand a jury to trials by military commission, or to have required that offenses against the law of war not triable by jury at common law be tried only in the civil courts. . . . We conclude that the Fifth and Sixth Amendments did not restrict whatever authority was conferred by the Constitution to try offenses against the law of war by military commission, and that petitioners, charged with such an offense not required to be tried by jury at common law, were lawfully placed on trial by the Commission without a jury.

Petitioners, and especially petitioner Haupt, stress the pronouncement of this Court in the Milligan case that the law of war 'can never be applied to citizens in states which have upheld the authority of the government, and where the courts are open and their process unobstructed'. Elsewhere in its opinion, the Court was at pains to point out that Milligan, a citizen twenty years resident in Indiana, who had never been a resident of any of the states in rebellion, was not an enemy belligerent either entitled to the status of a prisoner of war or subject to the penalties imposed upon unlawful belligerents. We construe the Court's statement as to the inapplicability of the law of war to Milligan's case as having particular reference to the facts before it. From them the Court concluded that Milligan, not being a part of or associated with the armed forces of the enemy, was a non-belligerent, not subject to the law of war save as-in circumstances found not there to be present and not involved here-martial law might be constitutionally established.

The Court's opinion is inapplicable to the case presented by the present record. We have no occasion now to define with meticulous care the ultimate boundaries of the jurisdiction of military tribunals to try persons according to the law of war. It is enough that petitioners here, upon the conceded facts, were plainly within those boundaries, and were held in good faith for trial by military commission, charged with being enemies who, with the purpose of destroying war materials and utilities, entered or after entry remained in our territory without uniform-an offense against the law of war. We hold only that those particular acts constitute an offense against the law of war which the Constitution authorizes to be tried by military commission. . . .

SOURCE: http://caselaw.lp.findlaw.com/scripts/getcase.pl?court=US&vol=317&invol=1

ANALYSIS

This case concerns a failed attempt in June 1942 by Nazi agents to sabotage multiple targets in the United States. On the evening of June 13, 1942, Burger, Heinrich, Quirin, and Dasch landed near Long Island, New York, wearing German uniforms and hauling explosives. All eight conspirators were subsequently arrested and, on the orders of President Franklin Roosevelt, tried by military commission. The commission found all eight men guilty and sentenced them to death. Arguing that the president exceeded his power in ordering the commission and that the Fifth and Sixth Amendments to the Constitution protect their rights to a regular trial, seven of the eight conspirators filed petitions for a writ of habeas corpus in Federal District Court. Their claims were denied, and they appealed to the United States Court of Appeals for the District of Columbia. Before the court ruled, however, they filed for hearing before the Supreme Court and, separately, filed petitions for habeas corpus directly with the Court. The Court, sitting in a special term, agreed to hear the cases.

The Quirin majority addressed two central issues. The first was whether the Court had the power to hear the appeal of the habeas corpus petition, even though the Presidential Proclamation denied the Nazis the right to the writ of habeas corpus. The second issue was whether President Roosevelt had the power to submit the Nazi defendants to trial by military commission. The Court concluded that the petitioners could properly seek the assistance of the federal courts, despite the fact that President Roosevelt's Proclamation of July 2, 1942, seemed to deny the eight Nazi saboteurs access. Second, within Article XV in the Articles of War, the Court held that Congress explicitly granted the executive branch the right to set up military commissions. This case established the principle that, in times of war, unlawful combatants can be tried by military courts. Such individuals do not have the right to a civil jury trial, although the decisions of the military tribunal are subject to review by civilian courts. The Court also issued an opinion that was unanimous. Justice Jackson was the lone holdout and originally wrote a concurring opinion expressing a strong belief that the president had the authority to set up military tribunals regardless of congressional assent, but he was persuaded to sign onto the majority opinion.

This case also has ramifications for the war on terror. On November 13, 2001, President George W. Bush promulgated an executive order titled "Detention, Treatment, and Trial of Certain Noncitizens in the War Against Terrorism" that authorized the establishment and application of military commissions as well as purported to eliminate whatever jurisdiction federal courts might have by statute and to deny federal court access to individuals prosecuted or detained for terrorism. The Bush administration substantially premised the order and jurisdiction-stripping provision on *Ex parte Quirin*. It has also invoked the opinion on many occasions when adopting related measures that involve activities related to the war on terror and when litigating major terrorism cases. President Bush's executive order establishing military commissions was subsequently struck down in *Hamdan v. Rumsfeld*. The *Quirin* precedent is an important example of the judiciary acting as a check on the executive in order to prevent arbitrary state action and undermining our liberty in the United States.

FURTHER READING

Thysell, Joseph R., Jr., "Ex parte Quirin: The Case for Military Commissions," *Southern University Law Review*. 31 (2004): 129.

Japanese Curfew after the Bombing of Pearl Harbor

- ***Document:*** The Supreme Court case of *Hirabayashi v. United States*, Excerpt
- ***Date:*** 1943
- ***Where:*** Washington, D.C.
- ***Significance:*** This was the first case challenging the curfew of Japanese Americans after the bombing of Pearl Harbor. The Supreme Court held that President Roosevelt's orders and the implementation of a curfew on Japanese Americans in wartime were constitutional and not a violation of due process.

DOCUMENT

Hirabayashi v. United States, 320 U.S. 81 (1943)

Argued May 10, 11, 1943.

Decided June 21, 1943.

Mr. Chief Justice Stone delivered the opinion of the Court.

Appellant, an American citizen of Japanese ancestry, was convicted in the district court of violating the Act of Congress of March 21, 1942, 56 Stat. 173, 18 U.S.C.A. 97a, which makes it a misdemeanor knowingly to disregard restrictions made applicable by a military commander to persons in a military area prescribed by him as such, all as authorized by an Executive Order of the President.

The questions for our decision are whether the particular restriction violated, namely that all persons of Japanese ancestry residing in such an area be within their place of residence daily between the hours of 8:00 p.m. and 6:00 a.m., was adopted by the military commander in the exercise of an unconstitutional delegation by Congress of its legislative power, and whether the restriction unconstitutionally discriminated between citizens of Japanese ancestry and those of other ancestries in violation of the Fifth Amendment.

On December 8, 1941, one day after the bombing of Pearl Harbor by a Japanese air force, Congress declared war against Japan. On February 19, 1942, the President promulgated Executive Order No. 9066. The Order recited that 'the successful prosecution of the war requires every possible protection against espionage and against sabotage to national-defense material, national-defense premises, and national-defense utilities... By virtue of the authority vested in him as President and as Commander in Chief of the Army and Navy, the President purported to 'authorize and direct the Secretary of War, and the Military Commanders whom he may from time to time designate, whenever he or any designated Commander deems such action necessary or desirable, to prescribe military areas in such places and of such extent as he or the appropriate Military Commander may determine, from which any or all persons may be excluded, and with respect to which, the right of any person to enter, remain in, or leave shall be subject to whatever restrictions the Secretary of War or the appropriate Military Commander may impose in his discretion.'

An Executive Order of the President, No. 9102, of March 18, 1942, established the War Relocation Authority, in the Office for Emergency Management of the Executive Office of the President; it authorized the Director of War Relocation Authority to formulate and effectuate a program for the removal, relocation, maintenance and supervision of persons designated under Executive Order No. 9066, already referred to; and it conferred on the Director authority to prescribe regulations necessary or desirable to promote the effective execution of the program.

Congress, by the Act of March 21, 1942, 18 U.S.C.A. 97a, provided: 'That whoever shall enter, remain in, leave, or commit any act in any military area or military zone prescribed, under the authority of an Executive order of the President, by the Secretary of War, or by any military commander designated by the Secretary of War, contrary to the restrictions applicable to any such area or zone or contrary to the order of the Secretary of War or any such military commander, shall, if it appears that he knew or should have known of the existence and extent of the restrictions or order and that his act was in violation thereof, be guilty of a misdemeanor and upon conviction shall be liable' to fine or imprisonment, or both.

Appellant does not deny that he knowingly failed to obey the curfew order as charged in the second count of the indictment, or that the order was authorized by the terms of Executive Order No. 9066, or that the challenged Act of Congress purports to punish with criminal penalties disobedience of such an order. His contentions are only that Congress unconstitutionally delegated its legislative power to the military commander by authorizing him to impose the challenged regulation, and that, even if the regulation were in other respects lawfully authorized, the Fifth Amendment prohibits the discrimination made between citizens of Japanese descent and those of other ancestry.

The conclusion is inescapable that Congress, by the Act of March 21, 1942, ratified and confirmed Executive Order No. 9066. And so far as it lawfully could, Congress authorized and implemented such curfew orders as the commanding officer should promulgate pursuant to the Executive Order of the President. The question then is not one of Congressional power to delegate to the President the promulgation of the Executive Order, but whether, acting in cooperation, Congress and the Executive have constitutional authority to impose the curfew restriction here complained of. We must consider also whether, acting together, Congress and the Executive could leave it to the designated military commander to appraise the relevant conditions and on the basis of that appraisal to say whether, under the circumstances, the time and place were appropriate for the promulgation of the curfew order and whether the order itself was an appropriate means of carrying out the Executive Order for the 'protection against espionage and against sabotage' to national defense materials, premises and utilities. For reasons presently to be stated, we conclude that it was within the constitutional power of Congress and the executive arm of the Government to prescribe this curfew order for the period under consideration and that its promulgation by the military commander involved no unlawful delegation of legislative power.

Executive Order No. 9066, promulgated in time of war for the declared purpose of prosecuting the war by protecting national defense resources from sabotage and espionage, and the Act of March 21, 1942, ratifying and confirming the Executive Order, were each an exercise of the power to wage war conferred on the Congress and on the President, as Commander in Chief of the armed forces, by Articles I and II of the Constitution.

The war power of the national government is . . . not restricted to the winning of victories in the field and the repulse of enemy forces. It embraces every phase of the national defense, including the protection of war materials and the members of the armed forces from injury and from the dangers which attend the rise, prosecution and progress of war. Since the Constitution commits to the Executive and to Congress the exercise of the war power in all the vicissitudes and conditions of warfare, it has necessarily given them wide scope for the exercise of judgment and discretion in determining the nature and extent of the threatened injury or danger and in the selection of the means for resisting it. Where, as they did here, the conditions call for the exercise of judgment and discretion and for the choice of means by those branches of the Government on which the Constitution has placed the responsibility of war making, it is not for any court to sit in review of the wisdom of their action or substitute it judgment for theirs.

The actions taken must be appraised in the light of the conditions with which the President and Congress were confronted in the early months of 1942, many of which since disclosed, were then peculiarly within the knowledge of the military authorities. On December 7, 1941, the Japanese air forces had attacked the United States Naval Base at Pearl Harbor without warning, at the very hour when Japanese diplomatic representatives were conducting negotiations with our State Department ostensibly for the peaceful settlement of differences between the two countries.

Although the results of the attack on Pearl Harbor were not fully disclosed until much later, it was known that the damage was extensive, and that the Japanese by their successes had gained a naval superiority over our forces in the Pacific which might enable them to seize Pearl Harbor, our largest naval base and the last stronghold of defense lying between Japan and the west coast. That reasonably prudent men charged with the responsibility of our national defense had ample ground for concluding that they must face the danger of invasion, take measures against it, and in making the choice of measures consider our internal situation, cannot be doubted.

The challenged orders were defense measures for the avowed purpose of safeguarding the military area in question, at a time of threatened air raids and invasion by the Japanese forces, from the danger of sabotage and espionage. As the curfew was made applicable to citizens residing in the area only if they were of Japanese ancestry, our inquiry must be whether in the light of all the facts and circumstances there was any substantial basis for the conclusion, in which Congress and the military commander united, that the curfew as applied was a protective measure necessary to meet the threat of sabotage and espionage which would substantially affect the war effort and which might reasonably be expected to aid a threatened enemy invasion. The alternative which appellant insists must be accepted is for the military authorities to impose the curfew on all citizens within the military area, or on none. In a case of threatened danger requiring prompt action, it is a choice between inflicting obviously needless hardship on the many, or sitting passive and unresisting in the presence of the threat. We think that constitutional government, in time of war, is not so powerless and does not compel so hard a choice if those charged with the responsibility of our national defense have reasonable ground for believing that the threat is real.

In the critical days of March, 1942, the danger to our war production by sabotage and espionage in this area seems obvious. The German invasion of the Western European countries had given ample warning to the world of the menace of the 'fifth column.' Espionage by persons in sympathy with the Japanese Government had been found to have been particularly effective in the surprise attack on Pearl Harbor. At a time of threatened Japanese attack upon this country, the nature of our inhabitants' attachments to the Japanese enemy was consequently a matter of grave concern. Of the 126, 000 persons of Japanese descent in the United States, citizens and noncitizens, approximately 112,000 resided in California, Oregon and Washington at the time of the adoption of the military regulations. Of these approximately two-thirds are citizens because born in the United States. Not only did the great majority of such persons reside within the Pacific Coast states but they were concentrated in or near three of the large cities, Seattle, Portland and Los Angeles. . . .

There is support for the view that social, economic and political conditions which have prevailed since the close of the last century, when the Japanese began to come to this country in substantial numbers, have intensified their solidarity and have in large measure prevented their assimilation as an integral part of the white population. In addition, large numbers of children of Japanese parentage are sent to Japanese language schools outside the regular hours of public schools in the locality. Some of these schools are generally believed to be sources of Japanese nationalistic propaganda, cultivating allegiance to Japan. Considerable numbers, estimated to be approximately 10,000, of American-born children of Japanese parentage have been sent to Japan for all or a part of their education.

Congress and the Executive, including the military commander, could have attributed special significance, in its bearing on the loyalties of persons of Japanese descent, to the maintenance by Japan of its system of dual citizenship. Children born in the United States of Japanese alien parents, and especially those children born before December 1, 1924, are under many circumstances deemed, by Japanese law, to be citizens of Japan. No official census of those whom Japan regards as having thus retained Japanese citizenship is available, but there is ground for the belief that the number is large.

The association of influential Japanese residents with Japanese Consulates has been deemed a ready means for the dissemination of propaganda and for the maintenance of the influence of the Japanese Government with the Japanese population in this country. As a result of all these conditions affecting the life of the Japanese, both aliens and citizens, in the Pacific Coast area, there has been relatively little social intercourse between them and the white population. The restrictions, both practical and legal, affecting the privileges and opportunities afforded to persons of Japanese extraction residing in the United States, have been sources of irritation and may well have tended to increase their isolation, and in many instances their attachments to Japan and its institutions.

Viewing these data in all their aspects, Congress and the Executive could reasonably have concluded that these conditions have encouraged the continued attachment of members of this group to Japan and Japanese institutions. These are only some of the many considerations which those charged with the responsibility for the national defense could take into account in determining the nature and extent of the danger of espionage and sabotage, in the event of invasion or air raid attack. The extent of that danger could be definitely known only after the event and after it was too late to meet it. Whatever views we may entertain regarding the loyalty to this country of the citizens of Japanese ancestry, we cannot reject as unfounded the judgment of the military authorities and of Congress that there were disloyal members of that population, whose number and strength could not be precisely and quickly ascertained. We cannot say that the war- making branches of the Government did not have ground for believing that in a critical hour such persons could not readily be isolated and separately dealt with, and constituted a menace to the national defense and safety, which demanded that prompt and adequate measures be taken to guard against it.

Fred Tayama, chairperson of the Southern District Council of the Japanese American Citizens League (JACL) explaining curfew and travel laws to two fellow Japanese Americans in 1942. Founded in 1929, JACL stressed civil rights and Americanization. However, during World War II the organization decided to cooperate with the government's relocation policy. (Library of Congress.)

Our investigation here does not go beyond the inquiry whether, in the light of all the relevant circumstances preceding and attending their promulgation, the challenged orders and statute afforded a reasonable basis for the action taken in imposing the curfew. We cannot close our eyes to the fact, demonstrated by experience, that in time of war residents having ethnic affiliations with an invading enemy may be a greater source of danger than those of a different ancestry. Nor can we deny that Congress, and the military authorities acting with its authorization, have constitutional power to appraise the danger in the light of facts of public notoriety. We need not now attempt to define the ultimate boundaries of the war power. We decide only the issue as we have defined it-we decide only that the curfew order as applied, and at the time it was applied, was within the boundaries of the war power. In this case it is enough that circumstances within the knowledge of those charged with the responsibility for maintaining the national defense afforded a rational basis for the decision which they made. Whether we would have made it is irrelevant.

The military commander's appraisal of facts in the light of the authorized standard, and the inferences which he drew from those facts, involved the exercise of his informed judgment. But as we have seen, those facts, and the inferences which could be rationally drawn from them, support the judgment of the military commander, that the danger of espionage and sabotage to our military resources was imminent, and that the curfew order was an appropriate measure to meet it.

Where, as in the present case, the standard set up for the guidance of the military commander, and the action taken and the reasons for it, are in fact recorded in the military orders, so that Congress, the courts and the public are assured that the orders, in the judgment of the commander, conform to the standards approved by the President and Congress, there is no failure in the performance of the legislative function. The essentials of that function are the determination by Congress of the legislative policy and its approval of a rule of conduct to carry that policy into execution. The very necessities which attend the conduct of military operations in time of war in this instance as in many others preclude Congress from holding committee meetings to determine whether there is danger, before it enacts legislation to combat the danger.

The Constitution as a continuously operating charter of government does not demand the impossible or the impractical. The essentials of the legislative function are preserved when Congress authorizes a statutory command to become operative, upon ascertainment of a basic conclusion of fact by a designated representative of the Government. The present statute, which authorized curfew orders to be made pursuant to Executive Order No. 9066 for the protection of war resources from espionage and sabotage, satisfies those requirements. Under the Executive Order the basic facts, determined by the military commander in the light of knowledge then available, were whether that danger existed and whether a curfew order was an appropriate means of minimizing the danger. Since his findings to that effect were, as we have said, not without adequate support, the legislative function was performed and the sanction of the statute attached to violations of the curfew order. It is unnecessary to consider whether or to what extent such findings would support orders differing from the curfew order.

Affirmed.

SOURCE: http://caselaw.lp.findlaw.com/scripts/getcase.pl?navby=search&court=US&case=/data/us/320/81.html

---

ANALYSIS

The legal conditions which surrounded the conviction of Gordon Hirabayashi during World War II were already present during late 19th century. In 1880 and 1882, Congress passed the Chinese Exclusion Acts which blocked Chinese immigration for the next 60 years. The Gentlemen's Agreement, adopted in 1908, prevented male Japanese workers from entering the United States. In 1922, the Supreme Court ruled on the *Ozawa* case, prohibiting Japanese immigrants from becoming naturalized citizens, and in 1924 a new immigration law effectively ended Japanese immigration to the United States. After the Japanese attack on Pearl Harbor, President Roosevelt acted to prevent incidents of subversion and espionage from individuals of Japanese descent living in the United States. He issued two executive orders which were quickly enacted into law. One gave the secretary of war the power to designate certain parts of the country "military areas" and exclude certain persons from them. The second established the War Relocation Authority which had the power to remove, maintain, and supervise persons who were excluded from military areas within the United States. Gordon Hirabayashi, a student at the University of Washington, was convicted of violating the curfew order.

The Hirabayashi majority determined that the presidential curfew order was an appropriate exercise of war powers, as a defense measure implemented for the purpose of safeguarding an important military area from the danger of sabotage and espionage by sympathetic persons of Japanese ancestry, at a time of threatened air raids and invasion by Japanese forces. Further, the Court concluded that curfew order was not an unconstitutional discrimination against persons of Japanese ancestry, because the surrounding circumstances of the war and of Japanese communities in the United States afforded substantial basis for the military commander's belief that persons of Japanese ancestry required segregation from others. Mr. Hirabayashi's conviction was subsequently overturned in by the District Court in Seattle and the Federal Appeals Court in 1986 and 1987. Although the Supreme Court ruling remains intact because the government chose not to appeal the reversals, Hirabayashi's legal victories made history in disproving the government's contention of disloyalty. This case precedent demonstrates a willingness of the Court to defer to Congress during times of crisis at the expense of individual liberty.

FURTHER READING

Robinson, Greg. *By Order of the President: FDR and the Internment of Japanese Americans.* Cambridge, Mass.: Harvard University Press, 2001.

Habeas Corpus and Noncitizens

- ***Document:*** The Supreme Court case *Secretary of Defense Johnson, et al., v. Eisentrager et al.*, Excerpt
- ***Date:*** June 5, 1950
- ***Where:*** Washington, D.C.
- ***Significance:*** The Supreme Court held that the federal Constitution did not confer immunity from military trial and punishment for an alien enemy engaged in the hostile service of a government at war with the United States, thereby granting the military commission jurisdiction to try the prisoners and determine whether an offense against the laws of war had been committed.

DOCUMENT

Secretary of Defense Johnson, et al., v. Eisentrager et al., 339 U.S. 763 (1950)

Argued April 17, 1950.

Decided June 5, 1950.

Mr. Justice Jackson delivered the opinion of the Court.

The ultimate question in this case is one of jurisdiction of civil courts of the United States vis-a-vis military authorities in dealing with enemy aliens overseas.

I.

Modern American law has come a long way since the time when outbreak of war made every enemy national an outlaw, subject to both public and private slaughter, cruelty and plunder. But even by the most magnanimous view, our law does not abolish inherent distinctions recognized throughout the civilized world between citizens and aliens, nor between aliens of friendly and of enemy allegiance, nor between resident enemy aliens who have submitted themselves to our laws and non-resident enemy aliens who at all times have remained with, and adhered to, enemy governments.

With the citizen we are now little concerned, except to set his case apart as untouched by this decision and to take measure of the difference between his status and that of all categories of aliens. Citizenship as a head of jurisdiction and a ground of protection was old when Paul invoked it in his appeal to Caesar. The years have not destroyed nor diminished the importance of citizenship nor have they sapped the vitality of a citizen's claims upon his government for protection. If a person's claim to United States citizenship is denied by any official, Congress has directed our courts to entertain his action to declare him to be a citizen "regardless of whether he is within the United States or abroad." This Court long ago extended habeas corpus to one seeking admission to the country to assure fair hearing of his claims to citizenship and has secured citizenship against forfeiture by involuntary formal acts. Because the Government's obligation of protection is correlative with the duty of loyal support inherent in the citizen's allegiance, Congress has directed the President to exert the full diplomatic and political power of the United States on behalf of any citizen, but of no other, in jeopardy abroad. When any citizen is deprived of his liberty by any foreign government, it is made the duty of the President to demand the reasons and, if the detention appears wrongful, to use means not amounting to acts of war to effectuate his release. It is neither sentimentality nor chauvinism to repeat that "Citizenship is a high privilege."

The alien, to whom the United States has been traditionally hospitable, has been accorded a generous and ascending scale of rights as he increases his identity with our society. Mere lawful presence in the country creates an implied assurance of safe conduct and gives him certain rights; they become more extensive and secure when he makes preliminary declaration of intention to become a citizen, and they expand to those of full citizenship upon naturalization. During his probationary residence, this Court has steadily enlarged his right against Executive deportation except upon full and fair hearing. And, at least since 1886, we have extended to the person and property of resident aliens important constitutional guaranties—such as the due process of law of the Fourteenth Amendment. But, in extending constitutional protections beyond the citizenry, the Court has been at pains to point out that it was the alien's presence within its territorial jurisdiction that gave the Judiciary power to act.

Since most cases involving aliens afford this ground of jurisdiction, and the civil and property rights of immigrants or transients of foreign nationality so nearly approach equivalence to those of citizens, courts in peace time have little occasion to inquire whether litigants before them are alien or citizen.

It is war that exposes the relative vulnerability of the alien's status. The security and protection enjoyed while the nation of his allegiance remains in amity with the United States are greatly impaired when his nation takes up arms against us. While

DID YOU KNOW?

***Harris v. Nelson*, 1969**

In *Harris v. Nelson,* the Supreme Court affirmed that the writ of habeas corpus was a fundamental instrument for safeguarding a U.S. citizen's individual freedom against arbitrary and lawless action by the government. One of the underlying principles of the habeas right has been to provide prisoners with an adequate amount of information to meaningfully challenge the factual basis of their imprisonment and for the courts to have an opportunity to evaluate the legality of the imprisonment based on the facts that have been provided. In *Harris,* the Supreme Court recognized that "the writ of habeas corpus is the fundamental instrument for safeguarding individual freedom against arbitrary and lawless state action," and that therefore, the writ must be "administered with the initiative and flexibility essential to insure that miscarriages of justice within its reach are surfaced and corrected." This case acts as a reminder that the writ of habeas corpus serves as an essential check for citizens on the manner in which state courts pay respect to federal constitutional rights.

his lot is far more humane and endurable than the experience of our citizens in some enemy lands, it is still not a happy one. But disabilities this country lays upon the alien who becomes also an enemy are imposed temporarily as an incident of war and not as an incident of alienage.

American doctrine as to effect of war upon the status of nationals of belligerents took permanent shape following our first foreign war. Conscription, compulsory service and measures to mobilize every human and material resource and to utilize nationals—wherever they may be—in arms, intrigue and sabotage, attest the prophetic realism of what once may have seemed a doctrinaire and artificial principle. The alien enemy is bound by an allegiance which commits him to lose no opportunity to forward the cause of our enemy; hence the United States, assuming him to be faithful to his allegiance, regards him as part of the enemy resources. It therefore takes measures to disable him from commission of hostile acts imputed as his intention because they are a duty to his sovereign.

The essential pattern for seasonable Executive constraint of enemy aliens, not on the basis of individual prepossessions for their native land but on the basis of political and legal relations to the enemy government, was laid down in the very earliest days of the Republic and has endured to this day. It was established by the Alien Enemy Act of 1798. And it is to be noted that, while the Alien and Sedition Acts of that year provoked a reaction which helped sweep the party of Mr. Jefferson into power in 1800, and though his party proceeded to undo what was regarded as the mischievous legislation of the Federalists, this enactment was never repealed. Executive power over enemy aliens, undelayed and unhampered by litigation, has been deemed, throughout our history, essential to war-time security. This is in keeping with the practices of the most enlightened of nations and has resulted in treatment of alien enemies more considerate than that which has prevailed among any of our enemies and some of our allies. This statute was enacted or suffered to continue by men who helped found the Republic and formulate the Bill of Rights, and although it obviously denies enemy aliens the constitutional immunities of citizens, it seems not then to have been supposed that a nation's obligations to its foes could ever be put on a parity with those to its defenders.

The resident enemy alien is constitutionally subject to summary arrest, internment and deportation whenever a "declared war" exists. Courts will entertain his plea for freedom from Executive custody only to ascertain the existence of a state of war and whether he is an alien enemy and so subject to the Alien Enemy Act. Once these jurisdictional elements have been determined, courts will not inquire into any other issue as to his internment.

The standing of the enemy alien to maintain any action in the courts of the United States has been often challenged and sometimes denied.

But the nonresident enemy alien, especially one who has remained in the service of the enemy, does not have even this qualified access to our courts, for he neither has comparable claims upon our institutions nor could his use of them fail to be helpful to the enemy. Our law on this subject first emerged about 1813 when the Supreme Court of the State of New York had occasion, in a series of cases, to examine the foremost authorities of the Continent and of England. It concluded the rule of the common law and the law of nations to be that alien enemies resident in the country of the enemy could not maintain an action in its courts during the period of hostilities.

II.

The foregoing demonstrates how much further we must go if we are to invest these enemy aliens, resident, captured and imprisoned abroad, with standing to demand access to our courts.

We are here confronted with a decision whose basic premise is that these prisoners are entitled, as a constitutional right, to sue in some court of the United States for a writ of habeas corpus. To support that assumption we must hold that a prisoner of our military authorities is constitutionally entitled to the writ, even though he (a) is an enemy alien; (b) has never been or resided in the United States; (c) was captured outside of our territory and there held in military custody as a prisoner of war; (d) was tried and convicted by a Military Commission sitting outside the United States; (e) for offenses against laws of war committed outside the United States; (f) and is at all times imprisoned outside the United States.

We have pointed out that the privilege of litigation has been extended to aliens, whether friendly or enemy, only because permitting their presence in the country implied protection. No such basis can be invoked here, for these prisoners at no relevant time were within any territory over which the United States is sovereign, and the scenes of their offense, their capture, their trial and their punishment were all beyond the territorial jurisdiction of any court of the United States.

Another reason for a limited opening of our courts to resident aliens is that among them are many of friendly personal disposition to whom the status of enemy is only one imputed by law. But these prisoners were actual enemies, active in the hostile service of an enemy power. There is no fiction about their enmity. Yet the decision below confers upon them a right to use our courts, free even of the limitation we have imposed upon resident alien enemies, to whom we deny any use of our courts that would hamper our war effort or aid the enemy.

A basic consideration in habeas corpus practice is that the prisoner will be produced before the court. This is the crux of the statutory scheme established by the Congress; indeed, it is inherent in the very term "habeas corpus." And though production of the prisoner may be dispensed with where it appears on the face of the application that no cause for granting the writ exists, we have consistently adhered to and recognized the general rule. To grant the writ to these prisoners might mean that our army must transport them across the seas for hearing. This would require allocation of shipping space, guarding personnel, billeting and rations. It might also require transportation for whatever witnesses the prisoners desired to call as well as transportation for those necessary to defend legality of the sentence. The writ, since it is held to be a matter of right, would be equally available to enemies during active hostilities as in the present twilight between war and peace. Such trials would hamper the war effort and bring aid and comfort to the enemy. They would diminish the prestige of our commanders, not only with enemies but with wavering neutrals. It would be difficult to devise more effective fettering of a field commander than to allow the very enemies he is ordered to reduce to submission to call him to account in his own civil courts and divert his efforts and attention from the military offensive abroad to the legal defensive at home. Nor is it unlikely that the result of such enemy litigiousness would be a conflict between judicial and military opinion highly comforting to enemies of the United States.

Moreover, we could expect no reciprocity for placing the litigation weapon in unrestrained enemy hands. The right of judicial refuge from military action, which it is proposed to bestow on the enemy, can purchase no equivalent for benefit of our citizen soldiers. Except in England, whose law appears to be in harmony with the views we have expressed, and other English-speaking peoples in whose practice nothing has been cited to the contrary, the writ of habeas corpus is generally unknown.

The prisoners rely, however, upon two decisions of this Court to get them over the threshold—Ex parte Quirin, and In re Yamashita. Reliance on the Quirin case is clearly mistaken. Those prisoners were in custody in the District of Columbia. One was, or claimed to be, a citizen. They were tried by a Military Commission sitting in the District of Columbia at a time when civil courts were open and functioning normally. They were arrested by civil authorities and the prosecution was personally directed by the Attorney General, a civilian prosecutor, for acts committed in the United States. They waived arraignment before a civil court and it was contended that the civil courts thereby acquired jurisdiction and could not be ousted by the Military. None of the places where they were acting, arrested, tried or imprisoned were, it was contended, in a zone of active military operations or under martial law or any other military control, and no circumstances justified transferring them from civil to military jurisdiction. None of these grave grounds for challenging military jurisdiction can be urged in the case now before us.

Nor can the Court's decision in the Yamashita case aid the prisoners. This Court refused to receive Yamashita's petition for a writ of habeas corpus. For hearing and opinion, it was consolidated with another application for a writ of certiorari to review the refusal of habeas corpus by the Supreme Court of the Philippines over whose decisions the statute then gave this Court a right of review. By reason of our sovereignty at that time over these insular possessions, Yamashita stood much as did Quirin before American courts. Yamashita's offenses were committed on our territory, he was tried within the jurisdiction of our insular courts and he was imprisoned within territory of the United States. None of these heads of jurisdiction can be invoked by these prisoners.

Despite this, the doors of our courts have not been summarily closed upon these prisoners. Three courts have considered their application and have provided their counsel opportunity to advance every argument in their support and to show some reason in the petition why they should not be subject to the usual disabilities of nonresident enemy aliens. This is the same preliminary hearing as to sufficiency of application that was extended in Quirin.... and Yamashita. After hearing all contentions they have seen fit to advance and considering every contention we can base on their application and the holdings below, we arrive at the same conclusion the Court reached in each of those cases, viz.: that no right to the writ of habeas corpus appears.

III.

The Court of Appeals dispensed with all requirement of territorial jurisdiction based on place of residence, captivity, trial, offense, or confinement. It could not predicate relief upon any intraterritorial contact of these prisoners with our laws or institutions. Instead, it gave our Constitution an extraterritorial application to embrace our enemies in arms. Right to the writ, it reasoned, is a subsidiary procedural right that follows from possession of substantive constitutional rights. These prisoners, it considered, are invested with a right of personal liberty by our Constitution and therefore must have the right to the remedial writ.

The doctrine that the term "any person" in the Fifth Amendment spreads its protection over alien enemies anywhere in the world engaged in hostilities against us, should be weighed in light of the full text of that Amendment:

"No person shall be held to answer for a capital, or otherwise infamous crime, unless on a presentment or indictment of a Grand Jury, except in cases arising in the land or naval forces, or in the Militia, when in actual service in time of War or public danger; nor shall any person be subject for the same offense to be twice put in jeopardy of life or limb; nor shall be compelled in any criminal case to be a witness against himself, nor be deprived of life, liberty, or property, without due process of law; nor shall private property be taken for public use, without just compensation."

When we analyze the claim prisoners are asserting and the court below sustained, it amounts to a right not to be tried at all for an offense against our armed forces. If the Fifth Amendment protects them from military trial, the Sixth Amendment as clearly prohibits their trial by civil courts. The latter requires in all criminal prosecutions that "the accused" be tried "by an impartial jury of the State and district wherein the crime shall have been committed, which district shall have been previously ascertained by law." And if the Fifth be held to embrace these prisoners because it uses the inclusive term "no person," the Sixth must, for it applies to all "accused." No suggestion is advanced by the court below, or by prisoners, of any constitutional method by which any violations of the laws of war endangering the United States forces could be reached or punished, if it were not by a Military Commission in the theater where the offense was committed.

The decision below would extend coverage of our Constitution to nonresident alien enemies denied to resident alien enemies. The latter are entitled only to judicial hearing to determine what the petition of these prisoners admits: that they are really alien enemies. When that appears, those resident here may be deprived of liberty by Executive action without hearing. While this is preventive rather than punitive detention, no reason is apparent why an alien enemy charged with having committed a crime should have greater immunities from Executive action than one who it is only feared might at some future time commit a hostile act.

If the Fifth Amendment confers its rights on all the world except Americans engaged in defending it, the same must be true of the companion civil-rights Amendments, for none of them is limited by its express terms, territorially or as to persons. Such a construction would mean that during military occupation irreconcilable enemy elements, guerrilla fighters, and "werewolves" could require the American Judiciary to assure them freedoms of speech, press, and assembly as in the First Amendment, right to bear arms as in the Second, security against "unreasonable" searches and seizures as in the Fourth, as well as rights to jury trial as in the Fifth and Sixth Amendments.

Such extraterritorial application of organic law would have been so significant an innovation in the practice of governments that, if intended or apprehended, it could scarcely have failed to excite contemporary comment. Not one word can be cited. No decision of this Court supports such a view. None of the learned commentators on our Constitution has even hinted at it. The practice of every modern government is opposed to it. We hold that the Constitution does not confer a right of personal security or an immunity from military trial and punishment upon an alien enemy engaged in the hostile service of a government at war with the United States.

IV.

The Court of Appeals appears to have been of opinion that the petition shows some action by some official of the United States in excess of his authority which confers a private right to have it judicially voided. Its Second and Third propositions were that "action by Government officials in violation of the Constitution is void" and "a basic and inherent function of the judicial branch ... is to set aside void action by government officials...." For this reason it thought the writ could be granted.

The jurisdiction of military authorities, during or following hostilities, to punish those guilty of offenses against the laws of war is long-established. This Court has characterized as "well-established" the "power of the military to exercise jurisdiction over members of the armed forces, those directly connected with such forces, or enemy belligerents, prisoners of war, or others charged with violating the laws of war." And we have held in the Quirin and Yamashita cases, that the Military Commission is a lawful tribunal to adjudge enemy offenses against the laws of war.

It is not for us to say whether these prisoners were or were not guilty of a war crime, or whether if we were to retry the case we would agree to the findings of fact or the application of the laws of war made by the Military Commission. The petition shows that these prisoners were formally accused of violating the laws of war and fully informed of particulars of these charges.

That there is a basis in conventional and long-established law by which conduct ascribed to them might amount to a violation seems beyond question. Breach of the terms of an act of surrender is no novelty among war crimes. It being within the jurisdiction of a Military Commission to try the prisoners, it was for it to determine whether the laws of war applied and whether an offense against them had been committed.

We are unable to find that the petition alleges any fact showing lack of jurisdiction in the military authorities to accuse, try and condemn these prisoners or that they acted in excess of their lawful powers.

V.

For reasons stated, the judgment of the Court of Appeals is reversed and the judgment of the District Court dismissing the petition is affirmed.

Reversed.

SOURCE: http://caselaw.lp.findlaw.com/scripts/getcase.pl?court=US&vol=339&invol=763

ANALYSIS

Twenty-one German nonresident enemy aliens were captured in China by the United States Army and tried and convicted in China by an American military commission for violations of the laws of war committed in China prior to their capture. They were transported to the American-occupied part of Germany and imprisoned there in the custody of the Army. At no time were they within the territorial jurisdiction of any American civil court. Claiming that their trial, conviction, and imprisonment violated Articles I and III, the Fifth Amendment due process clause, and other provisions of our Constitution, laws of the United States and provisions of the Geneva Convention, they petitioned the District Court for the District of Columbia for a writ of habeas corpus directed to the secretary of defense, the secretary of the army, and several officers of the army having directive power over their custodian.

This is an important case because the Court's analysis focuses primarily on the differences between the legal rights afforded to citizens versus those afforded to aliens. The majority opinion noted that our law and the laws of most of the civilized world have long recognized distinctions between citizens and aliens. The Court makes clear that because the prisoners at issue had at no relevant time been within any territory over which the United States held sovereignty, and all other aspects of their crimes, capture, trial, and imprisonment, were well beyond the territorial jurisdiction of any U.S. court. The Court also discussed the impact their decision would have on the capabilities of commanders to prosecute war and ensure wartime security; including the impact on the war effort should the requested relief be granted to the petitioners. They appreciated the importance of preserving the president's power over enemy aliens without the possible constraints of continued litigation.

The Court also acknowledged that they could discover no instances where a court in the United States or any other country that employs the writ had issued it on behalf of an alien enemy who had at no time been within the country's territorial jurisdiction. The majority distinguishes *Quirin* arguing that the prisoners in that case were captured, tried, and convicted by a military commission inside the United States whereas in *Eisentrager* the petitioners were captured and tried in an active military zone. Similarly, in *Yamashita*, the petitioner had committed offenses and been tried within a U.S. territory. In the end, the Court in *Eisentrager* paid great deference to the executive branch during wartime, undermining individual liberties of noncitizens.

FURTHER READING

Posner, Richard A. *Not a Suicide Pact: The Constitution in a Time of National Emergency*. London: Oxford University Press, 2006.

Footnote 4 and Levels of Scrutiny for Equal Protection Analysis

- ***Document:*** The Supreme Court case *United States v. Carolene Products Company*, Excerpt
- ***Date:*** April 25, 1938
- ***Where:*** Washington, D.C.
- ***Significance:*** The holding of this case upholding the Filled Milk Act is not as significant as the language found in footnote four. In footnote four, Justice Stone suggests that there were justifications to apply a more "exacting standard" of judicial review for noneconomic cases. He contends that legislation aimed at "discrete and insular minorities," who lack the customary protections of the political process, should be an exception to the presumption of constitutionality, and a heightened standard of judicial review should be applied. This footnote has significantly influenced equal protection jurisprudence and judicial review.

DOCUMENT

United States v. Carolene Products Co., 304 U.S. 144 (1938)

Argued April 6, 1938.

Decided April 25, 1938.

Mr. Justice Stone delivered the opinion of the Court.

The question for decision is whether the "Filled Milk Act" of Congress of March 4, 1923 which prohibits the shipment in interstate commerce of skimmed milk compounded with any fat or oil other than milk fat, so as to resemble milk or cream, transcends the power of Congress to regulate interstate commerce or infringes the Fifth Amendment.

The power of the legislature to secure a minimum of particular nutritive elements in a widely used article of food and to protect the public from fraudulent substitutions was not doubted, and the Court thought that there was ample scope for the legislative judgment that prohibition of the offending article was an appropriate means of preventing injury to the public.

We see no persuasive reason for departing from that ruling here, where the Fifth Amendment is concerned, and since none is suggested, we might rest decision wholly on the presumption of constitutionality. But affirmative evidence also sustains the statute. In twenty years, evidence has steadily accumulated of the danger to the public health from the general consumption of foods which have been stripped of elements essential to the maintenance of health. The Filled Milk Act was adopted by Congress after committee hearings, in the course of which eminent scientists and health experts testified. An extensive investigation was made of the commerce in milk compounds in which vegetable oils have been substituted for natural milk fat, and of the effect upon the public health of the use of such compounds as a food substitute for milk.

Both committees concluded, as the statute itself declares, that the use of filled milk as a substitute for pure milk is generally injurious to health and facilitates fraud on the public.

There is nothing in the Constitution which compels a legislature, either national or state, to ignore such evidence, nor need it disregard the other evidence which amply supports the conclusions of the Congressional committees that the danger is greatly enhanced where an inferior product is indistinguishable from a valuable food of almost universal use, thus making fraudulent distribution easy and protection of the consumer difficult.

There is no need to consider it here as more than a declaration of the legislative findings deemed to support and justify the action taken as a constitutional exertion of the legislative power, aiding informed judicial review, as do the reports of legislative committees, by revealing the rationale of the legislation. Even in the absence of such aids, the existence of facts supporting the legislative judgment is to be presumed, for regulatory legislation affecting ordinary commercial transactions is not to be pronounced unconstitutional unless, in the light of the facts made known or generally assumed, it is of such a character as to preclude the assumption that it rests upon some rational basis within the knowledge and experience of the legislators. Footnote 4:

There may be narrower scope for operation of the presumption of constitutionality when legislation appears on its face to be within a specific prohibition of the Constitution, such as those of the first ten amendments, which are deemed equally specific when held to be embraced within the Fourteenth...

It is unnecessary to consider now whether legislation which restricts those political processes which can ordinarily be expected to bring about repeal of undesirable legislation, is to be subjected to more exacting judicial scrutiny under the general prohibitions of the Fourteenth Amendment than are most other types of legislation.

Nor need we inquire whether similar considerations enter into the review of statutes directed at particular religious . . . or national . . . or racial minorities . . . : whether prejudice against discrete and insular minorities may be a special condition, which tends seriously to curtail the operation of those political processes ordinarily to be relied upon to protect minorities, and which may call for a correspondingly more searching judicial inquiry.

Where the existence of a rational basis for legislation whose constitutionality is attacked depends upon facts beyond the sphere of judicial notice, such facts may properly be male the subject of judicial inquiry and the constitutionality of a statute predicated upon the existence of a particular state of facts may be challenged by showing to the court that those facts have ceased to exist.

The prohibition of shipment in interstate commerce of appellee's product, as described in the indictment, is a constitutional exercise of the power to regulate interstate commerce. As the statute is not unconstitutional on its face and the judgment will be Reversed.

SOURCE: http://caselaw.lp.findlaw.com/cgi-bin/getcase.pl?court=US&vol=304&invol=144

ANALYSIS

Footnote four is considered one of the most famous footnotes in constitutional law. In *Carolene Products*, the Supreme Court presumed the constitutionality of the economic law in question by applying minimal scrutiny, but footnote four presented reasons for using more rigorous scrutiny in other types of cases. The footnote discusses three such instances: first, that a narrower presumption of constitutionality exists when legislation addresses a specific prohibition of the Constitution, such as those set forth in the Bill of Rights; second, legislation that directly interferes with the political process; and third, legislation aimed at discrete and insular minorities might be subject to stricter judicial review. Discrete and insular minorities are groups that have suffered a long history of discrimination, are politically powerless, and have been unsuccessful at protecting their interests in the majoritarian democratic political process.

The highest level of scrutiny is called "strict scrutiny" and applies when classifications are based on race, national origin, or classifications impacting fundamental rights such as those involving the First Amendment. The second level of scrutiny is called intermediate scrutiny and applies when classifications are based on gender or illegitimacy. The third level of scrutiny is called rational basis and usually applies when dealing with economic legislation. *Carolene Products* is cited overwhelmingly as the source of equal protection analysis by the courts, but this was not always the case. The Supreme Court did not cite *Carolene* in an equal protection case until 1971, and its early references appeared in due process cases. However, over time the principles of footnote four have mostly influenced equal protection jurisprudence. This footnote has significantly broadened the protections of individual liberties and helped to eradicate state-based discrimination in the United States.

FURTHER READING

Ackerman, Bruce. "Beyond Carolene Products." *Harvard Law Review* 98 (1985): 713.

Equal Protection and Strict Scrutiny Analysis under *Korematsu*

- ***Document:*** The Supreme Court case *Korematsu v. United States*, Excerpt
- ***Date:*** December 18, 1944
- ***Where:*** Washington, D.C.
- ***Significance:*** The *Korematsu* decision is significant for being the first instance of the Supreme Court applying the strict scrutiny standard to racial discrimination by the government and for being one of only a small handful of cases in which the Court held that the government met that standard.

DOCUMENT

Toyosaburo Korematsu v. United States, 323 U.S. 214 (1944)

Argued October 11, 12, 1944.
Decided December 18, 1944.
Mr. Justice Black delivered the opinion of the Court.

The petitioner, an American citizen of Japanese descent, was convicted in a federal district court for remaining in San Leandro, California, a "Military Area," contrary to Civilian Exclusion Order No. 34 of the Commanding General of the Western Command, U.S. Army, which directed that after May 9, 1942, all persons of Japanese ancestry should be excluded from that area. No question was raised as to petitioner's loyalty to the United States. It should be noted, to begin with, that all legal restrictions which curtail the civil rights of a single racial group are immediately suspect. That is not to say that all such restrictions are unconstitutional. It is to say that courts must subject them to the most rigid scrutiny. Pressing public necessity may sometimes justify the existence of such restrictions; racial antagonism never can.

In the instant case prosecution of the petitioner was begun by information charging violation of an Act of Congress, of March 21, 1942, 56 Stat. 173, which provides that:

"...whoever shall enter, remain in, leave, or commit any act in any military area or military zone prescribed, under the authority of an Executive order of the President, by the Secretary of War, or by any military commander designated by the Secretary of War, contrary to the restrictions applicable to any such area or zone or contrary to the order of the Secretary of War or any such military commander, shall, if it appears that he knew or should have known of the existence and extent of the restrictions or order and that his act was in violation thereof, be guilty of a misdemeanor and upon conviction shall be liable to a fine of not to exceed $5,000 or to imprisonment for not more than one year, or both, for each offense."

Exclusion Order No. 34, which the petitioner knowingly and admittedly violated, was one of a number of military orders and proclamations, all of which were substantially based upon Executive Order No. 9066, 7 Fed. Reg. 1407. That order, issued after we were at war with Japan, declared that "the successful prosecution of the war requires every possible protection against espionage and against sabotage to national-defense material, national-defense premises, and national-defense utilities...."

One of the series of orders and proclamations, a curfew order, which like the exclusion order here was promulgated pursuant to Executive Order 9066, subjected all persons of Japanese ancestry in prescribed West Coast military areas to remain in their residences from 8 p.m. to 6 a.m. As is the case with the exclusion order here, that prior curfew order was designed as a "protection against espionage and against sabotage." In Hirabayashi v. United States, 320 U.S. 81, we sustained a conviction obtained for violation of the curfew order. The Hirabayashi conviction and this one thus rest on the same 1942 Congressional Act and the same basic executive and military orders, all of which orders were aimed at the twin dangers of espionage and sabotage.

The 1942 Act was attacked in the Hirabayashi case as an unconstitutional delegation of power; it was contended that the curfew order and other orders on which it rested were beyond the war powers of the Congress, the military authorities and of the President, as Commander in Chief of the Army; and finally that to apply the curfew order against none but citizens of Japanese ancestry amounted to a constitutionally prohibited discrimination solely on account of race. To these questions, we gave the serious consideration which their importance justified. We upheld the curfew order as an exercise of the power of the government to take steps necessary to prevent espionage and sabotage in an area threatened by Japanese attack.

In the light of the principles we announced in the Hirabayashi case, we are unable to conclude that it was beyond the war power of Congress and the Executive to exclude those of Japanese ancestry from the West Coast war area at the time they did. True, exclusion from the area in which one's home is located is a far greater deprivation than constant confinement to the home from 8 p.m. to 6 a.m. Nothing short of apprehension by the proper military authorities of the gravest imminent danger to the public safety can constitutionally justify either. But exclusion from a threatened area, no less than curfew, has a definite and close relationship to the prevention of espionage and sabotage. The military authorities, charged with the primary responsibility of defending our shores, concluded that curfew provided inadequate protection and ordered exclusion. They did so, as pointed out in our Hirabayashi opinion, in accordance with Congressional authority to the military to say who should, and who should not, remain in the threatened areas.

Like curfew, exclusion of those of Japanese origin was deemed necessary because of the presence of an unascertained number of disloyal members of the group, most of whom we have no doubt were loyal to this country. It was because we could not reject the finding of the military authorities that it was impossible to bring about an immediate segregation of the disloyal from the loyal that we sustained the validity of the curfew order as applying to the whole group. In the instant case, temporary exclusion of the entire group was rested by the military on the same ground. The judgment that exclusion of the whole group was for the same reason a military imperative answers the contention that the exclusion was in the nature of group punishment based on antagonism to those of Japanese origin....

We uphold the exclusion order as of the time it was made and when the petitioner violated it. In doing so, we are not unmindful of the hardships imposed by it upon a large group of American citizens. But hardships are part of war, and war is an aggregation of hardships. All citizens alike, both in and out of uniform, feel the impact of war in greater or lesser measure. Citizenship has its responsibilities as well as its privileges, and in time of war the burden is always heavier. Compulsory exclusion of large groups of citizens from their homes, except under circumstances of direst emergency and peril, is inconsistent with our basic governmental institutions. But when under conditions of modern warfare our shores are threatened by hostile forces, the power to protect must be commensurate with the threatened danger....

After May 3, 1942, the date of Exclusion Order No. 34, Korematsu was under compulsion to leave the area not as he would choose but via an Assembly Center. The Assembly Center was conceived as a part of the machinery for group evacuation. The power to exclude includes the power to do it by force if necessary. And any forcible measure must necessarily entail some degree of detention or restraint whatever method of removal is selected. But whichever view is taken, it results in holding that the order under which petitioner was convicted was valid.

It is said that we are dealing here with the case of imprisonment of a citizen in a concentration camp solely because of his ancestry, without evidence or inquiry concerning his loyalty and good disposition towards the United States. Our task would be simple, our duty clear, were this a case involving the imprisonment of a loyal citizen in a concentration camp because of racial prejudice. Regardless of the true nature of the assembly and relocation centers—and we deem it unjustifiable to call them concentration camps with all the ugly connotations that term implies—we are dealing specifically with nothing but an exclusion order. To cast this case into outlines of racial prejudice, without reference to the real military dangers which were presented, merely confuses the issue. Korematsu was not excluded from the Military Area because of hostility to him or his race. He was excluded because we are at war with the Japanese Empire, because the properly constituted military authorities feared an invasion of our West Coast and felt constrained to take proper security measures, because they decided that the military urgency of the situation demanded that all citizens of Japanese ancestry be segregated from the West Coast temporarily, and finally, because Congress, reposing its confidence in this time of war in our military leaders—as inevitably it must—determined that they should have the power to do just this. There was evidence of disloyalty on the part of some, the military authorities considered that the need for action was great, and time was short. We cannot—by availing ourselves of the calm perspective of hindsight—now say that at that time these actions were unjustified.

Affirmed.

Mr. Justice Murphy, dissenting.

This exclusion of "all persons of Japanese ancestry, both alien and non-alien," from the Pacific Coast area on a plea of military necessity in the absence of martial law ought not to be approved. Such exclusion goes over "the very brink of constitutional power" and falls into the ugly abyss of racism.

In dealing with matters relating to the prosecution and progress of a war, we must accord great respect and consideration to the judgments of the military authorities who are on the scene and who have full knowledge of the military facts. The scope of their discretion must, as a matter of necessity and common sense, be wide. And their judgments ought not to be overruled lightly by those whose training and duties ill-equip them to deal intelligently with matters so vital to the physical security of the nation.

At the same time, however, it is essential that there be definite limits to military discretion, especially where martial law has not been declared. Individuals must not be left impoverished of their constitutional rights on a plea of military necessity that has neither substance nor support. Thus, like other claims conflicting with the asserted constitutional rights of the individual, the military claim must subject itself to the judicial process of having its reasonableness determined and its conflicts with other interests reconciled. "What are the allowable limits of military discretion, and whether or not they have been overstepped in a particular case, are judicial questions."

The judicial test of whether the Government, on a plea of military necessity, can validly deprive an individual of any of his constitutional rights is whether the deprivation is reasonably related to a public danger that is so "immediate, imminent, and impending" as not to admit of delay and not to permit the intervention of ordinary constitutional processes to alleviate the danger. Civilian Exclusion Order No. 34, banishing from a prescribed area of the Pacific Coast "all persons of Japanese ancestry, both alien and non-alien," clearly does not meet that test. Being an obvious racial discrimination, the order deprives all those within its scope of the equal protection of the laws as guaranteed by the Fifth Amendment. It further deprives these individuals of their constitutional rights to live and work where they will, to establish a home where they choose and to move about freely. In excommunicating them without benefit of hearings, this order also deprives them of all their constitutional rights to procedural due process. Yet no reasonable relation to an "immediate, imminent, and impending" public danger is evident to support this racial restriction which is one of the most sweeping and complete deprivations of constitutional rights in the history of this nation in the absence of martial law.

It must be conceded that the military and naval situation in the spring of 1942 was such as to generate a very real fear of invasion of the Pacific Coast, accompanied by fears of sabotage and espionage in that area. The military command was therefore justified in adopting all reasonable means necessary to combat these dangers. In adjudging the military action taken in light of the then apparent dangers, we must not erect too high or too meticulous standards; it is necessary only that the action have some reasonable relation to the removal of the dangers of invasion, sabotage and espionage. But the exclusion, either temporarily or permanently, of all persons with

Japanese blood in their veins has no such reasonable relation. And that relation is lacking because the exclusion order necessarily must rely for its reasonableness upon the assumption that all persons of Japanese ancestry may have a dangerous tendency to commit sabotage and espionage and to aid our Japanese enemy in other ways. It is difficult to believe that reason, logic or experience could be marshalled in support of such an assumption.

That this forced exclusion was the result in good measure of this erroneous assumption of racial guilt rather than bona fide military necessity is evidenced by the Commanding General's Final Report on the evacuation from the Pacific Coast area. In it he refers to all individuals of Japanese descent as "subversive," as belonging to "an enemy race" whose "racial strains are undiluted," and as constituting "over 112,000 potential enemies . . . at large today" along the Pacific Coast. In support of this blanket condemnation of all persons of Japanese descent, however, no reliable evidence is cited to show that such individuals were generally disloyal, or had generally so conducted themselves in this area as to constitute a special menace to defense installations or war industries, or had otherwise by their behavior furnished reasonable ground for their exclusion as a group.

Justification for the exclusion is sought, instead, mainly upon questionable racial and sociological grounds not ordinarily within the realm of expert military judgment, supplemented by certain semi-military conclusions drawn from an unwarranted use of circumstantial evidence. Individuals of Japanese ancestry are condemned because they are said to be "a large, unassimilated, tightly knit racial group, bound to an enemy nation by strong ties of race, culture, custom and religion." They are claimed to be given to "emperor worshipping ceremonies" and to "dual citizenship." Japanese language schools and allegedly pro-Japanese organizations are cited as evidence of possible group disloyalty, together with facts as to certain persons being educated and residing at length in Japan. It is intimated that many of these individuals deliberately resided "adjacent to strategic points," thus enabling them "to carry into execution a tremendous program of sabotage on a mass scale should any considerable number of them have been inclined to do so."

The main reasons relied upon by those responsible for the forced evacuation, therefore, do not prove a reasonable relation between the group characteristics of Japanese Americans and the dangers of invasion, sabotage and espionage. The reasons appear, instead, to be largely an accumulation of much of the misinformation, half-truths and insinuations that for years have been directed against Japanese Americans by people with racial and economic prejudices—the same people who have been among the foremost advocates of the evacuation. A military judgment based upon such racial and sociological considerations is not entitled to the great weight ordinarily given the judgments based upon strictly military considerations. Especially is this so when every charge relative to race, religion, culture, geographical location, and legal and economic status has been substantially discredited by independent studies made by experts in these matters.

The military necessity which is essential to the validity of the evacuation order thus resolves itself into a few intimations that certain individuals actively aided the enemy, from which it is inferred that the entire group of Japanese Americans could not be trusted to be or remain loyal to the United States. No one denies, of course, that there were some disloyal persons of Japanese descent on the Pacific Coast who did all in their power to aid their ancestral land. Similar disloyal activities have been engaged in by many persons of German, Italian and even more pioneer stock in our country. But to infer that examples of individual disloyalty prove group disloyalty and justify discriminatory action against the entire group is to deny that under our system of law individual guilt is the sole basis for deprivation of rights. Moreover, this inference, which is at the very heart of the evacuation orders, has been used in support of the abhorrent and despicable treatment of minority groups by the dictatorial tyrannies which this nation is now pledged to destroy. To give constitutional sanction to that inference in this case, however well-intentioned may have been the military command on the Pacific Coast, is to adopt one of the cruelest of the rationales used by our enemies to destroy the dignity of the individual and to encourage and open the door to discriminatory actions against other minority groups in the passions of tomorrow. . . .

I dissent, therefore, from this legalization of racism. Racial discrimination in any form and in any degree has no justifiable part whatever in our democratic way of life. It is unattractive in any setting but it is utterly revolting among a free people who have embraced the principles set forth in the Constitution of the United States. All residents of this nation are kin in some way by blood or culture to a foreign land. Yet they are primarily and necessarily a part of the new and distinct civilization of the United States. They must accordingly be treated at all times as the heirs of the American experiment and as entitled to all the rights and freedoms guaranteed by the Constitution.

SOURCE: http://caselaw.lp.findlaw.com/scripts/getcase.pl?court=US&vol=323&invol=214

ANALYSIS

This case was similar to the *Hirabayashi* case and dealt with the issue of internment of individuals based on race. During World War II, Presidential Executive Order 9066 and congressional statutes gave the military authority to exclude citizens of Japanese ancestry from areas deemed critical to national defense and potentially vulnerable to espionage. Korematsu remained in San Leandro, California, and violated Civilian Exclusion Order No. 34 of the U.S. Army.

These orders involved a racial classification requiring the use strict scrutiny. This means that in order for the law or executive order to be constitutional, the state must provide a compelling state reason. Usually when the Court applies this standard, the legislation or executive order is determined to be unconstitutional. This is one of only a few cases where the Court upheld the law or executive order in question. The state's compelling interest included protecting national security during a time of war. In the light the *Hirabayashi* case, the Court determined that it was unable to conclude that it was beyond the war power of Congress and the executive to exclude those of Japanese ancestry from the West Coast war area at the time they did in this case. The Court found that here, as in the *Hirabayashi* case, it could not reject as unfounded the judgment of the military authorities and of Congress that there were disloyal members of the Japanese population, whose number and strength could not be precisely and quickly ascertained. The Court balanced the country's national security against the "suspect" curtailment of the rights of a particular racial group. Ultimately, the majority decided that the nation's security concerns outweighed the Constitutional protections afforded individuals in this country.

Justice Murphy dissented because he disagreed with the way in which the court balanced national security and constitutional rights. The main aspect of Justice Murphy's criticism is that while the military must be fully trusted to wage war, its actions cannot escape the later judicial review of the courts, which are mandated to balance the demands of military necessity with the countervailing demands of individual liberties. Finding no evidence tying Japanese Americans to sabotage or espionage, Murphy argued the internment was based on "the misinformation, half truths and insinuations that for years have been directed against Japanese Americans by people with racial and economic prejudices—the same people who have been among the foremost advocates of the evacuation." Murphy also compared the treatment of Japanese Americans, on the one hand, with persons of German and Italian ancestry, on the other, as evidence that race, rather than the emergency alone, led to the exclusion order which Korematsu was convicted of violating. This is because although German and Italian citizens were also interned, Japanese Americans were the group that was almost exclusively targeted by the government. Even though Korematsu's conviction was eventually overturned in 1983, the *Korematsu* ruling concerning the creation of exclusion orders has never been overturned and it has been used in a number of terrorism cases by the Bush administration following 9/11.

FURTHER READING

Gressman, Eugene. "Judgments Judged and Wrongs Remembered: Examining the Japanese American Civil Liberties Cases on their Sixtieth Anniversary: Korematsu: A Melange of Military Imperatives." *Law and Contemporary Problems* 68 (Spring 2005): 15.

The Clear and Present Danger Test for First Amendment Jurisprudence

- ***Document:*** The Supreme Court case *Schenck v. United States*, Excerpt
- ***Date:*** March 3, 1919
- ***Where:*** Washington, D.C.
- ***Significance:*** The Supreme Court held unanimously that in a time of war, extraordinary conditions may take effect where Congress has the right to forbid printed materials or speech aimed at hindering the war effort. The "clear and present danger" test was formulated by Justice Holmes to deal with questions concerning the First Amendment.

DOCUMENT

Schenck v. United States, 249 U.S. 47 (1919)

Argued January 9, 10, 1919.

Decided March 3, 1919.

Mr. Justice Holmes delivered the opinion of the court.

This is an indictment in three counts. The first charges a conspiracy to violate the Espionage Act of June 15, 1917 by causing and attempting to cause insubordination, &c., in the military and naval forces of the United States, and to obstruct the recruiting and enlistment service of the United States, when the United States was at war with the German Empire, to-wit, that the defendants wilfully conspired to have printed and circulated to men who had been called and accepted for military service under the Act of May 18, 1917, a document set forth and alleged to be calculated to cause such insubordination and obstruction. The count alleges overt acts in pursuance of the conspiracy, ending in the distribution of the document set forth.... The defendants were found guilty on all the counts. They set up the First Amendment to the Constitution forbidding Congress to make any law abridging the freedom of speech, or of the press....

According to the testimony Schenck said he was general secretary of the Socialist party and had charge of the Socialist headquarters from which the documents were sent. He identified a book found there as the minutes of the Executive Committee of the party. The book showed a resolution of August 13, 1917, that 15,000 leaflets should be printed on the other side of one of them in use, to be mailed to men who had passed exemption boards, and for distribution. Schenck personally attended to the printing.... No reasonable man could doubt that the defendant Schenck was largely instrumental in sending the circulars about....

The document in question upon its first printed side recited the first section of the Thirteenth Amendment, said that the idea embodied in it was violated by the Conscription Act and that a conscript is little better than a convict. In impassioned language it intimated that conscription was despotism in its worst form and a monstrous wrong against humanity in the interest of Wall Street's chosen few. It said "Do not submit to intimidation," but in form at least confined itself to peaceful measures such as a petition for the repeal of the act. The other and later printed side of the sheet was headed "Assert Your Rights." It stated reasons for alleging that any one violated the Constitution when he refused to recognize "your right to assert your opposition to the draft," and went on "If you do not assert and support your rights, you are helping to deny or disparage rights which it is the solemn duty of all citizens and residents of the United States to retain." It described the arguments on the other side as coming from cunning politicians and a mercenary capitalist press, and even silent consent to the conscription law as helping to support an infamous conspiracy. It denied the power to send our citizens away to foreign shores to shoot up the people of other lands, and added that words could not express the condemnation such cold-blooded ruthlessness deserves, &c., &c., winding up "You must do your share to maintain, support and uphold the rights of the people of this country." Of course the documents would not have been sent unless it had been intended to have some effect, and we do not see what effect it could be expected to have upon persons subject to the draft except to influence them to obstruct the carrying of it out. The defendants do not deny that the jury might find against them on this point.

But it is said, suppose that that was the tendency of this circular, it is protected by the First Amendment

DID YOU KNOW?

"Clear and Present Danger": *Debs v. United States,* 1919

In *Debs v. United States* (1919), the Supreme Court held unanimously that Eugene V. Debs—a charismatic labor organizer, Socialist, and five-time Socialist presidential candidate—had violated the Espionage Act of 1917. Using the "clear and present danger" test established in *Schenck,* the Court concluded that a speech Debs had given in just such circumstances had had the probable effect of discouraging recruitment for the war, and that therefore his speech was punishable under the act.

The Espionage Act made it a crime to "convey information with intent to interfere with the operation or success of the armed forces of the United States or to promote the success of its enemies," thus constraining political speech. On June 16, 1918, Debs gave a speech in Canton, Ohio, protesting the nation's involvement in World War I. In the speech he praised individuals who had been imprisoned for refusing to serve in the military and who had obstructed military recruiting. For his speech, Debs was arrested and charged with violating the Espionage Act.

The state linked its case against Debs to a report entitled "Anti-War Proclamation and Program," presented in a referendum by the Socialist Party in May 1917. The document affirmed the international solidarity of the working class and condemned the war in terms similar to those Debs used in his June speech. The state argued that Debs was attempting to arouse mutiny and treason by preventing the drafting of soldiers into the U.S. Army. The Court concluded that statements in Debs's speech posed a clear and present danger to the country under *Schenck,* and it upheld his conviction. On December 25, 1921, however, President Warren G. Harding freed Debs from prison, commuting his sentence to time served.

This was the last case in which Justice Oliver Wendell Holmes wrote for a unanimous Court upholding a conviction under the Espionage Act of 1917 against a defendant who had spoken or written in opposition to World War I. However, the Court continued to uphold convictions by deferring to Congress during wartime, significantly undermining speech rights and allowing the government to clamp down on any dissent in the United States about the war.

On June 25, 1976—nearly 50 years after his death—the Senate Judiciary Committee voted to restore Debs's citizenship rights.

to the Constitution. Two of the strongest expressions are said to be quoted respectively from well-known public men. It well may be that the prohibition of laws abridging the freedom of speech is not confined to previous restraints, although to prevent them may have been the main purpose, as intimated in Patterson v. Colorado.

We admit that in many places and in ordinary times the defendants in saying all that was said in the circular would have been within their constitutional rights. But the character of every act depends upon the circumstances in which it is done. The most stringent protection of free speech would not protect a man in falsely shouting fire in a theatre and causing a panic. It does not even protect a man from an injunction against uttering words that may have all the effect of force. *The question in every case is whether the words used are used in such circumstances and are of such a nature as to create a clear and present danger that they will bring about the substantive evils that Congress has a right to prevent. It is a question of proximity and degree.* When a nation is at war many things that might be said in time of peace are such a hindrance to its effort that their utterance will not be endured so long as men fight and that no Court could regard them as protected by any constitutional right. It seems to be admitted that if an actual obstruction of the recruiting service were proved, liability for words that produced that effect might be enforced.

The statute of 1917 punishes conspiracies to obstruct as well as actual obstruction. If the act, (speaking, or circulating a paper,) its tendency and the intent with which it is done are the same, we perceive no ground for saying that success alone warrants making the act a crime....

Judgments Affirmed.

SOURCE: http://caselaw.lp.findlaw.com/cgi-bin/getcase.pl?court=US&vol=249&invol=47

ANALYSIS

The Supreme Court has never held that freedoms of speech, press, and assembly are completely without limits. During World War I, Schenck mailed circulars to draftees. The circulars suggested that the draft was a monstrous wrong motivated by the capitalist system. The circulars urged "Do not submit to intimidation" but advised only peaceful action such as petitioning to repeal the Conscription Act. Schenck was charged with conspiracy to violate the Espionage Act by attempting to cause insubordination in the military and to obstruct recruitment.

The Court upheld the Espionage Act of 1917 and concluded that the defendant did not have a First Amendment right to free speech against the draft during World War I. One of the primary difficulties for the majority was settling on a general standard to be applied in determining when a form of expression becomes so threatening to society that it deserves no constitutional protection and must be controlled by government. The clear and present danger test effectively established a doctrine that allowed the government to suppress political speech under certain circumstances such as wartime. Holmes admitted that in peacetime Schenck's words would have been protected by the Constitution. The decision, in addition to sending Schenck to jail for six months, resulted in a pragmatic "balancing test" allowing the Supreme

Court to assess free speech challenges against the state's interests on a case-by-case basis. This balancing test seems to favor the state in relation to the First Amendment in times of war.

FURTHER READING

Parker, Richard A. (ed.). *Free Speech on Trial: Communication Perspectives on Landmark Supreme Court Decisions*. Tuscaloosa, Ala. and London: University of Alabama Press (2003).

Criminalizing Anti-American Speech

- ***Document:*** The Supreme Court case *Abrams v. United States*, Excerpt from the Dissent
- ***Date:*** November 10, 1919
- ***Where:*** Washington, D.C.
- ***Significance:*** The Supreme Court upheld the conviction of the defendants under the Espionage Act based on the principles underlining Schenck. Justice Holmes dissented, advancing a revised version of his clear and present danger test which provided for greater protection of political speech under the First Amendment, even during wartime.

DOCUMENT

Abrams et al. v. United States, 250 U.S. 616 (1919)

Argued October 21 and 22, 1919.

Decided November 10, 1919.

Mr. Justice Holmes dissenting.

I do not doubt for a moment that by the same reasoning that would justify punishing persuasion to murder, the United States constitutionally may punish speech that produces or is intended to produce a clear and imminent danger that it will bring about forthwith certain substantive evils that the United States constitutionally may seek to prevent. The power undoubtedly is greater in time of war than in time of peace because war opens dangers that do not exist at other times.

But as against dangers peculiar to war, as against others, the principle of the right to free speech is always the same. It is only the present danger of immediate evil or an intent to bring it about that warrants Congress in setting a limit to the expression of opinion where private rights are not concerned. Congress certainly cannot forbid all effort to change the mind of the country. Now nobody can suppose that the surreptitious publishing of a silly leaflet by an unknown man, without more, would present any immediate danger that its opinions would hinder the success of the government arms or have any appreciable tendency to do so. Publishing those opinions for the very purpose of obstructing however, might indicate a greater danger and at any rate would have the quality of an attempt. An actual intent in the sense that I have explained is necessary to constitute an attempt, where a further act of the same individual is required to complete the substantive crime. It is necessary where the success of the attempt depends upon others because if that intent is not present the actor's aim may be accomplished without bringing about the evils sought to be checked. An intent to prevent interference with the revolution in Russia might have been satisfied without any hindrance to carrying on the war in which we were engaged.

I do not see how anyone can find the intent required by the statute in any of the defendants' words. The second leaflet is the only one that affords even a foundation for the charge, and there, without invoking the hatred of German militarism expressed in the former one, it is evident from the beginning to the end that the only object of the paper is to help Russia and stop American intervention there against the popular government—not to impede the United States in the war that it was carrying on. To say that two phrases taken literally might import a suggestion of conduct that would have interference with the war as an indirect and probably undesired effect seems to me by no means enough to show an attempt to produce that effect.

Oliver Wendell Holmes and John Marshall are considered two of the greatest justices in Supreme Court history. Holmes become known as the "Great Dissenter" because of his exceptional legal reasoning and the literary quality of the 173 dissents that he wrote. (National Archives.)

I wholly disagree with the argument of the Government that the First Amendment left the common law as to seditious libel in force. History seems to me against the notion. I had conceived that the United States through many years had shown its repentance for the Sedition Act of 1798, by repaying fines that it imposed. Only the emergency that makes it immediately dangerous to leave the correction of evil counsels to time warrants making any exception to the sweeping command, "Congress shall make no law … abridging the freedom of speech." Of course I am speaking only of expressions of opinion and exhortations, which were all that were uttered here, but I regret that I cannot put into more impressive words my belief that in their conviction upon this indictment the defendants were deprived of their rights under the Constitution of the United States.

SOURCE: http://caselaw.lp.findlaw.com/scripts/getcase.pl?court=US&vol=250&invol=616

ANALYSIS

The defendants were convicted under the Espionage Act on the basis of two leaflets they printed and threw from windows of a building in New York City. One leaflet, signed "revolutionists," condemned the sending of American troops to Russia. The second leaflet, written in Yiddish, condemned the war and the United States' efforts to impede the Russian Revolution and advocated the end of the production of weapons to be used against Russian revolutionaries. The majority opinion has been associated with using the "bad tendency test," which allowed the government to punish speech that tended, even remotely, to encourage violations of the law. The Court therefore rejected the defendants' contention that their only intent was to prevent injury to the Russian cause, holding that men had to be held to have intended, and to be accountable for, the effects that their acts were likely to produce.

Justice Holmes dissented arguing that there was no danger that the defendants actually could damage the war effort. Some scholars believe that Justice Holmes did not change his position but that the facts in Abrams required a different result while others argue that Holmes altered his clear and present danger test established in *Schenck*. In *Abrams*, Holmes asserted that he was following the principles underscoring the *Schenck* decision. However, in restating the "clear and present danger" standard, Holmes argued that Congress may punish only speech that "is intended to produce a clear and imminent danger that it will bring about forthwith certain substantive evils." Justice Holmes exchanged the word "present" with "imminent" and added the word "forthwith" to the sentence. This would seem to make it more difficult for the government to convict an individual under the statute without a greater sense that what was being said would actually occur immediately.

Holmes believed that the government had failed to prove intent in this case. The word "intent," he argued, often was vaguely used to mean only that a certain act had a tendency to cause a certain effect. But "when words are used exactly, a deed is not done with intent to produce a consequence unless that consequence is the aim of the deed." Intent means, in other words, that an individual's goal is the proximate and immediate cause of a specific act. Holmes argued that nobody could expect that the publishing of a "silly" leaflet by an unknown man, without more, would present any immediate danger thereby hindering the success of the government or have any appreciable tendency to do so. In this instance, he believed that the defendant's convictions should be overturned because the suppression of free speech should only be permitted when necessary to immediately save the country.

FURTHER READING

Bollinger, Lee. *The Tolerant Society: Freedom of Speech and Extremist Speech in America*. London: Oxford University Press (1986).

Justice Brandeis's Concurring Opinion and the "Time to Answer" Test

- ***Document:*** The Supreme Court case *Whitney v. California:* Justice Brandeis's Concurrence
- ***Date:*** May 16, 1927
- ***Where:*** Washington, D.C.
- ***Significance:*** The Supreme Court in a unanimous opinion upheld Ms. Whitney's conviction for helping to establish the Communist Labor Party, whose purpose was devoted to teaching the violent overthrow of government in violation of the Criminal Syndicalism Act. The decision is most often acknowledged for Justice Brandeis's concurring opinion, which has been called one of the greatest defenses of freedom of speech ever written by a member of the Court.

DOCUMENT

Whitney v. California, 274 U.S. 357 (1927)

Argued October 6, 1925.
Reargued March 18, 1926.
Decided May 16, 1927.
Justice Brandeis, concurring.

Miss Whitney was convicted of the felony of assisting in organizing, in the year 1919, the Communist Labor Party of California, of being a member of it, and of assembling with it. These acts are held to constitute a crime, because the party was formed to teach criminal syndicalism. The statute which made these acts a crime restricted the right of free speech and of assembly theretofore existing. The claim is that the statute, as applied, denied to Miss Whitney the liberty guaranteed by the Fourteenth Amendment....

The right of free speech, the right to teach and the right of assembly are, of course, fundamental rights. These may not be denied or abridged. But, although the rights of free speech and assembly are fundamental, they are not in their nature absolute. Their exercise is subject to restriction, if the particular restriction proposed is required in order to protect the State from destruction or from serious injury, political, economic or moral. That the necessity which is essential to a valid restriction does not exist unless speech would produce, or is intended to produce, a clear and imminent danger of some substantive evil which the State constitutionally may seek to prevent has been settled....

This Court has not yet fixed the standard by which to determine when a danger shall be deemed clear; how remote the danger may be and yet be deemed present; and what degree of evil shall be deemed sufficiently substantial to justify resort to abridgement of free speech and assembly as the means of protection. To reach sound conclusions on these matters, we must bear in mind why a State is, ordinarily, denied the power to prohibit dissemination of social, economic and political doctrine which a vast majority of its citizens believes to be false and fraught with evil consequence.

Fear of serious injury cannot alone justify suppression of free speech and assembly. Men feared witches and burnt women. It is the function of speech to free men from the bondage of irrational fears. To justify suppression of free speech there must be reasonable ground to fear that serious evil will result if free speech is practiced. There must be reasonable ground to believe that the danger apprehended is imminent. There must be reasonable ground to believe that the evil to be prevented is a serious one. Every denunciation of existing law tends in some measure to increase the probability that there will be violation of it. Condonation of a breach enhances the probability. Expressions of approval add to the probability. Propagation of the criminal state of mind by teaching syndicalism increases it. Advocacy of law-breaking heightens it still further. But even advocacy of violation, however, reprehensible morally, is not a justification for denying free speech where the advocacy falls sort of incitement and there is nothing to indicate that the advocacy would be immediately acted on. The wide difference between advocacy and incitement, between preparation and attempt, between assembling and conspiracy, must be borne in mind. In order to support a finding of clear and present danger it must be shown either that immediate serious violence was to be expected or was advocated, or that the past conduct furnished reason to believe that such advocacy was then contemplated.

Those who won our independence by revolution were not cowards. They did not fear political change. They did not exalt order at the cost of liberty. To courageous, self-reliant men, with confidence in the power of free and fearless reasoning applied through the processes of popular government, no danger flowing from speech can be deemed clear and present, unless the incidence of the evil apprehended is so imminent that it may befall before there is opportunity for full discussion. If there be time to expose through discussion the falsehood and fallacies, to avert the evil by the processes of education, the remedy to be applied is more speech, not enforced silence. Only an emergency can justify repression. Such must be the rule if authority is to be reconciled with freedom. Such, in my opinion, is the command of the Constitution. It is therefore always open to Americans to challenge a law abridging free speech and assembly by showing that there was no emergency justifying it.

Moreover, even imminent danger cannot justify resort to prohibition of these functions essential to effective democracy, unless the evil apprehended is relatively serious. Prohibition of free speech and assembly is a measure so stringent that it would be inappropriate as the means for averting a relatively trivial harm to society. A police measure may be unconstitutional merely because the remedy, although effective as means of protection, is unduly harsh or oppressive. Thus, a State might, in the exercise of its police power, make any trespass upon the land of another a crime, regardless of the results or of the intent or purpose of the trespasser. It might, also, punish an attempt, a conspiracy, or an incitement to commit the trespass. But it is hardly conceivable that this Court would hold constitutional a statute which punished as a felony the mere voluntary assembly with a society formed to teach that pedestrians had the moral right to cross unenclosed, unposted, waste lands and to advocate their doing so, even if there was imminent danger that advocacy would lead to a trespass. The fact that speech is likely to result in some violence or in destruction of property is not enough to justify its suppression. There must be the probability of serious injury to the State. Among free men, the deterrents ordinarily to be applied to prevent crime are education and punishment for violations of the law, not abridgment of the rights of free speech and assembly. . . .

Whether in 1919, when Miss Whitney did the things complained of, there was in California such clear and present danger of serious evil, might have been made the important issue in the case. She might have required that the issue be determined either by the court or the jury. She claimed below that the statute as applied to her violated the Federal Constitution; but she did not claim that it was void because there was no clear and present danger of serious evil, nor did she request that the existence of these conditions of a valid measure thus restricting the rights of free speech and assembly be passed upon by the court or a jury. On the other hand, there was evidence on which the court or jury might have found that such danger existed. I am unable to assent to the suggestion in the opinion of the Court that assembling with a political party, formed to advocate the desirability of a proletarian revolution by mass action at some date necessarily far in the future, is not a right within the protection of the Fourteenth Amendment. In the present case, however, there was other testimony which tended to establish the existence of a conspiracy, on the part of members of the International Workers of the World, to commit present serious crimes; and likewise to show that such a conspiracy would be furthered by the activity of the society of which Miss Whitney was a member. Under these circumstances the judgment of the state court cannot be disturbed. . . .

SOURCE: http://caselaw.lp.findlaw.com/scripts/getcase.pl?court=US&vol=274&invol=357

ANALYSIS

Charlotte Anita Whitney, a member of the Communist Labor Party of California, was prosecuted under the state's Criminal Syndicalism Act. The act prohibited advocating, teaching, or aiding the commission of a crime, including "terrorism as a means of accomplishing a change in industrial ownership . . . or effecting any political change." The Court upheld Whitney's conviction and concluded that the act did not violate the due process clause or the equal protection clause, and reiterated that freedom of speech guaranteed by the First Amendment was not an absolute right. The Court used the bad tendency test as they did in *Abrams*. The majority again deferred to the state legislatures arguing that a state may punish those who abuse the freedom of speech by utterances which tend to endanger the foundations of organized government and threaten its overthrow by unlawful means.

Justice Brandeis filed a separate concurring opinion, joined by Justice Holmes, in which he took issue with the majority's interpretation of the First Amendment. As he had done in previous cases in which he had dissented, Brandeis argued that the government can prohibit speech that advocates violent revolution only if under the particular circumstances of the case the speech in question creates a clear and imminent danger of serious injury to the state. He further developed the immediacy principle, stating that there could be no "clear and present danger" unless the occurrence of the evil was so imminent that it may occur before there is opportunity for full discussion. Brandeis makes it clear for the legislature that while they have a right to curb truly dangerous expression, they must define clearly the nature of that danger. A meager fear of unpopular ideas is not enough to restrict speech. This case was eventually overruled in *Brandenburg v. Ohio*, 395 U.S. 444 (1969).

FURTHER READING

Blasi, Vincent. "The First Amendment and the Ideal of Civic Courage: The Brandeis Opinion in Whitney v. California," *William and Mary Law Review* 29 (1988): 653.

Modification of the Clear and Present Danger Test for First Amendment Analysis

- ***Document:*** The Supreme Court case *Dennis v. United States*, Excerpt
- ***Date:*** June 4, 1951
- ***Where:*** Washington, D.C.
- ***Significance:*** This case is significant because the Supreme Court began to modify the "clear and present danger" test established by Justice Holmes in *Schenck*.

DOCUMENT

Dennis v. United States, 341 U.S. 494 (1951)

Argued December 4, 1950.

Decided June 4, 1951.

Chief Justice Vinson announced the judgment of the Court.

Petitioners were indicted in July, 1948, for violation of the conspiracy provisions of the Smith Act, during the period of April, 1945, to July, 1948....

Sections 2 and 3 of the Smith Act provide as follows:

"SEC. 2. (a) It shall be unlawful for any person—

"(1) to knowingly or willfully advocate, abet, advise, or teach the duty, necessity, desirability, or propriety of overthrowing or destroying any government in the United States by force or violence, or by the assassination of any officer of any such government;

"(2) with intent to cause the overthrow or destruction of any government in the United States, to print, publish, edit, issue, circulate, sell, distribute, or publicly display any written or printed matter advocating, advising, or teaching the duty, necessity, desirability, or propriety of overthrowing or destroying any government in the United States by force or violence;

"(3) to organize or help to organize any society, group, or assembly of persons who teach, advocate, or encourage the overthrow or destruction of any government in the United States by force or violence; or to be or become a member of, or affiliate with, any such society, group, or assembly of persons, knowing the purposes thereof.

"(b) For the purposes of this section, the term 'government in the United States' means the Government of the United States, the government of any State, Territory, or possession of the United States, the government of the District of Columbia, or the government of any political subdivision of any of them.

"SEC. 3. It shall be unlawful for any person to attempt to commit, or to conspire to commit, any of the acts prohibited by the provisions of this title."

The indictment charged the petitioners with wilfully and knowingly conspiring (1) to organize as the Communist Party of the United States of America a society, group and assembly of persons who teach and advocate the overthrow and destruction of the Government of the United States by force and violence, and (2) knowingly and wilfully to advocate and teach the duty and necessity of overthrowing and destroying the Government of the United States by force and violence....

The structure and purpose of the statute demand the inclusion of intent as an element of the crime. Congress was concerned with those who advocate and organize for the overthrow of the Government. Certainly those who recruit and combine for the purpose of advocating overthrow intend to bring about that overthrow. We hold that the statute requires as an essential element of the crime proof of the intent of those who are charged with its violation to overthrow the Government by force and violence....

The obvious purpose of the statute is to protect existing Government, not from change by peaceable, lawful and constitutional means, but from change by violence, revolution and terrorism. That it is within the power of the Congress to protect the Government of the United States from armed rebellion is a proposition which requires little discussion. Whatever theoretical merit there may be to the argument that there is a "right" to rebellion against dictatorial governments is without force where the existing structure of the government provides for peaceful and orderly change. We reject any principle of governmental helplessness in the face of preparation for revolution, which principle, carried to its logical conclusion, must lead to anarchy. No one could conceive that it is not within the power of Congress to prohibit acts intended to overthrow the Government by force and violence. The question with which we are concerned here is not whether Congress has such power, but whether the means which it has employed conflict with the First and Fifth Amendments to the Constitution....

The rule... is that where an offense is specified by a statute in nonspeech or nonpress terms, a conviction relying upon speech or press as evidence of violation may be sustained only when the speech or publication created a "clear and present danger" of attempting or accomplishing the prohibited crime...

In this case we are squarely presented with the application of the "clear and present danger" test, and must decide what that phrase imports.... Overthrow of the Government by force and violence is certainly a substantial enough interest for the Government to limit speech. Indeed, this is the ultimate value of any society, for if a society cannot protect its very structure from armed internal attack, it must follow that no subordinate value can be protected. If, then, this interest may be protected, the literal problem which is presented is what has been meant by the use of the phrase "clear and present danger" of the utterances bringing about the evil within the power of Congress to punish.

Obviously, the words cannot mean that before the Government may act, it must wait until the putsch is about to be executed, the plans have been laid and the signal is awaited. If Government is aware that a group aiming at its overthrow is attempting to indoctrinate its members and to commit them to a course whereby they will strike when the leaders feel the circumstances permit, action by the Government is required. The argument that there is no need for Government to concern itself, for Government is strong, it possesses ample powers to put down a rebellion, it may defeat the revolution with ease needs no answer. For that is not the question. Certainly an attempt to overthrow the Government by force, even though doomed from the outset because of inadequate numbers or power of the revolutionists, is a sufficient evil for Congress to prevent. The damage which such attempts create both physically and politically to a nation makes it impossible to measure the validity in terms of the probability of success, or the immediacy of a successful attempt. In the instant case the trial judge charged the jury that they could not convict unless they found that petitioners intended to overthrow the Government "as speedily as circumstances would permit." This does not mean, and could not properly mean, that they would not strike until there was certainty of success. What was meant was that the revolutionists would strike when they thought the time was ripe. We must therefore reject the contention that success or probability of success is the criterion. . . .

Chief Judge Learned Hand, writing for the majority below, interpreted the phrase as follows: "In each case [courts] must ask whether the gravity of the 'evil,' discounted by its improbability, justifies such invasion of free speech as is necessary to avoid the danger." We adopt this statement of the rule. As articulated by Chief Judge Hand, it is as succinct and inclusive as any other we might devise at this time. It takes into consideration those factors which we deem relevant, and relates their significances. More we cannot expect from words . . .

The mere fact that from the period 1945 to 1948 petitioners' activities did not result in an attempt to overthrow the Government by force and violence is of course no answer to the fact that there was a group that was ready to make the attempt. The formation by petitioners of such a highly organized conspiracy, with rigidly disciplined members subject to call when the leaders, these petitioners, felt that the time had come for action, coupled with the inflammable nature of world conditions, similar uprisings in other countries, and the touch-and-go nature of our relations with countries with whom petitioners were in the very least ideologically attuned, convince us that their convictions were justified on this score. And this analysis disposes of the contention that a conspiracy to advocate, as distinguished from the advocacy itself, cannot be constitutionally restrained, because it comprises only the preparation. It is the existence of the conspiracy which creates the danger. If the ingredients of the reaction are present, we cannot bind the Government to wait until the catalyst is added. . . .

We hold that §§ 2 . . . and 3 of the Smith Act do not inherently, or as construed or applied in the instant case, violate the First Amendment and other provisions of the Bill of Rights, or the First and Fifth Amendments because of indefiniteness. Petitioners intended to overthrow the Government of the United States as speedily as the circumstances would permit. Their conspiracy to organize the Communist Party and to teach and advocate the overthrow of the Government of the United

States by force and violence created a "clear and present danger" of an attempt to overthrow the Government by force and violence. They were properly and constitutionally convicted for violation of the Smith Act. The judgments of conviction are affirmed.

SOURCE: http://caselaw.lp.findlaw.com/scripts/getcase.pl?court=us&vol=341&invol=494

ANALYSIS

This case concerns the Alien Registration Act of 1940, also known as the Smith Act, which made it a crime "to knowingly or willfully advocate, abet, advise, or teach the duty, necessity, desirability, or propriety of overthrowing or destroying any government in the United States by force or violence." In 1948, the leaders of the Communist Part of America (CPUSA) were arrested and charged with violating provisions of the Smith Act. Party leaders were found guilty and lower courts upheld the conviction. Publication or display of printed matter teaching or advocating overthrow of the government was forbidden, as was organizing any group that teaches, advocates, or encourages overthrow of government by force. In July of 1948, Eugene Dennis, general secretary of the Communist Party in the United States, and 10 other party leaders were indicted for violating the Smith Act by conspiring to organize groups that taught the overthrow of the government.

The evidence against them was not strong, as there was no proof that they agreed to overthrow or advocate overthrow of the government. Rather, the defendants' trial proceeded on the theory that, as leaders of the CPUSA, they taught Marxist-Leninist doctrine, which allegedly involved forcible overthrow as a necessary aspect of a communist revolution. The defendants were convicted and this conviction was upheld by the Supreme Court. Conventional wisdom condemns Dennis, attributing the result to a Cold War hysteria that gripped the country and influenced the Courts' reasoning.

The Court held that there was a distinction between the mere teaching of Communist philosophies and active advocacy of those ideas. Such advocacy created a "clear and present danger" that threatened the government. Given the gravity of the consequences, the Court held that success or probability of success was not necessary to justify restrictions on the freedom of speech. They say that where the speech is that of a subversive organization, the government need not prove a present danger of revolution but only that the organization intends to bring about the revolution as speedily as circumstances permit. The government is permitted to intervene early enough so that its own strength is still intact and that of the revolutionaries still small.

The Court therefore eliminated the imminence requirement of the clear and present danger test and replaced it with a formulation that measured the gravity of harm against its likelihood of occurring. The crux of Holmes's test had been the imminence or immediacy requirement. Speech might be punished only if so closely brigaded in time and space with criminal action that no intervening factor might abort the substantive evil. Altering the test to include a probable danger if the anticipated evil were serious enough the imminence requirement is greatly diminished. Since

Dennis, the Court has consistently avoided the precise language of the clear and present danger test and with few exceptions commentators announced its demise. Again, this case represents a significant trend by which the Court defers to the legislature especially in times of war.

FURTHER READING

Belfrage, Cedric. *The American Inquisition, 1945–1960*. Indianapolis, Ind.: Bobbs Merrill Co., 1973.

The Incitement Test Providing Greater Protection under the First Amendment

- ***Document:*** The Supreme Court case *Brandenburg v. Ohio*, Excerpt
- ***Date:*** June 9, 1969
- ***Where:*** Washington, D.C.
- ***Significance:*** The Supreme Court overruled the *Whitney v. California* decision setting a new precedent for the "clear and present danger." The Court held that an individual's words were protected as free speech as long as they did not directly incite unlawful action.

DOCUMENT

Brandenburg v. Ohio, 395 U.S. 444 (1969)

Argued April 6, 1938.
Decided June 9, 1969.

Per Curiam

The appellant, a leader of a Ku Klux Klan group, was convicted under the Ohio Criminal Syndicalism statute for "advocat[ing] ... the duty, necessity, or propriety of crime, sabotage, violence, or unlawful methods of terrorism as a means of accomplishing industrial or political reform" and for "voluntarily assembl[ing] with any society, group, or assemblage of persons formed to teach or advocate the doctrines of criminal syndicalism." The appellant challenged the constitutionality of the criminal syndicalism statute under the First and Fourteenth Amendments to the United States Constitution....

The Ohio Criminal Syndicalism Statute was enacted in 1919. In 1927, this Court sustained the constitutionality of California's Criminal Syndicalism Act, the text of which is quite similar to that of the laws of Ohio. The Court upheld the statute on the ground that, without more, "advocating" violent means to effect political and economic change involves such danger to the security of the State that the State may outlaw it. But *Whitney* has been thoroughly discredited by later decisions. These later decisions have fashioned the principle that the constitutional guarantees of free speech and free press do not permit a State to forbid or proscribe advocacy of the use of force or of law violation except where such advocacy is directed to inciting or producing imminent lawless action and is likely to incite or produce such action. "The mere abstract teaching ... of the moral propriety or even moral necessity for a resort to force and violence, is not the same as preparing a group for violent action and steeling it to such action." A statute which fails to draw this distinction impermissibly intrudes upon the freedoms guaranteed by the First and Fourteenth Amendments. It sweeps within its condemnation speech which our Constitution has immunized from governmental control.

Measured by this test, Ohio's Criminal Syndicalism Act cannot be sustained. The Act punishes persons who "advocate or teach the duty, necessity, or propriety" of violence "as a means of accomplishing industrial or political reform"; or who publish or circulate or display any book or paper containing such advocacy; or who "justify" the commission of violent acts "with intent to exemplify, spread or advocate the propriety of the doctrines of criminal syndicalism"; or who "voluntarily assemble" with a group formed "to teach or advocate the doctrines of criminal syndicalism." Neither the indictment nor the trial judge's instructions to the jury in any way refined the statute's bald definition of the crime in terms of mere advocacy not distinguished from incitement to imminent lawless action.

Accordingly, we are here confronted with a statute which, by its own words and as applied, purports to punish mere advocacy and to forbid, on pain of criminal punishment, assembly with others merely to advocate the described type of action. Such a statute falls within the condemnation of the First and Fourteenth Amendments. The contrary teaching of Whitney v. California cannot be supported, and that decision is therefore overruled.

Reversed.

SOURCE: http://caselaw.lp.findlaw.com/cgi-bin/getcase.pl?court=US&vol=395&invol=444

DID YOU KNOW?

Hess v. Indiana, 1973

The basic holding of *Hess* affirms the rule in *Brandenburg* that the First Amendment does not permit a state to forbid or proscribe advocacy of the use of force or of law violation except where such advocacy is directed to inciting or producing imminent lawless action and is likely to incite or produce such action. In *Hess,* a sheriff and his deputies were clearing the streets of antiwar protesters when Hess, one of the protesters, said, "we'll take the fucking street later," or "we'll take the fucking street again." Two witnesses testified that Hess was not urging the crowd to take the street back and that "his statement did not appear to be addressed to any particular person or group, and that his tone, although loud, was no louder than that of the other people in the area." The Court agreed, holding that Hess's words did not come within those narrowly limited classes of speech beyond the protection of the First Amendment. The Court found the evidence of both intent to incite and a call for immediate action insufficient. Even if Hess's statement was a call for future illegal action, the state failed to demonstrate any specific action or any imminent violence.

The *Hess* Court was unwilling to strip the speech of First Amendment protection merely because of its "tendency to lead to violence." The Court looked at the literal import of the speech, the nature of the audience, and the probability of immediate reaction in assessing incitement. The indefinite time period in which reaction could take place secured the speech's protection. This case demonstrates a trend in the Supreme Court's willingness to protect an individual's right of speech even during wartime. Taken together, the *Hess* and *Brandenburg* decisions illustrate an unwillingness to blindly defer to the legislature, thereby protecting individual liberty against arbitrary state action.

ANALYSIS

Brandenburg, a leader in the Ku Klux Klan, made a speech at a Klan rally and was later convicted under an Ohio criminal syndicalism law. The law made illegal advocating "crime, sabotage, violence, or unlawful methods of terrorism as a means of accomplishing industrial or political reform," as well as assembling "with any society, group, or assemblage of persons formed to teach or advocate the doctrines of criminal syndicalism." The Court reversed Brandenburg's conviction, holding that government cannot constitutionally punish abstract advocacy of force or law violation. *Brandenburg* addresses speech activity designed to persuade someone to commit an unlawful act, not speech designed to facilitate the commission of an unlawful act by a person who has already decided to act. This offers greater protection to the individual engaging in speech under the First Amendment.

Under *Brandenburg,* advocacy of violence can be prohibited only when a speaker (1) advocates imminent illegal conduct; (2) intends to incite either the use of force or illegal conduct; and (3) is highly likely to incite such conduct. The Court did not find that the words spoken by Brandenburg satisfied this test. The criminal syndicalism act made illegal the advocacy and teaching of doctrines while ignoring whether or not that advocacy and teaching would actually incite imminent lawless action. The failure to make this distinction rendered the law overly broad and in violation of the Constitution. The test allowed for a greater degree of political discussion. People have the right to discuss the possibility of using violence to address social and political ills. Only when their words lead to direct action is the law broken.

FURTHER READING

Sunstein, Cass R. "Is Violent Speech a Right?" *The American Prospect*, Summer 1995.

The "Right to Be Let Alone"

- ***Document:*** The Supreme Court case *Olmstead v. United States:* Justice Brandeis's Dissent, Excerpt
- ***Date:*** June 4, 1928
- ***Where:*** Washington, D.C.
- ***Significance:*** Justice Brandeis's dissent in *Olmstead* is important because it is considered the first articulation by the Supreme Court of a general right to privacy from government intrusion.

DOCUMENT

Olmstead v. United States, 277 U.S. 438 (1928)

Argued February 20, 21, 1928.

Decided June 4, 1928.

Mr. Justice Brandeis, dissenting.

The defendants were convicted of conspiring to violate the National Prohibition Act. Before any of the persons now charged had been arrested or indicted, the telephones by means of which they habitually communicated with one another and with others had been tapped by federal officers. To this end, a lineman of long experience in wiretapping was employed on behalf of the Government and at its expense. He tapped eight telephones, some in the homes of the persons charged, some in their offices. Acting on behalf of the Government and in their official capacity, at least six other prohibition agents listened over the tapped wires and reported the messages taken. Their operations extended over a period of nearly five months. The typewritten record of the notes of conversations overheard occupies 775 typewritten pages. By objections seasonably made and persistently renewed, the defendants objected to the admission of the evidence obtained by wiretapping on the ground that the

New York City Deputy Police Commissioner John A. Leach (right) watches agents pour confiscated liquor into a sewer following a raid during the height of prohibition. (Library of Congress.)

Government's wiretapping constituted an unreasonable search and seizure in violation of the Fourth Amendment, and that the use as evidence of the conversations overheard compelled the defendants to be witnesses against themselves in violation of the Fifth Amendment.

The Government makes no attempt to defend the methods employed by its officers. Indeed, it concedes that, if wiretapping can be deemed a search and seizure within the Fourth Amendment, such wiretapping as was practiced in the case at bar was an unreasonable search and seizure, and that the evidence thus obtained was inadmissible. But it relies on the language of the Amendment, and it claims that the protection given thereby cannot properly be held to include a telephone conversation.

When the Fourth and Fifth Amendments were adopted, "the form that evil had theretofore taken" had been necessarily simple. Force and violence were then the only means known to man by which a Government could directly effect self-incrimination.

It could compel the individual to testify—a compulsion effected, if need be, by torture. It could secure possession of his papers and other articles incident to his private life—a seizure effected, if need be, by breaking and entry. Protection against such invasion of "the sanctities of a man's home and the privacies of life" was provided in the Fourth and Fifth Amendments by specific language.

The protection guaranteed by the Amendments is much broader in scope. The makers of our Constitution undertook to secure conditions favorable to the pursuit of happiness. They recognized the significance of man's spiritual nature, of his feelings, and of his intellect. They knew that only a part of the pain, pleasure and satisfactions of life are to be found in material things. They sought to protect Americans in their beliefs, their thoughts, their emotions and their sensations. They conferred, as against the Government, the right to be let alone—the most comprehensive of rights, and the right most valued by civilized men. To protect that right, every unjustifiable intrusion by the Government upon the privacy of the individual, whatever the means employed, must be deemed a violation of the Fourth Amendment. And the use, as evidence in a criminal proceeding, of facts ascertained by such intrusion must be deemed a violation of the Fifth.

The door of a court is not barred because the plaintiff has committed a crime. The confirmed criminal is as much entitled to redress as his most virtuous fellow citizen; no record of crime, however long, makes one an outlaw. The court's aid is denied only when he who seeks it has violated the law in connection with the very transaction as to which he seeks legal redress. Then aid is denied despite the defendant's wrong. It is denied in order to maintain respect for law; in order to promote confidence in the administration of justice; in order to preserve the judicial process from contamination. The rule is one, not of action, but of inaction. It is sometimes spoken of as a rule of substantive law. But it extends to matters of procedure, as well. A defense may be waived. It is waived when not pleaded. But the objection that the plaintiff comes with unclean hands will be taken by the court itself. It will be taken despite the wish to the contrary of all the parties to the litigation. The court protects itself.

Decency, security and liberty alike demand that government officials shall be subjected to the same rules of conduct that are commands to the citizen. In a government of laws, existence of the government will be imperiled if it fails to observe the law scrupulously. Our Government is the potent, the omnipresent teacher. For good or for ill, it teaches the whole people by its example. Crime is contagious. If the Government becomes a lawbreaker, it breeds contempt for law; it invites every man to become a law unto himself; it invites anarchy. To declare that, in the administration of the criminal law, the end justifies the means—to declare that the Government may commit crimes in order to secure the conviction of a private criminal—would bring terrible retribution. Against that pernicious doctrine this Court should resolutely set its face.

SOURCE: http://www.law.cornell.edu/supct/html/historics/USSC_CR_0277_0438_ZS.html

---

ANALYSIS

Roy Olmstead was a suspected bootlegger. Without judicial approval, federal agents installed wiretaps in the basement where Olmstead worked and in the streets near his home. Olmstead was convicted with evidence obtained from the wiretaps.

This case was decided along with *Green v. United States* and *McInnis v. United States*. The Court held that neither the Fourth nor Fifth Amendment rights of the recorded parties were violated. The use of wiretapped conversations as incriminating evidence did not violate their Fifth Amendment protection against self-incrimination because they were not forced to make those conversations. The Court noted that the conversations were made voluntarily between the parties and their associates. The parties' Fourth Amendment rights were not infringed because mere wiretapping does not constitute a search and seizure under the meaning of the Fourth Amendment.

Justice Brandeis's dissent disagreed with the Court's analysis on both the construction of the Fourth Amendment and the relevance of the government's law breaking. Brandeis's dissent in *Olmstead* focused on new technology which allowed wiretapping of telephone lines by federal officers, and strongly believed that such an interception of communications even without a physical trespass or seizure of tangible property—constituted an illegal "search and seizure" under the Fourth Amendment. According to Brandeis, the underlying general purpose of the Fourth Amendment was the protection of the right to privacy, or what he called, "a right to be let alone," which was similar to the principles formulated in his article in the *Harvard Law Review* 37 years previously. Justice Brandeis was strongly aware of technological change in arguing that a right of privacy had come of age under the Fourth Amendment, particularly with respect to wire communications. It was this change in society's technological arsenal which enabled the government to intrude upon an individual's personal space at anytime unchecked. Modern Fourth Amendment jurisprudence has since drawn heavily from Brandeis's ideas, and Olmstead was overruled by *Katz v. United States* (1967).

FURTHER READING

Ohm, Paul. "The Olmsteadian Seizure Clause." *Stanford Technology Law Review* (January 2007).

The Constitutional Right to Privacy

- ***Document:*** The Supreme Court case *Griswold v. Connecticut*, Excerpt
- ***Date:*** June 7, 1965
- ***Where:*** Washington, D.C.
- ***Significance:*** This is the landmark case where the Supreme Court held a right to privacy was protected under the Constitution.

DOCUMENT

Griswold v. Connecticut, 381 U.S. 479 (1965)

Argued March 29, 1965.

Decided June 7, 1965.

Mr. Justice Douglas delivered the opinion of the Court.

Appellant Griswold is Executive Director of the Planned Parenthood League of Connecticut. Appellant Buxton is a licensed physician and a professor at the Yale Medical School who served as Medical Director for the League at its Center in New Haven—a center open and operating from November 1 to November 10, 1961, when appellants were arrested. They gave information, instruction, and medical advice to married persons as to the means of preventing conception. They examined the wife and prescribed the best contraceptive device or material for her use. Fees were usually charged, although some couples were serviced free.

The statutes whose constitutionality is involved in this appeal are 53-32 and 54-196 of the General Statutes of Connecticut (1958 rev.). The former provides: "Any person who uses any drug, medicinal article or instrument for the purpose of preventing conception shall be fined not less than fifty dollars or imprisoned not less than sixty days nor more than one year or be both fined and imprisoned."

Section 54-196 provides: "Any person who assists, abets, counsels, causes, hires or commands another to commit any offense may be prosecuted and punished as if he were the principal offender."

Estelle Griswold (left) and Mrs. Ernest Jahncke view a newspaper article heralding the Supreme Court decision in *Griswold v. Connecticut* (1965). The Supreme Court overturned the Connecticut statute of 1879 that made the use of birth control illegal. (© Bettmann/Corbis.)

The appellants were found guilty as accessories and fined $100 each, against the claim that the accessory statute as so applied violated the Fourteenth Amendment....

Coming to the merits, we are met with a wide range of questions that implicate the Due Process Clause of the Fourteenth Amendment. Overtones of some arguments suggest that Lochner v. New York, 198 U.S. 45, should be our guide. But we decline that invitation. We do not sit as a super-legislature to determine the wisdom, need, and propriety of laws that touch economic problems, business affairs, or social conditions. This law, however, operates directly on an intimate relation of husband and wife and their physician's role in one aspect of that relation.

The association of people is not mentioned in the Constitution nor in the Bill of Rights. The right to educate a child in a school of the parents' choice—whether public or private or parochial—is also not mentioned. Nor is the right to study any particular subject or any foreign language. Yet the First Amendment has been construed to include certain of those rights.

By Pierce v. Society of Sisters, the right to educate one's children as one chooses is made applicable to the States by the force of the First and Fourteenth Amendments. By Meyer v. Nebraska, the same dignity is given the right to study the German language in a private school. In other words, the State may not, consistently with the spirit of the First Amendment, contract the spectrum of available knowledge... And so we reaffirm the principle of the Pierce and the Meyer cases.

In NAACP v. Alabama we protected the "freedom to associate and privacy in one's associations," noting that freedom of association was a peripheral First Amendment right. Disclosure of membership lists of a constitutionally valid association, we held, was invalid "as entailing the likelihood of a substantial restraint upon the exercise by petitioner's members of their right to freedom of association." In other words, the First Amendment has a penumbra where privacy is protected from governmental intrusion. The right of "association," like the right of belief is more than the right to attend a meeting; it includes the right to express one's attitudes or philosophies by membership in a group or by affiliation with it or by other lawful means. Association in that context is a form of expression of opinion; and while it is not expressly included in the First Amendment its existence is necessary in making the express guarantees fully meaningful.

The foregoing cases suggest that specific guarantees in the Bill of Rights have penumbras, formed by emanations from those guarantees that help give them life and substance. Various guarantees create zones of privacy. The right of association contained in the penumbra of the First Amendment is one, as we have seen. The Third Amendment in its prohibition against the quartering of soldiers "in any house" in time of peace without the consent of the owner is another facet of that privacy. The Fourth Amendment explicitly affirms the "right of the people to be secure in their persons, houses, papers, and effects, against unreasonable searches and seizures." The Fifth Amendment in its Self-Incrimination Clause enables the citizen to create a zone of privacy which government may not force him to surrender to his detriment. The Ninth Amendment provides: "The enumeration in the Constitution, of certain rights, shall not be construed to deny or disparage others retained by the people."

The Fourth and Fifth Amendments were described . . . as protection against all governmental invasions "of the sanctity of a man's home and the privacies of life."

We have had many controversies over these penumbral rights of "privacy and repose." These cases bear witness that the right of privacy which presses for recognition here is a legitimate one.

The present case, then, concerns a relationship lying within the zone of privacy created by several fundamental constitutional guarantees. And it concerns a law which, in forbidding the use of contraceptives rather than regulating their manufacture or sale, seeks to achieve its goals by means having a maximum destructive impact upon that relationship. Such a law cannot stand in light of the familiar principle, so often applied by this Court, that a "governmental purpose to control or prevent activities constitutionally subject to state regulation may not be achieved by means which sweep unnecessarily broadly and thereby invade the area of protected freedoms." Would we allow the police to search the sacred precincts of marital bedrooms for telltale signs of the use of contraceptives? The very idea is repulsive to the notions of privacy surrounding the marriage relationship.

We deal with a right of privacy older than the Bill of Rights—older than our political parties, older than our school system. Marriage is a coming together for better or for worse, hopefully enduring, and intimate to the degree of being sacred. It is an association that promotes a way of life, not causes; a harmony in living, not political faiths; a bilateral loyalty, not commercial or social projects. Yet it is an association for as noble a purpose as any involved in our prior decisions.

Reversed.

SOURCE: http://caselaw.lp.findlaw.com/scripts/getcase.pl?court=US&vol=381&invol=479

ANALYSIS

Griswold was the executive director of the Planned Parenthood League of Connecticut. Both she and the medical director for the League gave information, instruction, and other medical advice to married couples concerning birth control. Griswold and her colleague were convicted under a Connecticut law that criminalized counseling about contraception to married persons. The Court struck down the law as a violation of the right to privacy between a husband and wife. Although the Bill of Rights does not explicitly mention a broad right to privacy, Justice Douglas wrote for the majority that the right was to be found in the "penumbras" and "emanations" from the Bill of Rights. This literally means the shadows of the Bill of Rights. These "shadows" include the First Amendment (free speech), Third Amendment (prohibition on the forced quartering of troops), Fourth Amendment (freedom from searches and seizures), Fifth Amendment (freedom from self-incrimination), and Ninth Amendment (other rights not specifically listed), as applied against the states by the Fourteenth Amendment.

This is a seminal decision that established a basic sphere or zone of personal privacy to which all individuals are entitled. As a precedent, it places the burden on the government to demonstrate why it is justified in interfering with your life rather than requiring you to demonstrate that the text of the Constitution specifically and narrowly prohibits the government's actions. For 50 years, *Griswold* has functioned as the legal basis for judicial rulings involving issues of sexual intimacy, reproductive rights, and family life. Even today, it continues to set the agenda for debates about privacy in American life and the limitations placed upon the government.

FURTHER READING

Kanter, Stephen. "The Griswold Diagrams: Toward a Unified Theory of Constitutional Rights." *Cardozo Law Review* 28 (November 2006): 623.

Reasonable Expectation of Privacy

- ***Document:*** The Supreme Court case *Katz v. United States*, Excerpt
- ***Date:*** December 18, 1967
- ***Where:*** Washington, D.C.
- ***Significance:*** The Supreme Court overruled *Olmstead*, and Justice Harlan's concurring opinion set forth a two-part test for determining whether police activity constitutes a search under the Fourth Amendment.

DOCUMENT

Katz v. United States, 389 U.S. 347 (1967)

Argued October 17, 1967.

Decided December 18, 1967.

Mr. Justice Stewart delivered the opinion of the Court.

The petitioner was convicted in the District Court for the Southern District of California under an eight-count indictment charging him with transmitting wagering information by telephone from Los Angeles to Miami and Boston, in violation of a federal statute. At trial the Government was permitted, over the petitioner's objection, to introduce evidence of the petitioner's end of telephone conversations, overheard by FBI agents who had attached an electronic listening and recording device to the outside of the public telephone booth from which he had placed his calls. In affirming his conviction, the Court of Appeals rejected the contention that the recordings had been obtained in violation of the Fourth Amendment, because "[t]here was no physical entrance into the area occupied by [the petitioner]." We granted certiorari in order to consider the constitutional questions thus presented.

We conclude that the underpinnings of Olmstead and Goldman have been so eroded by our subsequent decisions that the "trespass" doctrine there enunciated can no longer be regarded as controlling. The Government's activities in electronically listening to and recording the petitioner's words violated the privacy upon which he justifiably relied while using the telephone booth and thus constituted a "search and seizure" within the meaning of the Fourth Amendment. The fact that the electronic device employed to achieve that end did not happen to penetrate the wall of the booth can have no constitutional significance.

The question remaining for decision, then, is whether the search and seizure conducted in this case complied with constitutional standards. In that regard, the Government's position is that its agents acted in an entirely defensible manner: They did not begin their electronic surveillance until investigation of the petitioner's activities had established a strong probability that he was using the telephone in question to transmit gambling information to persons in other States, in violation of federal law. Moreover, the surveillance was limited, both in scope and in duration, to the specific purpose of establishing the contents of the petitioner's unlawful telephonic communications. The agents confined their surveillance to the brief periods during which he used the telephone booth, and they took great care to overhear only the conversations of the petitioner himself.

Accepting this account of the Government's actions as accurate, it is clear that this surveillance was so narrowly circumscribed that a duly authorized magistrate, properly notified of the need for such investigation, specifically informed of the basis on which it was to proceed, and clearly apprised of the precise intrusion it would entail, could constitutionally have authorized, with appropriate safeguards, the very limited search and seizure that the Government asserts in fact took place.

The Government urges that, because its agents relied upon the decisions in Olmstead and Goldman, and because they did no more here than they might properly have done with prior judicial sanction, we should retroactively validate their conduct. That we cannot do. It is apparent that the agents in this case acted with restraint. Yet the inescapable fact is that this restraint was imposed by the agents themselves, not by a judicial officer. They were not required, before commencing the search, to present their estimate of probable cause for detached scrutiny by a neutral magistrate. They were not compelled, during the conduct of the search itself, to observe precise limits established in advance by a specific court order. Nor were they directed, after the search had been completed, to notify the authorizing magistrate in detail of all that had been seized. In the absence of such safeguards, this Court has never sustained a search upon the sole ground that officers reasonably expected to find evidence of a particular crime and voluntarily confined their activities to the least intrusive means consistent with that end.

Wherever a man may be, he is entitled to know that he will remain free from unreasonable searches and seizures. The government agents here ignored "the procedure of antecedent justification . . . that is central to the Fourth Amendment," a procedure that we hold to be a constitutional precondition of the kind of electronic surveillance involved in this case. Because the surveillance here failed to meet that condition, and because it led to the petitioner's conviction, the judgment must be reversed.

It is so ordered.

Mr. Justice Harlan, concurring.

I join the opinion of the Court, which I read to hold only (a) that an enclosed telephone booth is an area where, like a home, and unlike a field, a person has a constitutionally protected reasonable expectation of privacy; (b) that electronic as well as physical intrusion into a place that is in this sense private may constitute a violation of the Fourth Amendment; and (c) that the invasion of a constitutionally protected area by federal authorities is, as the Court has long held, presumptively unreasonable in the absence of a search warrant.

As the Court's opinion states, "the Fourth Amendment protects people, not places." The question, however, is what protection it affords to those people. Generally, as here, the answer to that question requires reference to a "place." My understanding of the rule that has emerged from prior decisions is that there is a twofold requirement, first that a person have exhibited an actual (subjective) expectation of privacy and, second, that the expectation be one that society is prepared to recognize as "reasonable." Thus a man's home is, for most purposes, a place where he expects privacy, but objects, activities, or statements that he exposes to the "plain view" of outsiders are not "protected" because no intention to keep them to himself has been exhibited. On the other hand, conversations in the open would not be protected against being overheard, for the expectation of privacy under the circumstances would be unreasonable.

SOURCE: http://caselaw.lp.findlaw.com/cgi-bin/getcase.pl?court=US&vol=389&invol=347

ANALYSIS

Federal agents placed an electronic listening and recording devise on the outside of the public telephone booth from which Katz had placed calls. Based on the information obtained from his phone calls, Katz was charged with transmitting wagering information by telephone from Los Angeles to Miami and Boston, in violation of a federal statute. At trial he sought to have the conversations excluded, claiming it was a violation of the Fourth Amendment. Despite his objections the conversations were admitted and Katz was convicted. The Court held that Katz was entitled to Fourth Amendment protection for his conversations and that a physical intrusion into an area occupied by Katz was not necessary for the state to be in violation of the Fourth Amendment. The majority articulated an important principle that the "the Fourth Amendment protects people, not places." This was a significant development of constitutional law because the court abandoned the common law trespass doctrine that previously required a physical intrusion by the government in order to be found in violation. Before Katz, electronic surveillance was permissible because that type of spying did not involve any type of physical intrusion. The key question after Katz became whether the individual was entitled to a "reasonable expectation of privacy" under the circumstances. This is an objective standard. The Court found that the government violated the Constitution even though its electronic device did not physically penetrate the wall of the telephone booth.

Justice Harlan's concurrence in Katz, rather than the majority opinion, has provided the basis for the test that eventually emerged from the decision. Justice Harlan attempted to define more clearly the privacy concepts that the majority had discussed in a general sense. Recognizing that any Fourth Amendment inquiry must also make reference to a place, Justice Harlan proposed a two-part test to determine if an individual's privacy had been invaded. First, the person must have exhibited either an actual or subjective expectation of privacy. This is the subjective part of the test.

Second, society must recognize such an expectation as reasonable. This is the objective part of the test. It was held that Katz, by entering the phone booth and closing the door behind him, expressed his subjective intent to not have his conversation overheard. Further, the public phone booth became a temporary private place where it would be objectively reasonable for one to expect freedom from intrusion, and any violation of this expectation, by police officers, would constitute a search and seizure within the meaning of the Fourth Amendment. In so ruling, the Court overturned the 40 years of Fourth Amendment case law that had developed since *Olmstead*. This significantly curtailed state action and further protected our individual liberties.

FURTHER READING

Swire, Peter P. "Katz Is Dead. Long Live Katz." *Michigan Law Review* 102 (March 2004): 904.

The Fourth Amendment and Domestic Surveillance

- ***Document:*** The Supreme Court case *United States v. U.S. District Court*
- ***Date:*** June 19, 1972
- ***Where:*** Washington, D.C.
- ***Significance:*** This unanimous decision upheld the requirements of the Fourth Amendment in cases of domestic surveillance targeting a domestic threat.

DOCUMENT

United States v. United States District Court, 407 U.S. 297 (1972)

Argued February 24, 1972.

Decided June 19, 1972.

Mr. Justice Powell delivered the opinion of the Court.

The issue before us is an important one for the people of our country and their Government. It involves the delicate question of the President's power, acting through the Attorney General, to authorize electronic surveillance in internal security matters without prior judicial approval. Successive Presidents for more than one-quarter of a century have authorized such surveillance in varying degrees, without guidance from the Congress or a definitive decision of this Court. This case brings the issue here for the first time. Its resolution is a matter of national concern, requiring sensitivity both to the Government's right to protect itself from unlawful subversion and attack and to the citizen's right to be secure in his privacy against unreasonable Government intrusion.

I

Title III of the Omnibus Crime Control and Safe Streets Act, 18 U.S.C. 2510–2520, authorizes the use of electronic surveillance for classes of crimes carefully specified in 18 U.S.C. 2516. Such surveillance is subject to prior court order. Section 2518 sets forth the detailed and particularized application necessary to obtain such an order as well as carefully circumscribed conditions for its use. The Act represents a comprehensive attempt by Congress to promote more effective control of crime while protecting the privacy of individual thought and expression.

The express grant of authority to conduct surveillances is found in 2516, which authorizes the Attorney General to make application to a federal judge when surveillance may provide evidence of certain offenses. These offenses are described with meticulous care and specificity.

Where the Act authorizes surveillance, the procedure to be followed is specified in 2518. Subsection (1) thereof requires application to a judge of competent jurisdiction for a prior order of approval, and states in detail the information required in such application. Subsection (3) prescribes the necessary elements of probable cause which the judge must find before issuing an order authorizing an interception. Subsection (4) sets forth the required contents of such an order.

Subsection (5) sets strict time limits on an order. Provision is made in subsection (7) for "an emergency situation" found to exist by the Attorney General (or by the principal prosecuting attorney of a State) "with respect to conspiratorial activities threatening the national security interest." In such a situation, emergency surveillance may be conducted "if an application for an order approving the interception is made... within forty-eight hours." If such an order is not obtained, or the application therefore is denied, the interception is deemed to be a violation of the Act.

In view of these and other interrelated provisions delineating permissible interceptions of particular criminal activity upon carefully specified conditions, it would have been incongruous for Congress to have legislated with respect to the important and complex area of national security in a single brief and nebulous paragraph. This would not comport with the sensitivity of the problem involved or with the extraordinary care Congress exercised in drafting other sections of the Act. We therefore think the conclusion inescapable that Congress only intended to make clear that the Act simply did not legislate with respect to national security surveillances.

II

It is important at the outset to emphasize the limited nature of the question before the Court. It addresses a question left open by Katz: "Whether safeguards other than prior authorization by a magistrate would satisfy the Fourth Amendment in a situation involving the national security."

The determination of this question requires the essential Fourth Amendment inquiry into the "reasonableness" of the search and seizure in question, and the way in which that "reasonableness" derives content and meaning through reference to the warrant clause.

We begin the inquiry by noting that the President of the United States has the fundamental duty, under Art. II, 1, of the Constitution, to "preserve, protect and defend the Constitution of the United States." Implicit in that duty is the power to protect our Government against those who would subvert or overthrow it by unlawful means. In the discharge of this duty, the President—through the Attorney General—may find it necessary to employ electronic surveillance to obtain intelligence information on the plans of those who plot unlawful acts against the Government. The use of such surveillance in internal security cases has been sanctioned more or less continuously by various Presidents and Attorneys General since July 1946. Herbert Brownell, Attorney General under President Eisenhower, urged the use of electronic surveillance both in internal and international security matters on the grounds that those acting against the Government "turn to the telephone to carry on their intrigue. The success of their plans frequently rests upon piecing together shreds of information received from many sources and many nests. The participants in the conspiracy are often dispersed and stationed in various strategic positions in government and industry throughout the country."

Though the Government and respondents debate their seriousness and magnitude, threats and acts of sabotage against the Government exist in sufficient number to justify investigative powers with respect to them. The covertness and complexity of potential unlawful conduct against the Government and the necessary dependency of many conspirators upon the telephone make electronic surveillance an effective investigatory instrument in certain circumstances. The marked acceleration in technological developments and sophistication in their use have resulted in new techniques for the planning, commission, and concealment of criminal activities. It would be contrary to the public interest for Government to deny to itself the prudent and lawful employment of those very techniques which are employed against the Government and its law-abiding citizens.

Our decision in Katz refused to lock the Fourth Amendment into instances of actual physical trespass. Rather, the Amendment governs "not only the seizure of tangible items, but extends as well to the recording of oral statements... without any 'technical trespass under ... local property law.'" That decision implicitly recognized that the broad and unsuspected governmental incursions into conversational privacy which electronic surveillance entails necessitate the application of Fourth Amendment safeguards.

III

As the Fourth Amendment is not absolute in its terms, our task is to examine and balance the basic values at stake in this case: the duty of Government to protect the domestic security, and the potential danger posed by unreasonable surveillance to individual privacy and free expression. If the legitimate need of Government to safeguard domestic security requires the use of electronic surveillance, the question is whether the needs of citizens for privacy and free expression may not be better protected by requiring a warrant before such surveillance is undertaken. We must also ask whether a warrant requirement would unduly frustrate the efforts of Government to protect itself from acts of subversion and overthrow directed against it.

The warrant clause of the Fourth Amendment is not dead language. Rather, it has been "a valued part of our constitutional law for decades, and it has determined the result in scores and scores of cases in courts all over this country. It is not an inconvenience to be somehow 'weighed' against the claims of police efficiency. It is, or should be, an important working part of our machinery of government, operating as a matter of course to check the 'well-intentioned but mistakenly overzealous executive officers' who are a part of any system of law enforcement."

Over two centuries ago, Lord Mansfield held that common-law principles prohibited warrants that ordered the arrest of unnamed individuals who the officer might conclude were guilty of seditious libel. "It is not fit," said Mansfield, "that the receiving or judging of the information should be left to the discretion of the officer. The magistrate ought to judge; and should give certain directions to the officer." Lord Mansfield's formulation touches the very heart of the Fourth Amendment directive: that, where practical, a governmental search and seizure should represent both the efforts of the officer to gather evidence of wrongful acts and the judgment of the magistrate that the collected evidence is sufficient to justify invasion of a citizen's private premises or conversation. Inherent in the concept of a warrant is its issuance by a "neutral and detached magistrate." The further requirement of "probable cause" instructs the magistrate that baseless searches shall not proceed.

These Fourth Amendment freedoms cannot properly be guaranteed if domestic security surveillances may be conducted solely within the discretion of the Executive Branch. The Fourth Amendment does not contemplate the executive officers of Government as neutral and disinterested magistrates. Their duty and responsibility are to enforce the laws, to investigate, and to prosecute. But those charged with this investigative and prosecutorial duty should not be the sole judges of when to utilize constitutionally sensitive means in pursuing their tasks. The historical judgment, which the Fourth Amendment accepts, is that unreviewed executive discretion may yield too readily to pressures to obtain incriminating evidence and overlook potential invasions of privacy and protected speech.

It may well be that, in the instant case, the Government's surveillance of Plamondon's conversations was a reasonable one which readily would have gained prior judicial approval. But this Court "has never sustained a search upon the sole ground that officers reasonably expected to find evidence of a particular crime and voluntarily confined their activities to the least intrusive means consistent with that end." The Fourth Amendment contemplates a prior judicial judgment, not the risk that executive discretion may be reasonably exercised. This judicial role accords with our basic constitutional doctrine that individual freedoms will best be preserved through a separation of powers and division of functions among the different branches and levels of Government. The independent check upon executive discretion is not satisfied, as the Government argues, by "extremely limited" post-surveillance judicial review. Indeed, post-surveillance review would never reach the surveillances which failed to result in prosecutions. Prior review by a neutral and detached magistrate is the time-tested means of effectuating Fourth Amendment rights.

We recognize, as we have before, the constitutional basis of the President's domestic security role, but we think it must be exercised in a manner compatible with the Fourth Amendment. In this case we hold that this requires an appropriate prior warrant procedure.

We cannot accept the Government's argument that internal security matters are too subtle and complex for judicial evaluation. Courts regularly deal with the most difficult issues of our society. There is no reason to believe that federal judges will be insensitive to or uncomprehending of the issues involved in domestic security cases. Certainly courts can recognize that domestic security surveillance involves different considerations from the surveillance of "ordinary crime." If the threat is too subtle or complex for our senior law enforcement officers to convey its significance to a court, one may question whether there is probable cause for surveillance.

Nor do we believe prior judicial approval will fracture the secrecy essential to official intelligence gathering. The investigation of criminal activity has long involved imparting sensitive information to judicial officers who have respected the confidentialities involved. Judges may be counted upon to be especially conscious of security requirements in national security cases.

Thus, we conclude that the Government's concerns do not justify departure in this case from the customary Fourth Amendment requirement of judicial approval prior to initiation of a search or surveillance. Although some added burden will be imposed upon the Attorney General, this inconvenience is justified in a free society to protect constitutional values. Nor do we think the Government's domestic surveillance powers will be impaired to any significant degree. A prior warrant establishes presumptive validity of the surveillance and will minimize the burden of justification in post-surveillance judicial review. By no means of least importance will be the reassurance of the public generally that indiscriminate wiretapping and bugging of law-abiding citizens cannot occur.

IV

We do not attempt to detail the precise standards for domestic security warrants any more than our decision in Katz sought to set the refined requirements for the specified criminal surveillances which now constitute Title III. We do hold, however, that prior judicial approval is required for the type of domestic security surveillance involved in this case and that such approval may be made in accordance with such reasonable standards as the Congress may prescribe.

Affirmed.

SOURCE: http://caselaw.lp.findlaw.com/scripts/getcase.pl?court=US&vol=407&invol=297

ANALYSIS

In this case, the government was investigating three individuals it suspected of conspiring to destroy government property and bombing a Central Intelligence Agency office. Specifically, government agents used electronic surveillance to record the suspects' conversations. The wiretapping was conducted without a search warrant. The Court held that the government officials were obligated to obtain a warrant before beginning electronic surveillance even if domestic security issues were involved. The "inherent vagueness of the domestic security concept" and the potential for abusing it to suppress political dissent made the Fourth Amendment protections especially important when the government engaged in spying on its own citizens.

In examining privacy concerns raised in the context of domestic security operations, the Court found that the Fourth Amendment should be flexible in its application. The government interest in protecting national security is to be balanced against the danger to individual privacy and free expression posed by unreasonable surveillance. The Court therefore concluded that neither the national security interest of the government nor the privacy interest of individual citizens is absolute.

Both interests must be balanced to afford individuals sufficient constitutional protection and to give the government the ability to protect national security. National security is not a sufficient interest to overcome Fourth Amendment protections due to the historic abuses of the search and surveillance power purportedly exercised for national security reasons. This established the precedent that a warrant needed to be obtained before beginning electronic surveillance even if domestic security issues were involved. The decision only applied to domestic issues; foreign intelligence operations were not bound by the same standards. The governing law for electronic surveillance of foreign intelligence information between or among foreign powers is the Foreign Intelligence Surveillance Act (FISA) of 1978 which was discussed earlier in chapter 3.

FURTHER READING

Cinquegrana, Americo R. "The Walls (And Wires) Have Ears: The Background and First Ten Years of the Foreign Intelligence Surveillance Act of 1978." *University of Pennsylvania Law Review* 137 (1989): 793.

5

21ST-CENTURY ENACTMENTS CONCERNING THE WAR ON TERROR

Congress Responds to September 11: The Authorization for Use of Military Force

- ***Document:*** Joint Resolution, Authorization for Use of Military Force against Terrorists (AUMF)
- ***Date:*** September 18, 2001
- ***Where:*** Washington, D.C.
- ***Significance:*** This joint resolution from Congress granted the president the authority to use all "necessary and appropriate force" against those whom he determined "planned, authorized, committed or aided" the September 11 attacks, or who harbored said persons or groups.

DOCUMENT

Joint Resolution

To authorize the use of United States Armed Forces against those responsible for the recent attacks launched against the United States.

Whereas, on September 11, 2001, acts of treacherous violence were committed against the United States and its citizens; and

Whereas, such acts render it both necessary and appropriate that the United States exercise its rights to self-defense and to protect United States citizens both at home and abroad; and

Whereas, in light of the threat to the national security and foreign policy of the United States posed by these grave acts of violence; and

Whereas, such acts continue to pose an unusual and extraordinary threat to the national security and foreign policy of the United States; and

Whereas, the President has authority under the Constitution to take action to deter and prevent acts of international terrorism against the United States: Now, therefore, be it

Resolved by the Senate and House of Representatives of the United States of America in Congress assembled,

Section 1. Short title.

This joint resolution may be cited as the 'Authorization for Use of Military Force'.

Sec. 2. Authorization for use of united states armed forces.

(a) IN GENERAL—That the President is authorized to use all necessary and appropriate force against those nations, organizations, or persons he determines planned, authorized, committed, or aided the terrorist attacks that occurred on September 11, 2001, or harbored such organizations or persons, in order to prevent any future acts of international terrorism against the United States by such nations, organizations or persons.

(b) War Powers Resolution Requirements-

(1) SPECIFIC STATUTORY AUTHORIZATION—Consistent with section 8(a) (1) of the War Powers Resolution, the Congress declares that this section is intended to constitute specific statutory authorization within the meaning of section 5(b) of the War Powers Resolution.

(2) APPLICABILITY OF OTHER REQUIREMENTS—Nothing in this resolution supercedes any requirement of the War Powers Resolution.

Approved September 18, 2001.

SOURCE: http://news.findlaw.com/wp/docs/terrorism/sjres23.es.html

DID YOU KNOW?

A Lone Voice: Representative Barbara Lee

Barbara Lee, a Democratic member of Congress representing California's ninth congressional district, was the only person in either chamber of Congress to vote against the authorization of use of force following the September 11, 2001, attacks. Lee voted against the Authorization to Use Military Force (AUMF) not because she opposed military action but because she believed the AUMF, as written, granted overly broad powers to wage war to the president at a time when the facts regarding the attacks on 9/11 were not yet clear. Lee explained, "It was a blank check to the president to attack anyone involved in the September 11 events—anywhere, in any country, without regard to our nation's long-term foreign policy, economic and national security interests, and without time limit. In granting these overly broad powers, the Congress failed its responsibility to understand the dimensions of its declaration.... The president has the constitutional authority to protect the nation from further attack and he has mobilized the armed forces to do just that. The Congress should have waited for the facts to be presented and then acted with fuller knowledge of the consequences of our action." Lee's vote made national news and brought about a huge and an exceedingly polarized response, with the quantity of calls congesting the switchboard of her Capitol Hill office.

ANALYSIS

In response to the terrorist attacks against the United States on September 11, 2001, the Congress passed a joint resolution on September 14, 2001, authorizing the president to "use all necessary and appropriate force against those nations, organizations, or persons he determines planned, authorized, committed, or aided the terrorist attacks that occurred on September 11, 2001, or harbored such organizations or persons...." The vote in the Senate was 98 to 0 while the vote in the House of Representatives was 420 to 1. The one vote against was cast by Representative Barbara Lee. The Authorization to Use Military Force (AUMF) was signed by President Bush on September 18, 2001.

The AUMF has been controversial because the language of the resolution is broad and therefore provides for multiple interpretations. This is further complicated by the fact that in the area of foreign affairs, and particularly that of war powers and national security, congressional enactments are usually broadly construed where they indicate support for authority typically asserted and exercised by the executive. It is Congress's war powers under Article I, Section 8 of the Constitution that empower Congress to legislate regarding the raising, regulation, and material support of the armed forces and related matters, rather than the prosecution of military campaigns, and the AUMF seemed to indicate Congress's endorsement of the president's use of his constitutional war powers.

The Bush administration took advantage of this ambiguity by citing the resolution as an authority for several controversial policies. First, the Bush administration argued that the AUMF authorized the president to detain U.S. citizens designated as an enemy combatant even though federal law states that the U.S. government cannot detain an American citizen except by an act of Congress. In *Hamdi v. Rumsfeld*, a plurality of the Supreme Court concluded that the AUMF authorized President Bush to detain "enemy combatants" until the hostilities concluded, even if they were U.S. citizens. Justice O'Connor reasoned that the phrase "all necessary and appropriate force" in the 2001 AUMF included all the incidents of presidential war making that have been informed by executive branch practice, including the power to detain enemy combatants until the end of hostilities. Justice O'Connor found support for her decision in a number of areas including executive branch practice, judicial precedent, the international laws of war, and the need to stop combatants from returning to the battlefield. Based on similar factors, the plurality also concluded that the AUMF authorized the president to detain enemy combatants, like Hamdi, who were American citizens. The plurality limited the AUMF to individuals engaged in armed conflict against the United States in Afghanistan.

The Bush administration also argued that the AUMF partly provided support for the executive to establish military commissions for enemy combatants held at Guantanamo Bay. A plurality of the Court in *Hamdan*, held that Congress never intended for the AUMF resolution to be used for the president to establish military commissions because the structure and procedures of the commissions violated the Uniform Code of Military Justice (UCMJ) and the Geneva Conventions. The Court held that the president's commission was unlawful based on two legal theories. First, in UCMJ Article 21, Congress authorized military commissions, but with the condition that the commissions comply with the law of war, which includes the Geneva Conventions. Common Article 3 of the Geneva Conventions requires that sentences be passed by "a regularly constituted court" providing all the judicial guarantees which are recognized as vital by civilized peoples. The Court concluded that courts martial are the regularly constituted courts of the United States applicable to persons in Hamdan's position. Comparatively, military commissions are considered "regularly constituted" only if there is some practical need that clearly explains the deviation from court-martial practice. The Court believed that the president had not demonstrated such a need. Thus, because the president's commission was not a regularly constituted court under Common Article 3, the Court concluded, the commission violated the law of war and therefore violated the UCMJ Article 21.

The administration also argued that AUMF provided support for the Terrorist Surveillance program (TSP) to engage in electronic surveillance against possible terrorists. The exact scope of the TSP is not known, but the NSA is or was provided total, unsupervised access to all fiber-optic communications going between some of the nation's major telecommunication companies' major interconnect locations, including phone conversations, e-mail, web browsing, and corporate private network traffic. This surveillance took place outside the framework of the Foreign Intelligence Surveillance Act (FISA), which makes it illegal to intentionally engage in electronic surveillance under appearance of an official act or to disclose or use information obtained by electronic surveillance under appearance of an official act knowing that it was not authorized by statute. FISA provides two avenues for the authorization of surveillance.

First, FISA allows the Justice Department to obtain warrants from the Foreign Intelligence Surveillance Court (FISC) before or up to 72 hours after the beginning of the surveillance. FISA authorizes a FISC judge to issue a warrant for the electronic cameras if "there is probable cause to believe that . . . the target of the electronic surveillance is a foreign power or an agent of a foreign power." Second, FISA permits the president or his delegate to authorize warrantless surveillance for the collection of foreign intelligence if "there is no substantial likelihood that the surveillance will acquire the contents of any communication to which a U.S. person is a party." Critics of the TSP argued that any "domestic" intercepts required FISC authorization under the FISA.

The interpretive conflict arises because other provisions of FISA, including the criminal sanctions, include an "unless authorized by statute" provision, raising the issue of statutory ambiguity. The administration's position is that the AUMF is such an authorizing statute that satisfies the FISA requirement. On August 17, 2006, the U.S. District Court for the Eastern District of Michigan ruled in *ACLU v. NSA* that the TSP was unconstitutional under the Fourth and First Amendments and enjoined the NSA from using the program to conduct electronic surveillance in violation of FISA. This ruling was appealed to the Sixth Circuit Court of Appeals which dismissed the case, ruling the plaintiffs in the case—which includes scholars, journalists, and national nonprofit organizations—had no standing to sue because they could not state with certainty that they have been wiretapped by the NSA. On February 19, 2008, the Supreme Court without comment turned down an appeal from the ACLU.

Congress also responded to the TSP by enacting the Protect America Act of 2007. The act clarifies that FISA's definition of "electronic surveillance" does not include surveillance directed at a person reasonably believed to be located outside of the United States. This clarification at the very least frees the government from having to obtain a FISA warrant to intercept foreign-to-foreign communications. Concern about the scope of the act, compounded by the extraordinary speed with which it was enacted, led Congress to include a sunset provision which expired on February 17, 2008.

FURTHER READING

Sunstein, Cass R. "Administrative Law Goes to War." *Harvard Law Review* 118 (2005): 2663.

Tushnet, Mark. "Controlling Executive Power in the War on Terrorism." *Harvard Law Review* 118 (2005): 2673.

The President Responds to September 11: President Bush Signs Executive Order Authorizing Military Tribunals (Commissions)

- ***Document:*** Presidential Military Order: Detention, Treatment, and Trial of Certain Noncitizens in the War against Terrorism
- ***Date:*** November 13, 2001
- ***Where:*** Washington, D.C.
- ***Significance:*** This executive order authorizes the creation of military commissions for the detention, treatment, and trial of certain noncitizens in the war against terrorism.

DOCUMENT

President Issues Military Order Detention, Treatment, and Trial of Certain Non-Citizens in the War against Terrorism

By the authority vested in me as President and as Commander in Chief of the Armed Forces of the United States by the Constitution and the laws of the United States of America, including the Authorization for Use of Military Force Joint Resolution (Public Law 107-40, 115 Stat. 224) and sections 821 and 836 of title 10, United States Code, it is hereby ordered as follows:

Section 1. Findings

(a) International terrorists, including members of al Qaida, have carried out attacks on United States diplomatic and military personnel and facilities abroad and on citizens and property within the United States on a scale that has created a state of armed conflict that requires the use of the United States Armed Forces.

(b) In light of grave acts of terrorism and threats of terrorism, including the terrorist attacks on September 11, 2001, on the headquarters of the United States Department of Defense in the national capital region, on the World

Trade Center in New York, and on civilian aircraft such as in Pennsylvania, I proclaimed a national emergency on September 14, 2001 (Proc. 7463, Declaration of National Emergency by Reason of Certain Terrorist Attacks).

(c) Individuals acting alone and in concert involved in international terrorism possess both the capability and the intention to undertake further terrorist attacks against the United States that, if not detected and prevented, will cause mass deaths, mass injuries, and massive destruction of property, and may place at risk the continuity of the operations of the United States Government.

(d) The ability of the United States to protect the United States and its citizens, and to help its allies and other cooperating nations protect their nations and their citizens, from such further terrorist attacks depends in significant part upon using the United States Armed Forces to identify terrorists and those who support them, to disrupt their activities, and to eliminate their ability to conduct or support such attacks.

(e) To protect the United States and its citizens, and for the effective conduct of military operations and prevention of terrorist attacks, it is necessary for individuals subject to this order pursuant to section 2 hereof to be detained, and, when tried, to be tried for violations of the laws of war and other applicable laws by military tribunals.

(f) Given the danger to the safety of the United States and the nature of international terrorism, and to the extent provided by and under this order, I find consistent with section 836 of title 10, United States Code, that it is not practicable to apply in military commissions under this order the principles of law and the rules of evidence generally recognized in the trial of criminal cases in the United States district courts.

(g) Having fully considered the magnitude of the potential deaths, injuries, and property destruction that would result from potential acts of terrorism against the United States, and the probability that such acts will occur, I have determined that an extraordinary emergency exists for national defense purposes, that this emergency constitutes an urgent and compelling govern-ment interest, and that issuance of this order is necessary to meet the emergency.

Sec. 2. Definition and Policy.

(a) The term "individual subject to this order" shall mean any individual who is not a United States citizen with respect to whom I determine from time to time in writing that:

  (1) there is reason to believe that such individual, at the relevant times,

    (i) is or was a member of the organization known as al Qaida;
    (ii) has engaged in, aided or abetted, or conspired to commit, acts of international terrorism, or acts in preparation therefor, that have caused, threaten to cause, or have as their aim to cause, injury to or adverse effects on the United States, its citizens, national security, foreign policy, or economy; or
    (iii) has knowingly harbored one or more individuals described in subparagraphs (i) or (ii) of subsection 2(a)(1) of this order; and

(2) it is in the interest of the United States that such individual be subject to this order.

(b) It is the policy of the United States that the Secretary of Defense shall take all necessary measures to ensure that any individual subject to this order is detained in accordance with section 3, and, if the individual is to be tried, that such individual is tried only in accordance with section 4.
(c) It is further the policy of the United States that any individual subject to this order who is not already under the control of the Secretary of Defense but who is under the control of any other officer or agent of the United States or any State shall, upon delivery of a copy of such written determination to such officer or agent, forthwith be placed under the control of the Secretary of Defense.

Sec. 3. Detention Authority of the Secretary of Defense. Any individual subject to this order shall be—

(a) detained at an appropriate location designated by the Secretary of Defense outside or within the United States;
(b) treated humanely, without any adverse distinction based on race, color, religion, gender, birth, wealth, or any similar criteria;
(c) afforded adequate food, drinking water, shelter, clothing, and medical treatment;
(d) allowed the free exercise of religion consistent with the requirements of such detention; and
(e) detained in accordance with such other conditions as the Secretary of Defense may prescribe.

Sec. 4. Authority of the Secretary of Defense Regarding Trials of Individuals Subject to this Order.

(a) Any individual subject to this order shall, when tried, be tried by military commission for any and all offenses triable by military commission that such individual is alleged to have committed, and may be punished in accordance with the penalties provided under applicable law, including life imprisonment or death.
(b) As a military function and in light of the findings in section 1, including subsection (f) thereof, the Secretary of Defense shall issue such orders and regulations, including orders for the appointment of one or more military commissions, as may be necessary to carry out subsection (a) of this section.
(c) Orders and regulations issued under subsection (b) of this section shall include, but not be limited to, rules for the conduct of the proceedings of military commissions, including pretrial, trial, and post-trial procedures, modes of proof, issuance of process, and qualifications of attorneys, which shall at a minimum provide for—

(1) military commissions to sit at any time and any place, consistent with such guidance regarding time and place as the Secretary of Defense may provide;

(2) a full and fair trial, with the military commission sitting as the triers of both fact and law;

(3) admission of such evidence as would, in the opinion of the presiding officer of the military commission (or instead, if any other member of the commission so requests at the time the presiding officer renders that opinion, the opinion of the commission rendered at that time by a majority of the commission), have probative value to a reasonable person;

(4) in a manner consistent with the protection of information classified or classifiable under Executive Order 12958 of April 17, 1995, as amended, or any successor Executive Order, protected by statute or rule from unauthorized disclosure, or otherwise protected by law, (A) the handling of, admission into evidence of, and access to materials and information, and (B) the conduct, closure of, and access to proceedings;

(5) conduct of the prosecution by one or more attorneys designated by the Secretary of Defense and conduct of the defense by attorneys for the individual subject to this order;

(6) conviction only upon the concurrence of two-thirds of the members of the commission present at the time of the vote, a majority being present;

(7) sentencing only upon the concurrence of two-thirds of the members of the commission present at the time of the vote, a majority being present; and

(8) submission of the record of the trial, including any conviction or sentence, for review and final decision by me or by the Secretary of Defense if so designated by me for that purpose.

Sec. 5. Obligation of Other Agencies to Assist the Secretary of Defense.

Departments, agencies, entities, and officers of the United States shall, to the maximum extent permitted by law, provide to the Secretary of Defense such assistance as he may request to implement this order.

Sec. 6. Additional Authorities of the Secretary of Defense.

(a) As a military function and in light of the findings in section 1, the Secretary of Defense shall issue such orders and regulations as may be necessary to carry out any of the provisions of this order.

(b) The Secretary of Defense may perform any of his functions or duties, and may exercise any of the powers provided to him under this order (other than under section 4(c)(8) hereof) in accordance with section 113(d) of title 10, United States Code.

Sec. 7. Relationship to Other Law and Forums.

(a) Nothing in this order shall be construed to—

(1) authorize the disclosure of state secrets to any person not otherwise authorized to have access to them;

(2) limit the authority of the President as Commander in Chief of the Armed Forces or the power of the President to grant reprieves and pardons; or
(3) limit the lawful authority of the Secretary of Defense, any military commander, or any other officer or agent of the United States or of any State to detain or try any person who is not an individual subject to this order.

(b) With respect to any individual subject to this order—

(1) military tribunals shall have exclusive jurisdiction with respect to offenses by the individual; and
(2) the individual shall not be privileged to seek any remedy or maintain any proceeding, directly or indirectly, or to have any such remedy or proceeding sought on the individual's behalf, in (i) any court of the United States, or any State thereof, (ii) any court of any foreign nation, or (iii) any international tribunal.

(c) This order is not intended to and does not create any right, benefit, or privilege, substantive or procedural, enforceable at law or equity by any party, against the United States, its departments, agencies, or other entities, its officers or employees, or any other person.
(d) For purposes of this order, the term "State" includes any State, district, territory, or possession of the United States.
(e) I reserve the authority to direct the Secretary of Defense, at any time hereafter, to transfer to a governmental authority control of any individual subject to this order. Nothing in this order shall be construed to limit the authority of any such governmental authority to prosecute any individual for whom control is transferred.

Sec. 8. Publication.

This order shall be published in the Federal Register.
GEORGE W. BUSH
THE WHITE HOUSE,
November 13, 2001.

SOURCE: http://frwebgate.access.gpo.gov/cgi-bin/getdoc.cgi?dbname=2001_register&docid=01-28904-filed.pdf

ANALYSIS

Under this executive order, the Bush administration claimed constitutional authority to subject persons detained in the United States, including American citizens and legal-alien residents of the United States to trial by military commission if the executive branch decides that the detainee is an "unlawful enemy combatant" who has violated the law of war. Trials by military commissions, like trials by civilian courts, involve the exercise of judicial power under Article III of the Constitution.

The Constitution vests the judicial power "in one Supreme Court and in such inferior Courts as the Congress may from time to time ordain and establish." A military tribunal must therefore be authorized by either the Constitution or by Congress. Congress has established military commissions (courts-martial), but has limited their jurisdiction, primarily to offenses committed by members of the armed forces. The Bush administration argued that the president has authority to set up these commissions due to the president's constitutional authority as commander in chief of the armed forces, the Joint Resolution Authorizing the Use of Military Force (AUMF), and parts of the Uniform Code of Military Justice (UCJM).

The military commission is a special U.S. military court traditionally convened by the president for the purpose of trying enemy combatants for violations of the law of war. It is important to note that a military commission is a different military court system than a court-martial. A court-martial is restricted to jurisdiction over members of the U.S. military, while a military commission has jurisdiction over enemy combatants who have violated the laws of war. The procedures for courts-martial are prescribed in the UCMJ and they are almost exact replicas of the Federal Rules applicable to criminal trials. However, the procedure for military commissions was not regulated by statute until passage of the Military Commissions Act of 2006 (described in more detail later on); before that point, military commissions were governed by common law. Thus, procedures were often designed at the executive's discretion. Examples from history reveal that early executives implemented commission procedures that were identical to courts-martial, while later executives did not. As a result, the military commission has taken many forms throughout our history. It has been adapted in each instance to the need of the times. Thus, as a precedent it is inconsistent.

The Bush administration's executive order establishing military commissions was challenged in court. In *Hamdan v. Rumsfeld*, the Supreme Court held that the Bush administration did not have authority to set up these military commissions without congressional authorization, because they did not comply with the UCJM and the Geneva Convention. In *Ex parte Quirin*, the Court held that the military commission created by presidential order in that case was lawfully constituted. The Court explained that since Congress had authorized the trials before the military commissions, the Court did not rule on "to what extent the President as Commander in Chief has constitutional power to create military commissions without the support of Congressional legislation." The Court in *Hamdan* reaffirmed that Congress's power to create military tribunals, including military commissions, is subject to constitutional limitations. The Court's opinion in *Hamdan* has been interpreted as a check on the power of the president.

Interestingly, four of the justices in the majority opinion explained that "nothing prevents the president from returning to Congress to seek the authority he believes necessary" to lawfully try enemy combatants. After the *Hamdan* decision, President Bush, taking this advice, returned to Congress and obtained the legislative authority needed to strip the federal courts of their jurisdiction to hear any habeas petitions of the Guantanamo detainees. Congress responded to the *Hamdan* Court and President Bush by passing the Military Commissions Act (MCA). The MCA expressly granted the president the supreme authority to convene military commissions in order to prosecute those detainees found to be unlawful enemy combatants, and to limit their access to the federal courts.

FURTHER READING

Anderson, Kenneth. "The Military Tribunal Order: What to Do with Bin Laden and Al Qaeda Terrorists?: A Qualified Defense of Military Commissions and United States Policy on Detainees at Guantanamo Bay Naval Base." *Harvard Journal of Law and Public Policy* 25 (Spring 2002): 591.

Burris, Christopher. "Time for Congressional Action: The Necessity of Delineating the Jurisdictional Responsibilities of Federal District Courts, Courts-Martial, and Military Commissions to Try Violations of the Laws of War." *Federal Courts Law Review* (May 2005): 4.

Silliman, Scott L. "'Terrorism on Trial': On Military Commissions." *Case Western Reserve Journal of International Law* 36 (2004): 529.

Congress Responds to September 11: The USA PATRIOT Act

- ***Document:*** The USA PATRIOT Act of 2001 (table of contents and list of sections).
- ***Date:*** October 26, 2001
- ***Where:*** Washington, D.C.
- ***Significance:*** This controversial law greatly increased the capacity of the federal government to search telephone, e-mail communications, medical, financial, and other records; alleviated limitations on foreign intelligence gathering within the United States; increased the secretary of the treasury's authority to regulate financial transactions, particularly those involving foreign persons and entities; and the judgments of law enforcement and immigration authorities in holding and deporting immigrants suspected of engaging in terrorism related operations.

DOCUMENT

An Act

To deter and punish terrorist acts in the United States and around the world, to enhance law enforcement investigatory tools, and for other purposes.

Be it enacted by the Senate and House of Representatives of the United States of America in Congress assembled,

Section 1. Short title and table of contents.

(a) SHORT TITLE—This Act may be cited as the 'Uniting and Strengthening America by Providing Appropriate Tools Required to Intercept and Obstruct Terrorism (USA PATRIOT ACT) Act of 2001'.

Attorney General John Ashcroft, FBI Director Robert Mueller and Office of Homeland Security Director Tom Ridge, left to right, just before President Bush signs the PATRIOT Act into law, Friday, October 26, 2001. (AP Photo/J. Scott Applewhite.)

(b) TABLE OF CONTENTS—The table of contents for this Act is as follows:

Title I—Enhancing Domestic Security Against Terrorism

Title II—Enhanced Surveillance Procedures

Sec. 201. Authority to intercept wire, oral, and electronic communications relating to terrorism.

Sec. 202. Authority to intercept wire, oral, and electronic communications relating to computer fraud and abuse offenses.

Sec. 203. Authority to share criminal investigative information.

Sec. 204. Clarification of intelligence exceptions from limitations on interception and disclosure of wire, oral, and electronic communications.

Sec. 205. Employment of translators by the Federal Bureau of Investigation.

Sec. 206. Roving surveillance authority under the Foreign Intelligence Surveillance Act of 1978.

Sec. 207. Duration of FISA surveillance of non-United States persons who are agents of a foreign power.

Sec. 208. Designation of judges.

Sec. 209. Seizure of voice-mail messages pursuant to warrants.

Sec. 210. Scope of subpoenas for records of electronic communications.

Sec. 211. Clarification of scope.

Sec. 212. Emergency disclosure of electronic communications to protect life and limb.

Sec. 213. Authority for delaying notice of the execution of a warrant.

Sec. 214. Pen register and trap and trace authority under FISA.

Sec. 215. Access to records and other items under the Foreign Intelligence Surveillance Act.

Sec. 216. Modification of authorities relating to use of pen registers and trap and trace devices.

Sec. 217. Interception of computer trespasser communications.

Sec. 218. Foreign intelligence information.

Sec. 219. Single-jurisdiction search warrants for terrorism.

Sec. 220. Nationwide service of search warrants for electronic evidence.

Sec. 221. Trade sanctions.

Sec. 222. Assistance to law enforcement agencies.

Sec. 223. Civil liability for certain unauthorized disclosures.

Sec. 224. Sunset.

Sec. 225. Immunity for compliance with FISA wiretap.

Title III—International Money Laundering Abatement And Anti-Terrorist Financing Act Of 2001

Sec. 301. Short title.

Sec. 302. Findings and purposes.

Sec. 303. 4-year congressional review; expedited consideration.

Subtitle A—International Counter Money Laundering and Related Measures

Sec. 311. Special measures for jurisdictions, financial institutions, or international transactions of primary money laundering concern.

Sec. 312. Special due diligence for correspondent accounts and private banking accounts.

Sec. 313. Prohibition on United States correspondent accounts with foreign shell banks.

Sec. 314. Cooperative efforts to deter money laundering.

Sec. 315. Inclusion of foreign corruption offenses as money laundering crimes.

Sec. 316. Anti-terrorist forfeiture protection.

Sec. 317. Long-arm jurisdiction over foreign money launderers.

Sec. 318. Laundering money through a foreign bank.

Sec. 319. Forfeiture of funds in United States interbank accounts.

Sec. 320. Proceeds of foreign crimes.

Sec. 321. Financial institutions specified in subchapter II of chapter 53 of title 31, United States code.

Sec. 322. Corporation represented by a fugitive.

Sec. 323. Enforcement of foreign judgments.

Sec. 324. Report and recommendation.

Sec. 325. Concentration accounts at financial institutions.

Sec. 326. Verification of identification.

Sec. 327. Consideration of anti-money laundering record.

Sec. 328. International cooperation on identification of originators of wire transfers.

Sec. 329. Criminal penalties.

Sec. 330. International cooperation in investigations of money laundering, financial crimes, and the finances of terrorist groups.

Subtitle B—Bank Secrecy Act Amendments and Related Improvements

Sec. 351. Amendments relating to reporting of suspicious activities.

Sec. 352. Anti-money laundering programs.

Sec. 353. Penalties for violations of geographic targeting orders and certain recordkeeping requirements, and lengthening effective period of geographic targeting orders.

Sec. 354. Anti-money laundering strategy.

Sec. 355. Authorization to include suspicions of illegal activity in written employment references.

Sec. 356. Reporting of suspicious activities by securities brokers and dealers; investment company study.

Sec. 357. Special report on administration of bank secrecy provisions.

Sec. 358. Bank secrecy provisions and activities of United States intelligence agencies to fight international terrorism.

Sec. 359. Reporting of suspicious activities by underground banking systems.

Sec. 360. Use of authority of United States Executive Directors.

Sec. 361. Financial crimes enforcement network.

Sec. 362. Establishment of highly secure network.

Sec. 363. Increase in civil and criminal penalties for money laundering.

Sec. 364. Uniform protection authority for Federal Reserve facilities.

Sec. 365. Reports relating to coins and currency received in nonfinancial trade or business.

Sec. 366. Efficient use of currency transaction report system.

Subtitle C—Currency Crimes and Protection

Sec. 371. Bulk cash smuggling into or out of the United States.

Sec. 372. Forfeiture in currency reporting cases.

Sec. 373. Illegal money transmitting businesses.

Sec. 374. Counterfeiting domestic currency and obligations.

Sec. 375. Counterfeiting foreign currency and obligations.

Sec. 376. Laundering the proceeds of terrorism.

Sec. 377. Extraterritorial jurisdiction.

Title IV—Protecting The Border

Subtitle A—Protecting the Northern Border

Sec. 401. Ensuring adequate personnel on the northern border.

Sec. 402. Northern border personnel.

Sec. 403. Access by the Department of State and the INS to certain identifying information in the criminal history records of visa applicants and applicants for admission to the United States.

Sec. 404. Limited authority to pay overtime.

Sec. 405. Report on the integrated automated fingerprint identification system for ports of entry and overseas consular posts.

Subtitle B—Enhanced Immigration Provisions

Sec. 411. Definitions relating to terrorism.

Sec. 412. Mandatory detention of suspected terrorists; habeas corpus; judicial review.

Sec. 413. Multilateral cooperation against terrorists.

Sec. 414. Visa integrity and security.

Sec. 415. Participation of Office of Homeland Security on Entry-Exit Task Force.

Sec. 416. Foreign student monitoring program.

Sec. 417. Machine readable passports.

Sec. 418. Prevention of consulate shopping.

Subtitle C—Preservation of Immigration Benefits for Victims of Terrorism

Sec. 421. Special immigrant status.

Sec. 422. Extension of filing or reentry deadlines.

Sec. 423. Humanitarian relief for certain surviving spouses and children.

Sec. 424. 'Age-out' protection for children.

Sec. 425. Temporary administrative relief.

Sec. 426. Evidence of death, disability, or loss of employment.

Sec. 427. No benefits to terrorists or family members of terrorists.

Sec. 428. Definitions.

Title V—Removing Obstacles To Investigating Terrorism

Sec. 501. Attorney General's authority to pay rewards to combat terrorism.

Sec. 502. Secretary of State's authority to pay rewards.

Sec. 503. DNA identification of terrorists and other violent offenders.

Sec. 504. Coordination with law enforcement.

Sec. 505. Miscellaneous national security authorities.

Sec. 506. Extension of Secret Service jurisdiction.

Sec. 507. Disclosure of educational records.

Sec. 508. Disclosure of information from NCES surveys.

Title VI—Providing For Victims Of Terrorism, Public Safety Officers, And Their Families

Subtitle A—Aid to Families of Public Safety Officers

Sec. 611. Expedited payment for public safety officers involved in the prevention, investigation, rescue, or recovery efforts related to a terrorist attack.

Sec. 612. Technical correction with respect to expedited payments for heroic public safety officers.

Sec. 613. Public safety officers benefit program payment increase.

Sec. 614. Office of Justice programs.

Subtitle B—Amendments to the Victims of Crime Act of 1984

Sec. 621. Crime victims fund.

Sec. 622. Crime victim compensation.

Sec. 623. Crime victim assistance.

Sec. 624. Victims of terrorism.

Title VII—Increased Information Sharing For Critical Infrastructure Protection

Sec. 701. Expansion of regional information sharing system to facilitate Federal-State-local law enforcement response related to terrorist attacks.

Title VIII—Strengthening The Criminal Laws Against Terrorism

Sec. 801. Terrorist attacks and other acts of violence against mass transportation systems.

Sec. 802. Definition of domestic terrorism.

Sec. 803. Prohibition against harboring terrorists.

Sec. 804. Jurisdiction over crimes committed at U.S. facilities abroad.

Sec. 805. Material support for terrorism.

Sec. 806. Assets of terrorist organizations.

Sec. 807. Technical clarification relating to provision of material support to terrorism.

Sec. 808. Definition of Federal crime of terrorism.

Sec. 809. No statute of limitation for certain terrorism offenses.

Sec. 810. Alternate maximum penalties for terrorism offenses.

Sec. 811. Penalties for terrorist conspiracies.

Sec. 812. Post-release supervision of terrorists.

Sec. 813. Inclusion of acts of terrorism as racketeering activity.

Sec. 814. Deterrence and prevention of cyberterrorism.

Sec. 815. Additional defense to civil actions relating to preserving records in response to Government requests.

Sec. 816. Development and support of cybersecurity forensic capabilities.

Sec. 817. Expansion of the biological weapons statute.

Title IX—Improved Intelligence

Sec. 901. Responsibilities of Director of Central Intelligence regarding foreign intelligence collected under Foreign Intelligence Surveillance Act of 1978.

Sec. 902. Inclusion of international terrorist activities within scope of foreign intelligence under National Security Act of 1947.

Sec. 903. Sense of Congress on the establishment and maintenance of intelligence relationships to acquire information on terrorists and terrorist organizations.

Sec. 904. Temporary authority to defer submittal to Congress of reports on intelligence and intelligence-related matters.

Sec. 905. Disclosure to Director of Central Intelligence of foreign intelligence-related information with respect to criminal investigations.

Sec. 906. Foreign terrorist asset tracking center.

Sec. 907. National Virtual Translation Center.

Sec. 908. Training of government officials regarding identification and use of foreign intelligence.

Title X—Miscellaneous

Sec. 1001. Review of the department of justice.

Sec. 1002. Sense of congress.

Sec. 1003. Definition of 'electronic surveillance'.

Sec. 1004. Venue in money laundering cases.

Sec. 1005. First responders assistance act.

Sec. 1006. Inadmissibility of aliens engaged in money laundering.

Sec. 1007. Authorization of funds for dea police training in south and central asia.

Sec. 1008. Feasibility study on use of biometric identifier scanning system with access to the fbi integrated automated fingerprint identification system at overseas consular posts and points of entry to the United States.

Sec. 1009. Study of access.

Sec. 1010. Temporary authority to contract with local and State governments for performance of security functions at United States military installations.

Sec. 1011. Crimes against charitable Americans.

Sec. 1012. Limitation on issuance of hazmat licenses.

Sec. 1013. Expressing the sense of the senate concerning the provision of funding for bioterrorism preparedness and response.

Sec. 1014. Grant program for State and local domestic preparedness support.

Sec. 1015. Expansion and reauthorization of the crime identification technology act for antiterrorism grants to States and localities.

Sec. 1016. Critical infrastructures protection.

SOURCE: http://thomas.loc.gov/cgi-bin/cpquery/R?cp109:FLD010:@1(hr333)

ANALYSIS

The USA PATRIOT Act is an acronym for the "Uniting and Strengthening America by Providing Appropriate Tools Required to Intercept and Obstruct Terrorism Act of 2001." This controversial law greatly increases the capacity of the federal government to search telephone, e-mail communications, medical, financial, and other records; alleviates limitations on foreign intelligence gathering within the United States; increases the secretary of the treasury's authority to regulate financial transactions, particularly those involving foreign persons and entities; and the judgments of law enforcement and immigration authorities in holding and deporting immigrants suspected of engaging in terrorism related operations. The act also expands the definition of terrorism to include domestic terrorism; thereby increasing the number of activities to which law enforcement powers can be applied. There is an ongoing debate about the scope of the PATRIOT Act and the concerns surrounding the broad new legal and investigative authority given the federal government.

Though the PATRIOT Act made considerable changes to over 15 federal statutes, it was introduced and passed with little debate, and without a House, Senate, or conference report. As a result, it lacks background legislative history that often retrospectively provides necessary statutory interpretation. The PATRIOT Act was first introduced in the House of Representatives on October 2, 2001, and a similar bill was introduced in the Senate on October 4, 2001. The Senate version of the PATRIOT Act, which closely resembled the legislation requested by Attorney General John Ashcroft previously, was sent straight to the floor with no discussion, debate, or hearings. Many Senators complained that they had little chance to read it, much less analyze it, before having to vote. The House held hearings and constructed a compromise bill that emerged from the Judiciary Committee. But then, with no debate or consultation with rank-and-file members, the House leadership threw out the compromise bill and replaced it with legislation that mirrored the Senate version. Neither discussion nor amendments were permitted, and members barely had time to read the thick bill before they were required to cast an up-or-down vote on it. The vote was 357 to 66 in the House while the Senate passed the bill with a 96–1 vote. Senator Russell Feingold was the lone dissenter and spoke openly about his fears that the law would negatively impact civil liberties in the United States. There are many senators and representatives from both sides of the aisle that have publicly regretted their votes in support of the PATRIOT Act. The pressure of seeming unpatriotic so soon after the attacks on 9/11 placed a great deal of pressure to vote in favor of legislation that was seen as a way of preventing future attacks.

Several of the PATRIOT Act's provisions were set to expire on December 31, 2005. In July 2005, the Senate passed a reauthorization bill with substantial changes to several sections of the act, while the House reauthorization bill kept most of the act's original language. The two bills were then reconciled in a conference committee that removed most of the changes from the Senate version. After several extensions, the PATRIOT Act was reaffirmed March 10, 2006, making permanent 14 of the 16 provisions that were scheduled to expire. The reauthorization also included new apparatus designed to help law enforcement prevent the trafficking of methamphetamine, such as tracking the purchase of over-the-counter ingredients and increasing federal penalties for smuggling and selling the drug. The more controversial renewed provisions include the following:

Section 206 to create so-called roving wiretaps, which allow government agents to tap the devices associated with a suspected terrorist rather than a single device under certain circumstances. Section 206 states that roving wiretaps will be applicable to FISA "in circumstances where the Court finds that the actions of the target of the application may have the effect of thwarting the identification of a specified person." A roving wiretap will be granted in a FISA investigation based on everyday behavior. Each phone in a phone bank could be wiretapped if the FBI got a report that the target of a FISA investigation simply used one of those phones once. The conversations of Americans with completely no link to the investigation would be subject to government scrutiny. The advantage to law enforcement from a roving wiretap as compared to a static wiretap is that with a roving wiretap the federal government is not required to return to the court for a new order each time the target changes location, but instead can present the generic order to the new delivery service, landlord, or custodian, directing their assistance to assure that the surveillance may be undertaken as soon as technically possible. The reauthorization holds agencies to a slightly stricter standard with regard to when roving wiretaps can be used, requires reports to Congress on their use, and sets a sunset expiration of four years.

Section 213 to authorize government agents to obtain "sneak and peek" warrants that allow them to enter and search a premises (or sometimes a seizure) without immediately notifying the target on a finding that immediate notification might have "an adverse result." An "adverse result" is defined to include endangering the life or physical safety of an individual; flight from prosecution; destruction or tampering with evidence; intimidation of potential witnesses; or otherwise seriously jeopardize an investigation or unduly delay a trial. Extensions of the delay of notification may be provided in increments of 90 days, with no maximum time limit imposed. The delay in notification may be extended indefinitely if good cause is shown. The statute provides no time limit, the standard to be applied is fairly open ended, and notification of seizures as well as searches may be deferred. This broadening of the exception is not limited to investigations of suspected terrorist activity. The expansion includes searches of areas that contain material constituting evidence of any criminal offenses in violation of the laws of the United States. Under the reauthorization, officials must notify the person whose premises is being searched within a reasonable time that is not to exceed 30 days unless a longer time is expressly approved by the court issuing the warrant.

Section 215 authorizes the government to acquire records and tangible things from custodians—including educational or financial institutions, Internet service providers, or even indignant librarians—under a court order. The PATRIOT Act vastly expanded the kinds of records and objects the government could acquire under this provision, which now covers any type of record and tangible thing, and eliminated the requirement that the government demonstrate any form of individualized suspicion. The director of the FBI or a designee as low in rank as an assistant special agent in charge may apply for a court order requiring the production of "any tangible things" including books, records, papers, documents, and other items upon written statement that these items are being sought for an investigation "to protect against international terrorism or clandestine intelligence activities." A judge presented with an application under Section 215 is required to enter an order approving the release of records.

The predecessor to this section, enacted after the Oklahoma City and 1993 World Trade Center bombings, allowed the government to obtain travel records under the somewhat lenient procedures of the FISA on the basis of specific and articulable facts giving reason to believe that the person to whom the records pertain is a foreign power or agent of a foreign power. Now, under Section 215, the FBI may obtain sensitive personal records by simply certifying that they are sought for an investigation "to protect against international terrorism or clandestine intelligence activities." The FBI need not suspect the person whose records are being sought of any wrongdoing. Furthermore, the class of persons whose records are obtainable under Section 215 is no longer limited to foreign powers and their agents, but may include U.S. citizens and lawful permanent residents, or "United States persons" in the parlance of the FISA. Reauthorization requires agents to present the FISA court with new data proving how the evidence sought will apply to the relevant investigation and affords greater protections for library, medical, and educational records. It also provides the party forced to disclose the business information the right to seek the advice of an attorney and establishes a sunset expiration of four years.

Section 505 of the act amends the Fair Credit Reporting Act, the Financial Right to Privacy Act, and the Electronic Communications Privacy Act, to allow government access to personal information upon "certification" by an FBI agent that the records are relevant to "an investigation to protect against international terrorism or clandestine intelligence activities." This part of the law also provides for the use of National Security Letters (NSL), which is a type of subpoena that forces the party being subpoenaed into a nondisclosure agreement severely limiting any course of action in response. The request for records must notify the recipient of the nondisclosure provisions. Any disclosure to those assisting in the production, or to an attorney, must be accompanied by a notice of the nondisclosure requirement. Finally, any person making a disclosure, or intending to make a disclosure, must inform the director of the FBI, or his designee, if he so requests. The lack of judicial review afforded by NSL worried many lawmakers, and the reauthorization gives a specific right to legal counsel to the recipients of an NSL, and the right to challenge it in court. It also states that libraries cannot be subjected to an NSL, and that the government must present a report to Congress each year on the use of NSL.

FURTHER READING

Chang, Nancy. *Silencing Political Dissent: How Post 9-11 Anti-Terrorism Measures Threaten Our Civil Liberties*. New York: Seven Stories Press, 2002.

Cole, David, et al. *Terrorism and the Constitution: Sacrificing Civil Liberties in the Name of National Security*. New York: New Press, 2002.

Schulhofer, Stephen J. *The Enemy Within: Intelligence Gathering, Law Enforcement, and Civil Liberties in the Wake of September 11*. New York: Century Foundation Press, 2002.

Congress and the President Attempt to Circumvent the Judicial Review of Detainees

Document: The Detainee Treatment Act of 2005
Date: December 30, 2005
Where: Washington, D.C.
Significance: The Detainee Treatment Act of 2005 is part of the Department of Defense Appropriations Act of 2006. It prohibits the "cruel, inhuman, or degrading treatment or punishment" of detainees and provides for "uniform standards" for interrogation. The act also removed the federal courts' jurisdiction over detainees wishing to challenge the legality of their detention, stating that "no court, justice or judge shall have jurisdiction to hear or consider" applications on behalf of Guantanamo detainees.

DOCUMENT

Detainee Treatment Act of 2005

TITLE X—MATTERS RELATING TO DETAINEES

SEC. 1001. Short Title.

This title may be cited as the 'Detainee Treatment Act of 2005'.

SEC. 1002. UNIFORM STANDARDS FOR THE INTERROGATION OF PERSONS UNDER THE DETENTION OF THE DEPARTMENT OF DEFENSE.

(a) In General—No person in the custody or under the effective control of the Department of Defense or under detention in a Department of Defense facility shall be subject to any treatment or technique of interrogation not authorized by and listed in the United States Army Field Manual on Intelligence Interrogation.

An Afghan detainee being escorted to a security cell at the U.S. detention facility at Guantanamo Bay, Cuba, May 9, 2003. Guantanamo has held suspected Al Qaeda members since 2001, and has been widely criticized by human rights organizations for holding the prisoners without formal charge. (U.S. Department of Defense.)

(b) Applicability—Subsection (a) shall not apply with respect to any person in the custody or under the effective control of the Department of Defense pursuant to a criminal law or immigration law of the United States.

(c) Construction—Nothing in this section shall be construed to affect the rights under the United States Constitution of any person in the custody or under the physical jurisdiction of the United States.

Sec. 1003. Prohibition on cruel, inhuman, or degrading treatment or punishment of persons under custody or control of the united states government.

(a) In General—No individual in the custody or under the physical control of the United States Government, regardless of nationality or physical location, shall be subject to cruel, inhuman, or degrading treatment or punishment.

(b) Construction—Nothing in this section shall be construed to impose any geographical limitation on the applicability of the prohibition against cruel, inhuman, or degrading treatment or punishment under this section.

(c) Limitation on Supersedure—The provisions of this section shall not be superseded, except by a provision of law enacted after the date of the enactment of this Act which specifically repeals, modifies, or supersedes the provisions of this section.

(d) Cruel, Inhuman, or Degrading Treatment or Punishment Defined—In this section, the term 'cruel, inhuman, or degrading treatment or punishment' means the cruel, unusual, and inhumane treatment or punishment prohibited by the Fifth, Eighth, and Fourteenth Amendments to the Constitution of the United States, as defined in the United States Reservations, Declarations and Understandings to the United Nations Convention Against Torture and Other Forms of Cruel, Inhuman or Degrading Treatment or Punishment done at New York, December 10, 1984.

Sec. 1004. Protection of united states government personnel engaged in authorized interrogations.

(a) Protection of United States Government Personnel—In any civil action or criminal prosecution against an officer, employee, member of the Armed Forces, or other agent of the United States Government who is a United States person, arising out of the officer, employee, member of the

Armed Forces, or other agent's engaging in specific operational practices, that involve detention and interrogation of aliens who the President or his designees have determined are believed to be engaged in or associated with international terrorist activity that poses a serious, continuing threat to the United States, its interests, or its allies, and that were officially authorized and determined to be lawful at the time that they were conducted, it shall be a defense that such officer, employee, member of the Armed Forces, or other agent did not know that the practices were unlawful and a person of ordinary sense and understanding would not know the practices were unlawful. Good faith reliance on advice of counsel should be an important factor, among others, to consider in assessing whether a person of ordinary sense and understanding would have known the practices to be unlawful. Nothing in this section shall be construed to limit or extinguish any defense or protection otherwise available to any person or entity from suit, civil or criminal liability, or damages, or to provide immunity from prosecution for any criminal offense by the proper authorities.

(b) Counsel—The United States Government may provide or employ counsel, and pay counsel fees, court costs, bail, and other expenses incident to the representation of an officer, employee, member of the Armed Forces, or other agent described in subsection (a), with respect to any civil action or criminal prosecution arising out of practices described in that subsection, under the same conditions, and to the same extent, to which such services and payments are authorized under section 1037 of title 10, United States Code.

Sec. 1005. Procedures for status review of detainees outside the united states.

(a) Submittal of Procedures for Status Review of Detainees at Guantanamo Bay, Cuba, and in Afghanistan and Iraq—

(1) IN GENERAL—Not later than 180 days after the date of the enactment of this Act, the Secretary of Defense shall submit to the Committee on Armed Services and the Committee on the Judiciary of the Senate and the Committee on Armed Services and the Committee on the Judiciary of the House of Representatives a report setting forth—

(A) the procedures of the Combatant Status Review Tribunals and the Administrative Review Boards established by direction of the Secretary of Defense that are in operation at Guantanamo Bay, Cuba, for determining the status of the detainees held at Guantanamo Bay or to provide an annual review to determine the need to continue to detain an alien who is a detainee; and

(B) the procedures in operation in Afghanistan and Iraq for a determination of the status of aliens detained in the custody or under the physical control of the Department of Defense in those countries.

(2) DESIGNATED CIVILIAN OFFICIAL—The procedures submitted to Congress pursuant to paragraph (1)(A) shall ensure that the official of the Department of Defense who is designated by the President or Secretary of Defense to be the final review authority within the Department of Defense with respect to decisions of any such tribunal or board (referred to as the 'Designated Civilian Official') shall be a civilian officer of the Department of Defense holding an office to which appointments are required by law to be made by the President, by and with the advice and consent of the Senate.

(3) CONSIDERATION OF NEW EVIDENCE—The procedures submitted under paragraph (1)(A) shall provide for periodic review of any new evidence that may become available relating to the enemy combatant status of a detainee.

(b) Consideration of Statements Derived With Coercion—

(1) ASSESSMENT—The procedures submitted to Congress pursuant to subsection (a)(1)(A) shall ensure that a Combatant Status Review Tribunal or Administrative Review Board, or any similar or successor administrative tribunal or board, in making a determination of status or disposition of any detainee under such procedures, shall, to the extent practicable, assess—

(A) whether any statement derived from or relating to such detainee was obtained as a result of coercion; and
(B) the probative value (if any) of any such statement.

(2) APPLICABILITY—Paragraph (1) applies with respect to any proceeding beginning on or after the date of the enactment of this Act.

(c) Report on Modification of Procedures—The Secretary of Defense shall submit to the committees specified in subsection (a)(1) a report on any modification of the procedures submitted under subsection (a). Any such report shall be submitted not later than 60 days before the date on which such modification goes into effect.

(d) Annual Report—

(1) REPORT REQUIRED—The Secretary of Defense shall submit to Congress an annual report on the annual review process for aliens in the custody of the Department of Defense outside the United States. Each such report shall be submitted in unclassified form, with a classified annex, if necessary. The report shall be submitted not later than December 31 each year.

(2) ELEMENTS OF REPORT—Each such report shall include the following with respect to the year covered by the report:

(A) The number of detainees whose status was reviewed.
(B) The procedures used at each location.

(e) Judicial Review of Detention of Enemy Combatants—

(1) IN GENERAL—Section 2241 of title 28, United States Code, is amended by adding at the end the following:

(e) Except as provided in section 1005 of the Detainee Treatment Act of 2005, no court, justice, or judge shall have jurisdiction to hear or consider—

(1) an application for a writ of habeas corpus filed by or on behalf of an alien detained by the Department of Defense at Guantanamo Bay, Cuba; or

(2) any other action against the United States or its agents relating to any aspect of the detention by the Department of Defense of an alien at Guantanamo Bay, Cuba, who—

(A) is currently in military custody; or

(B) has been determined by the United States Court of Appeals for the District of Columbia Circuit in accordance with the procedures set forth in section 1005(e) of the Detainee Treatment Act of 2005 to have been properly detained as an enemy combatant.

(2) REVIEW OF DECISIONS OF COMBATANT STATUS REVIEW TRIBUNALS OF PROPRIETY OF DETENTION—

(A) IN GENERAL—Subject to subparagraphs (B), (C), and (D), the United States Court of Appeals for the District of Columbia Circuit shall have exclusive jurisdiction to determine the validity of any final decision of a Combatant Status Review Tribunal that an alien is properly detained as an enemy combatant.

(B) LIMITATION ON CLAIMS—The jurisdiction of the United States Court of Appeals for the District of Columbia Circuit under this paragraph shall be limited to claims brought by or on behalf of an alien—

(i) who is, at the time a request for review by such court is filed, detained by the Department of Defense at Guantanamo Bay, Cuba; and

(ii) for whom a Combatant Status Review Tribunal has been conducted, pursuant to applicable procedures specified by the Secretary of Defense.

(C) SCOPE OF REVIEW—The jurisdiction of the United States Court of Appeals for the District of Columbia Circuit on any claims with respect to an alien under this paragraph shall be limited to the consideration of—

(i) whether the status determination of the Combatant Status Review Tribunal with regard to such alien was consistent with the standards and procedures specified by the Secretary of Defense for Combatant Status Review Tribunals (including the requirement that the conclusion of the Tribunal be supported by a preponderance of the evidence and allowing a rebuttable presumption in favor of the Government's evidence); and

(ii) to the extent the Constitution and laws of the United States are applicable, whether the use of such standards and procedures to make the determination is consistent with the Constitution and laws of the United States.

(D) TERMINATION ON RELEASE FROM CUSTODY—The jurisdiction of the United States Court of Appeals for the District of Columbia Circuit with respect to the claims of an alien under this paragraph shall cease upon the release of such alien from the custody of the Department of Defense.

(3) REVIEW OF FINAL DECISIONS OF MILITARY COMMISSIONS—

(A) IN GENERAL—Subject to subparagraphs (B), (C), and (D), the United States Court of Appeals for the District of Columbia Circuit shall have exclusive jurisdiction to determine the validity of any final decision rendered pursuant to Military Commission Order No. 1, dated August 31, 2005 (or any successor military order).

(B) GRANT OF REVIEW—Review under this paragraph—

(i) with respect to a capital case or a case in which the alien was sentenced to a term of imprisonment of 10 years or more, shall be as of right; or

(ii) with respect to any other case, shall be at the discretion of the United States Court of Appeals for the District of Columbia Circuit.

(C) LIMITATION ON APPEALS—The jurisdiction of the United States Court of Appeals for the District of Columbia Circuit under this paragraph shall be limited to an appeal brought by or on behalf of an alien—

(i) who was, at the time of the proceedings pursuant to the military order referred to in subparagraph (A), detained by the Department of Defense at Guantanamo Bay, Cuba; and

(ii) for whom a final decision has been rendered pursuant to such military order.

(D) SCOPE OF REVIEW—The jurisdiction of the United States Court of Appeals for the District of Columbia Circuit on an appeal of a final decision with respect to an alien under this paragraph shall be limited to the consideration of—

(i) whether the final decision was consistent with the standards and procedures specified in the military order referred to in subparagraph (A); and

(ii) to the extent the Constitution and laws of the United States are applicable, whether the use of such standards and procedures to reach the final decision is consistent with the Constitution and laws of the United States.

(4) RESPONDENT—The Secretary of Defense shall be the named respondent in any appeal to the United States Court of Appeals for the District of Columbia Circuit under this subsection.

(f) Construction—Nothing in this section shall be construed to confer any constitutional right on an alien detained as an enemy combatant outside the United States.

(g) United States Defined—For purposes of this section, the term 'United States', when used in a geographic sense, is as defined in section 101(a)(38) of the Immigration and Nationality Act and, in particular, does not include the United States Naval Station, Guantanamo Bay, Cuba.

(h) Effective Date—

(1) IN GENERAL—This section shall take effect on the date of the enactment of this Act.

(2) REVIEW OF COMBATANT STATUS TRIBUNAL AND MILITARY COMMISSION DECISIONS—Paragraphs (2) and (3) of subsection (e) shall apply with respect to any claim whose review is governed by one of such paragraphs and that is pending on or after the date of the enactment of this Act.

Sec. 1006. Training of Iraqi forces regarding treatment of detainees.

(a) Required Policies—

(1) IN GENERAL—The Secretary of Defense shall ensure that policies are prescribed regarding procedures for military and civilian personnel of the Department of Defense and contractor personnel of the Department of Defense in Iraq that are intended to ensure that members of the Armed Forces, and all persons acting on behalf of the Armed Forces or within facilities of the Armed Forces, ensure that all personnel of Iraqi military forces who are trained by Department of Defense personnel and contractor personnel of the Department of Defense receive training regarding the international obligations and laws applicable to the humane detention of detainees, including protections afforded under the Geneva Conventions and the Convention Against Torture.

(2) ACKNOWLEDGMENT OF TRAINING—The Secretary shall ensure that, for all personnel of the Iraqi Security Forces who are provided training referred to in paragraph (1), there is documented acknowledgment of such training having been provided.

(3) DEADLINE FOR POLICIES TO BE PRESCRIBED—The policies required by paragraph (1) shall be prescribed not later than 180 days after the date of the enactment of this Act.

(b) Army Field Manual—

(1) TRANSLATION—The Secretary of Defense shall provide for the United States Army Field Manual on Intelligence Interrogation to

be translated into arabic and any other language the Secretary determines appropriate for use by members of the Iraqi military forces.

(2) DISTRIBUTION—The Secretary of Defense shall provide for such manual, as translated, to be provided to each unit of the Iraqi military forces trained by Department of Defense personnel or contractor personnel of the Department of Defense.

(c) Transmittal of Regulations—Not less than 30 days after the date on which regulations, policies, and orders are first prescribed under subsection (a), the Secretary of Defense shall submit to the Committee on Armed Services of the Senate and the Committee on Armed Services of the House of Representatives copies of such regulations, policies, or orders, together with a report on steps taken to the date of the report to implement this section.

(d) Annual Report—Not less than one year after the date of the enactment of this Act, and annually thereafter, the Secretary of Defense shall submit to the Committee on Armed Services of the Senate and the Committee on Armed Services of the House of Representatives a report on the implementation of this section.

SOURCE: http://thomas.loc.gov/cgi-bin/query/R?r109:FLD001:S10909

ANALYSIS

The Detainee Treatment Act of 2005 (DTA) prohibits inhumane treatment of prisoners, including prisoners at Guantanamo Bay; requires military interrogations to be performed according to the United States Army Field Manual for Human Intelligence Collector Operations; and strips federal courts of jurisdiction to consider habeas corpus petitions filed by prisoners in Guantanamo, or other claims asserted by Guantanamo detainees against the U.S. government, as well as limiting appellate review of decisions of the Combatant Status Review Tribunals and Military Commissions. The DTA was a response to the *Rasul v. Bush* 542 U.S. 466 (2004), holding that detainees at Guantanamo Bay would have access to civilian courts through the statutory writ of habeas corpus. The act attempted to strip habeas jurisdiction from the federal courts and substituted the Defense Department's Combatant Status Review Tribunals, with a limited appeal to the Court of Appeals for the District of Columbia. This appeal was limited to whether the Combatant Status Review Tribunal followed its own procedures and its decision was consistent with any other applicable laws. It provided for a rebuttable presumption in favor of the government's evidence. Congress and the administration were once again trying to head off any civilian review or oversight of Guantanamo Bay's prisoners.

The DTA was the result of a compromise within and among the political branches. On the one hand, spearheaded by Republican senator and former prisoner of war John McCain, the DTA went further in protecting detainees by establishing uniform standards for the interrogation of persons detained by the U.S. military and establishing minimum standards for the treatment of detainees of any U.S. agency. But at the same time, the DTA attempted to restrict the role of the judiciary in enforcing the norms it established. The act permits only the D.C. Circuit to review the detention of accused combatants at Guantanamo, and even then, only within certain narrow constraints.

Most important, notwithstanding the act's ban on torture, the president issued a signing statement (an official document in which a president lays out his interpretation of the new law) which said that the law shall be construed, "in a manner consistent with the constitutional authority of the President to supervise the unitary executive branch and as Commander in Chief and consistent with the constitutional limitations on judicial power." With this statement, President Bush was proclaiming that notwithstanding the DTA, he had the power to continue to order interrogations that included torture. Thus, even though the DTA claimed to prohibit torture and cruel, inhuman, and degrading treatment, President Bush claimed the right to continue the practice. The use of a signing statement in this way is seen as very controversial. This is true, probably not because of the actual effect of the signing statement, but the perceived effect. The perception by many is that the president is attempting to rewrite the legislation in question, or ignoring the intent of Congress.

The DTA was impacted significantly by two Supreme Court decisions. First, in *Hamdan v. Rumsfeld*, 548 U.S. 557 (2006), the Court held that the DTA's elimination of habeas corpus jurisdiction over petitions brought by noncitizens held at Guantanamo Bay did not apply retroactively to cases pending at the time of the enactment of the DTA. Second, in the case of *Boumediene v. Bush*, the majority ruled that the DTA unconstitutionally limited the detainees from having the right to challenge their detention in conventional civilian courts. The Court determined that if Congress intends to suspend the right of habeas corpus, an adequate substitute must offer the prisoner a meaningful opportunity to demonstrate he is held pursuant to an erroneous application or interpretation of relevant law, and the reviewing decision-making must have some ability to correct errors, to assess the sufficiency of the government's evidence, and to consider relevant exculpating evidence. The Court found that the petitioners had met their burden of establishing that DTA of 2005 failed to provide an adequate substitute for habeas corpus.

FURTHER READING

Suleman, Arsalan M. "Detainee Treatment Act of 2005." *Harvard Human Rights Journal* (Spring 2006): 257–65.

Congress Passes the Military Commissions Act of 2006

- ***Document:*** The Military Commissions Act of 2006 (table of contents and list of sections)
- ***Date:*** October 17, 2006
- ***Where:*** Washington, D.C.
- ***Significance:*** The Military Commissions Act was prompted, in part, by the Supreme Court's ruling in *Hamdan v. Rumsfeld* 548 U.S. 557 (2006), which rejected the president's creation of military commissions by executive order and held that the protections of the UCMJ and Common Article 3 of the Geneva Conventions applies in the context of the war on terror.

DOCUMENT

Military Commissions Act of 2006

An Act

To authorize trial by military commission for violations of the law of war, and for other purposes.

Be it enacted by the Senate and House of Representatives of the United States of America in Congress assembled,

Beginning

Section 1. Short title; table of contents.

Chapter 47a—Military Commissions

Subchapter I—General Provisions

Sec. 948a. Definitions

Sec. 948b. Military commissions generally

Sec. 948c. Persons subject to military commissions

Sec. 948d. Jurisdiction of military commissions

Sec. 948e. Annual report to congressional committees

Subchapter II—Composition Of Military Commissions

Sec. 948h. Who may convene military commissions

Sec. 948i. Who may serve on military commissions

Sec. 948j. Military judge of a military commission

Sec. 948k. Detail of trial counsel and defense counsel

Sec. 948l. Detail or employment of reporters and interpreters

Sec. 948m. Number of members; excuse of members; absent and additional members

Subchapter III—Pre-Trial Procedure

Sec. 948q. Charges and specifications

Sec. 948r. Compulsory self-incrimination prohibited; treatment of statements obtained by torture and other statements

Sec. 948s. Service of charges

Subchapter IV—Trial Procedure

Sec. 949a. Rules

Sec. 949b. Unlawfully influencing action of military commission

Sec. 949c. Duties of trial counsel and defense counsel

Sec. 949d. Sessions

Sec. 949e. Continuances

Sec. 949f. Challenges

Sec. 949g. Oaths

Sec. 949h. Former jeopardy

Sec. 949i. Pleas of the accused

Sec. 949j. Opportunity to obtain witnesses and other evidence

Sec. 949k. Defense of lack of mental responsibility

Sec. 949l. Voting and rulings

Sec. 949m. Number of votes required

Sec. 949n. Military commission to announce action

Sec. 949o. Record of trial

Subchapter V—Sentences

Sec. 949s. Cruel or unusual punishments prohibited

Sec. 949t. Maximum limits

Sec. 949u. Execution of confinement

Subchapter VI—Post-Trial Procedure And Review Of Military Commissions

Sec. 950a. Error of law; lesser included offense

Sec. 950b. Review by the convening authority

Sec. 950c. Appellate referral; waiver or withdrawal of appeal

Sec. 950d. Appeal by the United States

Sec. 950e. Rehearings

Sec. 950f. Review by Court of Military Commission Review

Sec. 950g. Review by the United States Court of Appeals for the District of Columbia Circuit and the Supreme Court

Sec. 950h. Appellate counsel

Sec. 950i. Execution of sentence; procedures for execution of sentence of death

Sec. 950j. Finality or proceedings, findings, and sentences

Subchapter VII—Punitive Matters

Sec. 950p. Statement of substantive offenses

Sec. 950q. Principals

President Bush prior to signing the Military Commissions Act of 2006. (AP Photo/Ron Edmonds.)

SOURCE: http://thomas.loc.gov/cgi-bin/query/D?c109:4:./temp/~c109d4Z01I::

ANALYSIS

There has been a consistent effort throughout American history to protect civilians from the use of military tribunals even when the nation was at war and threatened with invasion. Military commissions are common law war courts instituted during periods of hostilities, martial rule, or military government as mechanisms for the more efficient execution of the war powers vested in Congress and the president. On those rare occasions when the president has attempted to extend military-tribunal jurisdiction beyond its application to members of the U.S. or enemy armed forces, the Court has either struck it down as unconstitutional or found no congressional authorization. Historically, there have been three types of military commission: (1) commissions that substitute for civilian courts at times and places where martial law has been declared ("martial law tribunals"); (2) commissions to try civilians "as part of a temporary military government over occupied enemy territory or territory regained from an enemy where civilian government cannot and does not function" ("occupied territory tribunals"); and (3) commissions incident to the conduct of war when there is a need to seize and subject to disciplinary measures those enemies who have violated the law of war. It is the third type that was at issue here.

The Military Commissions Act (MCA) amends the Uniform Code of Military Justice (UCMJ) and the War Crimes Act. The MCA mandates that unlawful alien combatants be tried by military commission and lays out the procedures for these commissions, which, except for a few key exceptions, are based on UCMJ courts-martial rules. The statute defines "unlawful enemy combatants" as non-citizens who have engaged in hostilities or "purposefully and materially supported hostilities against the United States" and who are not lawful enemy combatants. The definition specifically includes members of the Taliban, al Qaeda, or any associated force. The Military Commissions Act also defines a lawful enemy combatant, though lawful enemy combatants will not be tried pursuant to the Military Commissions Act.

Some of the most controversial provisions include authorizing the president to define who is an "unlawful enemy combatant," eliminating the writ of habeas corpus for any alien combatant, and allowing an exception for the use of "reliable" coerced evidence. If unchallenged the MCA would have allowed the federal government to continue to hold hundreds of prisoners for more than five years without charges.

In *Boumediene v. Bush*, the Supreme Court held that aliens designated as enemy combatants and detained at the U.S. Naval Station in Guantanamo Bay, Cuba, have the constitutional privilege of habeas corpus. The Court also found that Section 7 of the Military Commissions Act (MCA), which limited judicial review of executive determinations of the petitioners' enemy combatant status, did not provide an adequate habeas substitute and therefore acted as an unconstitutional suspension of the writ of habeas. The immediate impact of the *Boumediene* decision was that detainees at Guantanamo were allowed to petition a federal district court for habeas review of the circumstances of their detention. While the petitioners in *Boumediene* sought habeas review of their designation as enemy combatants, the Court's ruling that the constitutional writ of habeas extends to Guantanamo suggests that detainees may also seek judicial review of claims concerning unlawful conditions of treatment or confinement or to protest a planned transfer to the custody of another country.

FURTHER READING

Schatz, Christopher J., and Noah A. F. Horst, "Will Justice Delayed Be Justice Denied? Crisis Jurisprudence, the Guantanamo Detainees, and the Imperiled Role of Habeas Corpus in Curbing Abusive Government Detention." *Lewis and Clark Law Review* 11 (Fall 2007): 539.

Stewart, James G. "The Military Commissions Act's Inconsistency with the Geneva Conventions: An Overview." *Journal of International Criminal Justice* 5 (March 1, 2007): 26.

6

21ST-CENTURY COURT RULINGS

Supreme Court Responds to September 11: An Examination of Habeas Corpus Petitions from U.S. Citizens Designated as Enemy Combatants

- ***Document:*** The Supreme Court case *Hamdi v. Rumsfeld*, Excerpt
- ***Date:*** January 28, 2004
- ***Where:*** Washington, D.C.
- ***Significance:*** *Hamdi* was the Supreme Court decision reversing the dismissal of a habeas corpus petition brought on behalf of Yaser Esam Hamdi, a U.S. citizen being detained indefinitely as an unlawful combatant. The Court recognized the power of the government to detain unlawful combatants, but ruled that detainees must have the ability to challenge their detention before an impartial judge.

DOCUMENT

Hamdi v. Rumsfeld, 542 U.S. 507 (2004)

Argued April 28, 2004.
Decided June 28, 2004.
Justice O'Connor announced the judgment of the Court.

The threshold question before us is whether the Executive has the authority to detain citizens who qualify as "enemy combatants." There is some debate as to the proper scope of this term, and the Government has never provided any court with the full criteria that it uses in classifying individuals as such. It has made clear, however, that, for purposes of this case, the "enemy combatant" that it is seeking to detain is an individual who, it alleges, was "'part of or supporting forces hostile to the United States or coalition partners'" in Afghanistan and who "'engaged in an armed conflict against the United States'" there. We therefore answer only the narrow question before us: whether the detention of citizens falling within that definition is authorized.

The Government maintains that no explicit congressional authorization is required, because the Executive possesses plenary authority to detain pursuant to Article II of the Constitution. We do not reach the question whether Article II provides such authority, however, because we agree with the Government's alternative position, that Congress has in fact authorized Hamdi's detention, through the AUMF....

Protesters outside of the U.S. Supreme Court. (AP Photo/Evan Vucci.)

The AUMF authorizes the President to use "all necessary and appropriate force" against "nations, organizations, or persons" associated with the September 11, 2001, terrorist attacks. There can be no doubt that individuals who fought against the United States in Afghanistan as part of the Taliban, an organization known to have supported the al Qaeda terrorist network responsible for those attacks, are individuals Congress sought to target in passing the AUMF. We conclude that detention of individuals falling into the limited category we are considering, for the duration of the particular conflict in which they were captured, is so fundamental and accepted an incident to war as to be an exercise of the "necessary and appropriate force" Congress has authorized the President to use.

The capture and detention of lawful combatants and the capture, detention, and trial of unlawful combatants, by "universal agreement and practice," are "important incident[s] of war." Ex parte Quirin. The purpose of detention is to prevent captured individuals from returning to the field of battle and taking up arms once again....

There is no bar to this Nation's holding one of its own citizens as an enemy combatant. In Quirin, one of the detainees, Haupt, alleged that he was a naturalized United States citizen. We held that "[c]itizens who associate themselves with the military arm of the enemy government, and with its aid, guidance and direction enter this country bent on hostile acts, are enemy belligerents within the meaning of... the law of war." While Haupt was tried for violations of the law of war, nothing in Quirin suggests that his citizenship would have precluded his mere detention for the duration of the relevant hostilities. Nor can we see any reason for drawing such a line here. A citizen, no less than an alien, can be "part of or supporting forces hostile to the United States or coalition partners" and "engaged in an armed conflict against the United States"; such a citizen, if released, would pose the same threat of returning to the front during the ongoing conflict.

In light of these principles, it is of no moment that the AUMF does not use specific language of detention. Because detention to prevent a combatant's return to the battlefield is a fundamental incident of waging war, in permitting the use of "necessary and appropriate force," Congress has clearly and unmistakably authorized detention in the narrow circumstances considered here.

It is a clearly established principle of the law of war that detention may last no longer than active hostilities. Hamdi contends that the AUMF does not authorize indefinite or perpetual detention. Certainly, we agree that indefinite detention for the purpose of interrogation is not authorized. Further, we understand Congress' grant of authority for the use of "necessary and appropriate force" to include the authority to detain for the duration of the relevant conflict, and our understanding is based on longstanding law-of-war principles. If the practical circumstances of a given conflict are entirely unlike those of the conflicts that informed the development of the law of war, that understanding may unravel. But that is not the situation we face as of this date. Active combat operations against Taliban fighters apparently are ongoing in Afghanistan. . . . If the record establishes that United States troops are still involved in active combat in Afghanistan, those detentions are part of the exercise of "necessary and appropriate force," and therefore are authorized by the AUMF.

Ex parte Milligan does not undermine our holding about the Government's authority to seize enemy combatants, as we define that term today. In that case, the Court made repeated reference to the fact that its inquiry into whether the military tribunal had jurisdiction to try and punish Milligan turned in large part on the fact that Milligan was not a prisoner of war, but a resident of Indiana arrested while at home there. That fact was central to its conclusion. Had Milligan been captured while he was assisting Confederate soldiers by carrying a rifle against Union troops on a Confederate battlefield, the holding of the Court might well have been different. The Court's repeated explanations that Milligan was not a prisoner of war suggest that had these different circumstances been present he could have been detained under military authority for the duration of the conflict, whether or not he was a citizen. . . .

Quirin was a unanimous opinion. It both postdates and clarifies Milligan, providing us with the most apposite precedent that we have on the question of whether citizens may be detained in such circumstances. Brushing aside such precedent–particularly when doing so gives rise to a host of new questions never dealt with by this Court–is unjustified and unwise. . . .

Even in cases in which the detention of enemy combatants is legally authorized, there remains the question of what process is constitutionally due to a citizen who disputes his enemy-combatant status. Hamdi argues that he is owed a meaningful and timely hearing and that "extra-judicial detention [that] begins and ends with the submission of an affidavit based on third-hand hearsay" does not comport with the Fifth and Fourteenth Amendments. The Government counters that any more process than was provided below would be both unworkable and "constitutionally intolerable." Our resolution of this dispute requires a careful examination both of the writ of habeas corpus, which Hamdi now seeks to employ as a mechanism of judicial review, and of the Due Process Clause, which informs the procedural contours of that mechanism in this instance.

Striking the proper constitutional balance here is of great importance to the Nation during this period of ongoing combat. But it is equally vital that our calculus not give short shrift to the values that this country holds dear or to the privilege that is American citizenship. It is during our most challenging and uncertain moments that our Nation's commitment to due process is most severely tested; and it is in those times that we must preserve our commitment at home to the principles for which we fight abroad.

With due recognition of these competing concerns, we believe that neither the process proposed by the Government nor the process apparently envisioned by the District Court below strikes the proper constitutional balance when a United States citizen is detained in the United States as an enemy combatant. That is, "the risk of erroneous deprivation" of a detainee's liberty interest is unacceptably high under the Government's proposed rule, while some of the "additional or substitute procedural safeguards" suggested by the District Court are unwarranted in light of their limited "probable value" and the burdens they may impose on the military in such cases.

We therefore hold that a citizen-detainee seeking to challenge his classification as an enemy combatant must receive notice of the factual basis for his classification, and a fair opportunity to rebut the Government's factual assertions before a neutral decisionmaker. "For more than a century the central meaning of procedural due process has been clear: 'Parties whose rights are to be affected are entitled to be heard; and in order that they may enjoy that right they must first be notified.' It is equally fundamental that the right to notice and an opportunity to be heard 'must be granted at a meaningful time and in a meaningful manner.'" These essential constitutional promises may not be eroded.

At the same time, the exigencies of the circumstances may demand that, aside from these core elements, enemy combatant proceedings may be tailored to alleviate their uncommon potential to burden the Executive at a time of ongoing military conflict. Hearsay, for example, may need to be accepted as the most reliable available evidence from the Government in such a proceeding. Likewise, the Constitution would not be offended by a presumption in favor of the Government's evidence, so long as that presumption remained a rebuttable one and fair opportunity for rebuttal were provided. Thus, once the Government puts forth credible evidence that the habeas petitioner meets the enemy-combatant criteria, the onus could shift to the petitioner to rebut that evidence with more persuasive evidence that he falls outside the criteria. A burden-shifting scheme of this sort would meet the goal of ensuring that the errant tourist, embedded journalist, or local aid worker has a chance to prove military error while giving due regard to the Executive once it has put forth meaningful support for its conclusion that the detainee is in fact an enemy combatant. In the words of Mathews, process of this sort would sufficiently address the "risk of erroneous deprivation" of a detainee's liberty interest while eliminating certain procedures that have questionable additional value in light of the burden on the Government.

We think it unlikely that this basic process will have the dire impact on the central functions of warmaking that the Government forecasts. The parties agree that initial captures on the battlefield need not receive the process we have discussed here; that process is due only when the determination is made to continue to hold those who have been seized.... This focus meddles little, if at all, in the strategy or conduct of war, inquiring only into the appropriateness of continuing to detain an individual claimed to have taken up arms against the United States. While we accord the greatest respect and consideration to the judgments of military authorities in matters relating to the actual prosecution of a war, and recognize that the scope of that discretion necessarily is wide, it does not infringe on the core role of the military for the courts to exercise their own time-honored and constitutionally mandated roles of reviewing and resolving claims like those presented here.

In sum, while the full protections that accompany challenges to detentions in other settings may prove unworkable and inappropriate in the enemy-combatant setting, the threats to military operations posed by a basic system of independent review are not so weighty as to trump a citizen's core rights to challenge meaningfully the Government's case and to be heard by an impartial adjudicator.

Whatever power the United States Constitution envisions for the Executive in its exchanges with other nations or with enemy organizations in times of conflict, it most assuredly envisions a role for all three branches when individual liberties are at stake....

Because we conclude that due process demands some system for a citizen detainee to refute his classification, the proposed "some evidence" standard is inadequate. Any process in which the Executive's factual assertions go wholly unchallenged or are simply presumed correct without any opportunity for the alleged combatant to demonstrate otherwise falls constitutionally short....

Plainly, the "process" Hamdi has received is not that to which he is entitled under the Due Process Clause.

SOURCE: http://caselaw.lp.findlaw.com/scripts/getcase.pl?court=us&vol=000&invol=03-6696

ANALYSIS

In 2001, Yaser Hamdi, an American citizen, was captured by Northern Alliance forces who were cooperating with the U.S. military in its campaign against the Taliban regime and Al Qaeda in Afghanistan. He was accused of fighting for the Taliban against the United States, declared an "enemy combatant," and transferred to a military prison in Virginia. Frank Dunham, Jr., a defense attorney in Virginia, filed a petition for a writ of certiorari in federal district court there in an attempt to have Hamdi's detention declared unconstitutional. He argued that the government had violated Hamdi's Fifth Amendment right to due process by holding him indefinitely and not giving him access to an attorney or a trial. The government answered that the executive branch had the right, during wartime, to declare people who fight against the United States "enemy combatants" and thus restrict their access to the court system.

In the plurality opinion that controlled the disposition of the case, Justice O'Connor was joined by Chief Justice Rehnquist, Justice Kennedy, and Justice Breyer. Justice O'Connor's plurality opinion focuses on the limited question of whether the executive has the authority to detain an American citizen who was engaged in armed conflict against the United States, by either supporting or affiliating with forces hostile to the United States in Afghanistan, as an enemy combatant. The plurality concluded that the Authorization for Use of Military Force (AUMF) allowed Hamdi's detention and constituted an act of Congress that negated Hamdi's rights as a citizen. Justice O'Connor's opinion calls the detention of enemy combatants "fundamental and accepted [as] an incident to war," and affirmatively states that "there is no bar to this Nation's holding one of its own citizens as an enemy combatant."

Based on a balancing of the citizen's constitutional rights against the government's interests in national security, the plurality concluded that a citizen-detainee must receive notice of the factual basis for his classification as an enemy combatant, as well as a fair opportunity to rebut the government's allegations before a neutral decision maker. To justify continued detention, the decision maker must find that the government has proven the enemy combatant status of the citizen beyond a mere "some evidence" standard. The plurality carefully noted, however, that citizen enemy combatant proceedings "may be tailored to alleviate their uncommon potential to burden the Executive at a time of ongoing military conflict." They found that the executive could lawfully detain enemy combatants, but that American citizens were entitled to an opportunity before a neutral decision maker to challenge the executive's facts.

The plurality also determined that the separation of powers doctrine does not preclude the courts from hearing challenges by citizens to classification as enemy combatants because a citizen is entitled to bring a habeas corpus proceeding in the absence of suspension of the writ by Congress. A plurality of the Court held that it would turn the system of checks and balances on its head to suggest that a citizen could not make his way to court with a challenge to the factual basis for his detention by his government simply because the executive opposed making available such a challenge and that absent suspension of the writ of habeas corpus by Congress, a citizen detained as an enemy combatant was entitled to that process.

Justice Souter, joined by Justice Ginsburg, concurred in the judgment that Yaser Hamdi should receive due process. Justice Souter based his opinion on the historical context of wartime citizen internment because Hamdi represented "nothing more than customary detention of a captive taken on the field of battle..." Justice Souter concluded however that the AUMF did not provide a clear statement of authority in Hamdi's case.

Justice Scalia, joined by Justice Stevens, dissented, asserting that the government could only detain citizens if the United States prosecuted them or lawmakers had suspended the writ of habeas corpus under Article I. He contended that while the plurality described wartime detention procedures that would apply to enemy aliens, Hamdi's status as a citizen should have left the government with two options—either charge Hamdi with treason or suspend the writ of habeas corpus. As the writ was not suspended, and since Hamdi challenged his classification as an enemy combatant, Justice Scalia concluded that Hamdi's citizenship entitled him to either a criminal trial or a judicial decree mandating his release. Justice Thomas also dissented, supporting the theory urged by the Department of Justice that the president had nearly unfettered authority over individuals designated as enemy combatants and that the judgment of the Fourth Circuit should be affirmed.

FURTHER READING

Perkins, Jared. "Note and Comment, Habeas Corpus in the War Against Terrorism: Hamdi v. Rumsfeld and Citizen Enemy Combatants." *Brigham Young University Journal of Public Law* 19 (2005): 437.

Supreme Court Reviews President Bush's Military Order Establishing Military Commissions for Enemy Combatants

- ***Document:*** The Supreme Court case *Hamdan v. Rumsfeld*, Excerpt
- ***Date:*** June 29, 2006
- ***Where:*** Washington, D.C.
- ***Significance:*** The Supreme Court held that neither an act of Congress nor the inherent powers of the executive laid out in the Constitution expressly authorized the sort of military commission established by the military order from President Bush. Absent that express authorization, the military commission had to comply with the ordinary laws of the United States and the laws of war. The Geneva Convention, as a part of the ordinary laws of war, could therefore be enforced by the Supreme Court, along with the statutory Uniform Code of Military Justice.

DOCUMENT

Hamdan v. Rumsfeld, 548 U.S. 557 (2006)

Argued March 28, 2006.

Decided June 29, 2006.

Justice Stevens announced the judgment of the Court.

On September 11, 2001, agents of the al Qaeda terrorist organization hijacked commercial airplanes and attacked the World Trade Center in New York City and the national headquarters of the Department of Defense in Arlington, Virginia. Americans will never forget the devastation wrought by these acts. Nearly 3,000 civilians were killed.

Congress responded by adopting a Joint Resolution authorizing the President to "use all necessary and appropriate force against those nations, organizations, or persons he determines planned, authorized, committed, or aided the terrorist attacks... in order to prevent any future acts of international terrorism against the United States by such nations, organizations or persons." Acting pursuant to the AUMF, and having determined that the Taliban regime had supported al Qaeda, the President ordered the Armed Forces of the United States to invade Afghanistan. In the ensuing hostilities, hundreds of individuals, Hamdan among them, were captured and eventually detained at Guantanamo Bay.

On November 13, 2001, while the United States was still engaged in active combat with the Taliban, the President issued a comprehensive military order intended to govern the "Detention, Treatment, and Trial of Certain Non-Citizens in the War Against Terrorism," 66 Fed. Reg. 57833 (hereinafter November 13 Order or Order). Those subject to the November 13 Order include any noncitizen for whom the President determines "there is reason to believe" that he or she (1) "is or was" a member of al Qaeda or (2) has engaged or participated in terrorist activities aimed at or harmful to the United States. Any such individual "shall, when tried, be tried by military commission for any and all offenses triable by military commission that such individual is alleged to have committed, and may be punished in accordance with the penalties provided under applicable law, including imprisonment or death." The November 13 Order vested in the Secretary of Defense the power to appoint military commissions to try individuals subject to the Order, but that power has since been delegated to John D. Altenberg, Jr., a retired Army major general and longtime military lawyer who has been designated "Appointing Authority for Military Commissions."

On July 3, 2003, the President announced his determination that Hamdan and five other detainees at Guantanamo Bay were subject to the November 13 Order and thus triable by military commission.

After this formal charge was filed, the United States District Court for the Western District of Washington transferred Hamdan's habeas and mandamus petitions to the United States District Court for the District of Columbia. Meanwhile, a Combatant Status Review Tribunal (CSRT) convened pursuant to a military order issued on July 7, 2004, decided that Hamdan's continued detention at Guantanamo Bay was warranted because he was an "enemy combatant." Separately, proceedings before the military commission commenced....

On November 7, 2005, we granted certiorari to decide whether the military commission convened to try Hamdan has authority to do so, and whether Hamdan may rely on the Geneva Conventions in these proceedings.

The military commission, a tribunal neither mentioned in the Constitution nor created by statute, was born of military necessity. Though foreshadowed in some

DID YOU KNOW?

Habeas Corpus Petitions by Guantánamo Detainees: *Rasul v. Bush,* 2004

In *Rasul v. Bush* 542 U.S. 466 (2004), the U.S. Supreme Court held that federal courts have jurisdiction over habeas corpus petitions filed by detainees at the U.S. naval base at Guantánamo Bay, Cuba. Four British and Australian citizens, one of whom was Shafiq Rasul, had been captured abroad during hostilities between the United States and the Taliban regime in Afghanistan. They were held in executive detention at the Guantánamo Bay Naval Base in Cuba. In challenging their detention, they claimed that the government's decision to deny them access to attorneys and to hold them indefinitely without access to a court violated the Fifth Amendment's due process clause. The government countered that the federal courts had no jurisdiction to hear the case because the prisoners were not American citizens and were being held in territory over which the United States did not have sovereignty.

The Court responded that the degree of control exercised by the United States over the Guantánamo Bay base was sufficient to trigger the application of habeas corpus rights. Justice Stevens, using a list of precedents dating back to mid-17th-century English common law cases, found that the right to habeas corpus can be exercised in "all... dominions under the sovereign's control." Because the United States exercised "complete jurisdiction and control" over the base, the fact that ultimate sovereignty remained with Cuba was irrelevant. Stevens also wrote that the right to habeas corpus is not dependent on citizenship status. The detainees were therefore free to bring suit in federal court challenging their detention as unconstitutional. This decision greatly expanded the protections of the Constitution and diminished the power of the federal government.

respects by earlier tribunals like the Board of General Officers that General Washington convened to try British Major John André for spying during the Revolutionary War, the commission "as such" was inaugurated in 1847. As commander of occupied Mexican territory, and having available to him no other tribunal, General Winfield Scott that year ordered the establishment of both "'military commissions'" to try ordinary crimes committed in the occupied territory and a "council of war" to try offenses against the law of war....

Exigency alone, of course, will not justify the establishment and use of penal tribunals not contemplated by Article I, §8 and Article III, §1 of the Constitution unless some other part of that document authorizes a response to the felt need. And that authority, if it exists, can derive only from the powers granted jointly to the President and Congress in time of war.

The Constitution makes the President the "Commander in Chief" of the Armed Forces, Art. II, §2, cl. 1, but vests in Congress the powers to "declare War... and make Rules concerning Captures on Land and Water...." The interplay between these powers was described by Chief Justice Chase in the seminal case of Ex parte Milligan: "The power to make the necessary laws is in Congress; the power to execute in the President. Both powers imply many subordinate and auxiliary powers. Each includes all authorities essential to its due exercise. But neither can the President, in war more than in peace, intrude upon the proper authority of Congress, nor Congress upon the proper authority of the President.... Congress cannot direct the conduct of campaigns, nor can the President, or any commander under him, without the sanction of Congress, institute tribunals for the trial and punishment of offences, either of soldiers or civilians, unless in cases of a controlling necessity, which justifies what it compels, or at least insures acts of indemnity from the justice of the legislature."

The Government would have us dispense with the inquiry that the Quirin Court undertook and find in either the AUMF or the DTA specific, overriding authorization for the very commission that has been convened to try Hamdan. Neither of these congressional Acts, however, expands the President's authority to convene military commissions. First, while we assume that the AUMF activated the President's war powers, see Hamdi v. Rumsfeld (2004), and that those powers include the authority to convene military commissions in appropriate circumstances, there is nothing in the text or legislative history of the AUMF even hinting that Congress intended to expand or alter the authorization set forth in Article 21 of the UCMJ.

Likewise, the DTA cannot be read to authorize this commission. Although the DTA, unlike either Article 21 or the AUMF, was enacted after the President had convened Hamdan's commission, it contains no language authorizing that tribunal or any other at Guantanamo Bay....

Together, the UCMJ, the AUMF, and the DTA at most acknowledge a general Presidential authority to convene military commissions in circumstances where justified under the "Constitution and laws," including the law of war. Absent a more specific congressional authorization, the task of this Court is, as it was in Quirin, to decide whether Hamdan's military commission is so justified. It is to that inquiry we now turn.

The common law governing military commissions may be gleaned from past practice and what sparse legal precedent exists. Commissions historically have been used in three situations. First, they have substituted for civilian courts at times and in places where martial law has been declared. Their use in these circumstances has raised constitutional questions, but is well recognized. Second, commissions have been established to try civilians "as part of a temporary military government over occupied enemy territory or territory regained from an enemy where civilian government cannot and does not function." Illustrative of this second kind of commission is the one that was established, with jurisdiction to apply the German Criminal Code, in occupied Germany following the end of World War II.

The third type of commission, convened as an "incident to the conduct of war" when there is a need "to seize and subject to disciplinary measures those enemies who in their attempt to thwart or impede our military effort have violated the law of war," has been described as "utterly different" from the other two. Not only is its jurisdiction limited to offenses cognizable during time of war, but its role is primarily a factfinding one—to determine, typically on the battlefield itself, whether the defendant has violated the law of war. The last time the U.S. Armed Forces used the law-of-war military commission was during World War II. In Quirin, this Court sanctioned President Roosevelt's use of such a tribunal to try Nazi saboteurs captured on American soil during the War.

Quirin is the model the Government invokes most frequently to defend the commission convened to try Hamdan. That is both appropriate and unsurprising. Since Guantanamo Bay is neither enemy-occupied territory nor under martial law, the law-of-war commission is the only model available. At the same time, no more robust model of executive power exists; Quirin represents the high-water mark of military power to try enemy combatants for war crimes...

The charge against Hamdan alleges a conspiracy extending over a number of years, from 1996 to November 2001. All but two months of that more than 5-year-long period preceded the attacks of September 11, 2001, and the enactment of the AUMF—the Act of Congress on which the Government relies for exercise of its war powers and thus for its authority to convene military commissions. Neither the purported agreement with Osama bin Laden and others to commit war crimes, nor a single overt act, is alleged to have occurred in a theater of war or on any specified date after September 11, 2001. None of the overt acts that Hamdan is alleged to have committed violates the law of war.

These facts alone cast doubt on the legality of the charge and, hence, the commission; the offense alleged must have been committed both in a theater of war and during, not before, the relevant conflict. But the deficiencies in the time and place allegations also underscore—indeed are symptomatic of—the most serious defect of this charge: The offense it alleges is not triable by law-of-war military commission.

There is no suggestion that Congress has, in exercise of its constitutional authority to "define and punish... Offences against the Law of Nations," U.S. Const., Art. I, §8, cl. 10, positively identified "conspiracy" as a war crime. As we explained in Quirin, that is not necessarily fatal to the Government's claim of authority to try the alleged offense by military commission; Congress, through Article 21 of the UCMJ, has "incorporated by reference" the common law of war, which may render triable by military commission certain offenses not defined by statute. When, however, neither the elements of the offense nor the range of permissible punishments is defined by statute or treaty, the precedent must be plain and unambiguous. To demand any less would be to risk concentrating in military hands a degree of adjudicative and punitive power in excess of that contemplated either by statute or by the Constitution.

This high standard was met in Quirin; the violation there alleged was, by "universal agreement and practice" both in this country and internationally, recognized as an offense against the law of war....

At a minimum, the Government must make a substantial showing that the crime for which it seeks to try a defendant by military commission is acknowledged to be an offense against the law of war. That burden is far from satisfied here. The crime of "conspiracy" has rarely if ever been tried as such in this country by any law-of-war military commission not exercising some other form of jurisdiction, and does not appear in either the Geneva Conventions or the Hague Conventions—the major treaties on the law of war. . . .

Finally, international sources confirm that the crime charged here is not a recognized violation of the law of war. As observed above, none of the major treaties governing the law of war identifies conspiracy as a violation thereof. And the only "conspiracy" crimes that have been recognized by international war crimes tribunals (whose jurisdiction often extends beyond war crimes proper to crimes against humanity and crimes against the peace) are conspiracy to commit genocide and common plan to wage aggressive war, which is a crime against the peace and requires for its commission actual participation in a "concrete plan to wage war."

Far from making the requisite substantial showing, the Government has failed even to offer a "merely colorable" case for inclusion of conspiracy among those offenses cognizable by law-of-war military commission. Because the charge does not support the commission's jurisdiction, the commission lacks authority to try Hamdan. . . .

Whether or not the Government has charged Hamdan with an offense against the law of war cognizable by military commission, the commission lacks power to proceed. The UCMJ conditions the President's use of military commissions on compliance not only with the American common law of war, but also with the rest of the UCMJ itself, insofar as applicable, and with the "rules and precepts of the law of nations"—including, inter alia, the four Geneva Conventions signed in 1949. The procedures that the Government has decreed will govern Hamdan's trial by commission violate these laws. . . .

We have assumed, as we must, that the allegations made in the Government's charge against Hamdan are true. We have assumed, moreover, the truth of the message implicit in that charge—viz., that Hamdan is a dangerous individual whose beliefs, if acted upon, would cause great harm and even death to innocent civilians, and who would act upon those beliefs if given the opportunity. It bears emphasizing that Hamdan does not challenge, and we do not today address, the Government's power to detain him for the duration of active hostilities in order to prevent such harm. But in undertaking to try Hamdan and subject him to criminal punishment, the Executive is bound to comply with the Rule of Law that prevails in this jurisdiction.

The judgment of the Court of Appeals is reversed, and the case is remanded for further proceedings.

It is so ordered.

SOURCE: http://caselaw.lp.findlaw.com/scripts/getcase.pl?court=us&vol=000&invol=05-184

ANALYSIS

Salim Ahmed Hamdan, Osama bin Laden's former chauffeur, was captured by Afghani forces and imprisoned by the U.S. military in Guantanamo Bay, Cuba. He filed a petition for a writ of habeas corpus in federal district court to challenge his detention. Before the district court ruled on the petition, he was given a hearing from a military tribunal, which designated him as an enemy combatant. A few months later, the district court granted Hamdan's habeas petition, holding that he must first be given a hearing to determine whether he was a prisoner of war under the Geneva Convention before he could be tried by a military commission. The Circuit Court of Appeals for the District of Columbia reversed the decision, however, finding that the Geneva Convention could not be enforced in federal court and that the establishment of military tribunals had been authorized by Congress and was therefore not unconstitutional. The Supreme Court overturned the decision of the court of appeals and invalidated the military commissions established by President Bush.

In *Hamdan*, the Court held that the Bush administration's military commissions at Guantanamo exceed the president's legal authorization given by Congress and violated the law of war, including Common Article 3 of the Geneva Convention. In particular, the Court made four main findings: (1) the Detainee Treatment Act (DTA) did not suspend judicial review of cases pending at the time the act was enacted; (2) the Court was not required to abstain from intervening in the ongoing military case; (3) the president did not have congressional authority to convene the military commissions under the Authorization for the Use of Military Force (AUMF), the DTA, or the Uniform Code of Military Justice (UCMJ); and (4) The military commissions violated the structure and procedures set up by the UCMJ and Common Article 3 of the Geneva Conventions; further, Common Article 3 applied to the conflict with Al Qaeda and was binding on the president and his subordinates.

Hamdan is one of the most significant Supreme Court rulings to date dealing with the war on terror. Immediately following the decision, speculation developed about the impact the ruling would have on Guantanamo Bay detainees and pending habeas corpus cases. The ruling had the consequence of suspending all other military commission proceedings at Guantanamo Bay and halted most pending cases until the government arrived at a solution. While the Court's decision limited the president's wartime powers, it rested entirely on statutory grounds. Thus, nothing prevented the president from returning to Congress to seek the necessary authority to convene the kind of military commission at issue in the *Hamdan* case. In October 2006, both Congress and the president responded to the Court's decision in *Hamdan* by passing the Military Commissions Act of 2006 (MCA) which is the subject of the *Boumediene v. Bush* case.

FURTHER READING

Baldrate, Brian C. "The Supreme Court's Role in Defining the Jurisdiction of Military Tribunals: A Study, Critique, and Proposal for *Hamdan v. Rumsfeld*." *Military Law Review* 186 (Winter 2005): 1.

The Military Commissions Act (MCA) and Habeas Corpus Petitions by Enemy Combatants at Guantanamo Bay, Cuba

- ***Document***: The Supreme Court case *Boumediene v. Bush*, Excerpt
- ***Date***: June 12, 2008
- ***Where***: Washington, D.C.
- ***Significance***: In *Boumediene*, the Supreme Court held that aliens detained at Guantanamo Bay as enemy combatants were entitled to petition for writs of habeas corpus to challenge the legality of their detention.

DOCUMENT

Boumediene v. Bush, 128 S. Ct. 2229 (2008)

Argued December 5, 2007.

Decided June 12, 2008.

Justice Kennedy delivered the opinion of the Court.

Petitioners are aliens designated as enemy combatants and detained at the United States Naval Station at Guantanamo Bay, Cuba. There are others detained there, also aliens, who are not parties to this suit.

Petitioners present a question not resolved by our earlier cases relating to the detention of aliens at Guantanamo: whether they have the constitutional privilege of habeas corpus, a privilege not to be withdrawn except in conformance with the Suspension Clause, Art. I, §9, cl. 2. We hold these petitioners do have the habeas corpus privilege. Congress has enacted a statute, the Detainee Treatment Act of 2005 (DTA), 119 Stat. 2739, that provides certain procedures for review of the detainees' status. We hold that those procedures are not an adequate and effective substitute for habeas corpus. Therefore §7 of the Military Commissions Act of 2006 (MCA), 28 U.S. C. A. §2241(e), operates as an unconstitutional suspension of the writ.

We granted certiorari.

As a threshold matter, we must decide whether MCA §7 denies the federal courts jurisdiction to hear habeas corpus actions pending at the time of its enactment. We hold the statute does deny that jurisdiction, so that, if the statute is valid, petitioners' cases must be dismissed....

In deciding the constitutional questions now presented we must determine whether petitioners are barred from seeking the writ or invoking the protections of the Suspension Clause either because of their status, i.e., petitioners' designation by the Executive Branch as enemy combatants, or their physical location, i.e., their presence at Guantanamo Bay. The Government contends that noncitizens designated as enemy combatants and detained in territory located outside our Nation's borders have no constitutional rights and no privilege of habeas corpus. Petitioners contend they do have cognizable constitutional rights and that Congress, in seeking to eliminate recourse to habeas corpus as a means to assert those rights, acted in violation of the Suspension Clause.

Drawing from its position that at common law the writ ran only to territories over which the Crown was sovereign, the Government says the Suspension Clause affords petitioners no rights because the United States does not claim sovereignty over the place of detention.

Guantanamo Bay is not formally part of the United States. And under the terms of the lease between the United States and Cuba, Cuba retains "ultimate sovereignty" over the territory while the United States exercises "complete jurisdiction and control." Under the terms of the 1934 Treaty, however, Cuba effectively has no rights as a sovereign until the parties agree to modification of the 1903 Lease Agreement or the United States abandons the base.

The United States contends, nevertheless, that Guantanamo is not within its sovereign control. This was the Government's position well before the events of September 11, 2001. And in other contexts the Court has held that questions of sovereignty are for the political branches to decide. Even if this were a treaty interpretation case that did not involve a political question, the President's construction of the lease agreement would be entitled to great respect.

As we did in Rasul, however, we take notice of the obvious and uncontested fact that the United States, by virtue of its complete jurisdiction and control over the base, maintains de facto sovereignty over this territory.

Were we to hold that the present cases turn on the political question doctrine, we would be required first to accept the Government's premise that de jure sovereignty is the touchstone of habeas corpus jurisdiction. This premise, however, is unfounded. For the reasons indicated above, the history of common-law habeas corpus provides scant support for this proposition; and, for the reasons indicated below, that position would be inconsistent with our precedents and contrary to fundamental separation-of-powers principles.

A

The Court has discussed the issue of the Constitution's extraterritorial application on many occasions. These decisions undermine the Government's argument that, at least as applied to noncitizens, the Constitution necessarily stops where de jure sovereignty ends.

In a series of opinions later known as the Insular Cases, the Court addressed whether the Constitution, by its own force, applies in any territory that is not a State. The Court held that the Constitution has independent force in these territories, a force not contingent upon acts of legislative grace. Yet it took note of the difficulties inherent in that position....

These considerations resulted in the doctrine of territorial incorporation, under which the Constitution applies in full in incorporated Territories surely destined for statehood but only in part in unincorporated Territories. It may well be that over time the ties between the United States and any of its unincorporated Territories strengthen in ways that are of constitutional significance.... Yet noting the inherent practical difficulties of enforcing all constitutional provisions "always and everywhere," the Court devised in the Insular Cases a doctrine that allowed it to use its power sparingly and where it would be most needed. This century-old doctrine informs our analysis in the present matter....

Practical considerations weighed heavily as well in Johnson v. Eisentrager, where the Court addressed whether habeas corpus jurisdiction extended to enemy aliens who had been convicted of violating the laws of war. The prisoners were detained at Landsberg Prison in Germany during the Allied Powers' postwar occupation. The Court stressed the difficulties of ordering the Government to produce the prisoners in a habeas corpus proceeding. It "would require allocation of shipping space, guarding personnel, billeting and rations" and would damage the prestige of military commanders at a sensitive time. In considering these factors the Court sought to balance the constraints of military occupation with constitutional necessities.

True, the Court in Eisentrager denied access to the writ, and it noted the prisoners "at no relevant time were within any territory over which the United States is sovereign, and [that] the scenes of their offense, their capture, their trial and their punishment were all beyond the territorial jurisdiction of any court of the United States." The Government seizes upon this language as proof positive that the Eisentrager Court adopted a formalistic, sovereignty-based test for determining the reach of the Suspension Clause. We reject this reading for three reasons.

First, we do not accept the idea that the above-quoted passage from Eisentrager is the only authoritative language in the opinion and that all the rest is dicta....

Second, because the United States lacked both de jure sovereignty and plenary control over Landsberg Prison, it is far from clear that the Eisentrager Court used the term sovereignty only in the narrow technical sense and not to connote the degree of control the military asserted over the facility....

Third, if the Government's reading of Eisentrager were correct, the opinion would have marked not only a change in, but a complete repudiation of, the Insular Cases' functional approach to questions of extraterritoriality. We cannot accept the Government's view. Nothing in Eisentrager says that de jure sovereignty is or has ever been the only relevant consideration in determining the geographic reach of the Constitution or of habeas corpus.... A constricted reading of Eisentrager overlooks what we see as a common thread uniting the Insular Cases, Eisentrager, and Reid: the idea that questions of extraterritoriality turn on objective factors and practical concerns, not formalism.

The Government's formal sovereignty-based test raises troubling separation-of-powers concerns as well. The political history of Guantanamo illustrates the deficiencies of this approach. The United States has maintained complete and uninterrupted control of the bay for over 100 years. At the close of the Spanish-American War, Spain ceded control over the entire island of Cuba to the United States and specifically "relinquishe[d] all claim[s] of sovereignty . . . and title." The Government's view is that the Constitution had no effect there, at least as to non-citizens, because the United States disclaimed sovereignty in the formal sense of the term. The necessary implication of the argument is that by surrendering formal sovereignty over any unincorporated territory to a third party, while at the same time entering into a lease that grants total control over the territory back to the United States, it would be possible for the political branches to govern without legal constraint.

Our basic charter cannot be contracted away like this. The Constitution grants Congress and the President the power to acquire, dispose of, and govern territory, not the power to decide when and where its terms apply. Even when the United States acts outside its borders, its powers are not "absolute and unlimited" but are subject "to such restrictions as are expressed in the Constitution." Abstaining from questions involving formal sovereignty and territorial governance is one thing. To hold the political branches have the power to switch the Constitution on or off at will is quite another. The former position reflects this Court's recognition that certain matters requiring political judgments are best left to the political branches. The latter would permit a striking anomaly in our tripartite system of government, leading to a regime in which Congress and the President, not this Court, say "what the law is."

These concerns have particular bearing upon the Suspension Clause question in the cases now before us, for the writ of habeas corpus is itself an indispensable mechanism for monitoring the separation of powers. The test for determining the scope of this provision must not be subject to manipulation by those whose power it is designed to restrain.

In light of this holding the question becomes whether the statute stripping jurisdiction to issue the writ avoids the Suspension Clause mandate because Congress has provided adequate substitute procedures for habeas corpus. The Government submits there has been compliance with the Suspension Clause because the DTA review process in the Court of Appeals provides an adequate substitute. . . .

The gravity of the separation-of-powers issues raised by these cases and the fact that these detainees have been denied meaningful access to a judicial forum for a period of years render these cases exceptional. The parties before us have addressed the adequacy issue. While we would have found it informative to consider the reasoning of the Court of Appeals on this point, we must weigh that against the harms petitioners may endure from additional delay. And, given there are few precedents addressing what features an adequate substitute for habeas corpus must contain, in all likelihood a remand simply would delay ultimate resolution of the issue by this Court. . . .

Our case law does not contain extensive discussion of standards defining suspension of the writ or of circumstances under which suspension has occurred. This simply confirms the care Congress has taken throughout our Nation's history to preserve the writ and its function. Indeed, most of the major legislative enactments pertaining to habeas corpus have acted not to contract the writ's protection but to expand it or to hasten resolution of prisoners' claims. . . .

The two leading cases addressing habeas substitutes . . . provide little guidance here. . . .

To the extent any doubt remains about Congress' intent, the legislative history confirms what the plain text strongly suggests: In passing the DTA Congress did not intend to create a process that differs from traditional habeas corpus process in name only. It intended to create a more limited procedure.

It is against this background that we must interpret the DTA and assess its adequacy as a substitute for habeas corpus....

We do not endeavor to offer a comprehensive summary of the requisites for an adequate substitute for habeas corpus. We do consider it uncontroversial, however, that the privilege of habeas corpus entitles the prisoner to a meaningful opportunity to demonstrate that he is being held pursuant to "the erroneous application or interpretation" of relevant law. And the habeas court must have the power to order the conditional release of an individual unlawfully detained—though release need not be the exclusive remedy and is not the appropriate one in every case in which the writ is granted. These are the easily identified attributes of any constitutionally adequate habeas corpus proceeding. But, depending on the circumstances, more may be required.

Indeed, common-law habeas corpus was, above all, an adaptable remedy. Its precise application and scope changed depending upon the circumstances....

There is evidence from 19th-century American sources indicating that, even in States that accorded strong res judicata effect to prior adjudications, habeas courts in this country routinely allowed prisoners to introduce exculpatory evidence that was either unknown or previously unavailable to the prisoner....

The idea that the necessary scope of habeas review in part depends upon the rigor of any earlier proceedings accords with our test for procedural adequacy in the due process context....

Where a person is detained by executive order, rather than, say, after being tried and convicted in a court, the need for collateral review is most pressing. A criminal conviction in the usual course occurs after a judicial hearing before a tribunal disinterested in the outcome and committed to procedures designed to ensure its own independence. These dynamics are not inherent in executive detention orders or executive review procedures. In this context the need for habeas corpus is more urgent. The intended duration of the detention and the reasons for it bear upon the precise scope of the inquiry. Habeas corpus proceedings need not resemble a criminal trial, even when the detention is by executive order. But the writ must be effective. The habeas court must have sufficient authority to conduct a meaningful review of both the cause for detention and the Executive's power to detain.

To determine the necessary scope of habeas corpus review, therefore, we must assess the CSRT process, the mechanism through which petitioners' designation as enemy combatants became final. Whether one characterizes the CSRT process as direct review of the Executive's battlefield determination that the detainee is an enemy combatant—as the parties have and as we do—or as the first step in the collateral review of a battlefield determination makes no difference in a proper analysis of whether the procedures Congress put in place are an adequate substitute for habeas corpus. What matters is the sum total of procedural protections afforded to the detainee at all stages, direct and collateral.

Petitioners identify what they see as myriad deficiencies in the CSRTs. The most relevant for our purposes are the constraints upon the detainee's ability to rebut the factual basis for the Government's assertion that he is an enemy combatant.

As already noted, see Part IV-C, supra, at the CSRT stage the detainee has limited means to find or present evidence to challenge the Government's case against him. He does not have the assistance of counsel and may not be aware of the most critical allegations that the Government relied upon to order his detention. The detainee can confront witnesses that testify during the CSRT proceedings. But given that there are in effect no limits on the admission of hearsay evidence—the only requirement is that the tribunal deem the evidence "relevant and helpful," the detainee's opportunity to question witnesses is likely to be more theoretical than real....

Although we make no judgment as to whether the CSRTs, as currently constituted, satisfy due process standards, we agree with petitioners that, even when all the parties involved in this process act with diligence and in good faith, there is considerable risk of error in the tribunal's findings of fact. This is a risk inherent in any process that, in the words of the former Chief Judge of the Court of Appeals, is "closed and accusatorial." And given that the consequence of error may be detention of persons for the duration of hostilities that may last a generation or more, this is a risk too significant to ignore.

For the writ of habeas corpus, or its substitute, to function as an effective and proper remedy in this context, the court that conducts the habeas proceeding must have the means to correct errors that occurred during the CSRT proceedings. This includes some authority to assess the sufficiency of the Government's evidence against the detainee. It also must have the authority to admit and consider relevant exculpatory evidence that was not introduced during the earlier proceeding. Federal habeas petitioners long have had the means to supplement the record on review, even in the postconviction habeas setting. Here that opportunity is constitutionally required....

The extent of the showing required of the Government in these cases is a matter to be determined. We need not explore it further at this stage. We do hold that when the judicial power to issue habeas corpus properly is invoked the judicial officer must have adequate authority to make a determination in light of the relevant law and facts and to formulate and issue appropriate orders for relief, including, if necessary, an order directing the prisoner's release.

We now consider whether the DTA allows the Court of Appeals to conduct a proceeding meeting these standards....

We do not imply DTA review would be a constitutionally sufficient replacement for habeas corpus but for these limitations on the detainee's ability to present exculpatory evidence. For even if it were possible, as a textual matter, to read into the statute each of the necessary procedures we have identified, we could not overlook the cumulative effect of our doing so. To hold that the detainees at Guantanamo may, under the DTA, challenge the President's legal authority to detain them, contest the CSRT's findings of fact, supplement the record on review with exculpatory evidence, and request an order of release would come close to reinstating the §2241 habeas corpus process Congress sought to deny them. The language of the statute, read in light of Congress' reasons for enacting it, cannot bear this interpretation. Petitioners have met their burden of establishing that the DTA review process is, on its face, an inadequate substitute for habeas corpus.

Although we do not hold that an adequate substitute must duplicate §2241 in all respects, it suffices that the Government has not established that the detainees' access to the statutory review provisions at issue is an adequate substitute for the writ of habeas corpus. MCA §7 thus effects an unconstitutional suspension of the writ....

The determination by the Court of Appeals that the Suspension Clause and its protections are inapplicable to petitioners was in error. The judgment of the Court of Appeals is reversed. The cases are remanded to the Court of Appeals with instructions that it remand the cases to the District Court for proceedings consistent with this opinion.

It is so ordered.

SOURCE: http://caselaw.lp.findlaw.com/scripts/getcase.pl?court=US&vol=000&invol=06-1195

ANALYSIS

In 2002, Lakhdar Boumediene and five other Algerian natives were seized by Bosnian police when American intelligence officers suspected their involvement in a plot to attack the U.S. embassy. The men were detained at the naval base at Guantanamo Bay, Cuba which is leased by the U.S. government. Boumediene filed a writ of habeas corpus challenging his detainment. The district court judge granted the government's motion to have the claim dismissed on the ground that Boumediene, as an alien detained at an overseas military base, had no right to a habeas petition. The United States Court of Appeals for the D.C. Circuit affirmed the dismissal but the Supreme Court reversed in *Rasul v. Bush,* which held that the habeas statute extends to noncitizen detainees at Guantanamo.

In response to the *Rasul* and *Hamdi* decisions, the Department of Defense established the Combatant Status Review Tribunals (CSRT). The function of the CSRTs was to determine whether individuals detained at Guantanamo were enemy combatants who had taken up arms against the United States. The Boumediene petitioners were identified as enemy combatants by the CSRTs. While Boumediene's case was pending, Congress passed the Detainee Treatment Act of 2005 (DTA). The DTA amended the habeas corpus statute (28 U.S.C. § 2241) to strip federal courts' jurisdiction to hear habeas corpus petitions from aliens who had been designated as enemy combatants and detained at Guantanamo. Furthermore, section 1005(e) of the DTA provided the D.C. Circuit exclusive jurisdiction to review enemy combatant designations made by the CSRTs.

During this time, *Hamdan* was also being appealed in the federal court system. The Supreme Court in *Hamdan* asserted its jurisdiction to decide Guantanamo Bay cases. First, the Court adhered to *Rasul* in that Guantanamo is U.S. territory for all practical purposes and that habeas corpus applies. Second, since Congress failed to include the cases that were currently pending within the portion of the DTA that stripped federal courts of Guantanamo jurisdiction, the Supreme Court found no jurisdictional problem. However, the effect of *Hamdan* was short-lived because President Bush approached Congress for a new law which led to the passage of the Military Commissions Act (MCA). The MCA amended the habeas corpus statute (28 U.S.C. § 2241(e)(1)) to deny federal courts jurisdiction in actions designed to secure habeas corpus rights for detained aliens adjudged by the CSRT to be enemy combatants.

When the case was appealed to the D.C. Circuit for the second time, Boumediene argued that the MCA did not apply to his petition, and that if it did, it was unconstitutional under the suspension clause. The suspension clause reads: "The Privilege of the Writ of Habeas Corpus shall not be suspended, unless when in Cases of Rebellion or Invasion the public Safety may require it." The D.C. Circuit agreed with the government and upheld the MCA ruling that the suspension clause only protects the writ of habeas corpus as it existed in 1789, and that the writ would not have been understood in 1789 to apply to an overseas military naval base leased from a foreign government. The D.C. Circuit therefore did not consider whether the DTA provided an adequate and effective substitute for habeas. The D.C. Circuit concluded that constitutional rights do not apply to aliens outside of the United States and the leased military base in Cuba does not qualify as inside the geographic borders of the United States.

Boumediene appealed this decision to the Supreme Court which granted certiorari after initially denying review of the case three months earlier. The Supreme Court held that Congress's passage of the MCA denied federal courts jurisdiction to hear habeas corpus actions. Habeas corpus related to any aspect of the detention, transfer, treatment, trial, or conditions of confinement of an alien who was detained as an enemy combatant by the CSRTs. Because the MCA failed to provide an adequate substitute to the constitutional writ of habeas corpus, as required by the suspension clause of the Constitution, the Court found the MCA to be an unconstitutional suspension of the writ of habeas corpus. The petitioners were therefore entitled to challenge the legality of their detention.

With Justice Kennedy writing for the majority, the opinion begins with a lengthy survey of historical habeas cases in which common law courts considered cases of noncitizens imprisoned without trial. The history of the writ, both before and after the adoption of the Constitution, and in the United States and the United Kingdom, was inconclusive as to its extraterritorial application to noncitizens. Acknowledging the distinctiveness of the administration's practices at Guantanamo, the Court found that no historical habeas case offered by either side was directly on point and, instead, turned to the fundamental principles underlying the purpose of habeas corpus to allow the courts to act as a check on the other two branches of government. The Court emphasized that the suspension clause of the federal Constitution was designed by the Founders to protect against the abuses of the writ by the executive and legislative branches.

The Court held that if the privilege of habeas corpus is denied to detainees at Guantanamo, Congress is required to proceed in accordance with the suspension clause. Within the MCA, the review process was governed by the DTA and was held to be constitutionally inadequate and in violation of the suspension clause. The Court stated that a habeas proceeding as well as any substitute must provide the petitioner an effective and meaningful ability to correct any errors in the decision under review and an opportunity to challenge the sufficiency of the government's evidence, and the opportunity to present and have a court consider exculpatory evidence not considered by the tribunal below. Specifically, the DTA statute failed to provide for release from custody as a remedy offers no procedures for petitioners to present new, exculpatory evidence and to bring the full range of legal challenges available in a habeas proceeding. The CSRT process in particular was deficient in denying a detainee the ability to present newly discovered and previously unavailable evidence. Although a detainee could petition the Deputy Secretary of Defense for a new CSRT, the determination to grant a new proceeding was wholly discretion, and the denial of a request was unreviewable.

FURTHER READING

Alexander, Janet Cooper. "Jurisdiction-Stripping in a Time of Terror." *California Law Review* 95 (Fall 2007): 1193.

The Sixth Circuit: The First Amendment and the Right to Access Deportation Hearings

- ***Document:*** The Supreme Court case *Detroit Free Press v. Ashcroft*, Excerpt
- ***Date*:** June 17, 2003
- ***Where*:** Washington, D.C.
- ***Significance*:** The Court of Appeals for the Sixth Circuit ruled that there is a First Amendment right of access to deportation proceedings that were classified by the attorney general as presenting a significant national security concern.

DOCUMENT

Detroit Free Press v. Ashcroft, 303 F.3d 681, 682 (6th Cir. 2002)

Argued November 18, 2002.

Decided June 17, 2003.

SENTELLE, Circuit Judge:

The Office of the Chief Immigration Judge, under the authorization of Attorney General John Ashcroft, designates certain cases to be special interest cases, conducted in secret, closed off from the public. Arguing that closure of these hearings was unconstitutional, plaintiffs in three separate cases sought an injunction against such action. The Government filed a motion to dismiss, arguing that closing special interest cases was not unconstitutional.

The district court granted the injunction, finding blanket closure of deportation hearings in "special interest" cases unconstitutional. For the reasons that follow, we AFFIRM the district court's order granting Plaintiffs a preliminary injunction.

We . . . consider whether the First Amendment affords the press and public a right of access to deportation hearings.

DID YOU KNOW?

Secret Hearings: *North Jersey Media Group, Inc. v. Ashcroft,* 2002

In *North Jersey Media Group, Inc. v. Ashcroft* (308 F.3d 198, 202 (3d Cir. 2002), the Third Circuit reached a different conclusion than did the Sixth Circuit in *Detroit Free Press,* but came to a similar conclusion on the threshold question of whether *Richmond Newspapers* applied to deportation proceedings. The Third Circuit had agreed with the Sixth Circuit that the *Richmond Newspapers* analysis was properly utilized. However, The Third Circuit held that the government's closing of immigration hearings in cases determined to be of special interest to the September 11 investigation was not a violation of the First Amendment. The Third Circuit reasoned that under the *Richmond Newspapers* test, no right of access existed, because there was an insufficient history of openness for deportation hearings and too many potentially negative ramifications from allowing media access to the proceedings.

Concerning the openness, the Third Circuit disagreed with the Sixth Circuit's conclusion that deportation proceedings have traditionally been open to the public and press. The court rejected the newspaper's argument that Congress's practice of closing exclusion proceedings while refraining from closing deportation proceedings indicated that Congress intended that these proceedings remain presumptively open to the public. The court asserted that there is evidence to indicate specifically that deportation proceedings have been closed to the public. The government had often held deportation proceedings in areas that are traditionally closed off to the public such as prisons, hospitals, and even private homes. Hearings involving abused alien children are closed to the public by regulation. The court therefore concluded that immigration proceedings were more administrative in nature, rather than judicial, and found a tradition of closing many other types of hearings before administrative agencies.

The Third Circuit also based its decision on the government's compelling interest in protecting national security. The court paid particular attention to the statement offered by Dale Watson, the FBI's executive assistant director for counterterrorism and counterintelligence. Watson contended that secrecy is justified because seemingly harmless pieces of information, when combined with other information, might allow a terrorist organization to thwart government investigations. In light of the profound and unknown dimension of terrorist threats, the court found that access did not on balance play a positive role in relation to national security. North New Jersey Media Group pursued a writ of certiorari from the Supreme Court, but the Court declined to hear the case.

a. Deportation Proceedings Have Traditionally Been Accessible to the Public

The parties first dispute whether this inquiry requires a significantly long showing that the proceedings at issue were historically open, such as a common law tradition. The government cites Richmond Newspapers for the proposition that the tradition of open hearings must have existed from the time "when our organic laws were adopted," presumably at the adoption of the Bill of Rights.

The Supreme Court effectively silenced this argument in Press-Enterprise II, where the Court relied on exclusively post-Bill of Rights history in determining that preliminary hearings in criminal cases were historically open. Courts of Appeals have similarly not required such a showing.

Justice Brennan's formulation of the "experience" prong of the test in his Richmond Newspapers concurrence, adopted as the prevailing view of how to approach the issue, speaks on this point. Specifically, Justice Brennan opined: First, the case for a right of access has special force when drawn from an enduring and vital tradition of public entree to particular proceedings or information. Such a tradition commands respect in part because the Constitution carries the gloss of history. More importantly, a tradition of accessibility implies the favorable judgment of experience. Second, the value of access must be measured in specifics. Analysis is not advanced by rhetorical statements that all information bears upon public issues; what is crucial in individual cases is whether access to particular government process is important in terms of that very process.

Therefore, although historical context is important, a brief historical tradition might be sufficient to establish a First Amendment right of access where the beneficial effects of access to that process are overwhelming and uncontradicted. Accordingly, the Supreme Court has called both prongs of the test "complimentary considerations." This comports with the Court's view that the First Amendment concerns "broad principles," to contexts not known to the Framers. However, we are mindful that "[a] historical tradition of at least some duration is obviously necessary, . . . [or] nothing would separate the judicial task of constitutional interpretation from the political task of enacting laws currently deemed essential."

Nonetheless, deportation proceedings historically have been open. The Government argues that the history of explicitly closing exclusion hearings, while not specifying that deportation hearings be closed, does not show that Congress intended deportation hearings to be open. Instead, the Government contends, this demonstrates that Congress took the INS's discretion away for exclusion hearings and specifically gave them discretion to open or close deportation hearings. We find the Government's reading unpersuasive. Having explicitly closed exclusion hearings, it would have been easy enough for Congress expressly to state that the Attorney General had such discretion with respect to deportation hearings. But it did not. The Immigration and Nationality Act is replete with examples where discretion is specifically delegated to the Attorney General.

Moreover, the history of immigration law informs Congress's legislation. Open hearings, apart from their value to the community, have long been considered to advance fairness to the parties. Additionally, Congress has long been aware that deportees are constitutionally guaranteed greater procedural rights than those excluded upon initial entry. Therefore, Congress likely legislated key differences between both procedures accordingly.

Next, relying on Capital Cities Media, Inc., the Government impermissibly expands the relevant inquiry by arguing that there was no common law right of access to administrative proceedings. First, this argument ignores the fact that the modern administrative state is an entity unknown to the Framers of the First Amendment. This argument also fails to recognize the evolving nature of our government. Administrative proceedings come in all shapes and sizes. To the extent that we look to similar proceedings, we should look to proceedings that are similar in form and substance. This was the approach taken by the Third Circuit in The First Amendment Coalition. In that case, when analyzing the history prong of the test, the Third Circuit compared an administrative disciplinary board's function to that of a grand jury because both could only recommend, not impose, punishment.

As stated earlier, to paraphrase the Supreme Court, deportation hearings "walk, talk, and squawk" very much like a judicial proceeding. Substantively, we look to other proceedings that have the same effect as deportation. Here, the only other federal court that can enter an order of removal is a United States District Court during sentencing in a criminal trial. At common law, beginning with the Transportation Act of 1718, the English criminal courts could enter an order of transportation or banishment as a sentence in a criminal trial. As Richmond Newspapers discussed in great length, these types of criminal proceedings have historically been open.

It bears note that the history of administrative proceedings is briskly evolving to embrace open hearings. Thus, the "favorable judgment of experience" counsels that openness better serves formal administrative hearings. As the Supreme Court aptly recognized in 1938:

The vast expansion of this field of administrative regulation in response to the pressure of social needs is made possible under our system by adherence to the basic principles that the legislature shall appropriately determine the standards of administrative action and that in administrative proceedings of a quasi-judicial character the liberty and property of the citizen shall be protected by the rudimentary requirements of fair play. These demand "a fair and open hearing,"—essential alike to the legal validity of the administrative regulation and to the maintenance of public confidence in the value and soundness of this important governmental process. Such a hearing has been described as an "inexorable safeguard."

Finally, to refute the history of open hearings, the government points to a single passage in a study about deportation of non-citizens to Europe during the 1920s and a single Second Circuit case, for the proposition that deportation hearings took place in a variety of settings, including prisons, hospitals, and homes. However, neither of these sources speak to the norm. Certainly, while these examples might have been exceptional cases, neither of these sources even hint that the public could not attend a hearing at a prison, hospital, or home. Certainly, one could imagine family and friends being present at some of these places. Finally, the study cited by the Government points out that members of Congress, like Plaintiff Conyers, sometimes attended, or sent representatives to, such hearings.

b. Public Access Plays a Significant Positive Role in Deportation Hearings

Public access undoubtedly enhances the quality of deportation proceedings. Much of the reasoning from Richmond Newspapers is also applicable to this context.

First, public access acts as a check on the actions of the Executive by assuring us that proceedings are conducted fairly and properly. In an area such as immigration, where the government has nearly unlimited authority, the press and the public serve as perhaps the only check on abusive government practices.

Second, openness ensures that government does its job properly; that it does not make mistakes. These first two concerns are magnified by the fact that deportees have no right to an attorney at the government's expense. Effectively, the press and the public may be their only guardian.

Third, after the devastation of September 11 and the massive investigation that followed, the cathartic effect of open deportations cannot be overstated. They serve a "therapeutic" purpose as outlets for "community concern, hostility, and emotions."

Fourth, openness enhances the perception of integrity and fairness. The most stringent safeguards for a deportee "would be of limited worth if the public is not persuaded that the standards are being fairly enforced. Legitimacy rests in large part on public understanding."

Fifth, public access helps ensure that "the individual citizen can effectively participate in and contribute to our republican system of self-government." When government selectively chooses what information it allows the public to see, it can become a powerful tool for deception.

Additionally, the Government has not identified one persuasive reason why openness would play a negative role in the process. Nothing like the excessive financial burdens noted by the Supreme Court in Houchins would be applicable here. Having found a First Amendment right of access to deportation hearings, we now determine whether the Government has made a sufficient showing to overcome that right.

4. Strict Scrutiny

Under the standard articulated in Globe Newspaper, government action that curtails a First Amendment right of access "in order to inhibit the disclosure of sensitive information" must be supported by a showing "that denial is necessitated by a compelling governmental interest, and is narrowly tailored to serve that interest." The Government's ongoing anti-terrorism investigation certainly implicates a compelling interest. However, the Creppy directive is neither narrowly tailored, nor does it require particularized findings. Therefore, it impermissibly infringes on the Newspaper Plaintiffs' First Amendment right of access.

a. The Government Cites Compelling Interests

We do not agree with the district court that the Government failed to demonstrate that there are compelling interests sufficient to justify closure. The Government contends that "[c]losure of removal proceedings in special interest cases is necessary to protect national security by safeguarding the Government's investigation of the September 11 terrorist attack and other terrorist conspiracies."

The Government certainly has a compelling interest in preventing terrorism. In addition to Mr. Reynold's affidavit, other affidavits have been provided that justify the Government's interest in closure. According to the additional affidavits, public access to removal proceedings would disclose the following information that would impede the Government's investigation:

"Bits and pieces of information that may appear innocuous in isolation," but used by terrorist groups to help form a "bigger picture" of the Government's terrorism investigation, would be disclosed. The Government describes this type of intelligence gathering as "akin to the construction of a mosaic," where an individual piece of information is not of obvious importance until pieced together with other pieces of information.

The identifications of the detainees, witnesses, and investigative sources would be disclosed. Terrorist groups could subject these individuals or their families to intimidation or harm and discourage them from cooperating with the Government.

Methods of entry to the country, communicating, or funding could be revealed. This information could allow terrorist organizations to alter their patterns of activity to find the most effective means of evading detection. "Information that is not presented at the hearings also might provide important clues to terrorist, because it could reveal what the investigation has not yet discovered." The Government provides this example: "If the government discloses the evidence it has about a particular member of a terrorist organization, but fails to mention that the detainee is involved in an impending attack, the other members of the organization may be able to infer that the government is not yet aware of the attack."

Inasmuch as these agents' declarations establish that certain information revealed during removal proceedings could impede the ongoing anti-terrorism investigation, we defer to their judgment. These agents are certainly in a better position to understand the contours of the investigation and the intelligence capabilities of terrorist organizations.

b. The Creppy Directive Does Not Require Particularized Findings

Although the Government is able to demonstrate a compelling interest for closure, the immigration judge, Defendant Hacker, failed to make specific findings before closing Haddad's deportation proceedings. Press-Enterprise II instructs that in cases where partial or complete closure is warranted, there must be specific findings on the record so that a reviewing court can determine whether closure was proper and whether less restrictive alternatives exist. Similarly, the Creppy directive fails this requirement.

c. The Creppy Directive is Not Narrowly Tailored

Finally, the blanket closure rule mandated by the Creppy directive is not narrowly tailored. The Government offers no persuasive argument as to why the Government's concerns cannot be addressed on a case-by-case basis. The Newspaper Plaintiffs argue, and the district court agreed, that the Creppy directive is ineffective in achieving its purported goals because the detainees and their lawyers are allowed to publicize the proceedings. According to the Newspaper Plaintiffs, to the extent that Haddad had discussed his proceedings (and disclosed documents) with family, friends and the media, the information that the Government seeks to protect is disclosed to the public anyway. We are not persuaded by the Government's argument in response that few detainees will disclose any information and that their disclosure will be less than complete public access. This contention is, at best, speculative and belies the Government's assertion that any information disclosed, even bits and pieces that seem innocuous, will be detrimental to the anti-terrorism investigation.

Moreover, we find unpersuasive the Government's argument that the closure of special interest hearings has been accomplished on a case-by-case basis. In its reply, the Government alleges that "[e]ach special interest detainee has been evaluated and designated on the basis of the government's ongoing investigative interest in him and his relationship to the ongoing anti-terrorism investigation." Assuming such an evaluation has occurred, we find that problems still remain. The task of designating a case special interest is performed in secret, without any established standards or procedures, and the process is, thus, not subject to any sort of review, either by another administrative entity or the courts. Therefore, no real safeguard on this exercise of authority exists. The Government states that special interest cases represent "a small, carefully chosen subset of the universe of aliens facing removal proceedings." Yet, to date, the Government has failed to disclose the actual number of special interest cases it has designated.

Lastly, the public's interests are best served by open proceedings. A true democracy is one that operates on faith—faith that government officials are forthcoming and honest, and faith that informed citizens will arrive at logical conclusions. This is a vital reciprocity that America should not discard in these troubling times. Without question, the events of September 11, 2001, left an indelible mark on our nation, but we as a people are united in the wake of the destruction to demonstrate to the world that we are a country deeply committed to preserving the rights and freedoms guaranteed by our democracy. Today, we reflect our commitment to those democratic values by ensuring that our government is held accountable to the people and that First Amendment rights are not impermissibly compromised. Open proceedings, with a vigorous and scrutinizing press, serve to ensure the durability of our democracy.

IV. Conclusion

For the foregoing reasons, we AFFIRM.

SOURCE: http://fl1.findlaw.com/news.findlaw.com/hdocs/docs/aclu/dfpashcrft40302ord.pdf

ANALYSIS

On September 21, 2001, at the direction of Attorney General John Ashcroft, Chief Immigration Judge Michael Creppy issued a memorandum to all immigration judges and court administrators requiring that certain "special interest cases" be held in closed proceedings and with strict confidentiality. The memo stated that Attorney General Ashcroft had established additional security procedures applicable when such cases came before the court. The procedures included the requirement that only judges with security clearances hear special interest cases, that INS employees not comment on a special interest alien's appearance before the court, and, most significantly, that all proceedings be closed to visitors, family, and press. A lawsuit was filed by both the *Detroit Free Press* and the North Jersey Media Group because they were being closed out of certain deportation proceedings in the New Jersey area as a consequence of the Creppy directive. The cases were appealed to the Sixth and Third Circuit Courts respectively.

Both circuit courts addressed the right of access issue under the Supreme Court's decision in *Richmond Newspapers, Inc. v. Virginia*, which recognized a First Amendment right to attend criminal trials. Under the test set forth in *Richmond Newspapers*, a court must decide: whether the particular proceeding has "historically been open to the press and general public," and whether the "public access plays a significant positive role in the functioning" of that proceeding. Assuming both parts have been met, access cannot be denied absent a showing that denying access serves a compelling governmental interest, and is narrowly tailored to serve that interest. The circuit court holdings utilized the *Richmond Newspapers* precedent with contradictory decisions.

The *Detroit Free Press* case started with a series of hearings in the deportation action for Rabih Haddad, an alien who overstayed his tourist visa. Based on the Creppy directive, this case was designated as a special interest because of the government's suspicion that the Islamic charity Haddad operated supplies funds to terrorist organizations. Consequently, the hearings in Haddad's case were closed to the public and the press. An action was commenced against Attorney General John Ashcroft, Chief Immigration Judge Creppy, and the immigration judge presiding over Haddad's case, seeking injunctive and declaratory relief that the Creppy directive, facially and as applied, violated their First Amendment rights of access.

The U.S. District Court for the Eastern District of Michigan held for the plaintiffs, holding that the ban on access to the proceedings constituted an unconstitutional abridgment of the plaintiff's First Amendment right of access. The government appealed the decision. The Sixth Circuit, however, affirmed the district court's holding reasoning that, under the *Richmond Newspapers* test, there was a sufficient history of openness in deportation hearings and significantly positive effects from allowing media access to create a right of access under the First Amendment. The Sixth Circuit advanced five positive effects from openness including: (1) public access acts as a check on the actions of the executive by assuring us that proceedings are conducted fairly and properly; (2) openness ensures that government does its job properly; (3) the hearings have a "cathartic effect" on people's raw emotions in the wake of September 11; (4) openness enhances the perception of integrity and fairness; (5) and public access ensures the ability of citizens to participate in and contribute to our republican system of government. The Court went on to conclude that the government's national security concerns did not survive strict scrutiny, reasoning that although national security is a compelling interest, the ban was not narrowly tailored.

FURTHER READING

Ferrell, Meaghan E. "Balancing the First Amendment and National Security: Can Immigration Hearings be Closed to Protect the Nation's Interest." *Catholic University Law Review* 52 (Summer 2003): 981.

Free Speech and a Designated Demonstration Zone for the 2004 National Democratic Convention

- ***Document:*** The First Circuit case *Black Tea Society v. City of Boston*, Excerpt
- ***Date:*** July 30, 2004
- ***Where:*** Boston, Massachusetts
- ***Significance:*** The First Circuit upheld the use of a designated demonstration zone at the 2004 National Democratic Convention.

DOCUMENT

Black Tea Society v. City of Boston, 370 F. 3d 8 (2004)

Decided July 30, 2004.

SELYA, Circuit Judge.

This appeal arose in connection with demonstrations planned for the 2004 Democratic National Convention (the Convention). The appellant, the Bl(a)ck Tea Society, seeks review of an order denying its request to modify a designated demonstration zone (DZ) set aside by municipal officials. We summarily affirmed the order on July 26, 2004 (coincident with the start of the Convention). This opinion limns the basis for our ruling.

The facts surrounding this litigation are thoroughly canvassed in the district court's comprehensive opinion and it would serve no useful purpose to rehearse them in exegetic detail. Suffice it to say that the Convention was held at the Fleet Center, in Boston, Massachusetts, on July 26–29, 2004. Security at national political conventions is always tight and that was especially so this year in light of heightened sensitivity to security concerns following the terrorist attacks of September 11, 2001.

Security precautions at the Convention operated on two different levels. The City established a highly secure hard zone in the area immediately surrounding the Fleet Center (a zone for which the U.S. Secret Service assumed principal responsibility) and a less secure soft zone extending several blocks south in the area commonly known as Bullfinch Triangle. Only candidates, delegates, staff, press, and other specially authorized classes of persons were permitted into the hard zone—and even they had to pass through magnetometers before entering. By contrast, pedestrian access to and through the soft zone was generally unrestricted (although vehicles were not allowed to enter). This dual arrangement left little opportunity for groups wishing to demonstrate to do so within sight and sound of the delegates (especially since chartered buses, which loaded and unloaded within the hard zone, ferried the delegates to and from the Fleet Center).

In an effort to facilitate demonstrators' access to the delegates, the City established the DZ on the edge of the hard zone and allowed demonstrations within it. The DZ itself was far from a perfect solution. It comprised a heavily secured space, approximately 90 feet by 300 feet, located for the most part underneath unused rail tracks. It was surrounded by two rows of jersey barriers topped with eight-foot chainlink fencing; the perimeter was further surrounded by a semitransparent liquid dispersion mesh fabric; and a widely-woven mesh fabric was hung above the DZ between the rail tracks and the fence. Finally, the City placed coiled razor wire along the edges of the rail tracks in the vicinity of the Fleet Center (including the area above the DZ) in order to inhibit access to the tracks. Although there were three routes of ingress and egress to and from the DZ, the aggregate effect of the security measures was to create an enclosed space that the appellant likens to a pen.

The appellant filed suit in the United States District Court for the District of Massachusetts on July 21, 2004, seeking, inter alia, a preliminary injunction requiring the City to modify the DZ in certain respects. The next day, the district judge personally inspected the DZ; held a hearing; entertained an ex parte proffer of evidence from federal authorities concerning security matters; and, ruling ore sponte, denied the requested injunction. On July 23, he filed the memorandum opinion previously cited. The Bl(a)ck Tea Society appealed. We have jurisdiction...

We review the district court's grant or denial of a preliminary injunction for abuse of discretion. Within this sphere, the district court's conclusions of law are reviewed de novo and its findings of fact are reviewed for clear error.

Freedom of expression, especially expression of political views, ranks near the top of the hierarchy of constitutional rights. That freedom "is designed and intended to remove governmental restraints from the arena of public discussion, putting the decision as to what views shall be voiced largely into the hands of each of us, in the hope that use of such freedom will ultimately produce a more capable citizenry and more perfect polity and in the belief that no other approach would comport with the premise of individual dignity and choice upon which our political system rests."

The right to freedom of expression is secured principally by the First Amendment. U.S. Const. amend. I. Despite the importance of that right, the prophylaxis of the First Amendment is not without limits. Reasonable restrictions as to the time, place, and manner of speech in public fora are permissible, provided that those restrictions "are justified without reference to the content of the regulated speech,...are narrowly tailored to serve a significant governmental interest, and...leave open ample alternative channels for communication of the information."

A regulation is narrowly tailored if "the means chosen are not substantially broader than necessary to achieve the government's interest." To satisfy this benchmark, a regulation need not be the least restrictive alternative available to the government. Put another way, the validity of time, place, or manner regulations is not subject to "'a judge's agreement with the responsible decisionmaker concerning the most appropriate method for promoting significant government interests' or the degree to which those interests should be promoted."

An inquiry into the validity of time-place-manner regulations generally commands what we have termed "intermediate scrutiny." In this case, however, the appellant endeavors to ratchet up this level of scrutiny by characterizing the security measures (particularly the total prohibition of demonstrations in the hard zone) as a prior restraint on speech. We reject this approach: here, the City has not sought to prevent speech, but, rather, to regulate the place and manner of its expression. The Supreme Court has explicitly rejected attempts to analyze security-based time-place-manner restrictions as prior restraints . . . and those cases are controlling here. If content-neutral prohibitions on speech at certain places were deemed prior restraints, the intermediate standard of review prescribed in the time-place-manner jurisprudence would be eviscerated.

Having settled upon the appropriate level of scrutiny, we move the inquiry forward. The answers to some issues are indisputable: the challenged security precautions are plainly content-neutral and there can be no doubting the substantial government interest in the maintenance of security at political conventions. What remains, therefore, is whether the City's array of security precautions were narrowly tailored and whether those precautions left ample alternative avenues of communication.

We deem it appropriate to start a narrow tailoring analysis by examining the speech-related burdens that the challenged regulation imposes. It cannot be gainsaid that the security measures attendant to the Convention dramatically limited the possibilities for communicative intercourse between the demonstrators and the delegates. The measures allowed no opportunity for physical interaction (such as the distribution of leaflets) and severely curtailed any chance for one-on-one conversation. Visual communication using signs or other media was not prevented but was hampered to some extent by the cramped space and the mesh screening. And while the direct limits on aural communication seem minor, even this form of interaction may have been less effective because of the restrictions on other modes of expression. In sum, the challenged regulation imposed a substantial burden on free expression.

We turn next to the City's goal, mindful that the government's judgment as to the best means for achieving its legitimate objectives deserves considerable respect. Here, the City's overall goal was to maintain security at the Convention. But security simpliciter is too broad a rubric to be useful in this analysis. Security is not a talisman that the government may invoke to justify any burden on speech (no matter how oppressive). Thus, the question of narrow tailoring must be decided against the backdrop of the harms that a particular set of security measures are designed to forfend.

The City claims that the risk of harm was substantial. It designed the elaborate security measures here at issue in light of recent past experience with large demonstrations, including those at the 2000 Democratic National Convention in Los Angeles. The double ranks of fencing were meant to deter attempts to break through the fence; the liquid dispersal mesh was intended to protect the delegates from being sprayed with liquids; and the overhead netting was added to prevent demonstrators from hurling projectiles. Conduct of this type admittedly has occurred at a number of recent protests.

The appellant points out, correctly, that there is no evidence in the record that the City had information indicating that demonstrators intended to use such tactics at the Convention. Building on this foundation, the appellant maintains that the City may not implement security requirements that substantially burden speech on the basis of unrelated past experiences. It further argues that most protesters do not engage in such conduct, and that the First Amendment rights of the majority of protesters should not be curtailed because of the potential for unlawful actions by a rowdy minority. In the absence of event-specific threat evidence, the appellant says, the City should have been limited to arresting miscreants and punishing unlawful conduct after it occurred.

We do not believe a per se rule barring the government from using past experience to plan for future events is consistent with the approach adopted in the Court's time-place-manner jurisprudence. The question is not whether the government may make use of past experience—it most assuredly can—but the degree to which inferences drawn from past experience are plausible. While a government agency charged with public safety responsibilities ought not turn a blind eye to past experience, it likewise ought not impose harsh burdens on the basis of isolated past events. And in striking this balance, trial courts should remember that heavier burdens on speech must, in general, be justified by more cogent evidentiary predicates.

Tonia Vamont of the Black Tea Society. (AP Photo/Elise Amendola.)

On this hastily assembled record, the quantum of "threat" evidence was sufficient to allow the trier to weigh it in the balance. For now, we do not purpose to determine how that factor should be weighed either in future cases or in connection with better-developed factual proffers. We instead assess only whether the district court's balance of this and other factors was so unreasonable as to constitute an abuse of discretion. We conclude that it did not, and, thus, we uphold the district court's determination that the security measures undertaken by the City, though extreme, were nonetheless narrowly tailored.

Having left intact the district court's conclusions anent narrow tailoring, we briefly address the availability of alternative avenues for expression. The district court perspicaciously noted that many other opportunities for demonstrations existed in the vicinity of the Fleet Center and throughout Boston. The City allowed informal demonstrations within the soft zone without a permit so long as those demonstrations involved fewer than 20 people (and allowed up to 50 people with a permit). Several other public spaces throughout Boston remained available for demonstrations, subject to existing regulations and content-neutral permitting requirements.

The appellant's chief rejoinder is that these alternatives were not sufficient because none of them were within sight and sound of the delegates assembled at the Fleet Center. We disagree with that premise: the DZ did provide an opportunity for expression within sight and sound of the delegates, albeit an imperfect one. There are, moreover, two other pertinent considerations. First, although the opportunity to interact directly with the body of delegates by, say, moving among them and distributing literature, would doubtless have facilitated the demonstrators' ability to reach their intended audience, there is no constitutional requirement that demonstrators be granted that sort of particularized access. Second, we think that the appellant's argument greatly underestimates the nature of modern communications. At a high-profile event, such as the Convention, messages expressed beyond the first-hand sight and sound of the delegates nonetheless have a propensity to reach the delegates through television, radio, the press, the internet, and other outlets. On this record, then, we cannot say that the district court erred in concluding that viable alternative means existed to enable protesters to communicate their messages to the delegates.

Let us be perfectly clear: this is a close and difficult case. The district court, however, dealt with matters at first hand and concluded that the appellant had not shown a likelihood of success on the merits. On this record and at this preliminary litigation stage, we find that conclusion reasonable.

We have frequently said that likelihood of success is an essential prerequisite for the issuance of a preliminary injunction. In the interests of completeness, however, we briefly mention the remaining three parts of the preliminary injunction calculus.

A burden on protected speech always causes some degree of irreparable harm. Here, however, the safety, security, and logistical concerns voiced by the City were real, and the district court was correct in giving those concerns due consideration. Thus, the balance of harms is inconclusive in this case. Similarly, the public interest cuts both ways. On the one hand, freedom of expression, especially freedom of political expression, is vital to the health of our democracy. On the other hand, making public safety a reality and ensuring that important political events are able to proceed normally are also valuable. Moreover, a determination of the public interest necessarily encompasses the practical effects of granting or denying preliminary injunctive relief. Here, the district court was constrained by the physical limitations of the Fleet Center venue and by the timing of the suit (which, despite considerable advance notice of the planned security measures, was brought less than a week before the Convention was scheduled to open).

We mention these constraints because it is readily evident that they sharply limited the remedial options available to the district court. Considering these factors in the aggregate, we find the equities closely matched, and we come away sharing the district court's concern with the impracticability of eleventh-hour injunctive relief.

We need go no further. With the Convention looming and with few options at its disposal, we think the district court's resolution of the preliminary injunction request was fully supportable. The court did yeoman's work in holding a prompt hearing, mastering the complexity of the issues and the physical shortcomings of the site, deciding the motion in a timeous fashion, and writing a thoughtful rescript that explained its findings and its rationale. Dealing with the record as it stands, the temporal constraints under which the district court labored, and the deferential standard of review, we have no principled choice but to uphold the challenged order.

Affirmed.

SOURCE: http://openjurist.org/378/f3d/8/blck-tea-society-v-city-of-boston

ANALYSIS

In *Black Tea Society v. City of Boston,* the First Circuit upheld the City of Boston's Designated Demonstration Zone (DZ), during the 2004 Democratic National Convention. The court had to balance two competing interests: (1) the constitutional guarantee to peaceably assemble and protest, and (2) the necessity of keeping delegates, public figures, and citizens safe from domestic and international terrorist threats. The court had less than five days to rule.

The Democratic National Convention had been designated a National Special Security Event by the federal government. During the convention, security was divided into two sections. The first consisted of a high security zone which the Secret Service controlled. The second section included a soft security zone located some distance away from the convention site and was secured by local authorities. General access was prohibited in the high security zone but pedestrian traffic was freely allowed in the soft security zone. Due to this security arrangement, there were limited opportunities for protestors to protest within sight and sound of the delegates.

The city, wanting to accommodate the large numbers of demonstrators, created a protest area that was close to the hard security zone, in order to permit demonstrators to assemble close to the Fleet Center, which was the location of the convention. This site was not chosen by local, state, and federal security officials alone but in fact was selected with the input of organizations such as the American Civil Liberties Union (ACLU) and the National Lawyers Guild. Due to the harshness of the area, the district court described the DZ as an internment camp. The zone itself was 90 feet by 300 feet, under an elevated railroad track, and heavily fortified. The area that contained the demonstrators included cement barriers, mesh fencing, and an eight-foot high chain-link fence. The top edges of the enclosed space were also covered with coiled razor wire.

On July 21, 2004, just five days before the start of the convention, the Black Tea Society filed suit in the U.S. District Court for the District of Massachusetts seeking a preliminary injunction against the city and its protest zone. Under strict time constraints, the district judge personally went to the DZ on July 22, held a hearing with the parties. On July 23, 2004, Judge Woodlock upheld the use of the DZ. The First Circuit agreed with the lower court ruling that the security interests alleged by the city were enough to justify the regulation, even though the expression was burdened. The First Circuit concluded that the regulations were narrowly tailored because of the realistic security concerns. The demonstrators, according to the First Circuit, were not constitutionally entitled to closer access to their intended audience. The court recognized in its holding that these restrictions were indeed extreme, but because time limits prohibited a full examination of threat evidence, they were nonetheless narrowly tailored.

The opposite result happened in *Stauber v. City of New York*, No. 03–9162, 2004 WL 1593870 (S.D.N.Y. Jul. 16, 2004) when protestors challenged the New York City Police Department's use of "pens" to forcibly assemble protestors in specific locations during the 2004 Republican National Convention. After an extensive review of mass gatherings where pens were used, the court held that the NYPD's current policy was not narrowly tailored, and the use of the pens unreasonably limited the movement of demonstrators. The courts have split on these types of DZs, but a majority have upheld such practices after balancing the First Amendment rights of the protesters with that of national security.

FURTHER READING

Cheh, Mary M. "In the Aftermath of September 11: Defending Civil Liberties: Demonstrations, Security Zones, and First Amendment Protection of Special Places." *The University of the District of Columbia David A. Clarke School of Law Law Review* 8 (2004): 53.

The Right to Privacy in the Technological Age

- ***Document:*** The Supreme Court case *Kyllo v. United States*, Excerpt
- ***Date:*** June 11, 2001
- ***Where:*** Washington, D.C.
- ***Significance:*** In *Kyllo*, the Supreme Court held that government use of sensory enhancing devices not in "general public use" which can be used to view the intimate details of a home constitutes a search within the meaning of the Fourth Amendment and therefore requires a warrant.

DOCUMENT

Kyllo v. United States, 533 U.S. 27 (2001)

Argued February 20, 2001.

Decided June 11, 2001.

Justice Scalia delivered the opinion of the Court.

This case presents the question whether the use of a thermal-imaging device aimed at a private home from a public street to detect relative amounts of heat within the home constitutes a "search" within the meaning of the Fourth Amendment.

I

In 1991 Agent William Elliott of the United States Department of the Interior came to suspect that marijuana was being grown in the home belonging to petitioner Danny Kyllo, part of a triplex on Rhododendron Drive in Florence, Oregon. Indoor marijuana growth typically requires high-intensity lamps. In order to determine whether an amount of heat was emanating from petitioner's home consistent with the use of such lamps, at 3:20 a.m. on January 16, 1992, Agent Elliott and Dan Haas used an Agema Thermovision 210 thermal imager to scan the triplex. Thermal imagers detect infrared radiation, which virtually all objects emit but which is not visible to the naked eye. The imager converts radiation into images based on relative warmth-black is cool, white is hot, shades of gray connote relative differences; in that respect, it operates somewhat like a video camera showing heat images. The scan of Kyllo's home took only a few minutes and was performed from the passenger seat of Agent Elliott's vehicle across the street from the front of the house and also from the street in back of the house. The scan showed that the roof over the garage and a side wall of petitioner's home were relatively hot compared to the rest of the home and substantially warmer than neighboring homes in the triplex. Agent Elliott concluded that petitioner was using halide lights to grow marijuana in his house, which indeed he was. Based on tips from informants, utility bills, and the thermal imaging, a Federal Magistrate Judge issued a warrant authorizing a search of petitioner's home, and the agents found an indoor growing operation involving more than 100 plants. Petitioner was indicted on one count of manufacturing marijuana, in violation of 21 U.S. C. §841(a)(1). He unsuccessfully moved to suppress the evidence seized from his home and then entered a conditional guilty plea....

II

The Fourth Amendment provides that "[t]he right of the people to be secure in their persons, houses, papers, and effects, against unreasonable searches and seizures, shall not be violated." "At the very core" of the Fourth Amendment "stands the right of a man to retreat into his own home and there be free from unreasonable governmental intrusion." With few exceptions, the question whether a warrantless search of a home is reasonable and hence constitutional must be answered no.

On the other hand, the antecedent question of whether or not a Fourth Amendment "search" has occurred is not so simple under our precedent. The permissibility of ordinary visual surveillance of a home used to be clear because, well into the 20th century, our Fourth Amendment jurisprudence was tied to common-law trespass. We have since decoupled violation of a person's Fourth Amendment rights from trespassory violation of his property, but the lawfulness of warrantless visual surveillance of a home has still been preserved. As we observed, "[t]he Fourth Amendment protection of the home has never been extended to require law enforcement officers to shield their eyes when passing by a home on public thoroughfares."

One might think that the new validating rationale would be that examining the portion of a house that is in plain public view, while it is a "search" despite the absence of trespass, is not an "unreasonable" one under the Fourth Amendment. But in fact we have held that visual observation is no "search" at all-perhaps in order to preserve somewhat more intact our doctrine that warrantless searches are presumptively unconstitutional....As Justice Harlan's oftquoted concurrence described it, a Fourth Amendment search occurs when the government violates a subjective expectation of privacy that society recognizes as reasonable. We have subsequently applied this principle to hold that a Fourth Amendment search does not occur-even when the explicitly protected location of a house is concerned-unless "the individual manifested a subjective expectation of privacy in the object of the challenged search," and "society [is] willing to recognize that expectation as reasonable...."

The present case involves officers on a public street engaged in more than naked-eye surveillance of a home. We have previously reserved judgment as to how much technological enhancement of ordinary perception from such a vantage point, if any, is too much. While we upheld enhanced aerial photography of an industrial complex in Dow Chemical, we noted that we found "it important that this is not an area immediately adjacent to a private home, where privacy expectations are most heightened."

III

It would be foolish to contend that the degree of privacy secured to citizens by the Fourth Amendment has been entirely unaffected by the advance of technology. The question we confront today is what limits there are upon this power of technology to shrink the realm of guaranteed privacy.

The Katz test-whether the individual has an expectation of privacy that society is prepared to recognize as reasonable-has often been criticized as circular, and hence subjective and unpredictable. While it may be difficult to refine Katz when the search of areas such as telephone booths, automobiles, or even the curtilage and uncovered portions of residences are at issue, in the case of the search of the interior of homes-the prototypical and hence most commonly litigated area of protected privacy-there is a ready criterion, with roots deep in the common law, of the minimal expectation of privacy that exists, and that is acknowledged to be reasonable. To withdraw protection of this minimum expectation would be to permit police technology to erode the privacy guaranteed by the Fourth Amendment. We think that obtaining by sense-enhancing technology any information regarding the interior of the home that could not otherwise have been obtained without physical "intrusion into a constitutionally protected area," constitutes a search-at least where (as here) the technology in question is not in general publicuse. This assures preservation of that degree of privacy against government that existed when the Fourth Amendment was adopted. On the basis of this criterion, the information obtained by the thermal imager in this case was the product of a search.

The Government maintains, however, that the thermal imaging must be upheld because it detected "only heat radiating from the external surface of the house." The dissent makes this its leading point, see post, at 1, contending that there is a fundamental difference between what it calls "off-the-wall" observations and "through-the-wall surveillance." But just as a thermal imager captures only heat emanating from a house, so also a powerful directional microphone picks up only sound emanating from a house-and a satellite capable of scanning from many miles away would pick up only visible light emanating from a house. We rejected such a mechanical interpretation of the Fourth Amendment in Katz, where the eavesdropping device picked up only sound waves that reached the exterior of the phone booth. Reversing that approach would leave the homeowner at the mercy of advancing technology-including imaging technology that could discern all human activity in the home. While the technology used in the present case was relatively crude, the rule we adopt must take account of more sophisticated systems that are already in use or in development.... As for the dissent's extraordinary assertion that anything learned through "an inference" cannot be a search, that would validate even the "through-the-wall" technologies that the dissent purports to disapprove. Surely the dissent does not believe that the through-the-wall radar or ultrasound technology produces an 8-by-10 Kodak glossy that needs no analysis.

The Government also contends that the thermal imaging was constitutional because it did not "detect private activities occurring in private areas." The Fourth Amendment's protection of the home has never been tied to measurement of the quality or quantity of information obtained. In Silverman, for example, we made clear that any physical invasion of the structure of the home, "by even a fraction of an inch," was too much, and there is certainly no exception to the warrant requirement for the officer who barely cracks open the front door and sees nothing but the nonintimate rug on the vestibule floor. In the home, our cases show, all details are intimate details, because the entire area is held safe from prying government eyes.

Limiting the prohibition of thermal imaging to "intimate details" would not only be wrong in principle; it would be impractical in application, failing to provide "a workable accommodation between the needs of law enforcement and the interests protected by the Fourth Amendment." To begin with, there is no necessary connection between the sophistication of the surveillance equipment and the "intimacy" of the details that it observes-which means that one cannot say (and the police cannot be assured) that use of the relatively crude equipment at issue here will always be lawful. The Agema Thermovision 210 might disclose, for example, at what hour each night the lady of the house takes her daily sauna and bath—a detail that many

Danny Lee Kyllo. (AP Photo/Don Ryan.)

would consider "intimate"; and a much more sophisticated system might detect nothing more intimate than the fact that someone left a closet light on. We could not, in other words, develop a rule approving only that through-the-wall surveillance which identifies objects no smaller than 36 by 36 inches, but would have to develop a jurisprudence specifying which home activities are "intimate" and which are not. And even when (if ever) that jurisprudence were fully developed, no police officer would be able to know in advance whether his through-the-wall surveillance picks up "intimate" details-and thus would be unable to know in advance whether it is constitutional. . . .

We have said that the Fourth Amendment draws "a firm line at the entrance to the house." That line, we think, must be not only firm but also bright-which requires clear specification of those methods of surveillance that require a warrant. While it is certainly possible to conclude from the videotape of the thermal imaging that occurred in this case that no "significant" compromise of the homeowner's privacy has occurred, we must take the long view, from the original meaning of the Fourth Amendment forward.

Where, as here, the Government uses a device that is not in general public use, to explore details of the home that would previously have been unknowable without physical intrusion, the surveillance is a "search" and is presumptively unreasonable without a warrant.

Since we hold the Thermovision imaging to have been an unlawful search, it will remain for the District Court to determine whether, without the evidence it provided, the search warrant issued in this case was supported by probable cause-and if not, whether there is any other basis for supporting admission of the evidence that the search pursuant to the warrant produced.

The judgment of the Court of Appeals is reversed; the case is remanded for further proceedings consistent with this opinion.

SOURCE: http://caselaw.lp.findlaw.com/scripts/getcase.pl?court=us&vol=000&invol=99-8508

ANALYSIS

A government agent suspicious that Danny Kyllo was growing marijuana, used a thermal-imaging device to scan his triplex. The imaging was to be used to determine if the amount of heat emanating from the home was consistent with the high-intensity lamps typically used for indoor marijuana growth. Subsequently, the imaging revealed that relatively hot areas existed, compared to the rest of the home. Based on informants, utility bills, and the thermal imaging, a federal magistrate judge issued a warrant to search Kyllo's home. The search unveiled growing marijuana. After Kyllo was indicted on a federal drug charge, he unsuccessfully moved to suppress the evidence seized from his home and then entered a conditional guilty plea. Kyllo appealed to the Ninth Circuit Court on the grounds that observations with a thermal-imaging device constituted a search under the Fourth Amendment. At the court of appeals, the conviction was upheld and Kyllo petitioned a writ of certiorari to the Supreme Court. The Supreme Court agreed to hear the case and reversed the circuit court ruling that the use of a thermal imaging device not found in general public use to monitor the radiation of heat from a person's home was a "search" within the meaning of the Fourth Amendment and therefore required a warrant.

Before the decision of the Supreme Court in the Kyllo case, there was a split among the circuits regarding whether thermal imaging constituted a search under the Fourth Amendment. The lower courts were leaning heavily toward holding that that the warrantless use of thermal imaging on properties was constitutional under the Fourth Amendment. Justice Scalia, who wrote the majority opinion, held that a person has a reasonable expectation of privacy, especially in the home, because that was what the Fourth Amendment was adopted to protect. The Court explained that a search occurs when government agents use sense-enhancing technology not available in general public use to collect any information regarding the interior of a home that could not otherwise be obtained without a physical invasion.

Justice Scalia also discussed how future technology can invade one's privacy and therefore authored the opinion so that it protected against more sophisticated surveillance equipment. As a result, Justice Scalia asserted that the difference between "off the wall" surveillance and "through the wall" surveillance was nonexistent because both methods physically intruded upon the privacy of the home.

The Court criticized the Ninth Circuit's rationale by arguing that the appropriate inquiry must not be whether or not the technology reveals intimate details of the subject's life. The court further held that to limit the prohibition of thermal imaging to "intimate details" would not only have been wrong in principle but would also have been impracticable in application. It argued that this type of standard is impractical in application because the government can never know in advance whether or not the technology will reveal such details. The Fourth Amendment's protection of the home had never been tied to measurement of the quality or quantity of information obtained. In the home, all details were intimate details, because the entire area was held safe from prying government eyes.

Writing for the dissenters, Justice Stevens would not treat surveillance technology as a search unless it provided its user with the functional equivalent of actual presence in the area being searched. Unlike a device such as an X-ray, that can accomplish a physical penetration, the dissent posited that the thermal imaging device was merely passive and only measured heat on the exterior surfaces of the home, failing to reveal any details of the home's interior. Justice Stevens further argued that the use of thermal imaging does not constitute a search, which requires a warrant, because any person could detect the heat emissions. He believed that this could be done by simply feeling that some areas in or around the house are warmer than others or observing that snow was melting more quickly on certain sections of the house. Since the public could gather this information, Stevens argued, there is no need for a warrant and the use of this technique is not unconstitutional.

FURTHER READING

Kleppetsch, Paul. "Comment, In the Wake of *Kyllo v. United States:* The Future of Thermal Imaging Cameras." *John Marshall Law Review* 36 (Winter 2003): 507.

Kobos, Jessica T. "Note, *Kyllo v. United States:* A Lukewarm Interpretation of the Fourth Amendment." *Montana Law Review* 64 (Summer 2003): 519.

7

ARBITRARY STATE ACTION AND POLITICS

2008 Democratic Party Platform Concerning Civil Liberties

- ***Document:*** The 2008 Democratic Party Platform, Excerpt
- ***Date:*** August 25, 2008
- ***Where:*** Denver, Colorado
- ***Significance:*** The Democratic Party platform concerning civil liberties and arbitrary state action emphasized the importance of national security without diminishing our individual rights vis-à-vis the government. Concerning social issues, the platform provided inclusive language concerning the definition of family and also protected marginalized groups from discrimination.

DOCUMENT

2008 Democratic Party Platform "Renewing America's Promise"

Reclaiming Our Constitution and Our Liberties

As we combat terrorism, we must not sacrifice the American values we are fighting to protect. In recent years, we've seen an Administration put forward a false choice between the liberties we cherish and the security we demand. The Democratic Party rejects this dichotomy. We will restore our constitutional traditions, and recover our nation's founding commitment to liberty under law.

We support constitutional protections and judicial oversight on any surveillance program involving Americans. We will review the current Administration's warrantless wiretapping program. We reject illegal wire-tapping of American citizens.

We reject the use of national security letters to spy on citizens who are not suspected of a crime. We reject the tracking of citizens who do nothing more than protest a misguided war. We reject torture. We reject sweeping claims of "inherent" presidential power. We will revisit the Patriot Act and overturn unconstitutional executive decisions issued during the past eight years. We will not use signing statements to nullify or undermine duly enacted law. And we will ensure that law-abiding Americans of any origin, including Arab-Americans and Muslim-Americans, do not become the scapegoats of national security fears.

We believe that our Constitution, our courts, our institutions, and our traditions work. In its operations overseas, while claiming to spread freedom throughout the world, the current Administration has tragically helped give rise to a new generation of potential adversaries who threaten to make America less secure. We will provide our intelligence and law enforcement agencies with the tools to hunt down and take out terrorists without undermining our Constitution, our freedom, and our privacy.

To build a freer and safer world, we will lead in ways that reflect the decency and aspirations of the American people. We will not ship away prisoners in the dead of night to be tortured in far-off countries, or detain without trial or charge prisoners who can and should be brought to justice for their crimes, or maintain a network of secret prisons to jail people beyond the reach of the law. We will respect the time-honored principle of habeas corpus, the seven century-old right of individuals to challenge the terms of their own detention that was recently reaffirmed by our Supreme Court. We will close the detention camp in Guantanamo Bay, the location of so many of the worst constitutional abuses in recent years. With these necessary changes, the attention of the world will be directed where it belongs: on what terrorists have done to us, not on how we treat suspects.

Sen. Barack Obama (D-Ill.) and Sen. Hillary Rodham Clinton (D-N.Y.) during a presidential campaign stop, 2008. (Shutterstock.)

We recognize what leaders on the front lines of the struggle against terrorism have long known: to win this fight, we must maintain the moral high ground. When millions around the world see America living up to its highest ideals, we win friends and allies in this struggle for our safety and our lives, and our enemies lose ground.

For our Judiciary, we will select and confirm judges who are men and women of unquestionable talent and character, who firmly respect the rule of law, and who listen to and are respectful of different points of view and who represent the diversity of America.

We support the appointment of judges who respect our system of checks and balances and the separation of power among the Executive Branch, Congress, and the Judiciary—and who understand that the Constitution protects not only the powerful, but also the disadvantaged and the powerless.

Our Constitution is not a nuisance. It is the foundation of our democracy. It makes freedom and self-governance possible, and helps to protect our security. The Democratic Party will restore our Constitution to its proper place in our government and return our Nation to our best traditions—including our commitment to government by law, and not by men.

A More Perfect Union

We believe in the essential American ideal that we are not constrained by the circumstances of birth but can make of our lives what we will. Unfortunately, for too many, that ideal is not a reality. When our laws, our leaders or our government are out of alignment with our ideals, the dissent and activism of ordinary Americans becomes the truest expression of patriotism. We have more work to do. Democrats will fight to end discrimination based on race, sex, ethnicity, national origin, language, religion, sexual orientation, gender identity, age and disability in every corner of our country, because that's the America we believe in.

It is not enough to look back in wonder of how far we have come; those who came before us did not strike a blow against injustice only so that we would allow injustice to fester in our time. That means removing the barriers of prejudice and misunderstanding that still exist in America. We support the full inclusion of all families in the life of our nation, and support equal responsibility, benefits, and protections. We will enact a comprehensive bipartisan employment non-discrimination act. We oppose the Defense of Marriage Act and all attempts to use this issue to divide us.

SOURCE: http://www.democrats.org/a/party/platform.html

ANALYSIS

A national party platform is a document produced every four years by the representatives of a political party leading up to its national convention to nominate a presidential candidate. The platform submits to the public that party's vision, beliefs, and values, as well as its legislative plan and policy positions on important issues of the day such as education, the environment, national security, and social issues with the positions sometimes being altered to meet changing values and emerging global issues. Typically each political party has a platform, and individual members of that party have their own platforms which are often closely aligned with the party platform. The broad scope of the national party platform is designed to attract a broad range of voters to that party, in the hopes of generating party loyalty and potentially creating voters who will automatically select candidates associated with that party. In effect, the platforms can act as a cue for the electorate to use when voting.

A specific position set forth in a platform is called a "plank," and platforms today are made up from dozens of planks. Platforms are usually altered from election to election, and decade to decade. Sometimes these modifications come about because a party modifies its opinions on a subject. On other occasions, a plank may be added to address a new and compelling issue. For example, same-sex marriage was not addressed by the Republican platform until 1992 and the Democrats have never mentioned it directly but allude to this issue for the first time in 2004. The Republicans were and continue to be strong opponents of same-sex marriage while in 2004 the Democrats focused on whether the federal or state governments should legislate in this area without specifically mentioning same-sex marriage. The interest from Republicans started because of a number of court cases from the early 1990s challenging a state's ability to exclusively recognize heterosexual marriage. The Democrats' platform has never formally supported same-sex marriage, demonstrating the continuing divide within the party over this issue.

The 2008 Democratic Party platform concerning civil liberties focuses on national security and discrimination. In terms of national security, the democratic platform stresses that national security and civil liberties are not mutually exclusive. In order to be successful at protecting the United States from future attacks, the Democrats contend that we as a nation must cling to our beliefs in liberty and freedom. Responding to the previous administration, the Democrats reject the use of illegal wiretaps, indefinite detention of enemy combatants, torture, and the use of executive signing statements to nullify or undermine a duly enacted law. The Democratic Party believes that individuals should have a right to privacy, and generally supports laws that place restrictions on law-enforcement and intelligence-agency monitoring of American citizens. In order to uphold these principles, the Democrats support the appointment of judges who will value our system of checks and balances and the separation of power among the executive, Congress, and the judiciary. As part of these goals, the Democratic platform includes a section on revisiting the USA PATRIOT Act. Even though most Democrats voted for this legislation, they want to revisit certain sections which have been used to greatly expand the powers of the federal government in terms of domestic surveillance. Many of the goals from the platform are an attempt to undo much of what the party believes was committed by the previous administration concerning the war on terror.

The Democratic Party supports equal opportunity for all Americans regardless of sex, age, race, ethnicity, sexual orientation, gender identity, religion, creed, or national origin. This is different from the Republican Party platform because it includes sexual orientation. The Democratic Party also supports affirmative action programs to further this goal as well as a broad and more inclusive definition of family. Democrats also strongly support the Americans with Disabilities Act to prohibit discrimination against people on the basis of physical or mental disability. Even though they have been more supportive of gay rights generally, the Democratic Party has been largely divided on the subject of same-sex marriage; though support for it has been increasing and most of the support for same-sex marriage has come from the

Democrats. Some members favor civil unions for same-sex couples, others favor full and equal legalized marriage, and others are opposed to same-sex marriage on religious or ideological grounds. The party opposes the Federal Defense of Marriage Act and supports its repeal. However, President Obama supports civil unions and believes that marriage should be between a man and a woman.

FURTHER READING

Piven, Frances Fox. *The War at Home: The Domestic Causes and Consequences of Bush's Militarism*. New York: New Press, 2004.

Watson, Robert P., Tom Lansford, and Jack Covarrubias, (eds.). *America's War on Terror*. 2nd ed. Aldershot, UK: Ashgate Publishing, 2009.

2008 Republican Party Platform Concerning Civil Liberties

- ***Document:*** The 2008 Republican Party Platform, Excerpt
- ***Date:*** September 1, 2008
- ***Where:*** St. Paul, Minnesota
- ***Significance:*** The Republican Party platform concerning civil liberties emphasized the importance of national security but acknowledged that sometime threats can be homegrown and need to be dealt with by our intelligence agencies. They also focused on the importance of supporting judges who based their decisions on the language of the constitution and not their personal preferences. Concerning social issues, the platform supported marriage only between a man and a woman and the support for the free exercise of religion in the public policy arena.

DOCUMENT

2008 Republican Party Platform

Appointing Constitutionalist Judges for the Nation's Courts

Judicial activism is a grave threat to the rule of law because unaccountable federal judges are usurping democracy, ignoring the Constitution and its separation of powers, and imposing their personal opinions upon the public. This must stop.

We condemn the Supreme Court's disregard of homeowners' property rights in its Kelo decision and deplore the Court's arbitrary extension of Americans' habeas corpus rights to enemy combatants held abroad. We object to the Court's unwarranted interference in the administration of the death penalty in this country for the benefit of savage criminals whose guilt is not at issue. We lament that judges have denied the people their right to set abortion policies in the states and are undermining traditional marriage laws from coast to coast. We are astounded that four justices of the Supreme Court believe that individual Americans have no individual right to bear arms to protect themselves and their families.

Republicans will insist on the appointment of constitutionalist judges, men and women who will not distort our founding documents to deny the people's right

Securing Our Civil Liberties

Because our Constitution is based on the principles of individual liberty and limited government, we must always ensure that law enforcement respects the civil and constitutional rights of the people. While we wage war on terrorism in foreign lands, it is sometimes necessary for intelligence agencies and law enforcement officials to pursue terrorist threats at home.

Ensuring Equal Treatment for All

Individual rights—and the responsibilities that go with them—are the foundation of a free society. From the time of Lincoln, equality of individuals has been a cornerstone of the Republican Party. Our commitment to equal opportunity extends from landmark school-choice legislation for the students of Washington D.C. to historic appointments at the highest levels of government. We consider discrimination based on sex, race, age, religion, creed, disability, or national origin to be immoral, and we will strongly enforce anti-discrimination statutes. We ask all to join us in rejecting the forces of hatred and bigotry and in denouncing all who practice or promote racism, anti-Semitism, ethnic prejudice, or religious intolerance. As a matter of principle, Republicans oppose any attempts to create race-based governments within the United States, as well as any domestic governments not bound by the Constitution or the Bill of Rights.

Precisely because we oppose discrimination, we reject preferences, quotas, and set-asides, whether in education or in corporate boardrooms. The government should not make contracts on this basis, and neither should corporations. We support efforts to help low-income individuals get a fair shot based on their potential and merit, and we affirm the commonsense approach.

Preserving Traditional Marriage

Because our children's future is best preserved within the traditional understanding of marriage, we call for a constitutional amendment that fully protects marriage as a union of a man and a woman, so that judges cannot make other arrangements equivalent to it. In the absence of a national amendment, we support the right of the people of the various states to affirm traditional marriage through state initiatives.

Republicans recognize the importance of having in the home a father and a mother who are married. The two-parent family still provides the best environment of stability, discipline, responsibility, and character. Children in homes without fathers are more likely to commit a crime, drop out of school, become violent, become teen parents, use illegal drugs, become mired in poverty, or have emotional or behavioral problems. We support the courageous efforts of single-parent families to provide a stable home for their children. Children are our nation's most precious resource. We also salute and support the efforts of foster and adoptive families.

Republicans have been at the forefront of protecting traditional marriage laws, both in the states and in Congress. A Republican Congress enacted the Defense of Marriage Act, affirming the right of states not to recognize same-sex "marriages" licensed in other states. Unbelievably, the Democratic Party has now pledged to repeal the Defense of Marriage Act, which would subject every state to the redefinition of marriage by a judge without ever allowing the people to vote on the matter. We also urge Congress to use its Article III, Section 2 power to prevent activist federal judges from imposing upon the rest of the nation the judicial activism in Massachusetts and California. We also encourage states to review their marriage and divorce laws in order to strengthen marriage.

As the family is our basic unit of society, we oppose initiatives to erode parental rights.

SOURCE: http://www.gop.com/2008Platform/2008platform.pdf

ANALYSIS

A national party platform is a document produced every four years by the representatives of a political party leading up to its national convention to nominate a presidential candidate. The platform submits to the public that party's vision, beliefs, and values, as well as its legislative plan and policy positions on important issues of the day such as education, the environment, national security, and social issues with the positions sometimes being altered to meet changing values and emerging global issues. Typically each political party has a platform, and individual members of that party have their own platforms which are often closely aligned with the party platform. The broad scope of the national party platform is designed to attract a broad range of voters to that party, in the hopes of generating party loyalty and potentially creating voters who will automatically select candidates associated with that party. In effect, the platforms can act as a cue for the electorate to use when voting.

A specific position set forth in a platform is called a "plank," and platforms today are made up from dozens of planks. Platforms are usually altered from election to election, and decade to decade. Sometimes these modifications come about because a party modifies its opinions on a subject. On other occasions, a plank may be added to address a new and compelling issue. For example, same-sex marriage was not addressed by the Republican platform until 1992 and the Democrats have never mentioned it directly but allude to this issue for the first time in 2004. The Republicans were and continue to be strong opponents of same-sex marriage while in 2004 the Democrats focused on whether the federal or state governments should legislate in this area without specifically mentioning same-sex marriage. The interest from Republicans started because of a number of court cases from the early 1990s challenging a state's ability to exclusively recognize heterosexual marriage. The Democrats' platform has never formally supported same-sex marriage, demonstrating the continuing divide within the party over this issue.

The 2008 Republican Party platform concerning civil liberties focused on selection of judges, national security, discrimination, and preserving traditional marriage.

The Republican Party believes that judges should make decisions based on the theory of original intent and not make decisions based on their personal beliefs or that the constitution is a living document that changes with the times. Original intent includes a close examination of the language from the constitution or statute and the framers intent behind the words. This is sometimes difficult to determine if there was more than one person who drafted the language. The Republican Party believes this form of interpretation will prevent activist judges from making decisions that undermine our individual rights.

The Republican platform also highlights the importance of maintaining the rule of law but acknowledges that the country, our intelligence agencies, and law enforcement officials should also be concerned about domestic terrorism. The platform does not provide many more details about how the government might respond to this possibility. This lack of specificity might be due in part to the previous administration policies concerning the capturing and confinement of enemy combatants, the wiretapping and tracking of American citizens, and the torture of terrorist suspects.

The Republican Party believes that discrimination based on sex, race, age, religion, creed, disability, or national origin to be immoral and they will continue to enforce antidiscrimination laws based on these characteristics. The party rejects the use of preferences, quotas, and set-asides in order to achieve equality and believes that the government and corporations should not enter into contracts on this basis. However, the party does not extend its position against discrimination to gays and lesbians. The new platform renews the call for a constitutional amendment banning gay marriage, even though their candidate Senator John McCain did not favor such an amendment because he favored this determination to be left to the states. In addition, the party platform included a reinforcing of the traditional family unit. The party believes in supporting the right of states to ban same-sex marriage and to promote traditional marriage between one man and one woman. The Republican Party believes contrary to evidence that this will be better for a child's development and stability.

FURTHER READING

Crotty, William J. *The Politics of Terror: The U.S. Response to 9/11*. Boston, Mass.: Northeastern University Press, 2004.

Frum, David. *An End to Evil: How to Win the War on Terror*. New York: Random House, 2003.

Advocacy Group Mission Statements

- ***Documents:*** Advocacy group mission statements focusing on civil liberties and arbitrary state action
- ***Date:*** various
- ***Where:*** various
- ***Significance:*** These groups are important because they lobby Congress, write and influence legislation, file lawsuits, and write amicus (friend of the court) legal briefs to support their positions.

DOCUMENT

Alliance for Justice

"The Alliance for Justice is a national association of environmental, civil rights, mental health, women's, children's and consumer advocacy organizations... the Alliance has worked to advance the cause of justice for all Americans, strengthen the public interest community's ability to influence public policy, and foster the next generation of advocates." http://www.afj.org

American Civil Liberties Union (ACLU)

"The American Civil Liberties Union (ACLU) is our nation's guardian of liberty, working daily in courts, legislatures and communities to defend and preserve the individual rights and liberties guaranteed to all people in this country by the Constitution and laws of the United States." http://www.aclu.org

American Enterprise Institute for Public Policy Research

The Institute "is dedicated to preserving and strengthening the foundations of freedom-limited government, private enterprise, vital cultural and political

Bob Kearney, Associate Director of the American Civil Liberties Union (ACLU), holds up a sign during a rally in front of the Federal Building in San Francisco on July 7, 2003 to protest the Domestic Security Enhancement Act, or Patriot Act II, currently awaiting congressional approval. The original USA PATRIOT Act (2001), drafted by the Justice Department in the wake of the September 11, 2001 World Trade Center and Pentagon attacks, granted the government broad and controversial powers to investigate, detain, and interrogate suspects. (AP Photo.)

institutions, and a strong foreign policy and national defense-through scholarly research, open debate, and publications." http://www.aei.org

Amnesty International, USA

"Amnesty International's vision is of a world in which every person enjoys all of the human rights enshrined in the Universal Declaration of Human Rights and other international human rights standards. Amnesty International undertakes research and action focused on preventing and ending grave abuses of the rights to physical and mental integrity, freedom of conscience and expression, and freedom from discrimination, within the context of its work to promote all human rights." http://www.amnestyusa.org

The Brookings Institution

"The Brookings Institution, one of Washington's oldest think tanks, is an independent, nonpartisan organization devoted to research, analysis, and public education with an emphasis on economics, foreign policy, and governance. The goal of Brookings activities is to improve the performance of American institutions and the quality of public policy by using social science to analyze emerging issues and to offer practical approaches to those issues in language aimed at the general public." http://www.brookings.edu

CATO Institute

"The Cato Institute seeks to broaden the parameters of public policy debate to allow consideration of the traditional American principles of limited government, individual liberty, free markets and peace. Toward that goal, the Institute strives to achieve greater involvement of the intelligent, concerned lay public in questions of policy and the proper role of government." http://www.cato.org

Citizens United

"Citizens United is an organization dedicated to restoring our government to citizens control. Through a combination of education, advocacy, and grass roots organization, Citizens United seeks to reassert the traditional American values of limited government, freedom of enterprise, strong families, and national sovereignty and security. Citizens United's goal is to restore the founding fathers vision of a free nation, guided by the honesty, common sense, and good will of its citizens." http://www.citizensunited.org/

Electronic Privacy Information Center (EPIC)

"EPIC is a public interest research center in Washington, D.C. It was established in 1994 to focus public attention on emerging civil liberties issues and to protect privacy, the First Amendment, and constitutional values." http://epic.org/epic/

First Amendment Center

"We support the First Amendment and build understanding of its core freedoms through education, information and entertainment. The center serves as a forum for the study and exploration of free-expression issues, including freedom of speech, of the press and of religion, and the rights to assemble and to petition the government." http://www.firstamendmentcenter.org/

First Amendment Coalition

"The First Amendment Coalition is an award-winning, nonprofit public interest organization dedicated to advancing free speech, more open and accountable government, and public participation in civic affairs." http://www.firstamendmentcoalition.org/

First Amendment Project

"The First Amendment Project is a nonprofit advocacy organization dedicated to protecting and promoting freedom of information, expression, and petition." http://thefirstamendment.org/

The Freedom Forum

"The Freedom Forum, based in Washington, D.C., is a nonpartisan foundation that champions the First Amendment as a cornerstone of democracy." http://www.freedomforum.org/

Human Rights Watch

"Human Rights Watch is dedicated to protecting the human rights of people around the world. We stand with victims and activists to prevent discrimination, to uphold political freedom, to protect people from inhumane conduct in wartime, and to bring offenders to justice. We investigate and expose human rights violations and hold abusers accountable. We challenge governments and those who hold power to end abusive practices and respect international human rights law. We enlist the public and the international community to support the cause of human rights for all." http://www.hrw.org

Illinois First Amendment Center

"The Mission of the Illinois First Amendment Center is to promote First Amendment rights and responsibilities through education designed to raise awareness of the need to understand, preserve and protect the First Amendment of the United States Constitution." http://www.illinoisfirstamendmentcenter.com/

Institute for Justice

"Through strategic litigation, training, communication and outreach, the Institute for Justice advances a rule of law under which individuals can control their destinies as free and responsible members of society. IJ litigates to secure economic liberty, school choice, private property rights, freedom of speech and other vital individual liberties and to restore constitutional limits on the power of government. In addition, IJ trains law students, lawyers and policy activists in the tactics of public interest litigation. Through these activities, IJ challenges the ideology of the welfare state and illustrates and extends the benefits of freedom to those whose full enjoyment of liberty is denied by government." http://www.ij.org

Landmark Legal Foundation

"Founded in 1976, Landmark's long record of accomplishment has made it one of the nations most effective and successful conservative legal advocacy groups. We fight for the values and ideals the Founding Fathers gave voice to in the Declaration of Independence and the U.S. Constitution." http://www.landmarklegal.org

National Legal Center for the Public Interest

"The mission of the National Legal Center for the Public Interest is to foster knowledge about law and the administration of justice in a society committed to: the rights of individuals free enterprise private ownership of property balanced use of private and public resources limited government, and a fair and efficient judiciary." http://www.nndb.com/org/863/000126485/

Online Privacy Alliance

"The Online Privacy Alliance lead and supported self-regulatory initiatives that created an environment of trust and that foster the protection of individuals' privacy online and in electronic commerce." http://www.privacyalliance.org/

Pacific Legal Foundation

"Pacific Legal Foundation is America's trusted champion of constitutional rights, fighting and winning decisive actions in the courts of law and the court of public opinion to rescue liberty from the grasp of government power..." http://pacificlegal.org/

People for the American Way

"Our purpose is to meet the challenges of discord and fragmentation with an affirmation of "the American Way." By this, we mean pluralism, individuality, freedom of thought, expression and religion, a sense of community, and tolerance and compassion for others. People For the American Way will reach out to all Americans and affirm that in our society, the individual still matters; that there is reason to believe in the future—not to despair of it—and that we must strengthen the common cords that connect us as humans and citizens" http://www.pfaw.org

The Privacy Coalition

"The Privacy Coalition is a nonpartisan coalition of consumer, civil liberties, educational, family, library, labor, and technology organizations that have agreed to the Privacy Pledge." http://privacycoalition.org/

Privacy.org

"Privacy.Org is the site for daily news, information, and initiatives on privacy. This web page is a joint project of the Electronic Privacy Information Center (EPIC) and Privacy International. EPIC is a public interest research center in Washington, D.C. It was established in 1994 to focus public attention on emerging civil liberties issues and to protect privacy, the First Amendment, and constitutional values. Privacy International is a human rights group formed in 1990 as a watchdog on surveillance by governments and corporations. PI is based in London, England, and has an office in Washington, D.C. PI has conducted campaigns throughout the world on issues ranging from wiretapping and national security activities, to ID cards, video surveillance, data matching, police information systems, and medical privacy." http://privacy.org/

Washington Legal Foundation

"Since it was founded 27 years ago, WLF has developed into the nation's preeminent center for public interest law, advocating free-enterprise principles, responsible government, property rights, a strong national security and defense, and balanced civil and criminal justice system." http://www.wlf.org

---

ANALYSIS

These organizations seek to influence political and policy decisions as well as promote their issues. They usually have both well-defined political agendas and the financial resources necessary to exert broad influence on the political and regulatory process; utilizing direct lobbying, letter-writing campaigns, and voter turnout efforts during elections. Single-issue groups seek to influence policy in a particular area, such as gun laws (National Rifle Association), or animal rights (People for the Ethical Treatment of Animals). These tend to be aligned toward a specific political ideology or seek influence in specific policy areas. Interest groups play an important part in modern theories of democratic government. Elected leaders have an palpable stake in securing their own reelection, and they can be expected to act in ways that capitalize on their chances at the polls. In particular, politicians have an electoral motivation to steer clear of alienated organized constituencies that might rebuke them in the next election cycle. In this context, advocacy groups are a critical part of the political environment. Groups signal their commitment to a policy outcome by paying the costs of organizing and of monitoring politicians' performance. Since energized group members are likely to oppose politicians at the polls if they vote the "incorrect" way, elected leaders are cognizant of mobilized interest groups' policy preferences.

FURTHER READING

Brandt, Sanford F. *Advocacy is Sometimes an Agency's Best Service: Opportunities and Limits Within Federal Law*. Washington, D.C.: Independent Sector, 1984.

Hammack, David C. *Making the Nonprofit Sector in the United States*. Bloomington: Indiana University Press, 2000.

Reid, Elizabeth J. *Structuring the Inquiry Into Advocacy*. Washington, D.C. The Urban Institute, 2000.

CIVIL LIBERTIES RESOURCES

WEB SITES

There is an enormous amount of information available online concerning civil liberties. Below is a list of U.S. government Web sites, advocacy groups and films/documentaries that have a focus on these issues.

Government Agencies

The Central Intelligence Agency https://www.cia.gov/

The Department of Education—Office for Civil Rights http://ed.gov/about/offices/list/ocr/index.html

The Department of Defense http://www.defense.gov/

The Department of Homeland Security http://www.dhs.gov/index.shtm

The Department of Housing and Urban Development http://portal.hud.gov/portal/page/portal/HUD

The Department of Justice http://www.justice.gov/

The Department of Labor http://www.dol.gov/

The Equal Employment Opportunity Commission http://www.eeoc.gov/

The Federal Bureau of Investigation http://www.fbi.gov/

The Federal Trade Commission http://www.ftc.gov/

Intelligence Community Agencies http://www.intelligence.gov/

The National Security Agency http://www.nsa.gov/

The National Security Council http://www.whitehouse.gov/nsc/

The State Department http://www.state.gov/

United States Commission on Civil Rights http://www.usccr.gov/

Advocacy Groups

Alliance for Justice

"The Alliance for Justice is a national association of environmental, civil rights, mental health, women's, children's and consumer advocacy organizations . . . the Alliance has worked to advance the cause of justice for all Americans, strengthen the public interest community's ability to influence public policy, and foster the next generation of advocates."
http://www.afj.org

American Civil Liberties Union (ACLU)

"The American Civil Liberties Union (ACLU) is our nation's guardian of liberty, working daily in courts, legislatures and communities to defend and preserve the individual rights and liberties guaranteed to all people in this country by the Constitution and laws of the United States."
http://www.aclu.org

American Enterprise Institute for Public Policy Research

The Institute "is dedicated to preserving and strengthening the foundations of freedom-limited government, private enterprise, vital cultural and political institutions, and a strong foreign policy and national defense-through scholarly research, open debate, and publications."
http://www.aei.org

Amnesty International, USA

"Amnesty International undertakes research and action focused on preventing and ending grave abuses of the rights to physical and mental integrity, freedom of conscience and expression, and freedom from discrimination, within the context of its work to promote all human rights."
http://www.amnestyusa.org

The Brookings Institution

"The Brookings Institution, one of Washington's oldest think tanks, is an independent, nonpartisan organization devoted to research, analysis, and public education with an emphasis on economics, foreign policy, and governance."
http://www.brookings.edu

CATO Institute

"The Cato Institute seeks to broaden the parameters of public policy debate to allow consideration of the traditional American principles of limited government, individual liberty, free markets and peace."
http://www.cato.org

Citizens United

"Citizens United's goal is to restore the founding fathers vision of a free nation, guided by the honesty, common sense, and good will of its citizens."
http://www.citizensunited.org/

Electronic Privacy Information Center (EPIC)

"EPIC is a public interest research center in Washington, D.C. It was established in 1994 to focus public attention on emerging civil liberties issues and to protect privacy, the First Amendment, and constitutional values."
http://epic.org/epic/

First Amendment Center

"We support the First Amendment and build understanding of its core freedoms through education, information and entertainment."
http://www.firstamendmentcenter.org

First Amendment Coalition

"The First Amendment Coalition is an award-winning, nonprofit public interest organization dedicated to advancing free speech, more open and accountable government, and public participation in civic affairs."
http://www.firstamendmentcoalition.org/

First Amendment Project

"The First Amendment Project is a nonprofit advocacy organization dedicated to protecting and promoting freedom of information, expression, and petition."
http://thefirstamendment.org/

The Freedom Forum

"The Freedom Forum, based in Washington, D.C., is a nonpartisan foundation that champions the First Amendment as a cornerstone of democracy."
http://www.freedomforum.org/

Human Rights Watch

Human Rights Watch is dedicated to protecting the human rights of people around the world."
http://www.hrw.org

Illinois First Amendment Center

"The Mission of the Illinois First Amendment Center is to promote First Amendment rights and responsibilities through education designed to raise awareness of the need to understand, preserve and protect the First Amendment of the United States Constitution."
http://www.illinoisfirstamendmentcenter.com/

Institute for Justice

"Through strategic litigation, training, communication and outreach, the Institute for Justice advances a rule of law under which individuals can control their destinies as free and responsible members of society."
http://www.ij.org

Landmark Legal Foundation

"Founded in 1976, Landmark's long record of accomplishment has made it one of the nation's most effective and successful conservative legal advocacy groups. We fight for the values and ideals the Founding Fathers gave voice to in the Declaration of Independence and the U.S. Constitution."
http://www.landmarklegal.org

National Legal Center for the Public Interest

"The mission of the National Legal Center for the Public Interest is to foster knowledge about law and the administration of justice in a society committed to: the rights of individuals free enterprise private ownership of property balanced use of private and public resources limited government, and a fair and efficient judiciary."
http://www.nndb.com/org/863/000126485/

Online Privacy Alliance

"The Online Privacy Alliance led and supported self-regulatory initiatives that created an environment of trust and that foster the protection of individuals' privacy online and in electronic commerce."
http://www.privacyalliance.org/

Pacific Legal Foundation

"Pacific Legal Foundation is America's trusted champion of constitutional rights, fighting and winning decisive actions in the courts of law and the court of public opinion to rescue liberty from the grasp of government power..."
http://pacificlegal.org/

People for the American Way

"Our purpose is to meet the challenges of discord and fragmentation with an affirmation of 'the American Way.' By this, we mean pluralism, individuality, freedom of thought, expression and religion, a sense of community, and tolerance and compassion for others."
http://www.pfaw.org

The Privacy Coalition

"The Privacy Coalition is a nonpartisan coalition of consumer, civil liberties, educational, family, library, labor, and technology organizations that have agreed to the Privacy Pledge."
http://privacycoalition.org/

Privacy.org

"Privacy.Org is the site for daily news, information, and initiatives on privacy. It was established in 1994 to focus public attention on emerging civil liberties issues and to protect privacy, the First Amendment, and constitutional values."
http://privacy.org/

Washington Legal Foundation

"Since it was founded 27 years ago, WLF has developed into the nation's preeminent center for public interest law, advocating free-enterprise principles, responsible government, property rights, a strong national security and defense, and balanced civil and criminal justice system."
http://www.wlf.org

FILMS

Due Process and Equal Protection

Absence of Malice (1981)

The story of a man whose life is turned upside down after a reporter prints a story based on a false lead.

Come See the Paradise (1990)

This film tells the story of a man who falls in love with and marries a Japanese-American woman in the 1930s. Their relationship is tested when the man's wife and daughter are sent to an internment camp during World War II.

Of Civil Wrongs and Rights—The Fred Korematsu Story (2007)

Fred Korematsu challenged the forced internment of Japanese Americans during World War II. Korematsu lost his landmark Supreme Court case in 1944. Of Civil Wrongs and Rights is the untold history of the 40-year legal fight to vindicate Korematsu.

The Siege at Ruby Ridge (*Ruby Ridge: An American Tragedy*) (1996)

This TV movie dramatizes the 1992 raid by federal agents at the Idaho home of white supremacist and militia member Randy Weaver.

Snow Falling on Cedars (1999)

This movie tells the story of a Japanese American man accused of murder and the lingering anti-Japanese sentiment left behind after World War II.

Unconstitutional—The War on Our Civil Liberties (2004)

This film presents powerful and tragic examples of how the USA PATRIOT Act—passed with virtually no Congressional debate just 45 days after the terrorist attacks of 9/11/01.

Waco: The Rules of Engagement (1997)

This documentary chronicles the events of the 51-day stand-off at the Branch Davidian compound in Waco, Texas, through footage from the events, the subsequent congressional hearings, and from technology, religion and psychological experts.

First Amendment

Committing Poetry in Times of War (2007)
This documentary chronicles the firing of a New Mexico high school poetry teacher for his role in prompting the reading of one student's controversial work over the intercom. This documentary recounts the constitutional issues around the case.

Dirty Pictures (2000)
This TV movie dramatizes the 1990 trial of Cincinnati museum curator Dennis Barrie, who faced obscenity charges after his museum exhibited sexually graphic works by photographer Robert Mapplethorpe.

Fahrenheit 451 (1966)
Based on Ray Bradbury's 1951 novel, this film tells the story of a society in which reading material is banned and all books are burned.

The First Amendment Project (2004)
Freedom of speech and the press, to assemble peacefully, and to petition the government are all guaranteed in the Constitution, but how do those freedoms work in the 21st century, and are they in jeopardy? This documentary anthology explores these topics.

The Invisible Line: Teens and Censorship (2004)
Teen musicians, journalists, poets and artists discuss their feelings about censorship and how it affects their ability to express themselves. Comments from the adults who mentor these teens provide additional perspective.

The People vs. Larry Flynt (1996)
A movie chronicling controversial porn king Larry Flynt, whose publications have faced numerous obscenity challenges in court.

This Is What Democracy Looks Like (2000)
This documentary, shot by 100 amateur photographers, records the protests at the 1999 Seattle summit of the World Trade Organization.

Shut Up and Sing (2006)
In 2003, Natalie Maines, lead singer of the Dixie Chicks, stated: "Just so you know, we're ashamed the president of the United States is from Texas." The comment was delivered on the eve of the American invasion of Iraq, and drew cheers from the decidedly antiwar and anti-Bush British crowd. The documentary shows the band from their peak of popularity, through the now infamous anti-Bush comment, and on through the days, months, and years of mayhem.

Privacy

Brazil (1985)
This Orwellian tale centers on a futuristic society in which a paperwork error leads to the arrest of the wrong man, and attempts to correct the mistake only make the situation worse.

Enemy of the State (1998)
When an attorney is unknowingly given evidence in the assassination of a congressman, special agents use all the surveillance technology available to capture him.

Gattaca (1997)
In this futuristic film, humans are discriminated against based on their genes. Individuals predisposed to disease are blocked from important careers and powerful positions in society.

1984 (1984)
Based on George Orwell's novel of the same title, this movie tells the story of a dystopian society in which Big Brother watches everything and free thought and free speech are prohibited.

The Siege (1998)
In the film, New York City is reeling from a series of terrorist bombings perpetrated by a militant Arab group. As the government intensifies its search for the terrorists, martial law is implemented and Arab Americans are detained in prison camps.

The Truman Show (1998)
An insurance salesman, Truman Burbank, discovers his entire life is actually a television show that is following him 24/7.

BIBLIOGRAPHY

Abernethy, Thomas Perkins. *The Burr Conspiracy*. New York: Oxford University Press, 1954.

Ackerman, Bruce. "Beyond Carolene Products." *Harvard Law Review* 98 (1985): 713.

Ackerman, Bruce. *We the People: Foundations*. Cambridge: Harvard University Press, 1991.

Adams, George, and Robert Schuyler. *Constitutional History of England*. New York: H. Holt and Co., 1934.

Alderman, Ellen, and Caroline Kennedy. *The Right to Privacy*. New York: Vintage Books, 1995.

Alexander, Janet C. "Jurisdiction-Stripping in a Time of Terror." *California Law Review* 95 (2007): 1193.

Austin, Aleine. *Matthew Lyon: "New Man" of the Democratic Revolution, 1749–1822*. University Park: Pennsylvania State University Press, 1981.

Berger, Raoul. *The Fourteenth Amendment and the Bill of Rights*. Norman: University of Oklahoma Press, 1989.

Biskupic, Joan, and Elder Witt (eds.). *Congressional Quarterly's Guide to the U.S. Supreme Court*, 3rd ed. Washington, D.C.: Congressional Quarterly, Inc., 1996.

Blasi, Vincent. "The First Amendment & the Ideal of Civic Courage: The Brandeis Opinion in *Whitney v. California*." *William and Mary Law Review* 29 (1988): 653.

Bollinger, Lee, and Geoffrey Stone. *Eternally Vigilant: Free Speech in the Modern Era*, Chicago: University of Chicago Press, 2002.

Bond, James Edward. *No Easy Walk to Freedom: Reconstruction and the Ratification of the Fourteenth Amendment*, Westport, Conn.: Praeger, 1997.

Bosmajian, Haig. *Dissent: Symbolic Behavior and Rhetorical Strategies*. Boston, Mass.: Allyn and Bacon, 1972.

Bracken, Harry. *Freedom of Speech: Words Are Not Deeds*. Westport, Conn.: Praeger, 1994.

Brown, Christopher L. *Moral Capital: Foundations of British Abolitionism*. Chapel Hill: University of North Carolina Press, 2006.

Brown, Ralph S., Jr. *Loyalty and Security: Employment Tests in the United States*. New Haven, Conn.: Yale University Press, 1958.

Calabresi, Steven G. "The Tradition of the Written Constitution: Text, Precedent, and Burke." *Alabama Law Review* 57 (2006): 635.

Casto, William R. *The Supreme Court in the Early Republic: The Chief Justiceships of John Jay and Oliver Ellsworth*. Columbia: University of South Carolina Press, 1995.

Chafee, Zechariah. *Free Speech in the United States*. Cambridge, Mass.: Harvard University Press, 1941.

Chang, Nancy. *Silencing Political Dissent: How Post 9-11 Anti-Terrorism Measures Threaten Our Civil Liberties*. New York: Seven Stories Press, 2002.

Chiarella, Louis A., and Michael A. Newton. " 'So Judge, How Do I Get That FISA Warrant?': The Policy and Procedure for Conducting Electronic Surveillance." *Army Lawyer* (October 1997): 25–36.

Chernow, Ron. *Alexander Hamilton*. New York: Penguin Press, 2004.

Clancy, Thomas K. "What Is a "Search" within the Meaning of the Fourth Amendment?" *Alabama Law Review* 70 (2006): 1, 2.

Cole, David, et al. *Terrorism and the Constitution: Sacrificing Civil Liberties in the Name of National Security*. New York: New Press, 2002.

Cullen, Charles Thomas. *St. George Tucker and Law in Virginia, 1772–1804*. New York: Garland, 1987.

Curtis, Michael Kent. *No State Shall Abridge: The Fourteenth Amendment and the Bill of Rights*. Durham, N.C.: Duke University Press, 1986.

Cushman, Robert F. *Cases in Constitutional Law*. 7th ed. Englewood Cliffs, N.J.: Prentice-Hall, Inc., 1989.

Duker, William F. *A Constitutional History of Habeas Corpus*. Westport, Conn.: Greenwood Press, 1980.

Durey, Michael. *"With the Hammer of Truth": James Thomas Callender and America's Early National Heroes*. Charlottesville: University Press of Virginia, 1990.

Ellis, Joseph. *American Sphinx: The Character of Thomas Jefferson*. New York: Alfred A. Knopf, 1997.

Emerson, Thomas. *The System of Freedom of Expression*. New York: Random House, 1970.

Epps, Garrett. *Democracy Reborn: The Fourteenth Amendment and the Fight for Equal Rights in Post-Civil War America*. New York: H. Holt, 2006.

Epstein, David F. *The Political Theory of the Federalist*. Chicago: University of Chicago Press, 1984.

Epstein, Lee, and Thomas G. Walker. *Constitutional Law for a Changing America: Institutional Powers and Constraints*. 3rd ed. Washington, D.C.: Congressional Quarterly, 1998.

Federman, Cary. *The Body and the State: Habeas Corpus and American Jurisprudence*. SUNY Series in American Constitutionalism. Albany: State University of New York Press, 2006.

Fehrenbacher Don E. (ed.). *Abraham Lincoln: Speeches and Writings, 1859–1865*. New York: The Library of America, 1989, 456–457.

Forman, James D. *Anarchism: Political Innocence or Social Violence?* New York: Franklin Watts, Inc., 1975.

Furtwangler, Albert. *The Authority of Publius: A Reading of the Federalist Papers*. Ithaca, N.Y.: Cornell University Press, 1984.

Gerber, Scott D. "Privacy and Constitutional Theory." In *The Right To Privacy*, edited by Ellen Frankel Paul, Fred D. Miller, Jr., and Jeffrey Paul . Cambridge: Cambridge University Press, 2000.

Glenn, Richard A. *The Right to Privacy: Rights and Liberties under the Law*. Santa Barbara, Calif.: ABC-CLIO, 2003.

Gressman, Eugene. "Judgments Judged and Wrongs Remembered: Examining the Japanese American Civil Liberties Cases on their Sixtieth Anniversary: *Korematsu*: A Melange of Military Imperatives." *Law and Contemporary Problems* 68 (Spring 2005): 15.

Hallam, Henry. *The Constitutional History of England from the Accession of Henry VII to the Death of George II*. 2 vols. London: J. Murray, 1846. Reprint, Buffalo, N.Y.: W. S. Hein Co., 1989.

Hand, Learned. "Chief Justice Stone's Conception of the Judicial Function." *Colorado Law Review* 46 (1946): 696.

Handlin, Oscar, and Mary Flug Handlin. *The Popular Sources of Political Authority; Documents on the Massachusetts Constitution of 1780*. Cambridge, Mass.: Belknap Press of Harvard University Press, 1966.

Harman, Charles E. *Critical Commentaries on Blackstone: A Critique of Sir William Blackstone's Commentaries on the Laws of England*. Brookings, Or: Old Court Press, 2002.

Hay, Carla H. *James Burgh, Spokesman for Reform in Hanoverian England*. Washington, D.C.: University Press of America, 1979.

Haynes, John E. *Red Scare or Red Menace? American Communism and Anticommunism in the Cold War Era*. Chicago: Ivan R. Dee Publishers, 1996.

Holt, James Clarke. *Magna Carta*. Cambridge: Cambridge University Press, 1965.

Hoppit, Julian. *A Land of Liberty?: England 1689–1727*. The New Oxford History of England. Oxford [England]: Clarendon Press, 2000.

Hughes, Paul L., and Robert F. Fries. *Crown and Parliament in Tudor-Stuart England: A Documentary Constitutional History, 1485–1714*. New York: Putnam, 1959.

Jackson, Dick, et al. "The Law of War after the DTA, Hamdan and the MCA." *Army Law Review* (2007): 19.

Kanter, Stephen. "The Griswold Diagrams: Toward a Unified Theory of Constitutional Rights." *Cardozo Law Review* 28 (November 2006): 623.

Kenyon, J. P. *The Stuart Constitution, 1603–1688; Documents and Commentary*. Cambridge: Cambridge University Press, 1966.

Koppelman, Andrew. *The Gay Rights Question in Contemporary American Law*. Chicago: University of Chicago Press, 2002.

Lael, R. L., *The Yamashita Precedent: War Crimes and Command Responsibility*. Wilmington, Del.: Scholarly Resources, 1982.

Lane, Robert W. *Beyond the Schoolhouse Gate: Free Speech and the Inculcation of Values*. Philadelphia, Pa.: Temple University Press, 1995.

Levy, Leonard W. *Origins of the Fifth Amendment; The Right against Self-Incrimination*. New York: Oxford University Press, 1968.

Lewis, Gregory B. "Lifting the Ban on Gays in the Civil Service: Federal Policy Toward Gay and Lesbian Employees Since the Cold War." *Public Administration Review* 57, no. 5 (1997): 387–95.

Lockmiller, David A. *Sir William Blackstone*. Chapel Hill: University of North Carolina Press, 1938.

Macaulay, Thomas Babington, and C. H. Firth. *The History of England, From the Accession of James the Second*. London: Macmillan and Co., 1913.

Martin, Robert. *The Free and Open Press: The Founding of American Democratic Press Liberty, 1640–1800*. New York: New York University Press, 2001.

Mayer, David N. *The Constitutional Thought of Thomas Jefferson*. Charlottesville: University Press of Virginia, 1994.

McClellan, James. *Joseph Story and the American Constitution; A Study in Political and Legal Thought with Selected Writings*. Norman: University of Oklahoma Press, 1971.

Melton, Buckner F. *Aaron Burr: Conspiracy to Treason*. New York: Wiley, 2001.

Mian, Badshah K. *American Habeas Corpus: Law, History, and Politics*. San Francisco: Cosmos of Humanists Press, 1984.

Morgan, Ted. *Reds: McCarthyism in Twentieth-Century America*. New York: Random House, 2003.

Neely, Mark E. *The Fate of Liberty: Abraham Lincoln and Civil Liberties*. New York: Oxford University Press, 1991.

Nelson, William Edward. *The Fourteenth Amendment: From Political Principle to Judicial Doctrine*. Cambridge, Mass.: Harvard University Press, 1988.

Newmyer, R. Kent. *Supreme Court Justice Joseph Story: Statesman of the Old Republic*. Studies in Legal History. Chapel Hill: University of North Carolina Press, 1985.

Painter, Sidney. *The Reign of King John*. Baltimore: Johns Hopkins Press, 1949.

Paley, Ruth. "After *Somerset:* Mansfield, Slavery and the Law in England, 1772–1830." In *Law, Crime and English Society*, 1660–1830, ed. Norma Landau. New York: Cambridge University Press, 2002.

Pallister, Anne. *Magna Carta: The Heritage of Liberty*. Oxford: Clarendon Press, 1971.

Parker, Richard A. *Free Speech on Trial Communication Perspectives on Landmark Supreme Court Decisions*. Tuscaloosa, Ala. and London: University of Alabama Press, 2003.

Pasley, Jeffrey L. *The Tyranny of Printers: Newspaper Politics in the Early American Republic*. Charlottesville: University of Virginia Press, 2001.

Paulsen, Michael Stokes. "The Merryman Power and the Dilemma of Autonomous Executive Branch Interpretation." *Cardozo Law Review* 15 (1993): 81.

Peters, Ronald M. *The Massachusetts Constitution of 1780: A Social Compact*. Amherst: University of Massachusetts Press, 1978.

Peterson, H. C., and Gilbert C. Fite. *Opponents of War, 1917–1918*. Madison: University of Wisconsin Press, 1957.

Plamenatz, John P. *Man and Society: Political and Social Theory*. vol. 2. New York: McGraw-Hill, 1963.

Posner, Richard A. *Not a Suicide Pact: the Constitution in a Time of National Emergency*. New York: Oxford University Press: 2006.

Preston, William, Jr. *Aliens and Dissenters: Federal Suppression of Radicals, 1903–1933*. 2nd ed. Urbana: University of Illinois Press, 1994.

Reeves, Thomas C. *The Life and Times of Joe McCarthy: A Biography*. Madison, Wis.: Madison Books, 1997.

Robinson, Greg. *By Order of the President: FDR and the Internment of Japanese Americans*. Cambridge: Harvard University Press: 2001.

Rutland, Robert Allen. *The Ordeal of the Constitution: The Antifederalists and the Ratification Struggle of 1787–1788*. Boston: Northeastern University Press, 1983.

Saxton, A. *The Indispensable Enemy: Labor and the Anti-Chinese Movement in California*. Berkeley: University of California Press, 1971.

Schrecker, Ellen. *The Age of McCarthyism*. New York: St. Martin's, 1994.

Schulhofer, Stephen J. *The Enemy Within: Intelligence Gathering, Law Enforcement, and Civil Liberties in the Wake of September 11*. New York: Century Foundation Press, 2002.

Schwartz, Bernard. *Main Currents in American Legal Thought*. Durham, N.C.: Carolina Academic Press, 1993.

Semeraro, Steven. "Two Theories of Habeas Corpus." *Brooklyn Law Review* 71 (Spring 2006): 1233.

Shackleton, Robert. *Montesquieu: A Critical Biography*, London: Oxford University Press, 1961.

Simon, James F., *Lincoln and Chief Justice Taney: Slavery, Secession, and the President's War Powers*. New York: Simon and Schuster, 2006.

Stephenson, Carl, and Frederick George Marcham. *Sources of English Constitutional History; A Selection of Documents from A.D. 600 to the Present*. New York: Harper and Bros, 1937.

Sulmasy, Glenn M. *The National Security Court System: A Natural Evolution of Justice in an Age of Terror*. Oxford: Oxford University Press, 2009.

Sunstein, Cass. "Is Violent Speech a Right?" *The American Prospect*, Summer 1995.

Swire, Peter P. "Katz Is Dead. Long Live Katz." *Michigan Law Review* 102 (2004): 904.

Thompson, Faith. *Magna Carta; Its Role in the Making of the English Constitution, 1300–1629*. Minneapolis: University of Minnesota Press, 1948.

Tushnet, Mark. "Controlling Executive Power in the War on Terrorism." *Harvard Law Review* 118 (2005): 2673.

Walker, Robert S. *Habeas Corpus Writ of Liberty: English and American Origins and Development*. United States: BookSurge, 2006.

Westin, Alan, *Privacy and Freedom*. New York, Atheneum, 1967.

White, Morton Gabriel. *Philosophy, The Federalist, and the Constitution*. New York: Oxford University Press, 1987.

Witt, Elder (ed.). *The Supreme Court and Its Work*. Washington, D.C.: Congressional Quarterly, 1981.

INDEX

About the Author

CHRISTOPHER PETER LATIMER is Assistant Professor of Political Science at the State University of New York at Cortland. Dr. Latimer is also the Pre-Law Advisor for SUNY Cortland as well as Associate Director of the university's Institute for Civic Engagement.